On 18 September 2014, the Scots are to vote on their country's future. 'Should Scotland be an independent country?' is the question which will be put before them. *Annals of the Holyrood Parish* describes in ten chapters the 'Decade of Devolution' that has led up to this decisive moment, from the 'rainbow parliament' of 2003 which, a year later, moved into Enric Miralles' new parliament building at Holyrood, to the absolute majority of the Scottish National Party, covering elections, parliamentary bills, the ups and downs of parties and politicians, and what the Scottish people and the Scottish media have made of it all. A fascinating chronicle unfolds which charts the devolution journey so far, throws light on both campaigns – for and against independence – and sets the scene for 'Scotland's date with destiny'.

FRONT COVER:
9 June 2011 – First Minister's Question Time being held in the chamber of the Scottish Parliament. First Minister Alex Salmond was questioned by party leaders and eleven backbench MSPs. This session of Parliament was chaired by the Presiding Officer Trish Marwick MSP.

BACK COVER:
The Mace in the Debating Chamber of the Scottish Parliament was designed and crafted by Michael Lloyd. It is made from silver and of gold panned from Scottish rivers. The inlaid gold band symbolises the relationship between the Parliament, its people and the land. Engraved on the head of the mace are the words 'Wisdom, Justice, Compassion and Integrity' - these are a reference to the ideals that the people of Scotland aspire to for their Members of Parliament. The founding of the Scottish Parliament is commemorated by the words 'There shall be a Scottish Parliament – The Scotland Act 1998'. The mace was presented by Her Majesty The Queen at the opening ceremony of the Scottish Parliament, 1 July 1999. The gold was donated by Scottish Gold Panners.

THE ANNALS
OF THE
HOLYROOD
PARISH

THE ANNALS OF THE
HOLYROOD
PARISH

Eberhard Bort

Grace Note
Publications

The Annals of the Holyrood Parish:
A Decade of Devolution 2004-2014

First published 2014 by
Grace Note Publications
Grange of Locherlour,
Ochtertyre, PH7 4JS, Scotland
www.gracenotepublications.co.uk
books@gracenotereading.co.uk

ISBN: 978-1-907676-50-5

British Library Cataloguing-in-Publications Data
A catalogue record for this book is available from the British Library

Typesetting by Grace Note Publications

A Scottish Parliament. Not an end: a means to greater ends.

Donald Dewar
(Speech at the Opening of the Scottish
Parliament,
1 July 1999)

An upturned boat
— a watershed.

Kathleen Jamie
'For a new Scottish Parliament', 2000

For in the end a Parliament is not
a building, but a voyage of intent,
a journey to whatever we might be.
This is our new departure, this is what
we opted for, solid and permanent,
yet tenuous with possibility.

James Robertson
'The Voyage', 2005

CONTENTS

TABLES AND GRAPHS

ACKNOWLEDGEMENTS

Thanks are due to Lindsay Paterson, the editor of *Scottish Affairs*, and to Margaret MacPherson, who for years edited the Institute of Governance's 'Parliamentary News', thus providing an immensely useful source for the 'Annals'.

Thanks, too, to Chris Harvie who allowed me to use our collaborative piece 'After the Albatross' as Chapter I of this book. I'm also hugely indebted to all the MSPs who have participated in the Parliamentary Programme, as well as my students, for their feedback and comment.

I am hugely grateful to Gonzalo Mazzei, the finest publisher I know in Scotland. And we happily acknowledge Andrew Cowan and the Scottish Parliament Corporate Body as the source of the images used on the front and back covers of this book:

Image © Scottish Parliamentary Corporate Body – 2012.
Licensed under the Open Scottish Parliament Licence v1.0. <www.scottish.parliament.uk/Corporateandlegalresources/Open_Licence.pdf>.

The first nine chapters were originally published in *Scottish Affairs*:

Chapter I	No.50 (Winter 2005), pp.26-38.
Chapter II	No.53 (Autumn 2005), pp.136-152.
Chapter III	No.57 (Autumn 2006), pp.112-134.
Chapter IV	No.61 (Autumn 2007), pp.18-49.
Chapter V	No.65 (Autumn 2008), pp.1-37.
Chapter VI	No.69 (Autumn 2009), pp.1-39.
Chapter VII	No.73 (Autumn 2010), pp.61-101.
Chapter VIII	No.78 (Winter 2012), pp.37-85.
Chapter IX	No.82 (Winter 2013), pp.10-72.

The epigraphs by Donald Dewar, Kathleen Jamie and James Robertson come from the following sources:

- Donald Dewar , 'Speech at the opening of the Scottish Parliament, 1 July 1999, <www.scottish.parliament.uk/Education andCommunityPartnershipsresources/New_Parliament_Levels_A-F.pdf>.
- Kathleen Jamie, 'For a new Scottish Parliament', in Alec Finlay (ed.), *Without Day: proposals for a new Scottish Parliament*, Edinburgh: pocketbooks, 2000, p.9
- James Robertson, *Voyage of Intent: Sonnets and Essays from the Scottish Parliament*, Edinburgh: Scottish Book Trust and Luath Press, 2005, p.24.

PREFACE

When I arrived from Tübingen in Edinburgh in March 1995, the Constitutional Convention was finalising its 'blueprint' for the Scottish Parliament – which was eventually published on St Andrew's Day that year: *Scotland's Parliament, Scotland's Right*. At Westminster, of course, the Tories still ruled. For the past 16 years, they had rejected any move towards devolution. But now, the tide was turning. Change was in the air. And indeed, on 1 May 1997, the Labour 'landslide' victory ended 18 years of Tory rule – during the final ten of which they had returned only an average of 10 out of 72 Scottish MPs.

It was an exciting time to arrive in Scotland, after having observed Scottish politics through the office of Chris Harvie, Professor of British and Irish Studies at Tübingen, for the better part of ten years. So I was not completely unaware of the developments which were now coming to fruition, with the White Paper on Devolution in July 1997 and the referendum on 11 September of that year. Unlike 1979, this time over 74% agreed that there should be a Scottish Parliament, and 63.5% agreed that it should have tax-varying powers. In response, Westminster passed the Scotland Act in 1998, and on 6 May 1999 the Scottish electorate could vote for their first Scottish Parliament in nearly 300 years.

The University of Edinburgh acknowledged these momentous developments by founding, in 1998, an Institute which would engage with the evolving new political institutions. Under the directorship of Alice Brown and David McCrone, the Institute of Governance established itself as a research and liaison body, an interface between the University and the devolved polity.

The Institute also began, from the very start of Devolution, to offer a Parliamentary Programme in conjunction with the Parliament, combining academic tuition with practical research experience in the Parliament. As my contract as a researcher on the ESRC-funded European Borders project (under Professor Malcolm Anderson) was nearing its end, the Institute offered me a job with, at its core, responsibility for the Parliamentary Programme.

At about the same time, I was invited by Lindsay Paterson to join the editorial board of *Scottish Affairs* as Book Review Editor. And I began writing occasional pieces for the journal on the progress of the Parliament. After the 2003 election, Chris Harvie and I tried to assess the outcome and the move to the new Parliament building at Holyrood in a piece called 'After the Albatross', indicating the burden the difficult building process had been for the fledgling Parliament. The building's history may have been fraught with controversy but, like many others, I was bowled over when I first saw the inside of it. Seeing the MSPs settling in, and finding ever more evidence of Enric Miralles' ingenuity in designing his

Gesamtkunstwerk, I could perfectly understand how James Robertson, the first 'Writer in Residence' at Holyrood, described his experience:

> I arrived at the Parliament sceptical about both its location and its design. I left it filled with admiration for the building, and very conscious of the energy and enthusiasm that it seems to generate in those who work in it... It is not what one would expect a parliament to look like, and this is one of its strengths. It is impressive rather than magnificent, stylish rather than grand, humorous rather than staid, welcoming rather than imposing, celebratory rather than monumental. It invites comment and challenges preconceptions. It is a series of surprises, an assemblage of connected phrases rather than one big, bombastic statement. It honours history but projects itself into the future. It makes you think. It seems right for 21st-century Scotland.[1]

From 2004, I then embarked on my new role as chronicler of Holyrood. With a wee nod towards Scotland's first political novelist John Galt and his *Annals of a Parish* (1821) and a wink to all those who still tend to misquote Tony Blair as having compared the Scottish Parliament to a parish council,[2] I called my annual review of Scottish politics 'The Annals of the Parish'. Over the past decade, eight of these have appeared in *Scottish Affairs*. Due to the new time scale and greater space restrictions since the journal moved to Edinburgh University Press, the ninth instalment could not be accommodated in time before the referendum.

Both Gonzalo Mazzei of Grace Note Publications, with whom I've published three volumes on Hamish Henderson and the Scottish Folk Revival as well as *View from Zollernblick* (a Festschrift for Chris Harvie), and Lindsay Paterson encouraged me to collect the 'Annals' and publish them in book form, including the as yet unpublished latest chapter. The cut-off point for Chapter 10 could thus be moved to the end of May (rather than the end of March), coinciding with the start of the 'official' (i.e. regulated) 16-week referendum campaign. After the referendum, there will be the next chapter of the 'Annals', looking back on the referendum campaign and its result, in its usual place in *Scottish Affairs*.

---

[1] James Robertson, *Voyage of Intent: Sonnets and Essays from the Scottish Parliament*, Edinburgh: Scottish book trust and Luath Press, 2005, p.11.

[2] I leave it to Brian Taylor, the BBC's Scottish editor and author of two books about the Scottish Parliament, to explain: 'It is said to this day on sundry websites that Tony Blair compared the Scottish Parliament to a "parish council". That is simply not correct. He was speaking in the context of a debate about tax powers. He pointed out that it would be curious if the Scottish Parliament were to be denied the fiscal clout currently available to the humble Parish council. He was contrasting the two – not comparing them.' 'The Scottish legacy of Tony Blair', *BBC News Scotland*, 10 May 2007, <news.bbc.co.uk/1/hi/scotland/6639997.stm>.

The ten chapters in this book have only been very lightly edited. Some typos and factual mistakes were corrected, and the style of referencing was synchronised. The Annals are supposed to be a record of their time, not written from hindsight. The collaborative 'After the Albatross' is included to set the scene, the following nine chapters are charting what Henry McLeish, echoing James Mitchell, likes to call 'the evolution of devolution'.[3] They include the 2005 and 2010 UK General elections, the game-changing 2007 and 2011 Scottish Parliament elections, the local elections of 2003, 2007 and 2012 and the European elections of 2004, 2009 and 2014 – as well as a host of by-elections for Westminster and Holyrood. They also record the legislative process, with more than 150 bills passed by the Scottish Parliament in the period covered, the coming and going of politicians, and the odd wee scandal. Holyrood scandals have, by stark contrast with Westminster, mostly been of the small beer variety, from 'Taxi for Mr McLetchie' to Frank McAveety's 'pie-gate' or Alex Salmond's Holyrood lunch auctions...

Of John Galt it was said that, as a parliamentary lobbyist, he 'hung around the corridors of power' – my involvement on my frequent visits to Holyrood has had more to do with arranging placements for my students than 'nursing bills through parliament,'[4] but it has offered me some inside perspectives into the political processes at Holyrood. I do have my own opinions about Scottish politics, but for the purpose of these Annals it is perhaps not appropriate to wear them on my sleeves. A modicum of impartiality is called for – even if it might spur accusations of sitting on the fence.

The setting up and the early years of the Parliament were well-covered by Brian Taylor's *The Road to the Scottish Parliament* (Edinburgh University Press, 2002), and the 2007 election and the Parliament's tenth anniversary in 2009 triggered a trio of assessments: John Curtice, David McCrone, Nicola McEwen, Michael Marsh and Rachel Ormiston's *Revolution or Evolution?: The 2007 Scottish Elections* (Edinburgh University Press, 2009), Hamish Macdonell's *Uncharted Territory: The Story of Scottish Devolution, 1999-2009* (Politico's, 2009) and *The Scottish Parliament 1999-2009: The First Decade*, edited by Charlie Jeffery and James Mitchell (Luath and Hansard Society, 2009). The Constitution Unit at University College London has kept tabs on constitutional change across the UK in its *Monitor* series.[5] These Annals will, hopefully, stand alongside those publications as a record of a decade of Scottish devolution, which may help us understand how we've got to where we are in this year of the Scottish independence referendum.

---

[3] James Mitchell, 'The Evolution of Devolution: Labour's Home Rule Strategy in Opposition', *Government and Opposition*, vol.33, no.4 (Autumn 1998), pp.479-96.

[4] Carl MacDougall, *Writing Scotland: How Scotland's Writers Shaped the Nation*, Edinburgh: Birlinn, 2004, p.45.

[5] <www.ucl.ac.uk/constitution-unit/publications/tabs/monitor>.

Chapter I

AFTER THE ALBATROSS:
A NEW START FOR THE
SCOTTISH PARLIAMENT?

with Christopher Harvie

'OPEN THE DOORS AND BEGIN!'

To the words of the poet Edwin Morgan, on 9 October 2004 Holyrood the Building was officially opened.[1] Over the first term of the Scottish Parliament, its slow progress and escalating cost had hung like another poet's symbol, Coleridge's albatross, around the neck of the new Scottish politics, made heavier by part of the media which was only too willing to load it on to their anti-devolution polemic. After the elections of May 2003 George Reid, the second Presiding Officer, had apparently managed to avoid further delays and cost rises. Only weeks before the opening, the Fraser Inquiry had published its Final Report,[2] apportioning blame evenly across the board. The MSPs' collective sigh of relief was audible. No-one's severed head was going to decorate the portico.[3]

Once opened, folk were even positive. With no major teething problems, Enric Miralles' *Gesamtkunstwerk* proved a popular and critical success. Summing up the architectural response, Stuart MacDonald, the Director of the Lighthouse in Glasgow, spoke of 'a world-class, iconic parliament building ... with the undoubted power to express the complexity of our national identity.'[4] In the first three months, some 150,000 people visited.

---

[1] 'Open the Doors!', Edwin Morgan's poem for the opening of the Scottish Parliament, 9 October 2004, was published in *Scot Lit* (Association for Scottish Literary Studies), No.31, 2004, p.9; and subsequently included in Morgan's collection *A Book of Lives*, Manchester: Carcanet, 2007.

[2] Lord Fraser of Carmyllie QC, *The Holyrood Inquiry*, Edinburgh: Scottish Parliament, 2004.

[3] Richard Parry, 'The Verdict on Holyrood', *Scottish Affairs*, No.49 (Autumn 2004), pp.1-5.

[4] Stuart MacDonald, 'No place for a public hanging', *The Scotsman*, 11 December 2004.

The move was widely seen as a new start for the MSPs – 'Raising the Game' was a phrase frequently used – who would have to live up to the place.[5] Anecdotal evidence suggests the psychological process has already begun. Journalists and MSPs talk of an improvement in the quality of the debates and the confidence of committees, to match the improvement in working conditions. When journalists had all but withdrawn from the Commons, this was a modest advance for the parliamentary idea.[6] Creating too high expectations based on a new building alone could easily backfire, as with the newly-established Parliament in 1999. William McIlvanney has voiced his 'tattered dreams' gnawed by MSPs' feeble radicalism: 'It may be a new parliament, but it doesn't feel new enough.'[7] But there is now a realistic chance that Parliament will be judged for what it is – or is not – doing for Scotland, rather than through the distorted lens of an out-of-control building project.

So, what sort of political structures have walked through the doors? What is the outlook for Scottish politics in terms of issues and perspectives? And for self-government, 'a journey begun long ago and which has no end'?[8]

2003 – A SMALL EARTHQUAKE?

On 1 May 2003, the second elections for the Parliament took place. The polls were ambiguous, particularly over the Iraq war. The anti-war demo on 15 February 2003 was the largest staged in Glasgow in recent times, with around 100,000 participants, but by late April Labour seemed to profit from a 'Baghdad Bounce'; it was at least nine points ahead of its Nationalist rivals. Then, on 2 May, the Scots found they had, at a blow, received a six-party system and a possible Lib-Lab coalition with only a 5-seat majority. A small earthquake had happened.

The Coalition had enjoyed mixed fortunes: an accident-prone Executive went through three First Ministers in as many years, with the meter ticking on the Miralles building. *Spinmeisters*, all-conquering in London, bombed in Scotland. A mild reform, supposed to reverse Thatcher's homophobic Clause 28, saw Cardinal Winning and the evangelical Brian Souter of Stagecoach launch an illiberal backlash, steered by the *Daily Record*, and get a million signatures. Moreover, Gordon Brown's economics –

[5] Robin Dinwoodie and Douglas Fraser, 'Time to raise our game: Presiding Officer urges MSPs to look to the future', *The Herald*, 7 September 2004; see also Kenny MacAskill, *Building a Nation: Post-Devolution Nationalism in Scotland*, Edinburgh: Luath Press, 2004.2004, pp. 15, 78.

[6] Andrew Marr, *My Trade: A Short History of British Journalism*, London: Macmillan, 2004.

[7] William McIlvanney, 'Tattered Dreams', *The Sunday Times*, 28 November 2004.

[8] Donald Dewar, Speech at the Opening of Parliament, 1 July 1999, <www.scottish. parliament.uk/corporate/history/donaldDewar/>.

concentrating on the service sector and a house-price-driven high street boom – stumbled in Scotland. Most sectors were in or close to recession, with major closures not just in the few remaining traditional industries but in hi-tech 'Silicon Glen'. Farming, fishing and call centres were all in deep trouble, and the post 9/11 financial and tourism collapse was taking serious bites out of Edinburgh's economy. Following the fall of the Chancellor's protégé Henry McLeish, relations between Jack McConnell, Scotland's pawky First Minister, and Brown had grown notably distant: a prominent English Labourite remarked before the elections that the Chancellor and his friends were 'sitting on their hands'.

Scots electoral politics is a complex blend of regional and class loyalties, meriting a preliminary excursus into political geography. Three-quarters of Scots live in a thirty-mile-broad diagonal band between Ayr in the south and Aberdeen in the north. North-west and south east of this strip are thinly peopled rural areas directly represented by non-Labour parties. And within it? In 1996 the Scottish Council Foundation made out a useful threefold social division: between settled Scots, insecure Scots, and excluded Scots. This expressed itself on the voting map of central Scotland: the first group – voting Conservative, New Labour, Lib Dem and SNP – was present in the outlying towns, suburbs and counties. The 'insecure' – voting SSP, Greens, Old Labour – in the city centres; and the 'excluded' – Old Labour, SSP and (predominantly) non-voters – in the peripheral housing schemes.

The entrenched ruling group in Labour's 'fortresses' (Ayrshire, Lanarkshire, Mid- and East Lothian and, above all, Glasgow) was alienated, deeply opposed to McConnell's intention to bring in proportional representation for local elections, an obligation to his Liberal Democrat partners which would deprive Labour of (for example) a 90% dominance of Glasgow City Council on 47% of the vote. Allegations of multiple malpractice in such power-rich, member-poor areas refused to go away, although Scottish Labour was notably free from the through-and-through penetration by big business facilitated by Tony Blair's fund-raisers, described lapidarily by Henry Drucker, that much-missed Scottish Labour stalwart and effective founding-father of *Scottish Affairs*, as 'evil'.[9] Labour MPs at Westminster were in little better mood. Apart from ministers and notorious 'bomb-throwers' like Tam Dalyell and George Galloway (expelled in 2003), they had sunk out of sight, emerging only to carry unpopular legislation against their English comrades.

Most worrying of all, even a favourable poll showed that Labour might mobilise only 47% of its vote, against the Nationalists' 58%, particularly since towards the end of April Baghdad seemed to be retreating from the front pages of Scotland's populist tabloids, the *Record* and the Sun.

[9] David Osler, *Labour Party PLC: New Labour as a Party of Business*, Edinburgh: Mainstream, 2002.

Labour's coalition partners, the Liberal Democrats, had done well over the four years in being still there (unlike all of their Labour co-ministers bar McConnell), in the persons of Jim Wallace, Justice Minister and (twice) acting First Minister, and Ross Finnie, Rural Affairs Minister. In most respects left of Labour, they could claim responsibility for some of the Executive's more progressive acts – abolition of upfront tuition fees, free personal care for the elderly, the freedom of information act.[10] Their vote, however, remained static at around 15% and (ironically for a pro-PR party) they depended strongly on first-past-the-post seats (see Table 1) in rural Scotland. They were also losing patience. The Conservatives, surviving only because of PR, faced a new right-wing rival, the Scottish People's Alliance, to which three ex-MSPs had defected. Polls showed the Tories as low as 10%, though they argued that this ignored one by-election victory (Ayr in 2000), a string of council successes, and their leader David McLetchie, perhaps the most effective senior MSP, who had the downfall of Henry McLeish to his credit.

The Scottish National Party had lost – for reasons never wholly fathomed – the eloquent Alex Salmond to Westminster (he was returned by his Banff and Buchan constituency in the 2001 general election). It was now led by John Swinney, respected but somehow unmemorable. PR had allowed it to break out of its north-east and south-west rural reservations, though less dramatically than Plaid Cymru had done in 1999 in Wales. In 2003 it tried *both* to recruit from the disillusioned left and to offer a pro-business tax- reducing agenda. But it failed to realise it had to be centralised to master the regional list system. The selection exercise in 2002 left two of its best brains – education spokesman Mike Russell and economics spokesman Andrew Wilson – facing defeat and provoked the secession of the instantly recognisable Margo MacDonald. Although the SNP played down its goal of independence, presented its policies with flair, and had the reputation of getting its vote out, Swinney clocked up only half of McConnell's recognition factor, and *that* was not high. Most of all, the SNP had underestimated the competition from the fringe.

The polls showed a potential explosive power among the small parties and independent candidates. The Scottish Socialist Party, led by the eloquent Tommy Sheridan, 'the man with the tan' (non-smoking, non-drinking, but with an addiction to sunbeds: his recognition factor almost as good as McConnell's) was reaching 10% in some polls and possibly 22% in the Glasgow area (on 1 May it actually got nearly 16% in Glasgow). The Greens were getting around 6%. Both were pro-independence. Independents campaigning on local causes could eat deeply into Labour's support, and pensioners and hard-done-by fishermen were forming single-interest parties.

---

[10] Eberhard Bort, 'The new institutions: an interim assessment', in Michael O'Neill (ed.), *Devolution and British Politics*, Harlow: Pearson Longman, 2004, pp.295-318.

Table 1: Scottish Parliament Election Results 2003

Party	1st Vote %		Seats	2nd Vote %		Seats	Total Seats
Labour	34.62	(-4.18)	46 (-7)	29.62	(-3.98)	4 (+1)	50 (-6)
SNP	23.78	(-4.92)	9 (+2)	21.55	(-5.75)	18 (-10)	27 (-8)
Con	16.61	(+1.01)	3 (+3)	15.54	(+0.14)	15 (-3)	18 (0)
Lib Dem	15.36	(+1.16)	13 (+1)	11.64	(-0.76)	4 (-1)	17 (0)
SSP	6.2	(+5.2)	0 (0)	6.48	(+4.48)	6 (+5)	6 (+5)
Greens	0		0	6.46	(+2.86)	7 (+6)	7 (+6)
SSCUP*	0		0	1.47	(+1.47)	1 (+1)	1 (+1)
Others **	3.43	(+1.73)	2 (+1)	7.24	(+1.64)	1 (-1)	3 (0)

[* Scottish Senior Citizens Unity Party; ** two directly elected independent MSPs (Jean Turner and Dennis Canavan); one on the list (Margo MacDonald)]

This development seemingly reacted to the composition of the first parliament: overwhelmingly middle-class and young middle-aged. Despite the fact that the home rule campaign had been headed-up by the over-sixties (21% of the population) they had only a handful of MSPs; a similar population percentage between 18 and 29 was even worse represented, by only 2 MSPs.

Would dissent over the Iraq War, along with Scots irritation at London's dominance of British media, art and culture, further erode the Scottish intelligentsia's support for Labour, once 'their' party? Would 'doing less, better', McConnell's modest, populist credo – defending Scotland's traditionally high levels of public finance for schools and hospitals, throwing impressive sums at transport projects in Labour areas: trams for Edinburgh and Glasgow, railways to the airports – be enough to maintain Labour's grip on power?

McConnell ran with the issue of 'ned culture' – anti-social behaviour – which suited his tactical shrewdness and populist style. There certainly was a problem, as many of Scotland's 50,000 drug addicts and 200,000 alcoholics (three times the German level) were young, or were proving feckless parents of the young.[11] Some would have seen the root cause in third-generation unemployment, unadmitted by Brown, and the prospectless anomie that followed from this. McConnell's clampdown – electronic curfews for wayward teenagers, threats to jail their parents – disturbed his Liberal allies with their implications for civil liberties, something that even led to him clashing in public with Jim Wallace, but it strengthened Labour in the heartlands, and curbed any tendency to place second votes elsewhere.

The Greens played well tactically by concentrating precisely on this. Those who wanted to vote Green were guided direct to the list. They and the SSP also got through to an 18-26 year old group (what the

---

[11] Christopher Harvie, *Mending Scotland*, Glendaruel: Argyll, 2004, p.70.

writer Andrew O'Hagan called the chemical/hedonist generation) which otherwise polled less than 33 per cent.[12]

AFTERWARDS

The major issue handled by Parliament after the election had played no part in the campaign. The banning of smoking in enclosed public places was first tabled by Jack McConnell in October 2004, following a similar measure carried by Dáil Eireann and implemented in Ireland on 29 March 2004. Some observers thought this showed authority increasingly being concentrated in the Executive, with Parliament only reluctantly (if at all) being allowed to discuss such Scoto-Westminster decisions as the transfer of the Scotrail franchise from National Express to First Group, or the processing of schemes for new casinos through a Sewel motion:[13] a pseudo-federalism which was genuinely undemocratic.

Nevertheless, the coalition Executive proved stable (by the end of 2004 it had only lost two votes, on the competitive tendering of ferry routes and a symbolic one protesting against the reorganisation of Scotland's regiments). PR for local government, which could have split Labour, became law before the summer recess of 2004 – another feather in the Lib Dems' cap – and it outrode a series of embarrassing crises. Cathy Jamieson in Justice had to cope with the unreliability of Reliance in the privatised transport of prisoners; Frank McAveety in Culture was faced with, and blamed for, the financial malaise of Scottish Opera; Malcolm Chisholm in Health was attacked for controversial hospital closures. McConnell moved him to Communities in an October reshuffle, and replaced McAveety with Patricia Ferguson. But, overall, his resilient Executive contrasted dramatically with an unravelling Downing Street.

Because of opposition weakness? Alex Salmond's return from being 'king over the water' to lead the SNP (from Westminster) in September 2004, after Swinney was hounded out by the permanent bickering of some of his backbenchers, was fortified by a strong performance by his deputy and opposition leader in Holyrood, Nicola Sturgeon. But the SNP has still to come to terms with the bruising of May 2003, and with its devolution dilemma. 'The party must reflect the new political landscape. It must nurture and support the institution,' so reads Kenny MacAskill's

---

[12] John W. Robertson, Neil Blain and Paula Cowan, 'Naming the First Minister: Scottish Adolescents' Knowledge and Perceptions of Political Decision-Making Processes', *Scottish Affairs*, No.49 (Autumn 2004), pp.23-43.

[13] A legislative mode named after the Aberdeen academic John, Lord Sewel, whereby a matter of joint interest would be, for the sake of convenience, kicked back to Westminster (see Paul Cairney and Michael Keating, 'Sewel Motions in the Scottish Parliament', *Scottish Affairs*, No.47 (Spring 2004), pp.115-134).

prescription.[14] Regarding independence and interdependence as not being 'mutually irreconcilable', he urges his party to 'define itself as a mainstream European Social Democratic Party' committed to 'creating the best devolved Scotland there can be.' In other words, gradualism is the only game in town: 'The way forward will be incremental, building up both the Parliament as an institution and the powers to be exercised within it.'[15] More fundamentalist Nationalists think that such a successful devolved Parliament might divert Scots from demanding further constitutional change.

Amazingly, given the respect David McLetchie commands in- and outside the debating chamber, there have been persistent rumours of discontent with his leadership. This is probably linked to the unlikeliness of the Scottish Conservatives quitting their fringe ghetto, due to the dimness of their British prospects. The Greens, the big winners of 2003, have been lacklustre since. Their environmentalism may garner respect, but they have not found a 'big theme' that would extend their profile. The transition from one-man party (the colourful Robin Harper) to seven-member party group seems more difficult than perhaps expected. Such problems have become even more true for the SSP. In November 2004 they turned on their charismatic leader, Tommy Sheridan, over tabloid headlines about an alleged affair with a party member. By February 2005, according to a narrow party decision, a new leader will be elected. 'We are bigger than one person', an SSP member said.[16] Sure.

Initially, after the election, there was talk of a loose but activist rainbow coalition emerging among those in opposition with an independence commitment. So far, there has been little sign of this. But the agenda for it exists.

READING THE RUNES?

Has devolution strengthened the Union along proto-federal lines? There is still no elaborated structure of German-style cooperative federalism (Conferences of Minister Presidents, Bundesrat, etc.) and Westminster's authority is still represented in Cabinet by (in descending order of power) the Northern Ireland, Welsh and Scottish part-time secretaries. With the continuing impasse in Northern Ireland and the demolition of North-Eastern devolution on 4 November 2004, 'Home Rule

---

[14] Kenny MacAskill, *Building a Nation: Post-Devolution Nationalism in Scotland*, Edinburgh: Luath Press,.2004, p.79.

[15] *Ibid.*, pp. 31, 50, 78.

[16] Paul Hutcheon, 'Falling From Grace?; Tommy Sheridan's forced departure over allegations about his private life has left his party without a champion', *Sunday Herald*, 14 November 2004.

all round' seems dead.[17] Yet north-south tensions persist over Scotland's 'generous' treatment by the Barnett Formula (in place since 1978) for setting the block grant, whose restructuring, in a direction unfavourable to Scotland, seems inevitable.

Asked about the federal element, McConnell once said, not utterly provocatively, that he had more dealings with Brussels than with London. But his unobtrusive one-year presidency of RegLeg (the association of European regions with legislative powers) was crowned with little success. The proposed European Constitution may recognise the existence of sub- Member State governance, but it does not offer them a seat at the top table.[18]

Iraq has not faded into the background, but got tangled up with the exposure of the Black Watch to attack near Falluja and to amalgamation at home. The SNP has traditionally been an anti-nuclear, neutralist party; the SSP and the Greens even more determinedly so. Were these parties to dominate a future Parliament, the continuation of Britain's Trident nuclear submarines, based in the Clyde, and appallingly expensive to house elsewhere, would become problematic.[19] SNP coyness about a referendum on independence (which would probably still show a majority for the status quo) has been countered by broad and growing inter-party support for 'Fiscal Autonomy' (later and more euphoniously 'Fiscal Freedom' or 'Fiscal Independence') – meaning that Scotland should raise its own tax revenue, with sums precepted for 'British' purposes.[20] The Tories moved tentatively in the direction of giving the Scottish Parliament tax responsibility, and Wendy Alexander championed 'Fiscal Federalism' when summing up the series of Fraser of Allander lectures she had promoted.[21]

With a 'semi-fledged' six-party system, plus four independents, should we fear the 'Italianisation of Scottish politics'? A prospect made even less inspiring because Scotland lacks Italy's positive side: the strong local authority, micro-capitalist dimension. Yet politics *at* Holyrood looks like being more exciting than the first term. Some business is left pending. The Scots still have a 'white' Parliament – without a single ethnic minority MSP nor, despite the jostling for the Muslim vote in the war context, the prospect of one. By contrast, the gender balance, rather unexpectedly,

[17] Nigel Morris, 'Crushing "No" vote leaves devolution plans in ruins', *The Independent*, 6 November 2004.

[18] Eberhard Bort, 'Scotland and Europe, or: Room at the Top for "Constitutional Regions"', *Romanian Journal of European Affairs*, Vol.4, No.2, 2004, pp.55-64.

[19] William Walker and Malcolm Chalmers, *Uncharted Waters: The UK, Nuclear Weapons and the Scottish Question* , East Linton: Tuckwell, 2001.

[20] David Heald (ed.), *Scottish Affairs: Special Issue: Fiscal Autonomy*, No.41 (Spring 2002).

[21] Paul Hallwood and Ronald MacDonald, *Fiscal Federalism*, Glasgow: University of Strathclyde (The Allander Series), 2004.

improved (the Scottish Parliament is now 39.5% female, though the National Assembly in Cardiff actually reaches 50%). Labour has now a clear majority of women MSPs (28 out of 50), and the women of the SSP and the Greens compensated for the losses of the SNP. Scotland also got its first openly gay MSP, the Glasgow Green Patrick Harvie.

OUTLOOK

In a much-hyped address to the British Council on 8 July 2004, Chancellor Brown, *quondam* editor of *The Red Paper on Scotland* but sounding more like G. M. Trevelyan, lauded a Britishness to which fewer than 20% of Scots were committed;[22] yet a year earlier Matthew Parris, the *Times* columnist and by now dissident Tory, remarked on the way in which Scotland was concealed from London's purview (Parris 2003).[23] The fact that his was – even during an election campaign – a rare voice was proof enough of this. McConnell's cabinet, however, seems in its composition to confirm some perennial southern criticisms. It is overwhelmingly drawn from west central Scotland and from the Labour 'fortresses' which, on closer inspection, seem to exist only *there*. Henry McLeish may criticise the relative unimportance of 'Jack's lads', but then he himself tells us more about the royals than the Scottish cabinet.[24] Of the 'Edinburgh effect' – the high-profile 'culture-and-commerce' mix which had underwritten the city's success – there is scarcely a sign. Even McConnell's one radical policy, PR for local elections, has a commitment to STV (Single Transferable Vote) which guards against overmuch pluralism.

The Parliament may have delivered some landmark legislation, but is it fulfilling aspirations to a fundamentally open and inclusive polity? Or is it a mission to the 'insecure Scots', offering smart deals to secure middle class status, values and jobs? The decline in voter turnout (from 59 to 49% between 1999 and 2003) is an indication of the disappointment of the Scottish electorate with the results of the new politics in terms of industrial regeneration, combating poverty and addressing infrastructure deficits.[25] But the surveys also show that the principle of devolution has

[22] Gordon Brown, 'British Council Address', 8 July 2004, <politics.guardian.co.uk/labour/story/0,9061,1256550,00.html>.

[23] Matthew Parris, 'Here is a story about the Scots. It's no laughing matter', *The Times*, 17 May 2003.

[24] Henry McLeish, *Scotland First: Truth and Consequences*, Edinburgh: Mainstream, 2004.

[25] Both authors welcomed Sarah Boyack to the Freudenstadt Colloquium in 1999 as the first Scottish Minister to visit continental Europe. In 2004 not a single one of Boyack's railway projects had been realised. In 2003 the railway to Freudenstadt was electrified with an express service, a decision taken in 2001.

not lost popular support.[26] Those who welcomed McConnell's 2003 St Andrew's Day speech about the centrality of culture, the arts and creativity, have become deeply disappointed with the record of the Scottish Executive so far. Not just the starving of Scottish Opera, but the general perception that initiatives and consultations and strategies come and go, *because they are an end in themselves.*

This stasis may stem from forty years of de-industrialisation and external control, but cash as such has not been a major problem. Every spending review from 11 Downing Street has presented the Scottish Executive with new ways to throw money at structural problems – with limited success so far, particularly as regards delivery in the Scottish NHS. The debate about fiscal responsibility will not go away – a parliament without a fully-fledged budget debate and budgetary rights is, in the eyes of the public, no full parliament. The Holyrood inquiry spotlighted tensions between the political elite and the civil service. McConnell has tried to bind the Scottish bureaucracy closer to his Executive, stressing that it is answerable to him – yet it remains part of the UK civil service. Its whip is cracked by Whitehall.

But the situation could change, with the Treasury itself and Gordon Brown looking vulnerable. Should the concatenation of inflation, personal and public debt, tax increases, and corporate and pensions collapse kick in, and the Whitehall Scots not remedy matters, then fundamental trouble will face a far-from-monolithic Scots politics. The forthcoming UK general election is already straining the Executive coalition, with the Lib Dems claiming credit for the successes, and provoking intemperate Labour reactions.[27] That there is further potential for friction between the Blairite reform agenda and the Scottish Executive's approach became apparent when Tony Blair visited Bute House in December 2004 on one of his rare forays into Scotland.

Is the smoking ban really a new radical departure for McConnell & Co, as Iain Macwhirter and Brian Taylor suggest?[28] Or is it closer to William McIlvanney's 'indication of how tame our parliament has so far been?'[29] In 2000 the ever-readable Andrew Marr compared the infant Parliament with the other Scots mastering London and did not think the compromise

---

[26] Nicola McEwen, 'Is Devolution at Risk? Examining Attitudes Towards the Scottish Parliament in Light of the 2003 Election', *Scottish Affairs*, No. 44 (Summer 2003), pp. 54-73.

[27] Catherine MacLeod, 'Labour targets Lib Dems for poll attack', *The Herald*, 21 December 2004.

[28] Iain Macwhirter, 'Holyrood acts as London muddles', *The Herald*, 21 November 2004; Brian Taylor, 'Is Scotland too posh to puff?', *BBC News Scotland*, 17 December 2004, <news. bbc.co.uk/1/hi/scotland/4103301.stm>.

[29] William McIlvanney, 'Tattered Dreams', *The Sunday Times*, 28 November 2004.

would last,[30] with the decline of Scots expressing 'Britishness'.[31] Things have not changed, and with a quasi-federal Britain off the menu for the foreseeable future, Scotland (and Wales) will have to adjust to being on their own, not in the company of the English regions.

Perhaps as early as May 2005 we will find out what happens if Labour is returned to Westminster with a reduced majority based on Scottish (and Welsh) MPs, but with a minority of English MPs. The 'West Lothian Question' all over again. The Scots may be insignificant enough for the South not to get too steamed up about the Barnett formula and the few bawbees more per head spent on Scotland, but Scottish MPs deciding what is to be spent on English health, English education and English transport, perhaps enforcing cuts or additional fees the Scottish Parliament refuses to make in Scotland? Our guess is that the English will be less patient than the Scots were under Westminster rule. What then? Ban Scots MPs from voting on English matters – thus creating two classes of MPs and, de facto, an English Parliament? Perhaps with a Conservative majority? Or the need for a Labour–Lib Dem pact for English matters – while retaining a Labour majority for 'reserved' British affairs? At the price of PR for Westminster? Regional devolution could have been a way forward, but not after 4 November.

Finally, there is the question of Europe. What will happen in a UK referendum on the Constitution? Will the 'pro-European' SNP campaign shoulder to shoulder with UKIP and the Tories for a No-vote, trying to extract fisheries from the exclusive competence of the EU?[32] How would that play in the eyes of other mainstream European Social Democratic parties? And will there be, over time, a closer partnership between the 'regions' and the European institutions? Handing on the baton of RegLeg President to the Bavarian minister of European affairs, Eberhard Sinner, McConnell called for its recognition to be enhanced as a means of linking the EU to its citizens: 'The best way to do that is for devolved governments to have a stronger role in shaping and applying EU laws and regulations.'[33]

Despite the defeat for the SNP in 2003, the cause of independence was numerically boosted in the new Parliament. Given that some SNP MSPs might be shaky on independence, and some Labour MSPs might favour

---

[30] Andrew Marr, *The Day Britain Died*, London: Profile, 2000, pp. 65-72.

[31] David McCrone, *Understanding Scotland: the sociology of a nation*, London: Routledge, 2001, pp. 149-74.

[32] Hamish MacDonnell, 'Confusion as SNP threatens to fight against EU consitution', *The Scotsman*, 22 April 2004. They have a case, given that only seven of the 25 EU Member States now have a North Sea coastline, but whether this will change the sea's ecological crisis is another matter.

[33] Robbie Dinwoodie, 'McConnell calls for European recognition', *The Herald*, 1 December 2004.

it, 27 SNP MSPs, 6 SSP, 7 Greens, plus Margo MacDonald and Dennis Canavan made 42 – against 38 in 1999 (35 SNP plus 1 SSP, 1 Green and Canavan). But is arithmetic enough? Will these parties further the cause, or fragment and weaken it? Apart from this, will the increase on the left make a tangible difference in the policy-making process of the Scottish Parliament? And thus increase policy divergence between Scotland and the rest of the UK?

An 'admirable working legislature', in the words of Richard Parry, may, with Holyrood, have 'achieved its deserved physical embodiment.'[34] The albatross is off its neck. It will no longer obscure the achievements – and the shortcomings – of the Scottish Parliament and its Executive in fulfilling the aspirations which still focus on the devolved institution.

[December 2004]

---

[34] Richard Parry, 'The Verdict on Holyrood', *Scottish Affairs*, No.49 (Autumn 2004), p.5.

Chapter II

THE YEAR AT HOLYROOD
2004-2005

A NEW HOME

Any chronicling of the past year in Scottish politics would have to start with the official opening of the Holyrood Parliament on 9 October 2004. The ceremony itself, slightly more understated than the previous opening on the Mound, was a dignified celebration, with the Riding down the Royal Mile and the Gaelic psalm singing, Nicola Benedetti, and 'Makar' Edwin Morgan's gallus poem 'Open the Doors', read with esprit by Liz Lochhead. The Scottish thistle showed its best barbed charm by greeting Her Majesty the Queen with Copland's 'Fanfare for the Common Man'. And a cross-party rendering of Burns's 'Auld Lang Syne', led by Eddie Reader, brought the proceedings in the debating chamber to a rousing close.

The £416 mill Parliament was, by that time, already a working environment. The 129 MSPs and their staff had moved in at the beginning of September. On 15 September Lord Fraser had published the findings of his Holyrood Inquiry, which First Minister Jack McConnell had ordered before the 2003 elections and which had been hearing evidence at the Scottish Land Court in Edinburgh from more than sixty witnesses since October 2003. Lord Fraser's verdict was that he had found no single 'villain of the piece' who could be held responsible for the project's delays and escalating costs, but civil servants had to bear the brunt of the Lord's criticism for not informing ministers of the growing problems and increasing costs associated with the Holyrood project.[1]

In his response to the Inquiry Report, George Reid, the Parliament's Presiding Officer, expressed what the majority inside and outside of Holyrood seemed to share: a call for closure, a belief that Scotland now needed to look forward to the work the Parliament would do in its new environment, rather than looking back on the building itself.

The *Guardian*'s architectural critic got it right: 'The Scottish Parliament building is despised largely by mean-minded politicians. History will forget them as it learns to befriend this astonishing building that seems

---

[1] Lord Fraser, *The Holyrood Inquiry*, (2004), <www.holyroodinquiry.org/FINAL_report/report.htm>.

to have grown from the city's botanical gardens as much as it has from the architects' computer screens.'[2]

LEGISLATIVE PROGRAMME

At the beginning of September, Jack McConnell had announced the Executive's legislative programme 2004-2005. Twelve bills were to be introduced during the new Parliamentary session, and another five bills, already introduced before the summer, would complete their process. Tougher jail sentences for paedophiles and new powers to tackle failing schools, a Budget Bill providing 'efficiency savings', a bill to protect children from the crime of 'internet grooming' where children are preyed on by paedophiles, a Prevention of Female Genital Mutilation Bill to prohibit the sending of young Scots girls abroad for a what McConnell branded a 'grotesque crime', a 'comprehensive modernisation programme' of secondary schools, with the establishment of 'centres of excellence', but without 'elitist selection of pupils', a Licensing Bill, a Health Bill focusing on tissue and organ donation and transplants, a Housing Bill to strengthen the rights of private sector tenants and to assist councils in dealing with areas in decline, a Charity Bill to increase public confidence in charities, a Strategic Environmental Assessment Bill to regulate the assessment of the environmental impact of planning applications, a Transport Bill and a Gaelic Language Bill were announced as part of what the First Minister promised to be 'modern laws for a modern Scotland'.[3]

The five bills which would continue their passage through parliament involved tenement law reform, tougher penalties for attacks on emergency workers, new powers to enable ministers to intervene over failing schools, a new regulatory framework for the water industry and updating laws covering the fire service. McConnell also reassured that 'in this parliament we will take action to reduce the terrible toll that smoking takes on our people.'[4]

In her first reposte as the SNP's Holyrood leader, Nicola Sturgeon conceded that 'it is not that any of the proposed bills are particularly objectionable. On the contrary,' she said, 'many of them are eminently supportable.' But the legislative programme did 'not tackle the big challenges that we face as a nation,' and it 'lacks vision and a clear sense of purpose and direction for the nation.' Instead she proposed policies

---

[2] Jonathan Glancey, 'Building sights: Stirling shortlist unveiled', *The Guardian*, 28 July 2005.

[3] Jack McConnell, 'Legislative Speech', *BBC News Scotland*, 7 September. 2004, <news.bbc. co.uk/1/hi/scotland/3634150.stm>.

[4] *Ibid*

including a bullet train between Glasgow and Edinburgh and a Green Card scheme to attract foreign skilled workers.[5]

Shortly before he was moved to the Health portfolio, Finance Minister Andy Kerr announced at the end of September the Executive's spending plans for the next three years to the Parliament. Over 2005-06, 2006-07 and 2007-08, he said, more than £85 billion would be invested in Scotland.[6]

HOLYROOD SHUFFLE

On 4 October, Jack McConnell announced a Cabinet reshuffle, necessitated by the pressure the mass protests against hospital closures had heaped on Health Minister Malcolm Chisholm.[7] At the end of September, Chisholm had reversed the decision to close the Queen Mother's Hospital in Glasgow but, as Brian Ponsonby put it, 'the decision to breathe new life into the hospital gave the kiss of death to Mr Chisholm's career as health minister.[8] Andy Kerr, as already indicated, was moved from his previous post as Minister for Finance and Public Services to the post of Minister for Health and Community Care; Rhona Brankin was appointed to the post of Deputy Minister for Health and Community Care; Margaret Curran was moved from her previous post as Minister for Communities to the post of Minister for Parliamentary Business; Patricia Ferguson was moved from her previous post as Minister for Parliamentary Business to the post of Minister for Tourism, Culture and Sport; Malcolm Chisholm was moved from his previous post as Minister for Health to the post of Minister for Communities; Johann Lamont was appointed to the post of Deputy Minister for Communities; Tom McCabe was moved from his post as Deputy Minister for Health to the post of Minister for Finance and Public Service Reform; Alan Wilson was moved from his post as Deputy Minister for Environment and Rural Development to the post of Deputy Minister for Enterprise and Lifelong Learning; and Lewis Macdonald was moved from his post as Deputy Minister for Enterprise and Lifelong Learning to the post of Deputy Minister for Environment and Rural Development.

As Jack McConnell further explained, the posts of Tourism, Culture and Sport and Transport would now be fully salaried Cabinet posts to reflect

[5] 'Parties mull over series of bills', *BBC News Scotland*, 7 September 2004, <news.bbc. co.uk/1/hi/scotland/3635060.stm>.

[6] 'Spending promises under scrutiny', *BBC News Scotland*, 29 September 2004, <news.bbc. co.uk/1/hi/scotland/3701932.stm>.

[7] Liam McDougall, 'Health reform: no pain, no gain?', *Sunday Herald*, 12 September 2004.

[8] Brian Ponsonby, 'Politics review: July to September', *BBC News Scotland*, 30 December 2004, <news.bbc.co.uk/1/hi/scotland/4132963.stm>.

added responsibilities in the portfolios. Transport would now have the added responsibilities of Telecommunications and Post Offices, and the Tourism, Culture and Sport Minister would assist the First Minister with External Relations.

In June 2005, when the Liberal Democrats named Nicol Stephen as successor to Jim Wallace as their new party leader and Deputy First Minister, the new leadership team of McConnell and Stephen announced a further reshuffle. Nicol Stephen, in addition to his new role as Deputy First Minister was appointed Minister for Enterprise and Lifelong Learning; Tavish Scott was appointed Minister for Transport and Telecommunication (he was previously Deputy Minister for Finance); George Lyon joined the Cabinet as Deputy Minister for Finance and Parliamentary Business; Robert Brown joined the Cabinet as Deputy Minister for Education, replacing Euan Robson who left the Cabinet. Rhona Brankin, previously Deputy Minister for Health, was moved to the post of Deputy Minister for Environment and Rural Affairs; and Lewis Macdonald, previously Deputy Minister for Environment and Rural Affairs, was moved to the post of Deputy Minister for Health and Community Care.

While David McLetchie's leadership of the Scottish Tories came under considerable pressure, first, over his part-time status as an MSP while still practicing as a lawyer, then over the non-disclosure of taxi receipts (which allegedly were, in part, for his legal practice activities rather than his duties as an MSP), the Liberal Democrats, the SNP and the Scottish Socialist Party actually changed their leaders.

Most acrimoniously, and perhaps with the most serious consequences for the party's fortunes, the SSP dumped its charismatic founding figurehead Tommy Sheridan, the day before he announced in November 2004 that he would resign as convener for personal reasons, particularly to become 'a proper father'. He was replaced by Colin Fox MSP, who prevailed in a contest with Alan McCombes, the party's policy coordinator. Strangely enough, the SSP's website still gave (in September 2005) Tommy Sheridan as the party's convener... In August, the actor Peter Mullan, a high-profile supporter of the SSP, lambasted the party's ousting of Sheridan as 'disgraceful and disgusting'. In a TV interview he added: 'Their treatment of Tommy has as good as destroyed them for now.[9]

Jim Wallace, the Deputy First Minister, announced his resignation as leader of the Scottish Liberal Democrats who are partners with the Scottish Labour Party in the coalition that forms the Scottish government. He added that he would also relinquish his role as an MSP at the next election in 2007. According to the Partnership Agreement between the parties, the Liberal Democrat leader is appointed Deputy First Minister. Wallace, the MSP for Orkney, who was also Minister for Enterprise and

---

[9] Robbie Dinwoodie, 'Mullan launches attack on SSP', *The Herald*, 24 August 2005.

Lifelong Learning, stood down in June when Nicol Stephen was elected as his successor. Stephen saw off the challenge from fellow Lib Dem MSP Mike Rumbles.

After the disappointing result for the SNP in the 2004 European elections, John Swinney had announced his resignation and triggered a leadership competition which lasted all summer long. Roseanna Cunningham and Nicola Sturgeon looked like the frontrunners, with Cunningham poised to win when, at the last minute and in a spectacular U-turn, the former convener of the party, Alex Salmond MP, threw his hat into the ring, on a ticket with Nicola Sturgeon (whose leadership ambitions he had previously endorsed) as his deputy. He was duly elected in September, and the fears that his absenteeism from Holyrood would leave Nicola Sturgeon in a vulnerable and ineffective position have since dissipated. 'Already, Ruaridh Nicoll commented in an up-beat fashion by the end of September, 'Sturgeon seems adept at skewering McConnell at First Minister's questions, just as the Labour leader has raised his game in response.'[10]

TAXI FOR MCLETCHIE, THE RAFFAN MILES AND A FIRE-RAISING PEER

Scandals at Holyrood have so far been of thankfully moderate proportions or, seeing that the site was the home of a brewery, distinctly small beer. There was Frank McAveety losing his ministerial job over pies (and the never-ending crisis of Scottish Opera); then there was a bit of a hillaballoo about Jack McConnell's Wark holiday (blown up to 'Kirstygate' or 'Villagate'). Likewise without consequences have been the allegations against Tory leader David McLetchie's predilection for taxis. The attacks would perhaps have been less venomous and out of proportion, had it not been McLetchie who, in 2001, had been the scourge of Henry McLeish when his constituency sub-lettings had come under scrutiny. In February, after continued pressure and allegations of misconduct (he was cleared by the Standards Committee in September), McLetchie had given up his part-time legal work and resigned as a partner in the Edinburgh law firm Todd Murray.[11]

Liberal Democrat Keith Raffan clocked up an impressive number of miles in his wee Skoda – enough to circle the globe three times – criss-crossing his constituency even while, apparently, away on an official trip

---

[10] Ruaridh Nicoll, 'Let the good times roll', *The Observer*, 26 September 2004.

[11] Tom Gordon, 'McLetchie quits law firm after row over "interests"', *The Herald*, 19 February 2005.

to the Isle of Man.[12] All this is nicely listed by the Scottish Parliament under Freedom of Information legislation which had just come into effect and for which, of course, the Liberal Democrats claim credit. Not even MSPs have yet mastered the art of being in two places at the same time, so he had to go. And was replaced by Andrew Arbuckle who, after half a year in the job, complained that Scotland was 'overgoverned' and that an MSP's work did not make for a full-time occupation... [13] Maybe he should drive around a bit more?

And then, Labour Peer Lord Watson who, apparently frustrated at the 'Politician of the Year' awards last November, had a few drinks too many and tried to set the curtains at Prestonfield House alight, all meticulously documented on CCTV.[14] Mike Watson was, immediately after the incident, suspended by the Labour Party. In September 2005 he admitted to the deed, resigned from his MSP seat and thus triggered a by-election in Glasgow Cathcart on 29 September, the same day Livingstone would elect a successor to Robin Cook MP who had died suddenly while hiking in the Highlands in August.

EXTERNAL RELATIONS AND INTERNATIONAL DEVELOPMENT

In October of last year, Jack McConnell stated during a parliamentary debate that powers of devolution provide for specific ways in which Scotland's government can contribute to international development. He announced that the government would spend £3 million a year to help Scottish non-governmental organisations target their overseas work and promised that, at times of international crisis, the Scottish government would mobilise Scotland's response.

A cross-party group of six MSPs left in February 2005 for a 10-day visit to South Africa and Malawi. The visit was aimed at bringing together Scottish and African parliamentarians with Scottish charities and other overseas aid and education organisations and at developing sustainable links with South Africa and Malawi. In May, the First Minister himself travelled for five days to Malawi. On his return, he announced the creation of a National Fund – the Scottish Malawi Appeal Fund – to channel support to Malawi following his visit there. Jack McConnell made it clear

---

[12] Robbie Dinwoodie, 'The question Keith Raffan must answer: do the figures add up?', *The Herald*, 22 January 2005.

[13] Peter MacMahon, 'MSP is just a part-time job, claims new boy at Holyrood', *The Scotsman*, 12 August 2005.

[14] Paul Kelbie, 'MSP admits setting fire to hotel curtains', *The Independent*, 2 September 2005.

that the fund was not part of government and would have no direct relationship to ministers or politicians. In September it was wound up, having only collected a disappointing £30,000. The campaign is supposed to be relaunched as part of an international relief effort.

The early summer was dominated by the G8 summit, which was held in early July at Gleneagles in Perthshire. In the run-up, Sir Bob Geldof spoke at a special Executive-sponsored conference in the Parliament, saying that G8 leaders should stay away from Scotland in July if they were not prepared to actively tackle poverty in Africa. Other speakers included Kumi Naidoo, Secretary General and Chief Executive of CIVICUS, Salil Shetty, Director of the UN Millennium Development Goals Campaign, and Omar Kabbaj, President of the African Development Bank. Bob Geldof was one of 17 commissioners appointed by the UK government in 2004 to take a fresh look at the African continent and its problems and the international community's role in helping its development path. In June, the Parliament welcomed more than 80 international parliamentarians and policy-makers to the G8 International Parliamentarians' Conference on Development in Africa 2005. The main issues of the conference agenda were HIV/AIDS, sexual and reproductive health issues and the empowerment of women. Delegates debated the findings of the Report by the Commission for Africa, which was co-authored by Bob Geldof. The first weekend in July saw the biggest demonstrations in Edinburgh in living memory, 250,000 out to 'Make Poverty History', and a massive Live Concert at Murrayfield – 'Edinburgh 50,000: The Final Push' – on the eve of the Gleneagles summit.

To strengthen international trade and economic contacts, the First Minister, in October 2004, paid a five-day visit to Beijing and Shanghai. He expressed his support for a tourist agreement between China and Britain, which would allow Chinese tourists to travel to the UK for leisure. During his visit Jack McConnell announced that Scottish companies were to get extra government support to help them take advantage of opportunities offered by China's growing economy.

But, as Jim Wallace announced in December, while the EU market for Scotland is worth £10 billion and accounted for 54% of Scotland's total exports in 2003, with Germany and France the second and third largest export markets, Scotland's biggest single export market, worth £2.5 billion, is the USA.

That market is, since 1998, annually targeted during Tartan Week in early April. This year, a parliamentary delegation visited New York, Boston, Washington DC, Québec and Alabama, celebrating Scotland's cultural and historical links with Canada and the USA. As part of Tartan week, Tom McCabe, Minister for Finance and Public Service Reform, launched an event where Aberdeen, Dundee, Edinburgh and Glasgow Universities joined together to represent Scotland's expertise in life sciences at a specially created seminar in Cambridge, Massachusetts. They were aiming to secure business opportunities and strengthen US links through the event. As Patricia Ferguson, Minister for Tourism, announced later in April, a quarter of a million people had visited the Scottish Village in Grand Central Station in New York during Tartan Week – a purpose built structure featuring aspects of Scottish life and culture.

Closer to home, the fifth annual conference of the Presidents of Regions with Legislative Power (RegLeg) was held in Edinburgh on 30 November 2004. Jack McConnell had discussions with Commission Vice President Margo Wallström to develop a project that will improve the way the EU Commission works with devolved governments and regions across Europe. On the eve of the conference, the First Minister handed over the presidency of RegLeg to Eberhard Sinner, the Minister of Foreign Affairs of Bavaria. Despite the debate centred on the draft European Constitution, the Scottish RegLeg presidency seemed, overall, to have made little impact.[15]

Two of Scotland's regional partnerships were moved forward when, in January, an Action Plan between Scotland and the German State of North Rhine-Westphalia was signed in Edinburgh by Tom McCabe and Wolfram Kuschke from NRW. The key areas of co-operation of the Action Plan are renewable energy, biotechnology, regional policy and structural funds, entrepreneurship, European policy, administrative reform and infrastructure investment. A similar step was taken in May with the Scottish-Bavarian Action Plan, signed by McCabe and the Bavarian Minister for European Affairs and Regional Relations, Eberhard Sinner, at a formal ceremony in Munich.

In June, George Reid, the Scottish Parliament's Presiding Officer, welcomed a delegation from the Parliament of Catalonia led by its President, the Rt Hon Ernest Benach i Pascual. The delegation met with the Convener and members of the European and External Relations Committee to discuss 'the Promotion of Catalonia to the Wider World' and the role sub-national parliaments play in influencing European decisions.

CULTURE AND SOCIETY

After an interim report last November, the Cultural Commission published its Final Report on 23 June. Patricia Ferguson, Minister for Culture, welcomed the completion of the report and stated that she was pleased that the Commission had recommended the concept of cultural rights and entitlements which was a priority the Executive had

---

[15] Christopher Harvie, 'Destination Unknown', *Agenda* (Summer 2005), pp.4-9.

asked to be addressed. The Commission also recommended more links with the community planning process. Much more controversial was the suggestion to abolish the Scottish Arts Council, and give the Ministry direct control over the arts budget and its distribution through a new body, Culture Scotland. Other key suggestions are the introduction of a Culture Bill by 2007, the creation of a new Deputy Culture Minister and a tax support system for artists.

On 17 December, the Smoking, Health and Social Care Bill was published which aims to improve Scotland's health record by banning, as in Ireland since end of March 2004, smoking in enclosed public places in order to protect people from the effects of second hand smoke. In April, the bill was approved by 83 to 15 votes – only the Conservatives were against the compulsory ban.

The Gaelic Language (Scotland) Bill passed its third and final stage in Parliament on 21 April 2005. It establishes a body, Bòrd na Gàidhlig, to promote the use and understanding of the Gaelic language. Parity of esteem rather than equal legal status with English – but nonetheless significant progress for the recognition and support of Gaelic. For Education Minister Peter Peacock the unanimous passing of the bill marked a historic day for Gaelic. The SNP's Alex Neil said it was a day when the Gaelic language was going forward, not backward. Although the language still faced serious challenges – every year it currently loses 1500 speakers. Lord James Douglas Hamilton, the Tory education spokesman, called the bill a landmark for Gaels and their culture.

The Government also continued its efforts to combat racism and sectarianism in Scotland. In January, Jack McConnell and his Justice minister Cathy Jamieson met with supporters from both Rangers and Celtic football clubs to discuss ways of tackling sectarianism in Scotland. This was followed in February by a 'summit on sectarianism' in Glasgow's Kelvin Gallery, chaired by Jack McConnell, which brought together representatives from the 'Old Firm', the churches, local government, business, trade unions, police, youth groups and the media – as well as campaign groups against sectarianism and loyalist and republican organisations who insist in their right to march.

In November, MSPs passed the Breastfeeding (Scotland) Bill which makes it an offence to stop anyone feeding milk to children under two in public or in family-friendly licensed premises. The First Minister also announced a five-point plan aimed at tackling knife crime – including doubling the maximum jail term for possessing an offensive weapon from two to four years.

Just before Christmas, the long years of protest succeeded when the Skye Bridge tolls were abolished with immediate effect. They had been in place for the nine years since the Skye Bridge had been built as one of the first private finance projects. But there was a sting in the tail for the tax payer: the buy-back of the bridge cost £27 million.

PARLIAMENT AND POWER

St Andrews Day 2005 would mark the tenth anniversary since the Scottish Constitutional Convention published *Scotland's Parliament. Scotland's Right*, the 'blueprint' for the Scottish Parliament – time, in Jack McConnell's view, to look again at the range of powers devolved to Holyrood. In July, he ordered a review of the powers of the Scottish Parliament, looking at issues ranging from nuclear power stations, casinos, abortion and broadcasting to the electoral system, the size of the Scottish Parliament and the appointment and dismissal of Scottish civil servants, still a preserve of Whitehall.[16]

Tavish Scott, the Transport Minister, said he would welcome if some aviation powers were handed down from Westminster to Holyrood 'if it helped the executive in its attempt to reduce island air fares.' And former First Minister Henry McLeish called for the Scottish Parliament 'to have new powers, including on immigration, guns and drugs policy.'[17] Canon Kenyon Wright, the convener of the Constitutional Convention, favours Scotland taking control of any possible changes in the relationship between Westminster and Holyrood. He promoted his idea of a permanent constitutional commission to consider changes to Holyrood powers and procedures, which should not be imposed on Scotland by Westminster.

Public opinion in Scotland supports an increase of the powers of Holyrood. In the 2001 Scottish Social Attitudes Survey, 65% of Scots either agreed or strongly agreed that the Parliament's powers should be increased; a Mori poll in 2003 found 59%, and a poll for Scottish Television in September 2005, again by Mori, 58% in favour of more power to Holyrood.[18] But, as Allan Massie has pointed out, the appetite for more powers has been shrinking since the peak of 2001 and 2002, when 66 and 68% respectively were in support of increased powers.[19] The increase of powers also chimes with the findings of the Scottish Social Attitudes Survey that 52% trusted the Scottish Executive 'just about always' or 'most of the time', while 22% said the same of the UK government. A total of 67% said the executive should have the most influence over how Scotland is run, and 19% think the UK government should do so. But only

---

[16] Jason Allardyce, 'McConnell eyes greater powers', *The Sunday Times*, 24 July 2005.

[17] Douglas Fraser, 'Warning as McLeish says Holyrood should have new powers on guns', *The Herald*, 12 September 2005.

[18] Iain Macwhirter, 'Even Watson can't dent devolution support', *Sunday Herald*, 4 September 2005.

[19] Allan Massie, 'MSPs must earn powers', *The Sunday Times*, 4 September 2005.

19% think the executive has most influence, while 48% see Whitehall as dominant.[20]

While McConnell and his government stop short of demanding increased fiscal powers, these are being discussed by Labour backbenchers like Wendy Alexander. While she advocates a form of fiscal federalism, the Liberal Democrats are determined to make tax-raising powers a condition for any future coalition pact with Labour, focusing on the Scottish Parliament's right to levy greater proportions of income tax, corporation tax and VAT north of the border.[21] The Tories believe that devolving financial powers to Holyrood would make MSPs more accountable and more responsible in their spending decisions. In July, the Tories drew cup a plan for the 2007 election to lower the basic rate of income tax by three per cent.[22] After quitting his front-bench position as the party's spokesperson on finance in July (the post went to the party's newest MSP, Derek Brownlee), Brian Monteith MSP embarked on a tax-cutting campaign, promoting a flat-tax as pioneered in Estonia.[23] For the SNP, fiscal autonomy, apart from giving Scotland the leverage to lower corporate and business taxes in order to make its economy more competitive, is the logical next step towards independence. The debate will not go away. In his typical pointed way, Allan Massie, the literary face of Scottish Toryism, put it in a nutshell: 'If we want a real parliament rather than a toy one, a responsible executive rather than a play-acting one, then Holyrood has to be granted fiscal powers.'[24]

The Executive's Fresh Talents Initiative is one of the areas where the Parliament managed to extend its powers by negotiating special arrangements for Scotland in the area of immigration – a reserved matter. In January, Jack McConnell announced the next stage of the government's Fresh Talent project, which aims to help tackle Scotland's declining population by attracting people to live and work in Scotland. He revealed plans to extend Scotland's two-year student work scheme to overseas students who complete a Higher national diploma (HND), and a government fund to help universities and colleges support international students settle in Scottish communities. The First Minister also formally

---

[20] Scottish Centre for Social Research, 'Research out today shows that faith in devolution remains high, although people do not necessarily think it has changed things in Scotland', Press Release, 9 September 2005.

[21] Joanne Robertson, 'Lib Dems call for tax powers', The Sunday Times, 27 February 2005.

[22] Hamish MacDonell, 'Tories plan lower rate for Scotland', The Scotsman, 18 July 2005

[23] Brian Monteith, 'Why the flat tax is an idea whose time has come', The Scotsman, 12 September 2005.

[24] Allan Massie, 'MSPs must earn powers', The Sunday Times, 4 September 2005.

launched the new Relocation Advisory Service[25] that offers practical support and advice to people interested in living and working in Scotland.

Another area which has seen a transfer of power from Westminster to Holyrood is responsibility for railways. As part of the rail review, the Executive and the UK Government agreed in July that Scottish Ministers will take a greater responsibility for rail powers in Scotland. This includes full responsibility for specifying track and infrastructure improvements, as well as all of ScotRail's services.

UK ELECTIONS

The UK General Election on 5 May saw a reduction in the number of Scottish MPs from 72 to 59 in response to the establishment of the Scottish Parliament. In the campaign itself, there was no clear separation of reserved and devolved matters – the debates covered the economy, taxation, immigration and the war in Iraq as much as policies on health, education and crime.

The main question was, would the SNP under their returned leader make inroads into the Labour vote and position themselves as a credible challenger for the 2007 Holyrood election. They won six seats, gaining two, while Labour fared reasonably well, with its 41 seats (-5). But the SNP also slipped, with only 17.7%, into third place in the share of the vote (Labour: 39.5%; Lib Dems: 22.6%). The Tories (15.8%) stagnated, with a nominal gain of 1 (David Mundell MSP) – in practice holding their one seat, albeit not Peter Duncan's. The short-lived new Shadow Scottish Secretary's call for abolishing MSPs led to ruminations among Scottish Tories like Murdo Fraser MSP whether it was not time to break from the UK partry, becoming a 'separate party, separately funded, with separate responsibility for policy.'[26] The SSP's vote dropped dramatically to well below 50,000, nearly 30,000 votes less than in the 2001 elections.

Of potentially greater long-term impact could be another English poll – the referendum on a Northern Assembly which failed abysssmally on 4 November 2004, when only 22% (on a 48% turnout) voted in favour of an elected assembly in Newcastle.[27] This kicked regional devolution in England into the long grass, perhaps to remain there as long as it took Scotland and Wales to recover from the 1979 referendums – if it did not

---

[25] <www.scotlandistheplace.com>.

[26] Paul Hutcheon, 'Scottish Tories split over calls for break from UK party', The Herald, 22 May 2005.

[27] Peter Hetherington, 'Defeat halts Prescott's push for devolution', The Guardian, 6 November 2004.

indeed kill it off entirely.[28] This means that there is no short- to mid-term perspective any more for rolling devolution across the UK, a fact which might well affect attitudes towards devolution and independence in Wales and Scotland.

TOWARDS 2007

On 9 September, Jack McConnell opened the new session of Parliament by introducing 22 bills which would see the Parliament through the nineteen months until the next Scottish elections. The 'bombshell' was a promise to cut Scottish business rates by 10%, to the same level as in England and Wales.[29]

Other legislative proposals include legal reform, from a sentencing bill which will provide guidelines to judges on the granting of bail to football banning orders, council powers to ban sectarian parades and the outlawing of kerb crawling. McConnell also announced a new Police Services Authority and an independent Police Complaints Commissioner. There is to be a Human Rights Commission, and the summary courts are to be reformed and the children's hearing system overhauled.

The Executive plans a change, which will cause controversy with the churches, in the adoption law so that unmarried couples – including gay couples – will have the right to adopt a child. School forums will replace school boards, and school dinners are to be improved with a new nutritional standards bill. The sale of fizzy drinks on school premises will be banned.

A fish farming bill aims at controlling sea lice and escapes from fish farms. The planning law is to be streamlined. The definition of 'crofting' is to be made more flexible to allow different land use and to tackle the issue of absentee crofters. And an animal welfare bill will introduce a duty of care for those looking after animals.

The U-turn on business rates came as a surprise. Had the Executive in the past not rejected the opposition's repeated demands, claiming that it was actually lower than in England and, anyway, not important in the overall calculation of businesses? For Tory leader David McLetchie, the Executive had 'at last seen the Conservative light.'[30]

Had the Government hoped that the move would smoothen relations with the business community, they were in for an unpleasant surprise at the 'Business in the Parliament' conference in the debating chamber,

---

[28] Deborah Summers, 'English assemblies plan is dead', *The Herald*, 6 November 2004.

[29] John Knox, 'McConnell's legislative "splash"', *BBC News Scotland*, 10 September 2005, <news.bbc.co.uk/1/hi/scotland/4231666.stm>.

[30] *Ibid.*

which some 200 business people attended on the Thursday and Friday of the first session week in September to debate the future of the Scottish economy with MSPs, when business leaders lobbed a litany of complaints at the Scottish Executive. Apparently, there was some truth in the contention that business rates are not that important. Now, the attacks concentrated at tardy transport reforms and public procurement of goods and services from global players rather than Scottish firms. 'Scottish business had digested the good rates news,' Alf Young commented dryly, 'and moved on to fresh fare.' He felt compelled to remind the business sector that they have 'every right to expect that government will tax responsibly, operate efficiently and avoid unnecessary barriers to fair competition. But,' he added, 'government also has the right to expect that business will take its responsibilities equally seriously, that it will invest in the future as well as distribute profits in the here and now.'[31]

With the threatened takeover of Scottish Power by the German utility concern E.On, and the compliance of the Executive with the European Commission in putting the CalMac ferry services out to tender as well as the award of a major shipbuilding contract to a Polish shipyard, rather than Ferguson's of Port Glasgow, the SNP put 'economic patriotism' at the forefront of its challenge to the Labour-Liberal Democrat coalition. And with the price of oil at record highs, and secret Whitehall dossiers of thirty years ago, 'Scotland's Oil' seems back on the campaign agenda.

We have seen the return of Alex Salmond, even if not yet to the Scottish Parliament; John Swinney has returned to the SNP front bench as finance spokesman; Henry McLeish, while pocketing the erstwhile political enemy's Tory shilling, does not tire to urge a bigger international role for Scotland... Will we see the return of Tommy Sheridan? The door is not closed for a comeback, said Rosemary Byrne MSP at the end of August.[32]

While the Greens pledged their support for 'Independence First', a cross-party group campaigning for a referendum on independence already endorsed by the Scottish Socialists and a number of SNP MSPs,[33] Nicol Stephen ruled out a referendum on independence, which was a set back for a potential SNP-Lib Dem partnership. But the Lib Dems as well as Labour will want to sharpen their profile in the run-up to the May 2007 election.

Alex Salmond has called for his party to raise an extra £1 million for a strategy to win 20 seats in the next election, taking the SNP campaign

---

31 Alf Young, 'Rate cut is fine ... but what will business do in return?', *Sunday Herald*, 11 September 2005.

32 Paul Hutcheon, '"Door isn't closed" on Sheridan comeback', *Sunday Herald*, 28 August 2005.

33 Ian Swanson, 'Greens show their colours to back vote for independence', *Edinburgh Evening News*, 30 July 2005.

into the Labour heartlands of the Central Belt. Can the cash-strapped Nationalists come up with the goods? And what about the Tories? Still troubled by the occasional crossfire from north and south of the Border questioning their commitment to devolution, will there be a challenge to McLetchie's leadership, combined with a more radical Tory strategy? Will taxation powers for Holyrood be one of he dominant themes of the 2007 campaign?

2007, just a few weeks before the Holyrood elections, marks the tercentenary of the Act of Union. Will the Parliament pass up on the potential for academic and political assessment and commemoration, as it did in 2003, at the quartercentenary of the union of Crowns? No one needs to celebrate the Union if they do not wish to, but could there be an understanding to mark the occasion and use it to further Scotland's national and international profile?

BEYOND 2007

In his Donald Dewar lecture at the International Edinburgh Book Festival on 25 August, George Reid announced that he would step down as the Parliament's Presiding Officer at the next election. Last year, on 6 December, he had welcomed one hundred and forty experts from Scotland's blue chip companies, the arts, academia and civic Scotland, who joined MSPs to look at issues which will affect Scotland in the next ten years and beyond. They were joined in a day-long 'conversation' about a possible Futures Forum in Parliament by representatives from the Global Business Network in California, Stanford University, the Office of the Prime Minister of France and the Organisation for Economic Co-operation and Development.

Somewhat modelled on the Finnish Parliament's Committee for the Future, which helped the country to overcome the shock waves of the early 1990s by concentrating on electronic communications and public health, but taking cues from other countries as well, the Scottish Futures Forum was set up by George Reid in August. He summded up its credo: 'If we don't think from time to time out of the box and over the horizon, if we rely only on past experience, the danger is that we shall walk into the future backwards.'[34]

Holyrood, already a serial winner of architectural awards and shortlisted for the RIBA Stirling Prize, also hosted the first 'Festival of Politics' in August which played to packed houses. Together with the

---

[34] George Reid, 'The Donald Dewar Lecture 2005', Edinburgh Book Festival, 25 August 2005, <www.scottish.parliament.uk/nmCentre/news/news-05/dewar_lecture/print_version.htm>.

astonishing fact that, sinbce its opening in October 2004, over 500,000 visitors have come to see the new building from the inside, this shows that the Scottish Parliament is leading the way in opening up the process of public participation. Holyrood is the 'gathering place', the place where people meet, as George Reid said at the Book Festival: 'The bottom line, I suppose, is that politics is too important to be left just to the politicians.'[35]

[September 2005]

---

[35] *Ibid.*

Chapter III

THE YEAR AT HOLYROOD
2005-2006

The political year in Scotland, from September 2005 to September 2006, was the year of the smoking ban in enclosed public places, and of the official – and very successful – opening of the Scottish National Theatre; it was the year when bird flu' came and went, much like 2YK and Sars. Remember that swan in Cellardyke? It was also the year of the summer spectacular in the court room: Tommy Sheridan v. the *News of the World* (and most of his own party); it was the year of the McKie fingerprint controversy; the year that brought the whacking by-election defeat for Labour in Dunfermline and West Fife, with a 16% swing to the Liberal Democrats; the feverish identity debate – and the related, never-ending West Lothian Question – triggered by a wee football tournament in Germany and the vital support the English team apparently craved from their neighbours in the North, and which was denied them by no lesser figure than Jack 'Trinidad & Tobago' McConnell himself. It was the year of Tony Blair's long drawn-out (and continuing) farewell and the perspective of a Scottish UK prime minister (who in turn seemed to miss no opportunity to reaffirm his 'Britishness') and the impact of this disorderly transition on Labour's election prospects in Scotland; a summer of contradictory polls, once having the SNP, then Labour in the lead, which add to the rising temperature of the political climate as we edged closer towards the Holyrood elections of May 2007.

The past year has also seen the practical increase of the powers of the Scottish Parliament. In October 2005, Tavish Scott, Minister for Transport, announced the transfer of new rail powers to Scotland, which now allow the devolved government of Scotland to determine the long-term future for rail in Scotland, securing, managing and monitoring the performance of the rail franchise, and funding and controlling the tracks through Network Rail; enabled by a transfer of around £360 million to the Scottish Executive. In July, it was reported that UK and Scottish ministers had entered talks about whether to transfer control of the marine environment in Scotland to Holyrood. The debate about increased powers – fiscal autonomy, media, immigration – for Holyrood is ongoing, backed by surveys in which up to two-thirds of respondents express their favour for a further devolution of powers.

MEDIA TENSIONS

Also ongoing is the tension between the media and devolution. Just when we thought the Parliament building itself had left the headlines behind, the beam struck, and the media – especially Scotsman publications, antagonistic to the building from the start – had a field day. 'Holyrood scare as roof beam collapses over heads of MSPs,' titled the *Scotsman* in dramatic fashion;[1] 'Holyrood shut down after roof beam breaks free,' was the slightly less dramatic take by the *Herald*;[2] 'Holyrood is falling down,' blared the front page of the *Scottish Daily Mail* (3 March 2006),[3] topping that inside with the headline: 'Sorry, we've had to cancel Holyrood questions because the new £431m parliament is falling to bits.' Clearly, hopes that the editorial policy of Scotsman Publications would change under the new ownership (Johnson Press) remained unfulfilled. A beam had come lose; the chamber had to be temporarily closed; repairs were completed over the summer, and after the recess the MPS could move back in – embarrassing, annoying, particularly at a cost of over £500,000, but not exactly the collapse of the building!

Scotland has become 'inward-looking and slightly Anglophobic' since devolution – that was the gist of an article in the *Economist* by Johnny Grimond.[4] Reacting to the piece, Jack McConnell dismissed it as 'the rambling thoughts of someone on a day trip from London.'[5]

In August, Ian Bell attacked *BBC Newsnight* as 'failing Scotland'. Clearly miffed by the programme's output (and outlook) over the summer, he argued that the programme, broadcast since October 1999, 'has become home rule's most relentless, even obsessive, critic,' with an editorial policy 'to proceed from the assumption, on every possible occasion, that devolution has indeed failed.' He contended that a 'Scottish Six' – a main news bulletin edited and broadcast from Glasgow, as proposed and repeatedly rejected since 1999 – would never adopt this 'assumption that devolution is a wash-out [which] has become Newsnight Scotland's default position,' ignoring 'consistent polling evidence demonstrating that a majority of Scots want home rule and their parliament to continue, despite an understandable aversion to politicians.'[6]

[1] 'Holyrood scare as roof beam collapses over heads of MSPs', *The Scotsman*, 3 March 2006.

[2] 'Holyrood shut down after roof beam breaks free', *The Herald*, 3 March 2006.

[3] 'Holyrood is falling down', *Scottish Daily Mail*, 3 March 2006.

[4] Johnny Grimond, 'Home truths about home rule', *The Economist*, 18 May 2006.

[5] 'Magazine attacks Scots devolution', *BBC News Scotland*, 19 May 2006, <news.bbc.co.uk/1/hi/scotland/4997606.stm>.

[6] Ian Bell, 'Why the BBC is failing Scotland', *The Herald*, 26 August 2006.

On 12 July, BBC *Newsnight Scotland* reported on itself. Blair Jenkins had resigned from 'Current Affairs', which raised further questions concerning cutbacks in staffing and budget of BBC Scotland. The media pundit Philip Schlesinger saw this as casting doubts on the overall strategy of the BBC indicating a wider crisis of BBC management. Alex Neil MSP (SNP) saw it as raising 'a series of new questions about the BBC's position north of the border.' He was worried about the impact of cuts on the wider media landscape of Scotland – 'brain drain' or 'take-over' from the South? He saw 'the case for devolving media policy to the Scottish Parliament ... growing by the day.'[7]

LEGISLATION – SMOKING AND DRINKING

The Executive's legislative programme until the 2007 elections – fifteen bills overall – was already introduced last September. One of the most important pieces of legislation from the previous year, the banning of smoking in enclosed public places, came into force on 26 March of this year. The *Sunday Herald* dedicated a leader to the landmark legislation, calling it 'a triumph for health and a testament to the power of devolution.'[8]

In November, the third-stage debate of the reform of the Licensing Bill showed that Holyrood is still capable of living down to its bad press. It turned into, in the words of John Knox (the journalist, not the fire-and-brimstone reformer), 'a pantomime, a farce, a shambles, a comedy of error.'[9] After a shambolic debate, Labour backbenchers prevailed with a far more restrictive line on off-licence sales, to the chagrin of Labour's coalition partner who had backed the more liberal proposal of the Executive. 'It was supposed to be the biggest reform of Scotland's licensing laws for a generation,' so Knox: 'But, in the words of one MSP, it was as ill-organised as a proverbial booze-up in a brewery. It ended up with the sale of drink being banned in supermarkets and off-licences from 10pm to 10am, for no apparent reason.'[10] Five years of consultation ended in what the *Sunday Herald* called the 'licensing fiasco'.[11]

In December, the Family Law (Scotland) Bill was passed by Parliament. It provides rules for quicker divorces, regulates parental responsibilities

---

[7] BBC, *Newsnight Scotland*, 12 July 2006.

[8] 'A triumph for health and a testament to the power of devolution' (Leader), *Sunday Herald* 26 March 2006.

[9] John Knox, 'Drinking antics cause stir at Holyrood', *BBC News Scotland*, 18 November 2005, <news.bbc.co.uk/1/hi/scotland/4451106.stm>.

[10] *Ibid.*

[11] 'Licensing fiasco' (Leader), *Sunday Herald*, 20 November 2005.

and rights (PRRs) for fathers; raises protection against domestic abuse, as well as introducing new legal safeguards for cohabiting couples and their children. Particularly the cut in separation periods from five to two years in contested cases, and from two years to one in uncontested divorce cases, drew fire from the Catholic Church who accused the Executive as 'attacking the family' and 'dismantling marriage'.[12] Cardinal Keith O'Brien attacked MSPs for passing 'immoral' laws: 'It is all too easy to think of laws and proposed laws of our own Scottish parliament on marriage, the family, and the adoption of children, which come into this depressing category.'[13] The Cardinal's comments were rebutted robustly by MSPs from different parties. SNP justice spokesman Kenny MacAskill questioned whether O'Brien had yet fully arrived in the twenty-first century. But the selfsame accusations were to be repeated in September 2006 when the Parliament passed a new adoption law which allows same-sex partners to adopt children. Joseph Devine, the Bishop of Motherwell, claimed in a letter to MSPs that the 'distressing legislation' was a 'violation of family life'.[14] In the Chamber, too, the legislation was not uncontested. 'I hate to break the cosy consensus,' said the SNP's Roseanna Cunningham, speaking against the right of gay couples to adopt: 'I can't see how overturning tens of thousands of years of nature's design moves us forward.'[15] In the end, the bill was passed by 103 votes to eight.

At the end of March, the Parliament gave green light to Line One of Edinburgh's planned tram system. The line will form a loop from St Andrews Square, along Leith Walk to Leith, west to Granton, south to Haymarket and back to St Andrew Square along Princes Street. In June, the Waverley Railway (Scotland) Bill was passed, giving statutory authority to the Council and its successors for the construction of a railway from a point immediately south of Newcraighall to Tweedbank, largely following the route of the former Waverley railway line (which was closed over 35 years ago). In June, MSPs backed the £210m projected rail link between Glasgow airport and the city centre to be completed by 2009. Despite cost and efficiency concerns, the Parliament also approved of the £650m Edinburgh airport railway link. The SNP opposed the scheme, and its transport spokesman promised the scheme would be scrapped if his party gained power in 2007.

---

[12] Hamish Macdonell, 'Executive under fire after "quickie divorce" bill is passed', The Scotsman, 16 December 2005.

[13] Paul Hutcheon, 'Cardinal blasts Holyrood's "immoral" laws', Sunday Herald, 9 October 2005.

[14] Louise Gray, 'MSPs approve gay adoption but Church vows to fight on', The Scotsman, 14 September 2006.

[15] Robbie Dinwoodie, 'Adoption reforms provoke fury at Holyrood', The Herald, 14 September 2006.

FLAGSHIP POLICIES IN TROUBLE

A number of legislative projects encountered implementation problems. Free personal care for the elderly, one of Holyrood's flagship policies, made headlines for all the wrong reasons. Although two research reports, one in February from the Joseph Rowntree Foundation, one in June from a team of researchers at the University of Stirling, were very complimentary, calling the policy successful in improving the quality of life of older people and crediting it with the removal of many of their financial concerns as well as having the broad support of the electorate, they also pointed out that greater clarity was needed on how to calculate the costs of free personal care. Since its introduction in 2002, about 50,000 elderly people in Scotland have benefited from the policy. But the provision of care has been vastly different from council to council; there is controversy about the distinction between nursing and personal care. It was alleged that one-third of the 32 Scottish councils were charging for food preparation which should be covered by free care; worse, many councils were revealed as operating sometimes substantial waiting lists. The Executive was accused of having underestimated the costs involved in free care, and councils seem to have used funds allocated for free care to fill other gaps in their budgets. A report by the Health Committee revealed the 'postcode lottery experienced by some of Scotland's most vulnerable elderly.'[16]

Another of Holyrood's showcases lost some of its lustre. The £2.15bn investment into schools following the (Gavin) McCrone settlement of 2001, which gave teachers a 23% pay increase over the three years to 2004, and which limited class teaching to 22.5 hours per week (in force since August of this year) was criticised by Audit Scotland for the Executive's lack of proper assessment of cause and effect. No doubt the financial situation of teachers has been improved, but did the 'Deal' also improve education – there, the Audit Report published in May failed to find clear proof of improvement.

The Executive's antisocial behaviour legislation was branded a flop by opposition politicians when figures were released in August showing that, across the board, only little use was made of Asbos (Antisocial Behaviour Orders) and that, numerically, there were huge differences across different council areas. The Executive had to admit: 'We believe there can be more, and more appropriate use of these types of antisocial behaviour measures.'[17]

---

[16] Helen Puttick and Douglas Fraser, 'The personal care patchwork', *The Herald*, 20 September 2006.

[17] Ian Swanson, 'Low use of Asbos and tagging leaves powers branded a flop', *Edinburgh Evening News*, 30 August 2006.

Last September, Jack McConnell had surprised Parliament and public by announcing to bring down business rates to the level of England. He then added that he was prepared to look at a further reduction in business rates for firms investing in research and development. This plan to make Scotland, in McConnell's words, 'the most attractive place in the UK in which to invest in research and development' was effectively shelved after one year of inaction.[18]

NATIONAL THEATRE AND FRESH TALENTS

While there still is controversy about the Cultural Commission Report and the Executive's plan to fuse the Scottish Arts Council and Scottish Screen to form a new body, Culture Scotland, and take the national companies under its direct funding wing, Scotland's National Theatre, which was inaugurated on 24 February with performances under the collective title 'Home' at 10 different locations across the country, has been hailed a remarkable success. As a 'virtual' National Theatre, the organisation has an administrative base in Glasgow but no building of its own. It works with existing companies, tours Scotland and beyond, making use of venues as appropriate. Even if the Parliament closed its doors to a hilarious take on First Minister's Question Time as written by kids and performed by Alex Norton, Tam Dean Burn & Co, it was staged with great merriment at Edinburgh's Queen's Hall. Since then, the National Theatre has gone from strength to strength, culminating in the mega hit of this year's Edinburgh Festival, Gregory Burke's *Black Watch*.

The 'Working in Scotland' initiative, better known as the 'Fresh Talents' project, encouraging international students to stay in Scotland after finishing their studies on a two year visa without need for a work permit, has been, in Jack McConnell's words, 'one of the successes of this administration over the last few years.'[19] It started in June 2005, and more than 1,500 students from about 75 countries have since successfully applied for the scheme.

Until the elections, the Parliament's legislative agenda encompasses another 23 bills in progress, thirteen of them Executive bills, the rest Members' and Private bills. Among them are new regulations forbidding Christmas Day and New Year's Day trading, the St Andrew's Day Bank Holiday Bill, Mike Pringle's Environmental Levy on Plastic Bags (Scotland) Bill, the controversial Legal Profession and Legal Aid (Scotland) Bill

---

[18] Eddie Barnes, 'McConnell U-turn on business tax pledge', *Scotland on Sunday*, 17 September 2006.

[19] Rhiannon Edward, '1,500 take up Fresh Talent offer to stay on', *The Scotsman*, 7 March 2006.

which has already drawn flak from the legal profession, bills to introduce Commissioners for Older People and for Human Rights (controversial as the already existing tsars are deemed too costly by some critics).

The Planning Bill is controversial because the Greens and environmental organisations press for the right of third parties to appeal, which is rejected by the Executive. The Executive's Crofting Bill, which was heavily criticised in the Parliament's Environment and Rural Development Committee, particularly for a section which would have introduced a free market in croft tenancies, has already seen a 'major climbdown' by the Government, when Deputy Minister Rhona Brankin admitted that several key parts of the bill had been dropped and a wide-ranging inquiry into crofting issues was to be set up.[20] Committees at Holyrood are working at full throttle to cope with all these bills before the election campaign proper starts and Parliament is dissolved in early April.

BY-ELECTIONS 1: DUNFERMLINE AND WEST FIFE

While the Cathcart (Scottish Parliament) and Livingstone (Westminster) by-elections in September 2005, following the resignation of fire-raising Mike Watson and the death of Robin Cook, did not produce any great surprises, things were to change when a by-election for Dunfermline/West Fife became necessary following the death of Rachel Squire MP. It was scheduled for 9 February 2006.

Following the demise of Charles Kennedy as leader, described in an *Edinburgh Evening News* editorial as 'the brutal eviction of Ross, Skye and Lochaber MP Mr Kennedy by a cabal of conspirators,'[21] and the revelations of Mark Oaten and Simon Hughes about their sexual orientations, a *Scotsman* editorial spoke of the 'sobering prospect for Lib Dems';[22] and a *Herald* editorial saw 'The Lib Dems in crisis'.[23] Douglas Fraser even mused about Labour fears that the Lib Dems could come a poor fourth in Dunfermline, concerned 'that if its [i.e Labour's] partners lose momentum going into next year's Scottish elections, their joint majority could be at risk.'[24]

---

[20] John Ross, 'Ministers back down on crofting', *The Scotsman*, 22 September 2006.

[21] 'Revelations have destroyed progress made in recent years' (Leader), *Edinburgh Evening News*, 24 January 2006.

[22] 'Sobering prospect for Lib Dems' (Leader), *The Scotsman*, 9 January 2006.

[23] 'The Lib Dems in crisis' (Leader), *The Herald*, 27 January 2006.

[24] Douglas Fraser, 'Shattering result raises doubt over Brown's chances of No 10', *The Herald*, 10 February 2006.

But the actual campaign for the by-election, like the subsequent result, turned into a nightmare for Labour, starting with accusations of 'fixing' Catherine Stihler's candidature before she was duly selected. This came on top of the news of 700 job losses at the Lexmark factory and an embarrassing rift between Westminster Labour ministers and the Labour-led Executive at Holyrood, as the Forth bridge 'farrago' led to questions of 'who runs Scotland?' and 'who runs the Labour party in Scotland?'[25] Peter Jones saw the 'devolution concordat' crumbling, calling the 'Dunfermline by-election shenanigans' of London's 'meddling' and McConnell's 'resistance' no less than 'a defining moment in the relationship between the devolved government in Edinburgh and the UK government in London.'[26]

The turning point for the Lib Dems was undoubtedly Charles Kennedy's visit to Dunfermline on 2 February. After four weeks 'out of the spotlight,' Kennedy was the darling of the media, 'the day's true star.' The 'Kennedy factor' turned out trumps as TV screens and newspaper columns were full of the affection which was shown to 'the party's greatest asset and its greatest loss.'[27] More important, even, was Kennedy's signal that he did not bear grudges. So, no need for Lib Dem and Charles Kennedy supporters to punish the party for the treatment meted out to the former leader.

The by-election was won by Willie Rennie of the Liberal Democrats with a majority of 1,800 on a 16.24% swing. At the previous May's General Election Rachel Squire had won the seat for Labour with a majority of more than 11,500. The fall-out of this election result – Labour losing 'a safe seat in Gordon Brown's backyard' to the Lib Dems who had in the months leading up to the election been 'embroiled in back-stabbing, sniping and scandal'[28] – was seen as damaging to Gordon Brown's chances of, at least a quick, succession to No 10 Downing Street and coloured the spring party conference season.

While the Lib Dems celebrated, claiming that they now 'can win seats from the Labour Party in all parts of Scotland,'[29] Labour MPs (and some MSPs) cried foul over the Lib Dems' 'amoral campaign'; there were calls for a minority administration at Holyrood. Dishonest, dublicitous, untrustworthy, irresponsible, lack of discipline and 'no obvious sense

[25] Ian Bell, 'McConnell remains resolute as Forth bridge farrago takes its toll', *The Herald*, 27 January 2006.

[26] Peter Jones, 'The devolution concordat finally crumbles', *The Scotsman*, 31 January 2006.

[27] Tom Gordon, 'Kennedy factor still lights a fuse as the big guns shoot into town', *The Herald*, 3 February 2006.

[28] Ian Swanson, 'By-election sting for Sir Ming with new hearty party?', *Edinburgh Evening News*, 16 February 2006.

[29] Ian Swanson, 'Red Nose Day for Labour: Lib-Dems are jubilant after stunning by-election ambush', *Edinburgh Evening News*, 10 February 2006.

of honour'[30] were accusations hurled at the Lib Dems. As a *Scotsman* editorial put it: 'The Lib Dems have…managed to pull off the impressive trick of avoiding responsibility for the unpopular aspects of the Scottish Executive's record but claiming credit for the policies people like.[31] Or, in the relative moderate words of the Labour MSP Alasdair Morrison: 'We are scunnered that there are those in the Lib Dem party who think they can have their cake and eat it.'[32]

While the Lib Dems' celebrations continued at their conference, the aftermath of Dunfermline was less uplifting for the SNP and the Tories. Coming a poor third was 'grim news for Alex Salmond.'[33] The former SNP-leader Gordon Wilson launched 'a devastating attack' on his party leadership which he saw as having 'lost its way,' while the former MSP and SNP chief executive Michael Russell said that, after the by-election 'humiliation', the SNP 'is fighting for its survival,'[34] and the *Scotsman* columnist and ex-SNP MSP Duncan Hamilton saw his party 'in the doldrums.'[35]

Some 500 votes for ex-Labour MSP John McAllion, standing for the Scottish Socialist Party, did not augur well for the party's prospects for 2007. The Greens had kept out of the Dunfermline contest.

BY-ELECTIONS 2: MORAY

The media were united in their appreciation for the late Margaret Ewing – 'one of the few politicians without an enemy'[36] – whose death triggered another by-election, this time in Moray on 27 April. Tory Mary Scanlon was first to throw her hat into the ring. Both Scanlon and the SNP's candidate Richard Lochhead resigned their Holyrood list seats

---

[30] Catherine MacLeod, 'Angry Labour calls to break coalition with the Lib Dems', *The Herald*, 13 February 2006.

[31] 'The Lib Dems have done well out of the two coalition deals' (Leader), *The Scotsman*, 25 March 2006.

[32] Catherine MacLeod, 'Angry labour calls to break coalition with Lib Dems', *The Herald*, 13 February 2006.

[33] Douglas Fraser, 'Shattering result raises doubt over Brown's chances of No 10', *The Herald*, 10 February2006.

[34] Douglas Fraser, 'SNP has lost its way, ex-leader claims in wake of "humiliation"', *The Herald*, 4 March 2006.

[35] Duncan Hamilton, 'SNP's sails hang limply in the doldrums while other ships fly by', *The Scotsman*, 6 March 2006.

[36] Robbie Dinwoodie, 'One of the few politicians without an enemy', *The Herald*, 22 March 2006.

to contest the Moray seat (which Margaret Ewing had held with a 4,000 vote majority).

Even before the campaign had properly started, Mary Scanlon found herself enmeshed in problems. Letters of endorsement, allegedly by independent Moray councillors and distributed in leaflet form, were disowned by the councillors in question, and another leaflet, emphasising Scanlon's friendship with the late Margaret Ewing and presenting her as the 'continuity candidate' – but omitting the fact that she was a Tory – was fiercely criticised by the SNP.[37] Yet it was not only the 'Trojan Tory' who got into trouble, the Lib Dems were also accused of 'dirty tricks', as their candidate Linda Gorn and her team were likened to 'snake-oil salesmen' by the editor of the local weekly paper, the *Northern Scot*, for falsely suggesting in a leaflet that the paper was backing her candidature.[38]

The by-election was easily won by Richard Lochhead, with 12,653 votes. Mary Scanlon came a poor second with 6,268 votes. Richard Lochhead thus became a directly elected MSP. Maureen Watt took his list seat, and David Petrie of the Scottish Conservatives replaced Mary Scanlon. Maureen Watt took her oath of allegiance in the Doric dialect of the North-East as well as in English – a premiere at Holyrood.

PARTIES 1: SCOTTISH LABOUR

Dunfermline had sent Labour reeling. As the surprise defeat fed speculations about Brown and Blair, it became increasingly clear that Jack McConnell's biggest headache in the run-up to the forthcoming elections would be the fall-out of Blair's long farewell and the timetable of his succession. A *Herald* editorial spelled it out: 'Enduring the dog days of a premiership does not enthrall electorates, especially if tarnished by endless bickering about who will take over. This could be the baleful backdrop to next year's Holyrood poll.'[39]

Or, as Ian Bell pointedly observed: 'The prime minister is, after all, the single biggest reason for an outbreak of panic within Scottish Labour.'[40] The last thing McConnell wants is a Labour 'beauty contest' between leadership contenders overshadowing the Scottish election campaign –

---

[37] Frank Urquhart, 'Police urged to investigate "deceitful and dishonest" Tory election tactics', *The Scotsman*, 15 April 2006.

[38] Frank Urquhart, 'Now Lib Dems are accused of dirty tricks in bitter battle for Moray', *The Scotsman*, 19 April 2006.

[39] *The Herald*, 7 September 2006.

[40] Ian Bell, 'Policy that gives voters a chance to play havoc', *The Herald*, 9 May 2006.

a 'nightmare scenario' as one MSP put it.[41] From McConnell's perspective, the *Scotsman* concurred, 'diverting the attention of party activists and the media towards an internal beauty contest, smack in the middle of a fight to the death with the SNP, is plain electoral suicide.'[42]

Based on an analysis of current electoral trends, John Curtice projected in May that Labour could lose up to 15 seats in the 2007 election, and thus the power to continue the present coalition – even if the Lib Dems were up for it. McConnell tried to impart the seriousness of the situation to Tony Blair in June when he told him that the SNP could win next year's election, after private polling by Scottish Labour had revealed that the party could lose up to 12 seats in May 2007.

Labour's woes were compounded by revelations of a major cash crisis of the party, in London, with the potential of job losses in Scotland and considerably less money than anticipated for next year's campaign, and warnings by the Catholic hierarchy that the party was losing support among Catholic voters because, as Bishop Tartaglia of Paisley said, Catholics were 'tired of being bullied into accepting an intolerant new orthodoxy on issues such as homosexual unions while the family and marriage are constantly attacked by a very anti-family Labour party.'[43] Add to this protests about hospital closures and re-organisation, with the SNP and independents targeting Justice Minister Cathy Jamieson's seat over the Monklands A&E closure, and worries over the civil service relocation programme in Edinburgh, and it becomes clear that Labour has its work cut out for the 2007 campaign.

In response to the Dunfermline campaigning disaster, which was blamed on London's interference in devolved matters (like the Forth Bridge tolls and the building of a new Forth Bridge), McConnell increasingly distanced himself and Scottish Labour from 'ill-informed' Westminster politicians, stressing that he would in future be firm defending Scottish Executive business against interference from London.

When McConnell announced that (shock horror!) he would not support England in the World Cup, it earned him a bitter reprimand from Gordon Brown who accused him of 'draping himself in the Saltire' and 'pandering to nationalism.'[44] Does this and his support, all of a sudden, for St Andrew's Day as a national holiday, mean that 'Tartan Jack' is

---

[41] Hamish Macdonell, 'McConnell says Blair plans may harm election chances', *The Scotsman*, 14 September 2006.

[42] 'Blair and the Holyrood effect' (Leader), *The Scotsman*, 14 September 2006.

[43] Hamish Macdonell, 'Catholic vote at risk, bishop tells Labour', *The Scotsman*, 13 September.2006.

[44] Jason Allardyce, 'Brown: McConnell "panders to nationalism"', *The Sunday Times*, 28 May 2006.

'trying to out-nat the nats'?[45] Iain Macwhirter saw McConnell's changing stance as a consequence of devolution itself:

> Quietly, almost imperceptibly, Scotland is becoming more self-confident as a nation and clearer about what is required toi make it a better place to live. Jack McConnell is acutely conscious of this, which is why he is talking up his independence from London control.[46]

In August, a YouGov poll commissioned by the SNP saw Labour trailing its opponents, and ex-Minister Susan Deacon declared she would not seek reelection next year, expressing frustration and disappointment over the devolution process so far: 'Devolution hasn't delivered change on the scale or at the pace that it should have done.'[47] And the papers from the *Scotsman* stable splashed out stories about an internal rebellion against McConnell. There was even talk of a 'coup plotted amid election panic.'[48] While Susan Deacon bowed out of next year's contest, Lord Foulkes entered it, and Donald Anderson gave up his position as Council Leader in Edinburgh to contest Edinburgh South.

While speculation about the future of the Holyrood coalition flourished, particularly from quarters not too favourably disposed towards Labour and the Lib Dems, it is maybe worth while remembering that the coalition has been there before. Many media pundits saw it on its last legs from the start, and again in the run-up to the 2003 elections – oddly enough, it has, so far, proved remarkably resilient. That is realpolitik for you. But the Labour conference's adoption of nuclear power as an option for Scotland's energy policy seemed to put more potential obstacles in the way of the existing Holyrood partnership beyond May 2007, as the Lib Dem Conference clearly rejected nuclear energy.

Yet, after sitting on the fence on the question of new nuclear power stations for months, McConnell surprised he public by declaring in September that Scotland could meet its energy needs through a 'massive increase in renewable energy' which could 'replace nuclear entirely.'[49] This could ease dealing with the Lib Dems. But there remains the tricky issue of Trident's replacement, which Brown already endorsed in June –

---

[45] Joan McAlpine, 'Tartan Jack takes on the two-headed terrier', *The Herald*, 21 August 2006.

[46] Iain Macwhirter, 'Why our Jack the Lad has an air of Jack the Nat about him', *The Herald*, 1 February 2006.

[47] Peter MacMahon, 'McConnell fights for his political future as fears mount of uprising', *The Scotsman*, 21 August 2006.

[48] Eddie Barnes, 'McConnell warned: fail and you're out', *Scotland on Sunday*, 20 August 2006.

[49] Tom Gordon, 'Green power could replace nuclear, says McConnell', *The Herald*, 22 September 2006.

clearly a reserved matter, but a sensitive issue for 'all those veterans of the old "nuclear-free Scotland" campaigners on the Labour benches,' and particularly for the 'old unilateral disarmer' McConnell,[50] under incessant pressure from the SNP. Relief came only – and temporarily – when a TNS System Three survey published in early September saw Labour eight percentage points ahead of the SNP. Calculating on the basis of that poll, John Curtice had Labour on 49 seats (just one down) and the SNP at 24 seats (three down).

Labour commitments likely to be in the 2007 Manifesto were leaked in late September. Green issues, public health and law and order are, apparently, to dominate the agenda. Council tax discounts for making homes more environmentally friendly, the use of recycled materials in new roads and road repairs, trade academies for vocational training for 14 and 15-year-olds, cutting prices for sports facilities to encourage more people to use them in the fight against obesity, banning unhealthy snacks from sports centres, allowing local authorities to fluoridise water, investigating the possibility of a direct ferry link between Scotland and Denmark, a light rail link between Rosyth and Edinburgh, a one-stop Scotland-wide box office with tickets for all cultural events, and powers for ministers to compel local authorities to impose Asbos. While Labour sources are quoted as claiming that the draft manifesto 'represents a list of sensible and realistic policies which can be put into practice,' the oppositional view is that the leaked manifesto shows 'that First Minister Jack McConnell's party has run out of new ideas.'[51]

McConnell refused to even contemplate seat losses: 'We go into these elections more confident than I have ever been in my five years as First Minister. I believe we will have the better ideas, more of them, a greater clarity of vision in our manifesto.'[52]

PARTIES 2: SNP

After mixed fortunes in the by-elections of September and February, Alex Salmond demonstrated confidence at the SNP conference, sticking to his aim of 20 seats to be gained from Labour in the May 2007 elections. Lower taxation, public sector savings, replacement of the council tax by a local income tax, a legally binding waiting time guarantee,

---

[50] Ian Bell, 'Brown's nuclear intent leaves the First Minister sitting uncomfortably', The Herald, 23 June 2006.

[51] Murdo MacLeod, 'Tax breaks for going green top Jack's plan', Scotland on Sunday, 24 September 2006.

[52] Peter MacMahon and Louise Gray, 'Labour moves eight points clear of the SNP, says poll', The Scotsman, 5 September 2006.

and the publication of a referendum bill on independence were among the pledges unveiled in Dundee in April as cornerstones for a 2007 SNP Manifesto.

The YouGov poll in August showed the SNP four points ahead of Labour (33 to 29 %), Salmond ahead of his rivals on the question who would make the best First Minister (43%, compared to 27% for Jack McConnell, 13 % for Annabel Goldie, and 10% for Nicol Stephen) and public support for the SNP as the leading party in a coalition government after May 2007 – 28% for an SNP-Lib Dem pact, against 25% for the existing Holyrood coalition. The poll also endorsed the preliminary talks before Christmas between the SNP and the Greens, probing the possibilities for a coalition after the next elections: 66% agreed with the talks; just 14% disagreed.

The SNP used the summer for a series of policy announcements, including a pledge to cull quangos and slash bureaucracy and take local enterprise companies away from Scottish Enterprise and transfer them to councils, no more nuclear power stations, and ambitious targets for the reduction of greenhouse gas emissions, a total restructuring of the civil service, streamlining, cutting bureaucracy costs and focusing on three dominant departments: sustainable growth, health and education, slashing the size of government – fewer ministers, reducing civil service numbers in favour of 'small government', Irish-style tax breaks for artists, a pledge for old age pensioners to be exempt from council tax, a £100 m funding package to abolish the graduate endowment tax and return to free higher education, the slashing of business rates for 150,000 small businesses with a new Small Business Bonus Scheme worth £122m, and the vow to scrap the Edinburgh airport rail link.

The write-off of existing student debts and the scrapping of the graduate endowment tax came under double attack. The SNP's budgeted £100 were a massive underestimate – Labour politicians put the price tag between £1.7 and 3bn; and morally, Paul Hutcheon argued, wiping out existing debts of 'graduates in well-paid jobs is simply preposterous.' It would 'hand a £1bn plus subsidy to 300,000 people with more earning potential than anybody else.'[53] Tax-free OAPs, free higher education, tax exemption for artists, slashed business rates on the one hand – small government on the other. In the run-up to the election the SNP's financial probity will be examined in proportion to its likelihood of gaining power.

While Ian Bell pointed out that the YouGov poll was commissioned by the SNP, he led the speculation of what could happen if the SNP were the leading government party after May 2007, posing the question whether the SNP could win the election but perhaps fail in getting a yes vote in the promised independence referendum which would follow their electoral victory – and what the consequences of such a scenario might be.[54] The

---

[53] Paul Hutcheon, "'Wiping out debt of graduates is preposterous'", *Sunday Herald*, 30 July 2006.

[54] Ian Bell, 'Why SNP risks defeat over symbolic gesture', *The Herald*, 29 August 2006.

pledge to hold an independence referendum within four years of gaining power could become a major stumbling block if the SNP needs to form a coalition with the Lib Dems. While the Lib Dems have signalled that they are prepared to talk to all other parties about coalitions, Nicol Stephen expressly ruled out that the Lib Dems could consent to an independence referendum.

For Alex Salmond, the referendum is a *sine qua non*, but Mike Russell, who is expected to return to Holyrood in 2007, has just published different thoughts on the subject:[55] No referendum in the first term of an SNP-led government, and sharing of responsibility for foreign affairs and defence with England as part of the UK. This idea of a 'New Union' is, as Paul Hutcheon comments, likely to infuriate not just the 'fundamentalists' in the SNP – it is also in clear contradiction of Alex Salmond's stated policy.[56] Iain Macwhirter, on the other hand, suspects that a majority of SNP MSPs share Russell's scepticism regarding the referendum: 'after all, what is the point of having a referendum which the SNP are likely to lose?'[57]

But the conflict extends to other policies. Even in the existing parliamentary party there is an uneasy peace between the social democrats of Salmond's ilk, and the pro-business, low-tax free marketers like Kenny MacAskill and Jim Mather. The SNP expellee Campbell Martin accused his former party of having turned 'hard to the right', now sharing many policies with the Tories.[58] Jim Sillars claimed 'an independent Scotland must be right-thinking,'[59] and Mike Russell and Dennis MacLeod propose cuts in income tax and the abolition of corporation and inheritance taxes. They want Scotland to have its own currency, not joining the Euro (as is official SNP policy), a voucher-based system for education, privatisation of trunk roads and the water system, and an end of the party's bar on working with the Tories. Could this cast doubts on the SNP becoming the natural beneficiary of an electoral meltdown of the SSP as suggested by commentators over the summer?

[55] Michael Russell and Dennis MacLeod, *Grasping the Thistle: How Scotland Must React to the Three Key Challenges of the Twenty First Century*, Glendaruel: Argyll, 2006.

[56] Paul Hutcheon, 'Alternative blueprint for SNP future: let's stick with the union', *Sunday Herald*, 24 September 2006.

[57] Iain Macwhirter, 'Reservations about a referendum', *Sunday Herald*, 24 September 2006.

[58] Campbell Martin, 'Principles go overboard as SNP turns hard to the right', *The Herald*, 16 August 2006.

[59] Jim Sillars, 'An independent Scotland must be right-thinking', *The Scotsman*, 29 August 2006.

PARTIES 3: LIBERAL DEMOCRATS

After the Dunfermline boost, internal Liberal Democrat calculations this summer predicted an increase of seats for them from presently 17 to 25 after next year's election. They would then talk not just with the strongest party (Labour, as expected) but also with the SNP about forming a partnership government. They have clearly ruled out new nuclear power stations in Scotland and staked the claim at their autumn conference to become the greenest party, pledging that by 2050 all of Scotland's energy needs would be met from renewable sources. But that long-term focus was criticised by the Greens' co-convener Shiona Baird as deflecting scrutiny away from the party's current actions:

> The Lib Dems have utterly failed to take serious action to fast-track renewables. You only have to look at their record in office – of expanding motorways, aviation and even campaigning against congestion charging – to see that they will run a mile from the tough decisions that are really needed urgently.[60]

Other Lib Dem manifesto commitments include lowering the voting age in Scottish Parliament and local government elections to 16 and pupils' councils in every school and youth councils in every local authority area.

The recommendations of the Steel Commission, published in March, contained Lib Dem demands for greater powers for the Scottish Parliament, including new tax powers. This was seen, at least by the *Scotsman*, as 'a dramatic shift in the balance of Scottish politics,' splashing across its front page: 'Lib Dems open door to coalition with SNP.'[61] The Steel commission's report was, so Iain Macwhirter, 'little short of a declaration for independence.'[62]

In contrast to the Dunfermline scenario, the Lib Dems will have to defend the Executive's record next May. Souring relations with Labour, competition with the Greens over environmental credentials, and doubts anent their stance vis-à-vis a coalition with the SNP could make their task of gaining seats somewhat more difficult than anticipated.

---

[60] Gerri Peev and Tanya Thompson, 'Lib Dems stake claim to being greenest of the green', *The Scotsman*, 19 September 2006.

[61] 'Lib Dems open door to coalition with SNP', *The Scotsman*, 7 March 2006.

[62] Iain Macwhirter, 'Yet another step towards declaring independence?', *The Scotsman*, 8 March 2006.

PARTIES 4: SCOTTISH CONSERVATIVES

At the end of October of last year, David McLetchie MSP had to resign his post as leader of the Scottish Conservative party after continued pressure over his Holyrood taxi expenses. In November, Annabel Goldie MSP was elected as the new leader of the Scottish Tories. At the same time, Brian Monteith MSP resigned from the Scottish Conservative Party following his revelation that he had briefed against David McLetchie. He stated that he would remain at Holyrood as an independent MSP until the next election.

The Tories had hoped to improve their standing in Dunfermline, but they fell back from 10.3 to 7.8% of the vote. Addressing the Tory conference in Perth in March, UK party leader David Cameron, told the party to 'focus its fire on the Labour and Liberal Democrat politicians running Scotland, rather than the institution at Holyrood.'[63] Their only Scottish MP, David Mundell, said: 'For us as a party in Scotland, the time for whingeing about the Scottish Parliament is over. We have to focus all our time, energy and resources on making it better at delivering for the people of Scotland.'[64] Annabel Goldie demanded 'real devolution', as she formulated her 'strategic objective' to become the 'principal party of opposition' at Holyrood.[65] But her deputy, Murdo Fraser MSP, contended that the Tories would only regain power if they were prepared to enter into coalition, perhaps with a 'pro-business SNP', which led to speculations about a split on this strategic issue at the top of the Tories. Paul Hutcheon echoed David Mundell MP when he came to the conclusion that a Tory revival north of the border was 'still a long way off.'[66]

More controversy lay ahead as Annabel Goldie suggested the Tories could prop up Labour after the Holyrood elections for concessions on public service reforms and lower business rates – in order to keep the SNP out of power. At the same time, discussions in the SNP about a coalition with Labour were reported. 'Strange bedfellows emerge,' Douglas Fraser commented, 'when coalition fever grips the nation.'[67]

When Cameron returned to Scotland in September, he risked obesity – so much humble pie was he eating: he apologised for practically everything, from the Highland clearances to the poll tax and English

---

[63] Ian Swanson, 'Cameron brings big guns in hope of Scots fightback', *Edinburgh Evening News*, 2 March 2006.

[64] *Ibid.*

[65] Murdo MacLeod, 'Goldie's not for turning on devolution to the dismay of Tory hardliners', *Scotland on Sunday*, 5 March 2006.

[66] Paul Hutcheon, 'A Scottish Tory revival is still a long way off', *Sunday Herald*, 5 March 2006.

[67] Douglas Fraser, 'Strange bedfellows emerge when coalition fever grips the nation', *The Herald*, 6 June 2006.

prejudices against the Jocks. But it did not go down well: 'Go home Cameron to think again,' shouted an editorial leader in *Scotland on Sunday*: his speech was 'backward-looking, shallowly ingratiating and self-abasing,' it opined; 'to say that it was light on policy would be a charitable understatement.... a wasted opportunity.'[68]

So, no Cameron effect north of the Border. And, indeed, the biggest problem for the Tories is their stagnation, and the low esteem in which their MSPs are held, even among their own Holyrood candidates, who in August called for them to be de-selected to make space for fresh blood. Former deputy chairman Mars Goodman even spoke of the way the party was run at the moment as 'sheer lunacy'.[69] As a *Scotsman* editorial had it, 'Scottish Tories are all at sea.'[70] And Allan Massie's verdict was: 'No direction, no inspiration... no chance.'[71]

PARTIES 5: SCOTTISH SOCIALISTS

More headlines than all the other parties together were made by a court case which provided red tops as well as broadsheets and broadcast media with a summer extravaganza rivalling anything Big Brother and other celebrity TV shows could come up with. The mighty Tommy Sheridan MSP, founder of the Scottish Socialist Party, took on the *News of the World* (who had published a story about his alleged extramarital affairs in November 2004) and his own party, and won. Sexual capers – two, three, four in a bed (Tom Gordon commented on *Newsnight Scotland*, it could be 'sixes and sevens' before too long) – provided the voyeuristic novelty value. The problem was that Tommy Sheridan could only prove his case by proving his party to be a basket case. It was his word against that of four of his fellow MSPs – somebody had to be lying in court. The jury ruled in favour of Sheridan, who turned round calling his former comrades 'scabs' (a term he later regretted) and, on Sunday, 3 September, formed 'Solidarity', his own break-away socialist party.

Not only did this libel case and the party split totally overshadow any policies the SSP promotes as, for example, free prescriptions, a proposal which gained Committee backing at Holyrood and was then voted down in the Chamber by the Executive's majority. It also revealed a misogynist streak in the party. Most of the witnesses backing Sheridan were men,

---

[68] 'Go home Cameron to think again' (Leader), *Scotland on Sunday*, 17 September 2006.

[69] Hamish Macdonell, 'Top Tory adds "lunacy" jibe to rebellion against MSPs', *The Scotsman*, 29 August 2006.

[70] 'Scottish Tories are all at sea', *The Scotsman*, 28 August 2006.

[71] Allan Massie, 'No direction, no inspiration... no chance', *The Scotsman*, 1 September 2006.

most of those giving evidence against him women. It was ironic that 'the women giving evidence in court to support the NoTW case were portrayed as those the paper is usually out to get – feminists, hookers, gold-diggers, witches and man-haters. On Sheridan's side was his martyred mother and his near-perfect wife.' The whole affair 'cannot be described as one that has advanced the cause of women in any way.'[72]

The *Scotsman* predicted in an editorial leader that the most 'acrimonious' and 'bitter' contests in next year's election would be fought between these two rival socialist parties:

> The anti-Sheridan faction believes Mr Sheridan is an egotist and a liar and wants nothing to do with him. The pro-Sheridan faction believes he has been the victim of a vicious attempted coup and that he is still the best political leader in Scotland.[73]

In September, Arthur Scargill's Socialist Labour Party announced that it would also enter the fray and field candidates across Scotland, hoping to capitalise on the divisions and infighting between former members of the SSP. Sheridan may claim that 'Scotland is big enough for more than one socialist party,[74] but it is difficult to see any of them repeating the electoral success the SSP achieved in 2003.

PARTIES 6: GREENS

The sorry picture of the SSP at war contrasted sharply with the growing prospects of the Greens, from pre-Christmas coalition talks with the SNP to the mainstream parties' belief that they 'could play kingmaker after next year's poll.'[75] They share common ground with the SNP on the question of independence for Scotland, on more powers for Holyrood, a nuclear-free Scotland, more wave and wind power, third party (community) appeals on planning, asylum and rendition, and PFI/PPP government finance deals. But they differ on business-friendly policies, on major new road projects, on airport expansion, reliance on oil revenues, and fisheries conservation policies.

Solidly led by Robin Harper and Shiona Baird, with Mark Ballard winning the post of student and staff rector at Edinburgh University

---

[72] Julie Bindel, 'A win for machismo', *The Guardian*, 8 August 2006.

[73] 'Same old socialist stand-offs' (Leader), *The Scotsman*, 4 September 2006.

[74] Lynn Malone, '"Scotland is big enough for more than one socialist party. I predict thousands will join us": – interview with Tommy Sheridan', *Sunday Herald*, 20 August 2006.

[75] Paul Hutcheon, ''Greens ready to support SNP government', *Sunday Herald*, 7 May 2006.

(against Boris Johnston MP and Magnus Linklater), it is no pipedream when their election co-ordinator, Patrick Harvie MSP, says the Greens aim at winning ten parliamentary seats in May 2007. In any power deal after the election, they would prioritise assurances on key Green policies over cabinet posts. In September, the ex-leader of Edinburgh Council, Labour Holyrood hopeful Donald Anderson, lanced an invitation to his own party and to the Greens to consider a three-way coalition:

> I believe Labour needs to open a dialogue with the Green Party. There are successes in our relationship with the Lib Dems, but failures too. Weekend environmentalists, they are guilty of adopting gimmicks or policies they believe to be popular. A three-way coalition could give a real drive and strength to our environmental policies. (…) The Greens could play a role in delivering, rather than demanding, better policies for our environment. The question for us in the Labour Party is, are we bold enough to open up the dialogue, and, if we are, will the Greens respond?[76]

Their draft manifesto includes scrapping Asbos, allowing local authorities to introduce car parking charges, abolishing zoos, prohibiting the import of animals for circuses, banning coursing, live baiting and the use of whips in horse racing – 'none of which are likely to impress Mr McConnell or SNP leader Alex Salmond.'[77] But, then, not all of them might be signed off by the autumn party conference, and even fewer would perhaps survive power-broking talks after the election.

MAY 2007: THE HEAT IS ON

According to the *Scotsman*, 'normally, August is the "silly season",'

> But not this August, when the Scottish political scene has been anything but quiescent. The Scottish Socialist Party has self-destructed in the wake of the Tommy Sheridan trial. A new opinion poll gives the SNP a four point lead over Labour, and it is set to be the largest party next May. Meanwhile, inside Labour ranks, there is growing criticism of the First Minister. One political party alone seems to fail

[76] Donald Anderson, 'Why climate is right for Greens to join Holyrood coalition', *The Scotsman*, 12 September 2006.

[77] Paul Hutcheon, 'Scottish Green activists demand zoo and circus ban. Party's draft pledges may damage government hopes', *Sunday Herald*, 24 September 2006.

to capture any headlines – Scotland's Tories. The same poll that puts the SNP firmly ahead of Labour indicates a slump in Conservative fortunes – the party has dropped seven points to only 10%. At this rate, they could be overtaken by the Scottish Greens.[78]

What is true about August can be said of the entire year at Holyrood. Since last autumn, the political climate has warmed significantly. The political temperature is rising because the next Holyrood election, coinciding with the 300th anniversary of the Union, promises to be the most interesting since devolution. In 1999 and 2003 the polls predicted a pretty clear-cut majority for the Labour-Lib Dem partnership. This time, even if they had the numerical strength after the election, it is not sure whether the partners wish to continue. The SNP could be on the verge of a break-through, and Labour's hegemony in Scotland could come to a close. The rainbow Parliament could get a rainbow coalition government. Voter turn-out should, given these circumstances, be up – and election night next May should be well worth staying up for.

[September 2006]

---

[78] 'Scottish Tories are all at sea' (Leader), *The Scotsman*, 28 August 2006.

Chapter IV

THE YEAR AT HOLYROOD
2006-2007

The twelve months since the last instalment of the 'Annals' have seen astonishing changes in the political landscape – in Scotland and elsewhere in the UK. First and foremost on the chronicler's mind are the changes in Scotland: the elections in May which led to the end of Labour's rule in Scotland and the creation of an SNP minority government. But there were also the elections in Wales which resulted, after prolonged negotiations, in an unprecedented coalition between Labour and Plaid Cymru; that we have witnessed the emergence of a partnership government involving both the Democratic Unionists and Sinn Féin, with Ian Paisley and Martin McGuinness sharing the posts of First and Deputy First Ministers; the eventual transition from Tony Blair to Gordon Brown in the post of UK Prime Minister; and, most recently, the 'coronation' of Wendy Alexander as new Scottish Labour and Holyrood opposition leader. Truly, a remarkable year of change. One of the few things that did not change, it seems, was the Scottish football team's ability to beat the French – they did it last October at Hampden, and managed to repeat the feat this September in Paris.

SETTING THE SCENE

While until the spring of 2006, opinion polls had seen the SNP in the doldrums, the party entered last autumn on a high in the polls, clearly leading Labour. Their good fortunes continued. 'Who would have thought that the SNP would stage the most successful party conference of the season? Labour were at war with themselves, the Liberal Democrats shell-shocked, and the Tories accident-prone. The nationalists, by contrast, seemed united, confident, businesslike, purposeful.'[1] That is how Iain Macwhirter summed up the conference season.

Maybe the decisive moment in the run-up to the election campaign came when Jack McConnell gave the John P Macintosh Memorial

---

[1] Iain Macwhirter, 'The SNP seem to be on their way at last', *Sunday Herald*, 15 October 2006.

lecture in Haddington on 24 October, where he argued that the powers of Holyrood were sufficient and demands for further powers would lead to 'political paralysis'.[2] After the Dunfermline disaster for Scottish Labour, McConnell had repeatedly tried to put some red tartan between his government and Westminster, some media commentators even suggesting he was attempting to 'out-nat the nats.'[3] Had not McConnell himself initiated a review of the Parliament's powers, suggesting transfers in areas like immigration, broadcasting, control over firearms, casinos and drug policy?[4] Now, all of a sudden, Ron Davies's famous dictum that devolution was a process not an event seemed no longer the guiding principle of Labour. McConnell thus boxed Labour into a defensive corner reminiscent of the Tories' stance in the 1980s and '90s – the only party resisting change, as the Lib Dems had, earlier in the year, published their blueprint for change,[5] and Tory voices in favour of increased taxation responsibilities for the Scottish Parliament became more frequent as the campaign progressed.[6]

The *Edinburgh Evening News* challenged the 'superficial logic' of McConnell's stance. Tax powers, control of the electoral system, transport, medical contracts, energy policy, broadcasting, civil service responsibility – it saw 'no reason why responsibility for some of these other areas should not gradually be handed from London to Edinburgh if it becomes clear in time such a move makes sense.'[7] After all, as Ruth Wishart commented, 'the devolution settlement, like all politics, is a work in progress that must be adapted...'[8]

Henry McLeish, the former First Minister, added his critical voice:

> The first minister must do more to convince the electorate
> that Labour has the ability and the courage to provide a real
> alternative to the struggle that exists between the status

---

[2] 'McConnell warning on extra powers', BBC News Scotland, 24 October 2006, <news.bbc.co.uk/1/hi/scotland/6079026.stm>.

[3] Joan McAlpine, 'Can Jack shake off the nationalist terrier?, The Herald, 21 August 2006.

[4] Andrew McDonald and Robert Hazell, 'What happened next: constitutional change under New Labour', in Andrew McDonald (ed.), Reinventing Britain: Constitutional change under New Labour, London: Politico's, 2007, p.16.

[5] The Steel Commission, Moving to Federalism: A New Settlement for Scotland, Edinburgh: Scottish Liberal Democrats, (March) 2006.

[6] Hamish Macdonell, 'Tory shift on power leaves Labour isolated', The Scotsman, 5 March 2007.

7 'There is a case for giving Holyrood further tax powers' (Leader), Edinburgh Evening News, 30 October 2006.

8 Ruth Wishart, 'Oddly, Jack's going to tell why he's a Union man', The Herald, 24 October 2006.

quo and separatism and that means defying Westminister and demanding more powers for Holyrood.[9]

A *Scotsman* Leader warned McConnell that 'defending the status quo may not be an option.'[10] And Peter Jones commented that it could be 'a big mistake' for Labour to take 'no more constitutional change as a manifesto mantra.'[11]

On the 300th anniversary of Westminster's signing of the Act of Union, the *Edinburgh Evening News* summed up this debate:

> What is clear is that the devolution deal delivered in 1999 is far from the settled will of the Scottish people, but neither has it been proved to be the start of the inexorable slide towards independence. There is plenty of room for change, and giving Holyrood proper responsibility for raising the money it spends or answering the West Lothian question should not be regarded as the next stop to divorce.[12]

Labour concentrated on apocalyptic warnings should the SNP come to power, with Tony Blair and Dr John Reid leading the attack at the party conference in Oban: for Reid, the SNP was 'not fit for purpose',[13] for Blair, an SNP victory constituted a 'constitutional nightmare',[14] and Gordon Brown warned that 'everyone in the United Kingdom would suffer economically and culturally if Scotland voted for independence.'[15]

Labour in Scotland, Alex Salmond countered, are 'incapable of running their own campaign without remote control from their London masters'.[16] By contrast, the SNP stressed the offensive: 'We are preparing for government and we are preparing to win,' assured Salmond his delegated in Perth:

---

[9] Henry McLeish, 'The debate we should have', *The Sunday Times*, 5 November 2006.

[10] 'McConnell's election problem' (Leader), *The Scotsman*, 25 October 2006.

[11] Peter Jones, 'McConnell's "no more power" is a big gamble', *The Scotsman*, 24 October 2006.

[12] "We need to give devolution time to be a success" (Leader), *Edinburgh Evening News*, 16 January 2007.

[13] 'SNP "not fit for purpose" – Reid', *BBC News Scotland*, 26 November 2006, <news.bbc.co.uk/go/pr/fr/-/2/hi/uk_news/scotland/6184412.stm>.

[14] 'Blair urges "fight for Scotland"', *BBC News Scotland*, 24 November 2006, <news.bbc.co.uk/go/pr/fr/-/2/hi/uk_news/scotland/6178804.stm>.

[15] 'Scots split would harm UK – Brown', *BBC News Scotland*, 25 November 2006, <news.bbc.co.uk/go/pr/fr/-/2/hi/uk_news/6182762.stm>.

[16] *Ibid.*

We've now had seven years of devolution and I think there's a pretty overwhelming feeling in Scotland that now we've got a parliament, we may as well make it a real parliament with real powers, so it can do real things for Scotland.[17]

With a brilliantly staged autumn conference, the SNP cemented its lead, while Labour's gathering at Oban was overshadowed by Tony Blair's long farewell and the replacement of Trident (which Gordon Brown had committed himself to as early as July 2006). It looked as if the return of Alex Salmond as SNP leader in 2003 had truly galvanised the party (eventually, 'Alex Salmond for First Minister' would replace the party name on the ballot paper). Riding high in the polls, his claim that the SNP could win 20 extra seats in the election seemed increasingly more believable.

FLURRY OF LEGISLATION

While the upcoming election campaign made the headlines, the legislative machine at Holyrood went into nigh-overdrive, with committees and sub-committees working flat-out to get as much of the programme on the statute books as possible. As the Parliament's Annual Report, published on 19 June 2007, disclosed, during the period from September 2006 to end of March 2007 no fewer than 27 bills received Royal assent and became Acts of the Scottish Parliament. Of these Acts, twenty resulted from Executive bills, four from private bills, two had been Member's bills and one a Committee bill.

Their content ranged from the reorganisation of the Scottish tourist boards, including the official renaming of the Scottish Tourist Board as VisitScotland, the establishment of an independent Scottish Commissioner for Human Rights, a new Planning Bill, the establishment of St Andrew's Day as a bank holiday, the modernisation of the laws of personal bankruptcy, the Adoption and Children (Scotland) Bill, including adoption rights for same-sex couples, the reform of the system for handling complaints against lawyers through the creation of a new statutory body called the Scottish Legal Complaints Commission, reforms to ensure more efficient and effective summary justice, the Crofting Reform Bill, with the objective to simplify crofting legislation and the administration of crofting, to allow new crofts to be created, to allow crofters to undertake a wider range of activities on their crofts, and to

---

[17] '"Prepare for Power" says Salmond', *BBC News Scotland*, 11 October 2006, <news.bbc.co.uk/go/pr/fr/-/2/hi/uk_news/scotland/6038704.stm>.

modernise crofting legislation to take account of changes such as the increasing interest in renewable energy development in crofting areas.

In addition, the Transport and Works (Scotland) Bill was passed in February, as was the Budget Bill; the Adult Support and Protection Bill seeks to protect and benefit adults at risk of being abused, and the new law on prostitution makes it an offence for persons engaged in prostitution to cause nuisance, alarm or offence. Finally, the month before dissolution saw seven bills taking their final parliamentary hurdle. The Aquaculture and Fisheries Bill aims at improving the regulatory framework of aquaculture and enhances powers for controlling parasites affecting farmed salmon. The Christmas Day and New Year's Day Trading Bill prohibits large retail shops from opening for retail trading on Christmas Day and New Year's Day. The Protection of Vulnerable Groups Bill creates two lists – a Children's List and a new Adults' List – of people from working with vulnerable groups. Further legislation aimed at ensuring that food and drink supplied in local authority schools is nutritionally balanced, and more generally, that all schools increase their health promoting efforts; the Custodial Sentences and Weapons (Scotland) Bill ends automatic and unconditional early release of offenders and provides for the introduction of new restrictions on the sale of non-domestic knives and swords. The last two bills concerned the right of relatives who had died from Mesothelioma to claim damages; and green light for Network Rail to construct an electrified double track railway between Airdrie and Bathgate. All in all, the second session of the Scottish Parliament, from 2003 to 2007, passed 66 Bills, four more than the first session – 53 introduced by the Executive, one Committee Bill, three Members' and nine Private bills.[18]

In February, George Reid, the Presiding Officer, could announce to Members of the Parliament that the final cost of the Holyrood building had been reduced by £16.1m. The cost of the taxpayer therefore will fall from an estimated £431 to £414.4 million. With the dissolution of the 2003-2007 Parliament, George Reid took his final bow at Holyrood. Brian Taylor gave him a fine send-off in his blog:

> For this observer, George Reid's term of office has been a triumph. He sorted out the building project, he kept Holyrood's face turned upon the world (rather than internalised). More than that, he has been a splendid envoy for Scotland and Scottish politics.[19]

---

[18] <www.scottish.parliament.uk/business/bills/billSummaries.htm>.

[19] Brian Taylor *BBC Blog*, 29 March 2007, <www.bbc.co.uk/blogs/election07/scotland/>.

ELECTION CAMPAIGN

The election campaign proper started only with the dissolution of the Parliament at the end of March, but in reality it had all begun much earlier. The political temperature had continually risen, with speculation blossoming about possible coalitions and rumours galore.

Matters for Labour were not helped when Malcolm Chisholm resigned from his post in the Cabinet as Minister for Communities because he found himself unable to support the official Labour position on the issue of Trident, notwithstanding the fact that it is a reserved issue. Chisholm had been one of four Labour members who supported the SNP's motion opposing the replacement of the nuclear submarines.

The SNP started the New Year with a message posted on YouTube. Speaking from the Kinnaird Head Lighthouse in Fraserburgh, Alex Salmond said Scotland could increase its prosperity by learning from countries across the water, such as Norway. The SNP, he said, was working for peace because Scotland had been 'dragged into enough foolish, costly and illegal wars.'[20] Thematically, the Iraq war (and Trident) would never be to far from the centre of the election campaign. And the SNP seemed to set the agenda. On a BBC *Newsnight Scotland* programme on 4 January, commentators as different as Gerry Hassan and Katie Grant agreed that Labour was 'not in a good position' and that people were 'bored' or even 'fed up' with Labour. The SNP seemed 'to dominate the media agenda,' as Lorraine Davidson remarked on *Newsnight Scotland* on 23 January 2007, while Labour seemed to 'snooze'.

Against the backdrop of the Union's anniversary, a peculiar double-decker argument evolved – on the upper deck the debate about the Union and Scottish independence; on the lower deck the issues of devolved governance. Labour concentrated the big guns on the upper deck – repeating the mantra of 'divorce is expensive' which had been successful in 1999 and 2003, but also attacking the tax plans of the SNP, saying SNP policies would cost the equivalent of more than £5,000 for every household in Scotland.[21] What they did not fully grasp was that, on the one hand, the SNP had mastered the double-decker argument, taking the sting out of the independence issue by promising a separate referendum (and thus decoupling the issues of devolved government from the issue of independence), while at the same time playing on the unpopular reserved issues like the Iraq war, the replacement of Trident, Gordon Brown's role in the pensions crisis, and Blair's cash for peerages scandal, and that, on the other hand, an independence referendum and

---

[20] 'Salmond in New Year message first', *BBC News Scotland*, 31 December 2006, <news.bbc.co.uk/go/pr/fr/-/2/hi/uk_news/scotland/6219745.stm>.

[21] 'SNP "planning chaos and turmpoil"', *BBC News Scotland*, 19 March 2007, <news.bbc.co.uk/go/pr/fr/-/2/hi/uk_news/scotland/6467287.stm>.

the transfer of taxation powers from Westminster to Holyrood ranked only seventeenth and twenty-first respectively among twenty-five policy issues in an ICM poll for the BBC at the beginning of the campaign, way behind schools and hospitals, crime, farming and fishing.[22]

The SNP seemed to have taken aboard the fact that the election was about what almost all elections are about, viz. should the existing government be thrown out because it had outstayed its welcome.[23] And Labour, having been in power at Westminster since 1997, and in the driving seat at Holyrood since 1999 (and in hegemony in Scotland since the late 1950s), was widely perceived as having been there too long for a healthy democracy. The SNP threw a plethora of attractive – if uncosted – promises into the battle: scrapping the graduate endowment tax, wiping out student debt, replacing the 'unfair council tax' with a local income tax (the only dominant domestic theme in the elections), more teachers, smaller class sizes, more policemen, reduced business rates, abolition of road and bridge tolls.

In fairness, it has to be said that Jack McConnell tried hard to make education the central plank of Scottish Labour's election campaign – but Labour did not manage to make its themes the focus of the campaign. In the end, Blair's long good-bye, the ongoing fiasco in Iraq, Trident, cash for honours, nuclear power, pensions, treatment of asylum seekers, etc cast a long shadow over the campaign. Blair and Brown's presence in the campaign highlighted those 'reserved' matters – and reinforced the public perception of negativity about Labour. A Populus poll for *The Times* a fortnight before the election put Labour in the UK on 29%, showing support for the party falling to a level last seen when Michael Foot was leader in the 1980s.[24]

Labour got all worked up by the independence bogey, their apocalyptic rhetoric annoying at least as many voters as they were frightening into voting for the status quo. What worked in 1999 and 2003, now became increasingly counterproductive, but Labour kept ploughing on, not realising, or not wanting to realise, that there were seriously diminishing returns, while reminding the public constantly of those reserved Westminster political issues that highlighted the impotence of the Scottish Parliament in those reserved matters. Moreover, if Scotland was, as Labour argued, incapable of sustaining itself as an independent country, was that not Labour's fault in the first place – in government since 1997/1999? If Labour in Scotland and in the UK had done such a

[22] ICM Scottish Omnibus Poll (for the BBC), conducted 29-31 March 2007, <news.bbc.co.uk/2/hi/uk_news/scotland/6526715.stm#table>.

[23] See Owen Dudley Edwards, 'Election 2007: The Year of Courage?', *Scottish Affairs*, No.60 (Summer 2007), pp.115-39.

[24] The Populus poll was conducted for the *Times* between 13-15 April 2007. See Philip Webster, 'Blair prepares for final test as polls plunge to new low', *The Times*, 17 April 2007.

wonderful job over the last decade, why was Scotland still on the drip?

This 'Scotland is a basket case' rhetoric obviously alienated some influential Scottish business leaders so much that they publicly declared their support for the SNP – and filled the party's coffers to the brim. Among them the controversial bus-tycoon Brian Souter who donated £500,000, and Tom 'KwikFit' Farmer who was good for £100,000. The former Royal Bank of Scotland chairman Sir George Mathewson also endorsed the party's stance on independence. Through the Scottish Independence Convention and non-party campaign group Independence First (combining the pro-independence parties), cult author Irvine Welsh, his fellow-writer Alasdair Gray, and folk singer Dick Gaughan threw their weight behind demands for an independence referendum. Other prominent support came from Archbishop Keith O'Brien and the historian and former Tory candidate Michael Fry. A sign of the frustration with Labour, but also an indication of how far the SNP had travelled since 1999.

The same is true for endorsements by the media. While hitherto the Scottish political landscape was remarkable for the paradox that not a single paper supported the largest opposition party, this time a handful of national broadsheets recommended, even if sometimes couched in unionist caveats, a vote for change and for an SNP-led government.[25]

From the start of the campaign, it was clear that it would be a 'two-horse-race' between Labour and the SNP. It is generally agreed that Annabel Goldie had a good campaign for the Scottish Tories, with her 'touch of talking common sense and letting people remember afterwards she happens to be a Tory.'[26] But there was no sign of a Cameron effect north of the Border. The Lib Dems had lured themselves into the belief they could manage a major break through after Dunfermline, but they ran a bland campaign in which their new leader Nicol Stephen did not establish himself sufficiently.[27] They stood for an increase in the powers of the Parliament, based on the findings of their own Steel Commission. But the only issue involving them directly in the campaign was the

---

[25] *Scotland on Sunday* stated in an editorial that an SNP-led government 'offers the best chance of restoring public confidence in our democracy, and a new sense of possibility in the people of this country' (29 April 2007); *The Scotsman* also argued for an SNP role in government; The *Sunday Herald* editorialised that 'a vote for change is a leap of faith. It's a leap this newspaper is prepared to make.' (29 April 2007); and the *Sunday Times* concluded 'that an SNP-led coalition is the best option for voters' (29 April 2007). By contrast, most of the tabloids stuck with the Labour rhetoric about 'sleepwalking into independence' (*Daily Record*, 3 May 2007), while the *Scottish Sun*'s front page on election day carried the image of a noose – Salmond as the hangman and 'wrecker' of Scotland – and an editorial to the tune of 'only Labour can save us from a living nightmare' (3 May 2007).

[26] Owen Dudley Edwards, *op.cit.* p.134.

[27] See Peter Jones, 'The Smooth Wooing: the SNP's Victory in the 2007 Scottish Parliament Elections', *Scottish Affairs*, No.60 (Summer 2007), p.19.

possibility of a coalition with the SNP – and the potential stumbling block of the independence referendum, which the Lib Dems refused to even contemplate. Their relationship with Labour had, ever since Dunfermline, been strained.

And what happened to the 'rainbow'? The Scottish Socialists had torn themselves apart – in a very public split in 2006 following Tommy Sheridan's libel case against the *News of the World*. Both the SSP and Sheridan's new party, Solidarity, failed to have an impact on the campaign, fighting each other as much as their real political opponents. The Greens, by contrast, hoped to build on their successful transformation from a one-man-band to a fully-fledged parliamentary party. It remains their secret why they picked Mark Ruskell as their campaign manager – perhaps their least well-known MSP? Whether it would have made much of a difference if Robin Harper, Mark Ballard and Patrick Harvie had been more to the fore, is of course a matter of speculation – perhaps the focus on the two main contenders in this two-horse race would have crushed, or squeezed, the smaller parties anyway.

In contrast to 2003, there was not much talk about 'apathy' this time round. In STV's *Politics Now* on 29 March 2007, Lorraine Davidson praised the campaign as 'the real thing' and 'absolutely fascinating', even 'riveting'. This was also reflected in the huge international media interest in these elections. Many of the world's major newspapers as well as radio and television channels carried in-depth coverage of the issues facing Scottish voters during the four-week election campaign.

ELECTION RESULT

Coinciding with the tercentenary of the Union of Parliaments, the 2007 elections in Scotland on 3 May 2007 could not be other than special. The Parliament they returned looked more akin to the 1999 version – fewer parties, albeit with roles reversed between the two biggest contenders.[28] Arguably, the changes they brought mark the most important development in the evolution of devolution since the heady days of the late 1990s.

As, on the fourth of May 2007, the shock of the ballot paper fiasco was being digested – nearly 150 000 voting papers had been discarded

---

[28] A first analysis of the 2007 Scottish Parliament election result can be found in Stephen Herbert, Ross Burnside, Murray Earle, Tom Edwards, Tom Foley, Iain McIver (eds), *Election 2007*, Edinburgh: Scottish Parliament Information Centre (SPICe), 07/21 (8 May 2007), <www.scottish.parliament.uk/business/research/briefings-07/SB07-21.pdf>.

as spoilt, reducing the turn-out figure from just under 54 per cent[29] to an even more modest 51.7% in the constituency and 52.4% in the regional list vote[30] – it emerged that Scotland had voted for political change. By the narrowest of margins, but with surging momentum, the SNP had pipped Labour to the post, with 47 to 46 seats. Far from an overall majority. But that was to be expected. Under the Additional Member System (AMS), no party since 1999 had gained an outright majority.

Table 2: Scottish Parliament Election Results 2007 (Share of Seats)

Party	Constituency MSPs	Regional MSPs	Total
SNP	21	26	47
Labour	37	9	46
Conservatives	4	13	17
Lib Dems	11	5	16
Greens	0	2	2
Independent	0	1	1
Total	73	56	129

Forty-one of the 129 MSPs (31.8%) have not served in the previous term; 43 women (33.3% of MSPs) were elected to the third Scottish Parliament, down from 51 (39%) in the previous term. That figure increased to 44 when Shirley-Anne Somerville replaced Stefan Tymkewicz as an SNP Lothians list MSP in September.

Table 3: Scottish Parliament Election Results 2007 (Share of Vote)

Party	Constituency (%)	Regional List (%)
SNP	32.9	31.0
Labour	32.1	29.2
Conservatives	16.6	13.9
Lib Dems	16.2	11.3
Greens	0.1	4.0
Independent	2.1	10.6
Total	100	100

What the result also showed was that the AMS scraped by delivering – had Labour ended in front of the SNP, despite the Nationalists' gaining

---

[29] An increase of 4.2% on the 2003 figure. See David Denver, '"A Historic Moment"? The Results of the Scottish Parliament Elections 2007', *Scottish Affairs*, No.60 (Summer 2007), p.64.

[30] It is an oddity that spoilt ballots are not counted in the official turn-out figure. After all, had voters not turned out, their ballots could not have been spoilt. See Stephen Herbert and Tom Edwards, *Rejected Ballot Papers*, Edinburgh: Scottish Parliament Information Centre (SPICe), 07/36 (26 June 2007), <www.scottish.parliament.uk/business/research/briefings-07/SB07-36.pdf>.

most votes both at constituency and regional levels, this would have led to further criticism of the electoral system as being not proportional enough. As it was, the result seemed to please even those who had not voted for the SNP: change had been effected. Part of that was the realisation that the Scottish Parliament would only be able to prove itself purely devolved if the settlement was – as it would at some stage anyway – to be tested by different parties in power at Holyrood and Westminster. Simply put, London had to be forced to cease thinking of Edinburgh as a local *dependence* of the Labour Party. Joyce McMillan commented that 'no system of democratic government can be considered successful until it has achieved a peaceful transition of power.'[31]

The first act of the reconvened Parliament was, on 14 May, the election of Alex Ferguson MSP as the Parliament's Presiding Officer, which ended his Tory party affiliation. Alasdair Morgan (SNP), and Trish Godman (Labour) were elected as Deputy Presiding Officers.

Most pundits thought that, regardless of what they had said during the campaign, the SNP would form a government with the help of the Liberal Democrats. But as the Lib Dems set as a precondition that the Nationalists drop their plan for an independence referendum, and Alex Salmond refused to do that before talks started, talks were never even entered. As the SNP had ruled out the Tories (and the Tories had ruled themselves out for any coalition), the Lib Dems had no intention of continuing with Labour in any shape or form, and power-sharing between Labour and the SNP was not on the cards (even if Ian Paisley can tango with Gerry Adams, and Rhodri Morgan with Ieuan Wyn Jones, it is difficult to imagine such a 'cohabitation' in Scotland between Labour and the SNP), there remained only the Greens, and the prospect of a minority government.

Eventually, the SNP signed an agreement with the two Greens which ensured that their two MSPs voted for Alex Salmond as First Minister and supported his ministerial appointments. In return, the Nationalists gave their backing to a climate change bill as an early measure and nominated Patrick Harvie MSP as the convener of one of the Holyrood committees (Transport, Infrastructure and Climate Change). But it is not a coalition deal. No ministerial posts for the Greens. And they are not obliged to back Alex Salmond in a confidence vote or support the SNP's budget plans. It is an even looser arrangement than the 'confidence and supply' model of co-operation which the Greens had talked about during the campaign. And whether it is a good deal for the Greens remains to be seen – they could be hung for being perceived to be backing a government scrapping road tolls, building roads and scuppering public transport projects.

---

[31] Joyce McMillan, 'SNP's ascension has given us renewed hope', *The Scotsman*, 1 September 2007.

On 16 May, Alex Salmond, First Minister, announced his cabinet, comprising six Cabinet Secretaries (Cabinet Ministers): in addition to himself as First Minister there are Nicola Sturgeon (Health and Wellbeing, and Deputy First Minister), John Swinney (Finance and Sustainable Growth), Fiona Hyslop (Education and Lifelong Learning), Kenny MacAskill (Justice and Communities) and Richard Lochhead (Rural Affairs and Environment). At the junior level there are ten Ministers who report to a Cabinet Secretary: Bruce Crawford: (Parliamentary Business), Linda Fabiani (Europe, External Affairs and Culture), Jim Mather (Enterprise, Energy and Tourism), Stewart Stevenson (Transport, Infrastructure and Climate Change), Maureen Watt (Schools and Skills), Adam Ingram (Children and Early Years), Shona Robison (Public Health), Stewart Maxwell (Communities and Sport), Fergus Ewing (Community Safety) and Mike Russell (Environment).

The first domestic measures of Alex Salmond's government were populist and popular and consensual, at least among a majority of the Parliament – steps to prevent ship-to-ship oil transfer in the Firth of Forth, the abolition of the graduate endowment tax, the scrapping of the Forth bridge tolls.

The first 'foreign' visit of the First Minister saw him in Belfast, hobnobbing with Ian Paisley and Martin McGuinness. Could there be a concerted demand for a lower corporate tax for the 'Celtic' regions and nations, perhaps joined by Rhodri Morgan on behalf of Wales? Particularly with Plaid Cymru as part of his government? A ganging up by the Celts against London? An enhanced role for the British-Irish Council, as Tom Nairn had announced a tad prematurely at the turn of the century?[32] The *Irish Independent* seemed to hint at that possibility:

> Mr Salmond's visit to Belfast, in the early days of the new Executive and shortly after his own election as First Minister in Scotland, is an event of some political significance. It indicates the possibility of a shake-up of loosening ties in the centralised UK state, and the possibility of new relationships developing between the constituent parts (and indeed across national boundaries) as the regions, with new-found confidence, begin to flex their muscles.[33]

In February, the SNP had laid out its plan, based on the current British-Irish Council, formed after the Good Friday Agreement and involving

---

[32] See Tom Nairn, *After Britain: New Labour and the Return of Scotland*, London: Granta, 2000, pp.278, 305. Nairn revisited the idea in his *Gordon Brown: The Bard of Britishness*, Cardiff: Institute of Welsh Affairs, 2006, pp.27-29.

[33] 'Scottish neighbour Salmond may well be a friend in disguise', *Irish Independent*, 27 June 2007.

ministers from Scotland, Wales, Ireland and England as well as the crown dependencies (Channel Islands and Isle of Man) meeting to discuss areas of common concern. After Scottish independence, Salmond envisaged the convening of a 'beefed-up' version, modelled on the Nordic Council.[34]

THE HAPPY HONEYMOON

This summer saw a remarkable media honeymoon for Alex Salmond and his SNP minority government. 'The McConnell years seem a distant memory, the *Edinburgh Evening News* commented, such was the way Alex Salmond 'eased into his new role … as if he's been in the job for years.'[35] His first hundred days 'brought both a blast of refreshment and a lot of surprise' through the sense of energy and mission that the SNP has brought to an Executive that had come to look tired, mediocre and bereft of distinctiveness and purpose."[36] Otherwise critical commentators like Joyce McMillan (*The Scotsman*) or Iain Macwhirter (*The Herald/Sunday Herald*) heaped praise on the new administration, and especially on Alex Salmond. 'The effect of the last six weeks has been devastating,' Iain Macwhirter commented just before the summer recess: 'The SNP hasn't so much hit the ground running as lapped the political field on an almost daily basis. Opposition MSPs have been blown away at what has been happening.' Even some opposition MSPs, he continued,

> seem to agree the Scottish parliament has moved up a gear since the Nats took over. Debates are worth listening to; MSPs who were languishing in backbench obscurity have started making speeches that are intelligent and relevant. You could say the parliament has suddenly come alive.[37]

He compared Salmond's start with that of Blair in 1997: the same flurry of dramatic statements of intent changing the climate of public affairs. But, he reminds us, Blair did it with a huge majority, Salmond with a party that has never before been in government and holds only a minority of seats. 'Where the SNP has been unexpectedly lucky is in being a minority

---

[34] Eddie Barnes, 'SNP spells out 'Council of the Isles' plan', *Scotland on Sunday*, 25 February 2007.

[35] "'The McConnell years seem a distant memory'" (Leader), *Edinburgh Evening News*, 9 August 2007.

[36] 'Now for some tough choices' (Leader), *The Scotsman* 24 August 2007.

[37] Iain Macwhirter, 'The SNP didn't just hit the ground running, they lapped the political field', *Sunday Herald*, 24 June 2007.

government. It has allowed ministers to act swiftly,' concurred George Kerevan (aspiring SNP candidate for Westminster), 'with discipline and with a proactive media strategy.'[38] Crises like Foot & Mouth and the terrorist attacks on London and Glasgow airport saw the Scottish government acting promptly, wisely and in full accord with the UK government.

Ewan Crawford summed it all up neatly: 'In his first three months, Scotland's first minister has promoted consensus, won over the press and left Labour bewildered.' The Scottish press, he argued, 'so long antagonistic towards Salmond, has now fallen head over heels in love with the new first minister.'[39]

Salmond's honeymoon was mirrored down south by Gordon Brown's. Fearing he would sound 'naïve and even sycophantic,' Macwhirter sang the praises of both Gordon Brown and Alex Salmond as 'two astute and even visionary politicians at he very top of their game.' And

> ... we also have the makings of Scotland's first great political leader in 300 years in the shape of Alex Salmond. The First Minister has shown tactical genius and real political courage in the manner in which he has run an effective government in Scotland, with only 46 out of 129 MSPs and no coalition partner. (...) Above all, it is Salmond's sense of destiny that marks him out from other Scottish political figures of the modern age, He is the real deal; the first genuine political leader in Scottish democratic history.[40]

While the SNP soared in the media and in opinion polls,[41] questions were raised about the Labour Party. 'Dazed and unwilling to admit its defeat,'[42] was Labour in denial? 'Battered and bruised in the May elections,' so Hamish Macdonell, they had, in the six weeks leading up to the summer recess, 'been bulldozed by Alex Salmond in the chamber.... Some

[38] George Kerevan, 'The London media (and Brown) just don't get it', *The Scotsman*, 21 June 2007.

[39] Ewan Crawford, 'Governing well is worth a hundred freedom slogans', *The Guardian*, 15 August 2007.

[40] Iain Macwhirter, 'Salmond and Brown: the right men for these times', *The Herald*, 30 July 2007. Macwhirter prefaced his piece with a wee caveat that, 'like most political hacks, I tend to be a professional pessimist, if not a borderline depressive,' and that 'the reward for optimism about politicians is generally ridicule.' This might be 'one column I will probably regret writing.' Time will tell...

[41] A *Scottish Daily Mail* poll on 10 August 2007 put the SNP at 48% – but with only 31% in favour of independence.

[42] 'Labour fails to get the message' (Leader), *The Scotsman*, 22 June 2007.

observers have suggested the Labour Party is in denial over its election defeat. It's not: it's in shock.'[43]

'Labour lost votes in May,' argued the *Scotsman*, 'because – for the first time – it refused even to discuss more powers for Holyrood, thus conceding the constitutional debate to the SNP.'[44] Iain Macwhirter marvelled at Gordon Brown's constitutional review, announced as he took over from Tony Blair, including the replacement of the Scottish Secretary by a minister of the regions, reform of the House of Lords and, eventually, a written constitution: 'I can't for the life of me understand why Labour didn't announce this new constitutional settlement before, rather than after, the Scottish elections. It would have shot a number of Nationalist foxes.'[45]

The new Scottish Labour leader Wendy Alexander has a huge mountain to climb, if she wants to reconnect Labour with the electorate beyond its west of Scotland heartlands, reorganise the party at root and branch, redefine its relationship with the party hierarchy in London and bring the party back to power in Scotland. While Tom Gordon argued that Wendy Alexander was 'a liability to her party' and that her succession to Jack McConnell would give Alex Salmond 'the most pleasure,'[46] Eddie Barnes commented on the SNP's apparent glee about Wendy Alexander becoming Labour leader, citing her 'presentational style', but warned that her being a woman, being intelligent, and an accomplished strategist might yet give Salmond and the SNP headaches.[47] George Kerevan, too, warned his friends in the SNP: 'Don't assume that because Wendy is an intellectual she lacks backbone. She was the only Labour minister to stand up to her civil servants.'[48]

THE SCOTTISH SIX

Another hot topic during the summer was broadcasting in Scotland. In August, the SNP government started a major campaign for a 'Scottish Six' and for the devolution of control over broadcasting to Holyrood.

[43] Hamish Macdonell, 'Has anyone seen the Labour Party?', *The Scotsman*, 22 June 2007.

[44] 'Labour fails to get the message' (Leader), *The Scotsman*, 22 June 2007.

[45] Iain Macwhirter, 'Southern discomfort: an increasingly bitter taste', *The Herald*, 25 June 2007.

[46] Tom Gordon, 'White Hot Alex', *The Sunday Times*, 19 August 2007.

[47] Eddie Barnes, 'Wendy's house may be not so easy for the SNP to blow down', *Scotland on Sunday*, 29 July 2007.

[48] George Kerevan, 'The big tasks facing next Scottish Labour leader', *The Scotsman*, 9 August 2007.

In an intervention in the *Herald* in June, the former Head of News and Current Affairs at BBC Scotland, Blair Jenkins (he resigned in July 2006), commented on Ofcom's annual report for the nations and regions and was scathing in his criticism of the BBC's policy towards Scotland. He contended that: 'For a number of reasons, 2007 looks like a good year to have a proper national debate about what Scotland gets from television – and what television gets from Scotland.' He diagnosed 'serious structural and behavioural problems in how UK television networks engage with the production community in Scotland.'[49]

The spending on current affairs programmes between 2001 and 2006, taking BBC and STV together, 'declined by 45%':

> It seems incredible in the first decade of devolution, when a real and sizeable policy agenda has emerged for investigation and debate, that spending on TV current affairs should virtually be halved and spending on news should be reduced by more than a quarter. Is that really what Scottish viewers would have wished? Is it really what the parliament thinks is appropriate? Is it really public service broadcasting?[50]

He concluded that: 'Perhaps it's time to explore on an all-party basis the issue of whether broadcasting should become a devolved responsibility, to secure greater accountability and transparency from the broadcasters and put some political muscle behind the programme makers?' Alex Salmond asked him to chair his new commission on broadcasting, which also includes former First Minister Henry McLeish and former Green MSP Mark Ballard.

Conservative MSP Ted Brocklebank, a former TV producer, was outraged at the suggestion that Scotland's broadcasters were not talented enough (as argued by Michael Grade and Mark Thompson, ITV and BBC chief executive and director-general, respectively, at an Ofcom conference in Cardiff). He referred to the SNP's manifesto commitment to devolve broadcasting and concluded:

> The other parties should be warned. Whether or not they believe broadcasting should continue to be reserved, they cannot be seen to condone a situation where Scottish broadcasters, in-house as well as independents, continue

---

[49] Blair Jenkins, 'A nation deserves better from its broadcasters', *The Herald*, 18 June 2007.
[50] *Ibid.*

to be discriminated against by those who control national funding.[51]

Iain Macwhirter took up the baton:

> The first step must be the Scottish Parliament taking on responsibility for broadcasting. It makes no sense that this is a reserved power, except in the minds of paranoid Unionists who believe that BBC Scotland is a nationalist plot. ... Then there has to be a regulatory regime established that doesn't have the metrocentric blindness of Ofcom. The Scottish government also needs to lobby the BBC, north and south, to remind it of its charter obligations and its public service remit... The BBC has just opened one of the most advanced broadcasting facilities in Europe, in Pacific Quay. It would be nice if it found something useful to do in it.[52]

A Scottish Six would be, as the BBC's Brian Taylor explained in his blog, 'a TV news programme, made in Scotland, which covered global, UK and Scottish news. Contrary to some comments, it would not focus exclusively on Scottish news.'[53] But, he asked, has the issue not moved on? Do not more people decide for themselves, online, which news to watch rather than relying 'upon a running order of events chosen by someone else.' Was this not, he asked, 'an analogue debate in a digital age?'

Bill Jamieson advised caution as to the desirability of a 'Scottish Six'. He pointed out three caveats:

> One is to ensure that any new Scottish Six is not simply a stretching out or extension of the existing news service... Second, the Scottish Six should not cannibalise international news coverage in order to expand coverage of 'Holyrood' affairs... And third is the danger of a Scottish Six becoming a dependent bugle for 'Holyrood' proclamations and pronouncements. Mr Salmond insists that he has no intention of creating a Scottish Broadcasting Corporation. But that, I fear, is just where his rhetoric logically takes us.[54]

[51] Ted Brocklebank, 'Here is the news: Scots viewers deserve better', *The Herald*, 6 July 2007.

[52] Iain Macwhirter, 'Switching off Scotland's window on the world', *The Herald*, 23 July 2007.

[53] Brian Taylor, 'Broadcasting Scotland', *BBC Blog*, 8 August 2007, <www.bbc.co.uk/blogs/thereporters/briantaylor/2007/08/08/index.html>.

[54] Bill Jamieson, 'Cause for caution on devolution of broadcasting', *The Scotsman*, 10 August 2007.

'The last thing Scottish broadcasting needs,' according to Ted Brocklebank, 'is a blinkered Braveheart overview, or the world seen through tartan-tinted spectacles.'[55] Ian Macwhirter disagrees that that would be the consequence of a 'Scottish Six'. As someone who saw the pilots the BBC produced in 2004, he states:

> The programmes were well-presented and gave excellent UK and foreign coverage while treating devolved matters with the respect and authority they deserved. I can well understand why the BBC didn't show them to the public. As soon as you actually see a Scottish Six, you wonder how we could have tolerated the present arrangement for so long.[56]

George Kerevan, citing that in a survey in 2004 by the Scottish Consumer Council nearly 70% of viewers supported a 'Scottish Six',[57] added: 'As long as there is a licence fee, Scotland has a right to a say in how that money is spent. That is why it is still imperative that public service broadcasting is devolved to Holyrood.'[58]

Repeated gaffes in the last few months by the BBC have stoked the unease – the abrupt ending of a Kirsty Wark interview with Alex Salmond in June; Jeremy Paxman's assertion that 'not one' of fifty firms north and south of the Border supported independence (in fact only seven had replied to the survey at all), and then the claim that voters in Scotland in the Referendum of 1997 had rejected independence, although the question was not even asked. Having splashed this 'New BBC Blunder' over the entire front page, the *Sunday Herald* tried to put it into perspective:

> ...it would be a mistake to brand a massive national organisation the size of the BBC as being riddled with problems... The reality is that most of what the BBC does is first rate... So it is important that Thompson gets the

---

[55] Ted Brocklebank, 'Our TV talent has been abandoned', *Sunday Express*, 12 August 2007.

[56] Iain Macwhirter, 'And now for the news...broadcast from Scotland', *Sunday Herald*, 12 August 2007. For an exchange of views on Scottish broadcasting, see 'Broadcasting's devolution debate' in the *Guardian* of 13 August 2007, where the pro-side was taken by Alex Bell of <allmediascotland.com>, and the contra side by Brian McNair of Strathclyde University.

[57] But a YouGov poll for the *Sunday Times* in August 2007 showed 52% rejecting a 'Scottish Six' – *The Sunday Times*, 26 August 2007.

[58] George Kerevan, 'Here is the news... a "Scottish Six" is vital', *The Scotsman*, 6 August 2007.

message across: the BBC has to have standards or its public service mission is lost.[59]

WHITE PAPER ON INDEPENDENCE

The publication of the White Paper on Scottish independence[60] in August came in for a good deal of criticism, seeing that there was no chance of a parliamentary majority for the referendum envisaged in it. *Scotland on Sunday* begged to differ. It found 'hard to understand the vitriol that was poured on Alex Salmond;' after all he was only fulfilling a manifesto pledge. Citing the latest survey figure of 39% support for independence, it contended that 'Salmond himself expects that his White Paper will fall at the first hurdle,' but that he hopes that its failure will 'herald a more complex debate on Scotland's constitutional future.'[61] This debate, so the paper hoped, would result in 'Devolution Max' which would include 'new control over broadcasting, marine law, stamp duty and business taxation.' It continued:

> There must also be a debate on wider fiscal devolution, and the immediate policy focus must be the economy. Scotland needs specific policies for Scotland's particular economic strengths and weaknesses. There is a compelling argument that without access to all levers of economic power – including tax powers – the Scottish Parliament and the Scottish government will never be fully responsible for the Scottish economy. Instead, we will continue to blame Westminster for our own ills.[62]

While the opposition parties stuck to rejecting a referendum, the *Scotsman* disagreed, arguing for a referendum 'sooner rather than later' – 'Scotland's constitutional future can be determined only by her voters. They should be allowed to do so in the lifetime of this parliament.'[63] Picking up on Tory voices supporting a referendum now, the *Edinburgh*

---

[59] 'Ratings can never be worth losing the trust of the public' (Leader), *Sunday Herald*, 22 July 2007.

[60] Scottish Executive: *Choosing Scotland's Future: A National Conversation*, Edinburgh, 2007.

[61] 'Time to rethink devolution' (Leader), *Scotland on Sunday*, 29 July 2007

[62] *Ibid.*

[63] 'Referendum is the right way' (Leader), *The Scotsman*, 15 August 2007.

Evening News had pronounced back in June: 'Scotland needs stability and if that means an independence referendum, then better sooner than later.'[64]

A first result of the White Paper was the coming together of the three main opposition parties in an agreement to develop devolution within the UK. Commenting on the 'remarkable turnaround' of Labour, the *Sunday Herald* marvelled:

> It is another sign of how Salmond, as was always his intension, is changing Scottish politics out of all recognition: all mainstream parties now agree on the need for more powers, however much they might differ on the extent of change required. Like him or loathe him, Salmond is a first minister who is leading from the front.[65]

But there were also questions about the process of the 'national conversation'. The *Edinburgh Evening News* questioned the openness of the conversation, if Salmond was the chair: 'Mr Salmond may be genuine in his desire to have a "national conversation" about Scotland's future governance, but if he really wants an open debate it is not one he can chair and it must be one he is prepared to lose.'[66] Canon Kenyon Wright's Constitutional Commission[67] or, indeed, a new Constitutional Convention (as proposed by the Steel Commission's Report)[68] could prevent Salmond being all in one person: instigator, moderator and adjudicator of the 'national conversation' and its outcome.

Labour's 'most effective challenge to the Nationalists,' Iain Macwhirter pointed out, could one of the conundrums of the SNP:

> Why... does Scotland need independence when it has political autonomy under devolution? In a sense, the SNP's effective performance in government rather undermines the Nationalists' own case. The inventory of the first 100 days is pretty impressive – bridge tolls, hospitals, prescription charges, tuition fees, even doubling the subsidy to the Edinburgh Festival. If Salmond can do so

---

[64] 'Chance to kick independence out of bounds' (Leader), *Edinburgh Evening News*, 19 June 2007.

[65] 'Scotland's changed... so should unionist parties' attitudes' (Leader), *Sunday Herald*, 19 August 2007.

[66] 'It's not an open debate if Alex is the chairman' (Leader), *Edinburgh Evening News*, 15 August 2007.

[67] See <www.constitutionalcommission.org>.

[68] David Steel, 'A new convention? Now you're talking', *The Scotsman*, 25 August 2007.

much with the powers of the Parliament, what's the point of independence?[69]

Peter Jones looked at it from a different perspective of attack. Referring to the SNP's rejection of the Edinburgh Airport Rail Link (EARL), he asked: could the SNP 'deprive Scotland of the kind of big improvements that are eminently achievable now so that we become convinced that we must have independence in order to get them?'[70] On the other hand, the SNP's Peter Wishart MP warned that 'independence has become just an option when it should, of course, be *the* option,' warning his party to be 'careful that this key choice does not become obscured in a plethora of other options.'[71]

LEGISLATION LITE – THE END OF THE HONEYMOON?

In the run-up to the first disclosure of an SNP legislative programme, there were signs of the first cracks appearing in the armour of the seemingly unassailable SNP government, threatening an end to the 'easy ride'. The abolition of the council tax took its first hurdle, as the Lib Dems shared the SNP's intent, but as their model of local income tax is substantially different from the SNP's, one of them would have to give if a replacement was to pass in the Chamber.

Offering Northern Irish students free tuition at Scottish universities, while English and Welsh students would still have to pay, the *Scotsman* commented, was 'no longer education policy,' but 'talking about ways to dismember the United Kingdom,' and warned the Scottish government not to make Scottish universities 'a political football.'[72] The *Herald* took another target: 'It would be a matter of great regret if the debate about regulating firearms were to be muddied by a constitutional turf war.[73] Then the SNP was accused of 'watering down', 'back tracking' on or even 'dropping' their promise 'to make [St Andrew's Day] a new

---

[69] Iain Macwhirter, 'Why we haven't the constitution to go it alone', *The Herald*, 6 August 2007.

[70] Peter Jones, 'The conflict at the heart of SNP's programme', *The Scotsman*, 4 September 2007.

[71] Peter Wishart, 'Independence or nothing', *The Sunday Times*, 16 September 2007.

[72] 'Not the way, Mr Salmond' (Leader), *The Scotsman*, 20 June 2007. The policy was abandoned.

[73] 'Disarming debate' (Leader), *The Herald*, 27 August 2007.

bank holiday.'[74] And *Scotland on Sunday* revealed cash-for-access issues around the forthcoming SNP party conference in Aviemore in October – a meeting with Alex Salmond to be had at the price of £9,500...[75]

On 27 June, Cabinet Secretary John Swinney had accepted the first resounding defeat for the government – Labour, the Lib Dems and the Tories had supported an amendment in the name of Wendy Alexander MSP to keep the Edinburgh tram project on track and review the airport rail link until the autumn. Despite previous speculation to the contrary, nourished by remarks of Transport Minister Stewart Stevenson and Alex Salmond himself, the government declared it would respect the will of Parliament and act accordingly, thus avoiding the threat of a no-confidence vote.[76] That is the new politics for you... and it seemed not to dent the SNP's honeymoon.

It was perhaps Arthur Midwinter's prediction that the SNP was heading for a financial 'black hole' of £2bn which really signalled the beginning of the end for the honeymoon period.[77] Tough choices might be the order of the day. 'And it is in making these that real government is proven or broken.'[78] Labour and the Lib Dems accused the SNP of not delivering on pre-election pledges. And who would foot the bill for the council tax freeze the SNP plans to impose on (or, rather, negotiate with) local councils? Severin Carrell listed the deficiencies:·

> Watered-down promise to abolish all student debts; delayed pledge to remove business rates for small firms; held up plans to abolish council tax; failed to support marine national parks; abandoned deal to end automatic early release for prisoners.[79]

The announcement of the eleven bills in the SNP's legislative programme was greeted with comments of 'legislation lite' or 'semi-skimmed'. Arguing that the 'slighter legislative menu than we have been used to in previous years ... comes as no surprise,' being 'conditioned by the fact that Alex Salmond cannot command an overall majority in the Scottish

[74] Raymond Hainey, 'Salmond in St Andrew's Day holiday backtrack row', *The Scotsman*, 25 August 2007.

[75] Murdo MacLeod, 'Want to lobby a minister? Send £10,000 to the SNP', *Scotland on Sunday*, 2 September 2007.

[76] Douglas Fraser, 'Tram scheme goes ahead after SNP defeat', *The Herald*, 28 June 2007.

[77] Peter MacMahon, 'SNP: on brink of a financial "black hole"?', *The Scotsman*, 17 August 2007.

[78] 'Now for some tough choices' (Leader), *The Scotsman*, 24 August 2007.

[79] Severin Carrell, 'Salmond accused of spin as SNP reviews first 100 days in power', *The Guardian*, 24 August 2007.

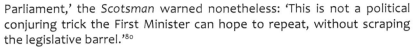

Parliament,' the *Scotsman* warned nonetheless: 'This is not a political conjuring trick the First Minister can hope to repeat, without scraping the legislative barrel.'[80]

What does the programme entail? Two bills prepared by the Scots Law Commission on the modernisation of legislation on rape and sexual offenses, lowering the level for convictions, and a technical bill on right to interest on personal debt; taking forward the Culture Scotland Bill prepared by the former Executive, including the merger of Scottish Screen with the Scottish Arts Council; bills on public health, on judicial appointments, flood prevention, a Commonwealth Games Bill (provided Glasgow's bid for 2014 is successful), and the statutory Budget Bill (after the Westminster spending review). That leaves only three bills delivering on SNP manifesto commitments: direct elections to health boards, abolishing tolls on the Tay and Forth bridges, and ending the graduate endowment scheme. 'The bigger ambitions,' Douglas Fraser noted, 'from local income tax to independence, have to wait for another day.'[81]

In Severin Carrell's view, 'Alex Salmond's honeymoon period ended abruptly' when he faced accusations of 'breaching a series of promises to voters.'[82] The *Daily Record* peppered its pages with headlines like 'Nats shelve anti-drugs commission' and 'Salmond silent on vows' and added a scathing editorial:

> After staying silent on many of his flagship policies the previous day, when e unveiled his programme for government, opposition MSPs scented blood. They went for him. They asked: Will he really deliver £2000 grants for first-time buyers? How will he guarantee a three-year council tax freeze? Is he going to give patients a right to sue hospitals if they are not treated on time? These were vote-winners for Salmond in May. Yet clear commitments were noticeable by their absence yesterday as Salmond dodged the questions.[83]

The veteran journalist Tom Brown, self-confessed 'very old Labour', spoke of 'Alex Salmond's sleight-of-hand government' pulling 'storybook-

---

[80] 'First Minister has to play safe' (Leader), *The Scotsman*, 6 September 2007.

[81] Douglas Fraser, 'Salmond unveils first eleven', *The Herald*, 6 September 2007.

[82] Severin Carrell, 'Opposition parties mock SNP as Salmond unveils reforms', *The Guardian*, 6 September 2007.

[83] 'No excuse for SNP silence' (Leader), *Daily Record*, 7 September 2007.

promises and fantasy policies out of the hat' which made Scotland look 'increasingly like make-believe land.'[84]

It may surprise how little effect any criticism of Salmond's decision to hang on to his Westminster seat until the next general election has provoked. Ian Bell was one of the few who openly criticised the decision: 'Isn't it beneath the dignity of the First Minister of Scotland,' he asked,

> to waste his time – my time, your time – as a Westminster bit-player? Doesn't Alex Salmond have a full-time job? I don't care about the money – can't afford the joke – but I care about Twa Jobs Eck. MP, MSP and First Minister of an entire nation to boot: it won't do.[85]

But he also lay his hand on a deeper problem. He sees Salmond becoming too powerful in his own party – 'Who within his party can now gainsay our Alex?' – as he 'has crushed all internal rivalry.' Has Scottish nationalism actually been reduced to 'Salmondism'?[86]

Contrarily, Allan Massie even suggests, Salmond should 'set aside his promise to give up his commons seat at the next General Election,' as 'one of the weaknesses of our political system is the clear division between different levels of government, with this weakness all the more apparent since devolution.'[87]

INDEPENDENCE IN BRITAIN?

Undoubtedly, 2006-2007 has been a year of change. We have seen the end of a beginning. Devolution has come of age.[88] Whether we have also witnessed the beginning of the end of the Union is less clear. According to a System 3 Poll at the beginning of September, only 35% of Scots would vote in favour of independence.[89] And, according to David

---

[84] Tom Brown, 'Salmon's Passport to Penicuik is an expensive forgery', *Scotland on Sunday*, 7 July 2007.

[85] Ian Bell, 'Salmondism: Is it really a substitute for nationalism?', *The Herald*, 7 July 2007.

[86] *Ibid.*

[87] Allan Massie, 'Politicians have a home in many Houses', *The Scotsman*, 27 July 2007.

[88] Eberhard Bort, 'Election 2007: Devolution Come of Age?, in Gilles Leydier (ed.), *La dévolution des pouvoirs à l'Écosse et au pays de Galles, 1966-1999*, Paris: Éditions Ellipses, 2007.

[89] Paul Hutcheon, 'If Alex Salmon's referendum was held today, 50% would vote NO to independence, 35% would vote YES', *Sunday Herald*, 2 September 2007.

McCrone and Frank Bechhofer, 'Britishness is still widespread in England and Scotland,'[90] despite a strengthening sense of Scottishness over the last thirty years.

In a new book Henry McLeish and Tom Brown promote their idea of a 'New Union', a Union which must adapt to survive.[91] The 'national conversation', they contend, must not be restricted to Scotland and increased powers for Holyrood alone. Are there signs of a convergence? Did not Mike Russell and Dennis McLeod also argue for a 'New Union',[92] where some remaining reserved matters could be shared at a UK level. And has not Alex Salmond for over ten years now talked about a 'British Association'?[93]

In 1992 the SNP adopted Jim Sillars's 'Independence in Europe' as its slogan – could now be the time for 'Independence in Britain' or, as McLeish calls it, 'small-i independence'.[94] After all, 'we live now in [a] very different kind of world – a world of federations and confederations of autonomous nations within states within the European Union. Self-government is a question of degree, not of kind.'[95] Will Hutton, in an intervention in the *Herald*, argued for 'Devolution-max', which would 'in effect create a Scottish state within Britain rather like Alberta or Ontario within Canada.' He contended that globalisation demanded management by 'bigger units, not small'. Independence would therefore be 'a 19th century response to 21st century dilemmas.'[96]

'Holyrood has become a fixture,' *Scotland on Sunday* declared in a leader marking the advent of the tenth anniversary of the devolution referendum, and

> there is a growing confidence about the place, in most quarters: after initial doubts, Labour is increasingly optimistic that Wendy Alexander can find the right structure and tone to prompt the party's recovery from May's humiliating defeat; the Lib Dems finally seem to be settling into opposition, with leader Nicol Stephen last week making a surprisingly aggressive and effective attack on the

[90] Frank Bechhofer and David McCrone, 'Being British: A Crisis of Identity?', *Political Quarterly*, Vol.78,No.2 (April-June 2007), p.259.

[91] Henry McLeish and Tom Brown, *Scotland: The Road Divides*, Edinburgh: Luath Press, 2007.

[92] Michael Russell and Dennis McLeod, *Grasping the Thistle: How Scotland Must React to the Three Key Challenges of the Twenty First Century*, Glendaruel: Argyll, 2006.

[93] Alex Salmond, 'Sotland and Ireland', *Scottish Affairs*, No.25 (Autumn 1998), pp.68-77.

[94] *BBC News at Ten*, 14 September 2007.

[95] David McCrone, 'Semi-detached', *Holyrood*, 162, 125 January 2007, p.45.

[96] Will Hutton, 'How Scotland could end up with best of both worlds', *The Herald*, 15 August 2007.

SNP's legislative programme; and, while the Tories remain bit-players in terms of numbers of MSPs, Annabel Goldie remains the strongest and most sensible advocate of the Union. And then there is the part played by Alex Salmond, whose optimism and sheer class infect everything his newly renamed Government does.[97]

'We know that Salmond is full of intelligence and political savvy,' the paper continued, 'but how far do these qualities spread through his ministerial team – and will they be enough to overcome the difficulties faced in this new parliamentary year?' It concluded:

> It won't be easy, but we urge the First Minister to be bold. Scotland voted for change and more vision in May and will not accept inaction, however hamstrung the government feels. For its part, the opposition must be helpful where there is scope for consensus, and constructive but combative where there is none. That is how democracy should work and – remarkably – 10 years on, devolution is strong enough to take it.[98]

'The stage is set for the most crucial period in Scottish politics since 1997,' dramatised the *Edinburgh Evening News*, 'not only because of the new personalities in the leading roles, but because the future of the country is at stake as it has never been in living memory.'[99] In a year's time we will have a much clearer picture as to where the new dispensation of power in Scotland and the UK will take us. And maybe, just maybe, the next 'Annals' will have a tale to tell about a UK General Election?

For the time being, one thing is for sure, astonishing as some observers may find it: even four months after the May election, 'wily Salmond is on a popularity roll,'[100] and there is still a palpable sense of change and optimism around. Joyce McMillan went so far as to talk of 'a smile on the face of the nation, and a spring in its step':

> … people seem energised, hopeful, even excited, as if some dead hand of cramped thinking and low expectation had been lifted at last, and it's a mood that has spread across

[97] 'Time to look ahead' (Leader), *Scotland on Sunday*, 9 September 2007.

[98] *Ibid.*

[99] 'Alexander has already scored a few hits' (Leader), *Edinburgh Evening News*, 25 August 2007.

[100] Michael White, 'Alexanders, children of the manse and Labour's third dynasty', *The Guardian*, 1 September 2007.

the whole field of Scottish public life, from politics and business to public service and the media.[101]

At First Minister's Questions on 13 September Alex Salmond claimed the Scottish football victory in Paris as part of the new optimism in the country. Anyone remember Argentina 1978?

[September 2007]

---

[101] Joyce McMillan, 'SNP's ascension has given us renewed hope', *The Scotsman*, 1 September 2007.

Chapter V

THE YEAR AT HOLYROOD
2007-2008

A QUIETER YEAR?

Scottish politics from September 2007 to September 2008 was 'a tale of two parties'[1] – one buoyant, riding high in the opinion polls, led by a hugely popular Alex Salmond, apparently unassailable; the other experiencing an 'annus horribilis', culminating in the resignation of Wendy Alexander, after only nine months in the post as Scottish Labour leader, and the crushing defeat in the Glasgow East by-election.

Remember? At the time of composing last year's 'Annals', Gordon Brown and Labour in the UK were 11 points ahead of David Cameron's Conservatives. A general election seemed a distinct possibility. Then came Northern Rock, the U-turn on inheritance tax, the election that never was – and from then on an astonishing downward spiral – 10p income tax, lost data, the Crewe by-election, the Glasgow East by-election, demands for a leadership challenge. Now, on the eve of Labour's autumn conference, after the demise of the Bank of Scotland and what looks like meltdown in the global financial system, Brown and Labour in the UK are more than 25% behind the Tories – the most unpopular UK government for generations.

In Scotland. some pundits had murmured that 2008 might be quieter year, a year where the dust of the upheavals of 2007 would be allowed to settle. Well, for a quiet year there has been quite a lot going on: two leadership contests, one attention-grabbing by-election under the belt, and another one looming on the horizon. Scottish politics seems to have lost none of its capacity to surprise and entertain – or to annoy, as the case may be.

Even when it rained gold medals for the British Olympians in Beijing during the summer, politicians north and south of the border managed to make a political football out of it. Literally – as Gordon Brown's

---

[1] The phrase comes from Henry McLeish, former Labour First Minister, on *Politics Now*, STV, 26 June 2008.

suggestion of a GB football team for the London games in 2012 was roundly rejected by the Scottish government and the Scottish FA (fearing it would endanger Scotland's presence at European and World Cup tournaments); while Scottish medal winners were sceptical about the SNP's demands for a separate Scottish team at the Olympics, given the training opportunities here, compared to what they enjoy as part of Team GB.

LEGISLATION LITE

As noted in the last instalment of the 'Annals', Alex Salmond's announcement in September 2007 of his Government's legislative programme had provoked comments about its 'liteness' – and, indeed, the list of bills passed by Parliament to be chronicled here is relatively short.

Just before Christmas, the SNP government fulfilled one of its manifesto pledges when, on 20 December, the Abolition Of Bridge Tolls (Scotland) Bill was passed by Parliament, scrapping the tolls on the Forth and Tay Road Bridges. The most important bill to pass, for a minority government, was the Budget Bill which got approval on 6 February. Another promise made good was the passing of the Graduate Endowment Abolition (Scotland) Bill on 28 February, abolishing the fee (or 'tax') known as the Graduate Endowment for all students who successfully completed their course on 1 April 2007 or thereafter.

The Glasgow Commonwealth Games Bill was passed on 30 April. Its primary policy aim is to meet the Scottish Government's obligations for the 2014 games under the Hosts City Contract and deliver the commitments in the Candidate City File, providing the Scottish Ministers and councils with the powers necessary to achieve this.

The Public Health Etc (Scotland) Bill was passed by Parliament on 12 June. The Bill redefines and clarifies the relationships between Ministers, health boards and local authorities in protecting public health. It strengthens the role of health boards, amends current arrangements for statutory notification of diseases and introduces statutory notification of organisms and health risk states. In addition, it aims at updating and improving the statutory nuisance regime in the Environmental Protection Act 1990. It also contains provisions to ensure that those who use sunbeds are advised of the associated skin cancer risks.

SCOTTISH BROADCASTING COMMISSION

The Scottish Broadcasting Commission, an independent body set up by the Scottish Government to investigate television production and broadcasting in Scotland, had its first meeting on 26 October 2007. It published its findings on 8 September 2008. The main point of the report was the proposal for a not-for-profit digital Scottish national channel – costs estimated at up to £75m – which would fill a 'missing piece of the public service jigsaw.'[2] The channel, the Commission said, would also provide crucial competition for the BBC, which suffered, according to the evidence it had collected, from a 'perceived lack of ambition' in Scottish productions. The proposed channel was widely welcomed by First Minister Alex Salmond, the BBC's Scotland controller Ken McQuarrie, and the political parties.

The BBC Trust should also ensure better news coverage of the devolved nations, and the Commission also called for a review of BBC Radio Scotland – currently the only Scotland-wide broadcasting service – amid criticism that it lacked ambition and space for new ideas.

The Commission, chaired by former BBC news boss Blair Jenkins, also called on the BBC to review its commissioning policy for Scottish programmes. Further, it recommended that some broadcasting powers should be devolved to Scotland. But the report also stated, counter to the wishes of the Scottish Government, that legislative powers for broadcasting should remain with the UK Government.[3]

'Holyrood supposedly has oversight of the creative industries,' Iain Macwhirter observed, 'and yet not of broadcasting, which is the key creative industry.'[4] He is not the only one to question the sense of such 'constitutional ring-fencing'. He argues that it is a 'constitutional anomaly' which 'will be addressed as part of the reassessment of devolution being conducted by the Calman Commission and the National Conversation.'[5] Scotland Office Minister David Cairns, on the other hand, backed the report's 'underlying principle' that Scottish broadcasting should remain an integral part of UK broadcasting. The Liberal Democrats warned that any new channel would have to be properly resourced, while the Tories said it should be paid for partly out of private funding.[6]

---

[2] 'Scotland "needs national channel"', *BBC News Scotland*, 8 September 2008. <news.bbc.co.uk/1/hi/scotland/7603396.stm>.

[3] <news.bbc.co.uk/1/shared/bsp/hi/pdfs/08_09_08_broacasting.pdf>.

[4] Iain Macwhirter, 'BBC Scotland needs to get with the programme', *The Herald*, 8 September 2008.

[5] *Ibid.*

[6] Phil Miller, 'Funding question for £75m Scots TV channel', *The Herald*, 9 September 2008.

In June, a review for the BBC Trust (which represents viewers) had found that the BBC needed to improve its coverage of the UK's nations and regions in its main news bulletins and factual programmes. Research found that 37% of people believed that BBC news reports were often not relevant to where they live.[7] The study included an analysis of UK-wide BBC coverage, including the main 6pm and 10pm bulletins, by media expert Professor Anthony King of Essex University. His research showed that during a month-long period last year all 136 items about health and education on the main BBC news related to England only – as separate policies applied in Scotland, Wales and Northern Ireland. Analysis of the BBC's coverage found one in five stories involving devolution were 'vague and confusing' or factually inaccurate.[8] Giving evidence to a Welsh Assembly inquiry into broadcasting, the BBC's director general Mark Thompson said, in response to the Trust's report, there needed to be 'significant improvement' in the BBC's network coverage of the UK's nations.[9]

In September, the new BBC Gaelic digital channel – *BBC Alba* – was launched. Besides enthusiastic welcomes, the cost of the new service also attracted criticism.[10] And, as the *Stornoway Gazette* reported, the local MSP Rob Gibson (SNP) appealed to the BBC and the UK government to make the new channel 'available to terrestrial viewers via freeview as soon as possible.' The paper quotes the MSP:

> Given the public money being spent on the channel and the fact that it is under the banner of [the] BBC, it strikes me as ridiculous that it will only be available to those that have private satellite rental. The fact that the appearance on freeview is subject to a review by the BBC Trust is a worry. If they do not give the go ahead then it could really stymie the development and impact that the channel could have.[11]

[7] 'BBC told to improve UK coverage', *BBC News Scotland*, 11 June 2008. <news.bbc.co.uk/1/hi/entertainment/7447985.stm>.

[8] 'BBC told to improve national coverage of Scottish news', *The Daily Record*, 12 June 2008.

[9] 'More devolved issues for BBC news', *BBC News Scotland*, 16 June 2008. <news.bbc.co.uk/go/pr/fr/-/2/hi/uk_news/wales/7457200.stm>.

[10] Liz Thomas, 'BBC launches controversial £21m Gaelic channel – costing £365 per native speaker', *Scottish Daily Mail*, 14 August 2008.

[11] Donnie Macinnes, 'Plea for more viewers to see Gaelic channel', *Stornoway Gazette*, 10 September 2008.

CALMAN COMMISSION

At perhaps the worst possible moment for her (due to the donations scandal hanging over her), Wendy Alexander delivered a major speech on the constitution at Edinburgh University on St Andrew's Day, setting out her plan to develop devolution through an independent Scottish Constitutional Commission, endorsed by the Scottish Parliament.[12] It put the seal on this constitutional U-turn for Scottish Labour, revising the position Jack McConnell had adopted before the May election.

Alexander singled out the strengthening of the financial accountability of the Parliament, including a review of the Barnett formula with a view to diminish the role of the block grant from Westminster through shared and assigned taxes, thus increasing the fiscal responsibility of the Scottish Parliament. While the Commission, endorsed by a parliamentary majority (the 'grand, if informal, Unionist coalition'[13]) on 6 December 2007, specifically excludes the independence option, it allows for discussion of wider areas of UK constitutional reform, with the aim of strengthening both Devolution and the Union. The SNP sticks by the government's 'National Conversation', which is limited to Scotland. The Commission was finally established on 28 April under the chairmanship of Sir Kenneth Calman, the Chancellor of the University of Glasgow.[14] The Calman Commission was, albeit with some caveats, widely welcomed as 'timely', and Brown's support for the 'review' was noted,[15] particularly after Scotland Office minister David Cairns's dismissal of more tax powers for Holyrood as being only of interest to the 'McChattering classes'.[16]

Now, Scotland has two constitutional discourses: the SNP government's 'National Conversation' (started by Alex Salmond in August 2007) and the Parliament's Calman Commission. This dual approach, having evolved 'for crude partisan ends,' has been criticised as divisive and confusing: 'All the parties are agreed that the experience to date with devolution has to be reviewed,' wrote the *Scotsman*: 'But instead of finding common ground to conduct such a review in a rational manner, and thus present a united

---

[12] Douglas Fraser, 'Alexander calls for tax powers to replace the Barnett formula', *The Herald*, 1 December 2007.

[13] Ian Bell, 'Can we plot a fourth way for Scotland?', *The Herald*, 8 December 2007.

[14] Other members include a childhood friend of Gordon Brown (Murray Elder), a former Deputy First Minister (Jim Wallace), two former Tory ministers (Lord Lindsay and Lord James Douglas Hamilton), a veteran trade union leader (Matt Smith of Unison) and a Big Brother contestant (John Loughton, chair of the Scottish Youth Parliament).

[15] Douglas Fraser, 'Brown promises extensive review of devolution', *The Herald*, 25 March 2008.

[16] Michael Settle, 'Minister dismisses more tax power for Holyrood', *The Herald*, 12 February 2008.

face to Westminster – the only body that can introduce constitutional change – we are left with rival projects.'[17]

For the SNP, the 'Constitutional Commission' heads in the right direction – more powers for the Parliament. An indication of this was Gordon Brown's (quasi) concession that Holyrood should have a greater say in setting taxes:

> The seemingly unstoppable march towards an independent Scotland took a massive step forward on Thursday night with Prime Minister Gordon Brown's hint that he was prepared to devolve tax-raising powers to the Scottish Parliament. ... Mr Brown is right to say that the economy is everything, so handing economic power to the Scottish Parliament means it is only a very short hop to full separation.[18]

Eddie Barnes is not alone in thinking that the 'Unionist pact may not just be seen in later years as a historic moment for devolution,' but also as 'the moment when a referendum on independence became inevitable.'[19]

A NEVER-ENDING SNP HONEYMOON?

With the main opposition party in turmoil and stumbling ever deeper into crisis, the Tories veering between co-operating with Salmond's government and opposing it, and the Lib Dems in their self-imposed wilderness, accentuated by the surprise resignation of Nicol Stephen at the beginning of July, the SNP minority government's honeymoon has, so far, shown no real signs of ending. Despite some criticisms, the general verdict after one year of SNP government in May 2008 was overwhelmingly positive. 'The honeymoon will end," stated Brian Taylor in his BBC blog: 'Right now, though, the first minister is able to mark the anniversary of his election victory with signs of continuing popular support.'[20]

Scotland on Sunday summed up 'a good year for Scotland,' asserting that 'the record of the SNP's first year in power is impressive':

---

[17] 'Dual approach to devolution debate can't succeed' (Leader), *The Scotsman*, 7 December 2007.

[18] 'It's only a very short hop to full separation' (Leader), *Edinburgh Evening News*, 6 September 2008.

[19] Eddie Barnes, 'Unionist pact to debate devolution may hasten independence vote', *Scotland on Sunday*, 9 December 2007.

[20] Brian Taylor, 'Making New Friends' (Blether with Brian), *BBC News Scotland*, 2 May 2008, <www.bbc.co.uk/blogs/thereporters/briantaylor/2008/05/making_new_friends.html>.

Policies such as freezing Council Tax, cutting prescription charges, scrapping bridge tolls, scrapping the graduate endowment and saving some local hospital units from downgrading have struck a chord with wide sections of the Scottish electorate. These were solid, tangible policies with a material effect on people's lives, and they left much of the electorate feeling that this was a Government that could get things done.[21]

It disagreed with some key policies of the SNP:

Its plans to scrap Council Tax and replace it with a Local Income Tax represent an unwelcome new burden on the Scottish middle classes. And we disagree with the SNP's aim of complete independence from the rest of the United Kingdom; a far more sensible – and popular – course of action would be to negotiate more powers for the Holyrood Parliament, especially the financial levers necessary to inject some dynamism into the Scottish economy.[22]

But it hailed the effect Alex Salmond and his government have had on the 'general mood of the Scottish people':

Today, Scotland feels more comfortable with itself than it was a year ago. There is a welcome air of confidence and ambition in the country that must, in some part, be the result of a new spirit in Scottish public life. For that reason alone, this has been a good year for the Scottish Government, and a good year for Scotland.[23]

Any opposition and media criticism seemed to pale in the face of success. Under Salmond, the party presented an absolutely coherent image – no indication of internal cracks or feuds which used to characterise the SNP in the past.

When John Swinney presented the first SNP budget on 14 November, following the tightest financial settlement from London since devolution,[24]

---

[21] 'A good year for Scotland' (Leader), *Scotland on Sunday*, 12 April 2008,

[22] *Ibid.*

[23] *Ibid.*

[24] Following the announcement of the Comprehensive Spending Review by the UK Government, Alex Salmond said that the Treasury's claim that the real-terms increase in Scotland over the next three years was 1.8% per annum was wrong – the actual, real-terms increase over the next 3 years was only 1.4% (the difference due to re-drawing the baseline for English health expenditure).

the attacks on 'broken promises' intensified. No sign any more of the £2000 for first-time house buyers. Where was the commitment to match the school-building programme of the previous administration 'brick by brick'? Insufficient funding for Scotland's universities? Not enough new teachers to allow primary school classes one, two and three to have no more than 18 pupils? Prescription charges to be phased out by 2011, but no immediate abolition for those with chronic conditions (as unequivocally promised in the party manifesto)?

Undoubtedly, the biggest coup for the SNP was getting its budget approved by the Parliament, with the help of the Tories. John Swinney and Alex Salmond triumphantly outmanoeuvred and humiliated the opposition (with Labour eventually abstaining on their own amendment!). Part of the package was that John Swinney had been able to negotiate an agreement – the much vaunted 'historic concordat' – with all 32 Scottish local councils to freeze the council tax.[25] Although criticised by the opposition and by academics as disproportionally benefiting the well-off and therefore directly contradicting, as David Bell argued, the SNP's 'cherished aim of reducing inequality,'[26] tax payers saw the measure as a huge relief on their pockets, with more promised when the unpopular council tax would be replaced with a local income tax.

WENDY ALEXANDER'S REFERENDUM CALL

Then came Wendy Alexander's astonishing 'shock U-turn' on the independence referendum,[27] when she gave Scottish politics that 'surreal turn',[28] announcing her conversion to an independence referendum live on the BBC's *Politics Show* on 4 May. One of the strangest weeks in Scottish politics ensued, 'with the situation becoming more bizarre by the minute.'[29]

Wendy's new departure had, quite obviously, created a 'major headache for Brown.'[30] Coming in the immediate wake of the local electoral disaster for Labour in England and Wales, it looked as if Brown

[25] Robbie Dinwoodie, 'Political coup for Swinney as councils all sign up to agreement for a tax freeze', *The Herald*, 17 November 2007.

[26] See Peter MacMahon, 'SNP in no position to claim moral high ground', *The Scotsman*, 4 December 2007.

[27] Douglas Fraser, 'Alexander backs independence referendum in shock U-turn', *The Herald*, 5 May 2008.

[28] Gordon Brewer on *BBC Newsnight Scotland*, 6 May 2008.

[29] David Perry, 'Wendy defiant in referendum row', *The Press and Journal*, 8 May 2008.

[30] Bill Jamieson, 'Wendy's cry brings on major headache for Brown', *The Scotsman*, 9 May 2008.

had 'lost patience with Ms Alexander,' as he refused to give her demand for a referendum his backing at Prime Minister's Questions: 'Far from endorsing her standpoint, he went out of his way to dilute it.'[31] That Alexander insisted on her demand when appearing at First Minister's Questions at Holyrood the following day, led the *Scotsman* to ask whether Brown was 'losing his grip on Scotland.'[32]

The *Press and Journal* saw her coming 'within an inch of landing a blow, of sorts, on Salmond,' only to be 'pulled out of the ring by Gordon Brown.'[33] The paper conceded, 'it might have been the master stroke,' but now 'it looks like Mr Salmond will come out of the fight better off, again, and continue with his policy of a referendum in 2010.' Brian Taylor added, 'The manner of executing this plan, if such a description can be used, has been utterly abominable.'[34] He saw Labour's 'new-found support for a referendum' driven by 'calculation and fear.'[35] Fear of electoral defeat, calculation that being blamed for not letting the Scottish people have a say could rebound on the party in the 2011 election and that, at least for the time being, the Scots would reject the independence option in a referendum. 'Wendy Alexander's backing of an early referendum on independence is hugely significant,' editorialised the *Scottish Daily Mail*:

> It signals the Labour Party's first signs of life in a year. And it presents Alex Salmond with a dilemma. How does he oppose a referendum without damaging the validity of his party's claims that increasing numbers of Scots favour wrecking the Union?[36]

The *Daily Telegraph*, too, was prepared to give Miss (sic) Alexander 'some credit' for her 'tacit acknowledgement that Labour has been wrong-footed,' but called her move 'bluffing for base political advantage' and 'dangerous tinkering with the constitutional settlement.'[37] All of a sudden, a referendum seemed a question of when and how, rather than

---

[31] Brian Taylor, 'Where's your referendum now?' (Blether with Brian), *BBC News Scotland*, 7 May 2008, <www.bbc.co.uk/blogs/thereporters/briantaylor/2008/05/wheres_your_referendum_now.html>.

[32] David Maddox, 'Losing his grip on Scotland', *The Scotsman*, 9 May 2008.

[33] 'Referendum announcements' (Leader), *The Press and Journal*, 8 May 2008.

[34] Brian Taylor, 'Not just any referendum' (Blether with Brian), *BBC News Scotland*, 8 May 2008, <www.bbc.co.uk/blogs/thereporters/briantaylor/2008/05/not_just_any_referendum.html>.

[35] Brian Taylor, 'Calculation and fear' (Blether with Brian), *BBC News Scotland*, 5 May 2008, <www.bbc.co.uk/blogs/thereporters/briantaylor/2008/05/calculation_and_fear.html>.

[36] 'Labour is alive again. But it may be too late' (Leader), *Scottish Daily Mail*, 7 May 2008.

[37] 'Union put in peril by Labour's electoral games' (Leader), *The Daily Telegraph*, 7 May 2008.

if. Strangely, having been the brainchild of Wendy Alexander, the Calman Commission seemed to be totally sidelined by Labour's referendum U-turn.

LEADERSHIP RESIGNATIONS

Still reeling from the turmoil following that U-turn, on 28 June, Wendy Alexander bowed out. In the end, it was the unnecessary donations for her unnecessary leadership campaign which added the final straw. The Parliament's Standards Committee had decided, while the Chamber had already packed up for the summer, to recommend a day's suspension from Parliament for Wendy Alexander for not declaring the donations as personal gifts in the MSPs' register, following the advice of Standards Commissioner John Dyer, but contradicting the advice the Clerks of the Parliament had given Wendy Alexander. The Parliament would have to vote on that recommendation – after the summer recess....[38] The issue seemed to just not go away. And Wendy Alexander seemed to have had enough.

But, as Douglas Fraser commented, her resignation had deeper reasons than just the Parliament's Standards Commission decision:

> Although her resignation was in response to the committee vote, it set out her case for why it had been wrong, partisan ad against natural justice. So why resign at all? Because the standards ruling was the final straw. Ms Alexander's leadership negatives heavily outweighed her positives.[39]

Her leadership, long overshadowed by the illegal donations row,[40] only temporarily relieved by the Electoral Commission's clearance of her (branded a 'whitewash' by SNP MSP Alex Neil),[41] had come under attack long before that shambolic manoeuvre. In a widely noticed leader back in January, the (usually) Labour-supporting *Daily Record* had been scathing about the leadership of the Scottish Labour leader.

---

[38] Which the Scottish Parliament did at the beginning of September, overruling the Committee.

[39] Douglas Fraser, 'The final straw for Wendy Alexander', *The Herald*, 30 June 2008.

[40] Campbell Gunn, 'Wendy's woes are not going away', *The Sunday Post*, 13 January 2008.

[41] Ian Swanson, 'MSP says ruling on Wendy donation is "a whitewash"', *Edinburgh Evening News*, 8 February 2008.

> These are very difficult times for Scots Labour leader Wendy Alexander. (...) During her reign, she has so far failed to land a blow on First Minister Alex Salmond. (...) Labour's first year in opposition was always going to be tough. But no one could have predicted how far their fortunes would slump in just nine months.[42]

Wendy Alexander seemed to have made some progress by the time of the Labour conference in March. Eddie Barnes commented that she 'appears to have found a clearer message to sell to the party,' and 'she has bought herself some time.'[43] Hamish Macdonell's verdict was: 'The Scottish Labour Party landed itself in a pretty big hole last May. It's not out of it yet, but at least it has stopped digging.'[44]

But it was a false dawn. 'Alexander's record as leader failed to live up to the expectations,' wrote James Mitchell in the *Observer*:

> Her performances at First Minister's questions were poor. ... When she stunned the country – and her colleagues in London – with support for a referendum on independence, she had once again failed to prepare the ground, having not thought through the implications of her U-turn.[45]

All commentators stressed the impact on Gordon Brown. 'Just when it seemed things could hardly get worse for Gordon Brown, Wendy Alexander resigns in a sleaze row over donations to her leadership campaign,'[46] but not all reactions were outright and relentlessly negative. *Scotland on Sunday* conceded:

> This is not to say that Alexander did not have a vision for her party and Scotland. She was quietly modernising the former while trying to outline the latter. Most notably, this included the brave decision to take on her colleagues at Westminster in an attempt to effectively federalise the party and get it to look seriously at devolving further powers to Holyrood. This newspaper backed that approach, which took form in the

---

[42] 'Alexander yet to score point' (Leader), *Daily Record*, 28 January 2008.

[43] Eddie Barnes, 'It may sound cuckoo, but Labour thinks spring has sprung', *Scotland on Sunday*, 30 March 2008.

[44] Hamish Macdonell, 'Still in a hole, but they might have found a way out', *The Scotsman*, 1 April 2008.

[45] James Mitchell, 'Great expectations came to nothing', *The Observer*, 29 June 2008.

[46] 'Now Wendy adds to Gordon's many woes' (Leader), *Scottish Daily Mail*, 30 June 2008.

> cross-party Calman Commission. ... Last week 's standards
> committee suspension *was* politically motivated and she
> has paid a price way out of proportion with her 'offence',
> of not registering donations to her leadership campaign.[47]

'Wendy Alexander may have lacked many of the skills necessary for
political leadership,' so the verdict of Iain Macwhirter,

> but her analysis of the political situation in Scotland was
> sound. To meet the Nationalist challenge, Labour has to
> detach itself from Westminster and become more of a
> Scottish party. It can only do this by adopting an explicit
> federal agenda, calling for an autonomous Scottish
> parliament, with economic powers.[48]

Macwhirter probably wrote the *Herald*'s editorial on Wendy Alexander's
demise:

> Ms Alexander may have been among the strongest
> intellectually of her party north of the border, but she
> failed on the key public front of at least breaking even in
> the weekly cut-and-thrust of First Minister's questions.
> There were ample openings for point-scoring, for example,
> on the SNP's proposals for local income tax. But when she
> lost her voice in the final week of her tenure as party leader,
> it was only the physical manifestation of what had been
> happening anyway when it came to unequal sparring in the
> debating chamber. More tellingly, her bungled attempt to
> unsettle the SNP by insisting on an immediate referendum
> against the wishes of 10 Downing Street showed all the
> hallmarks of an ambitious politician seeking to throw off
> the image of being a mere Brownite 'puppet'. It backfired
> badly, and the absence of more than tepid backing by the
> Prime Minister left her weaker to resist the forces, including
> some in her own party, actively plotting her downfall.[49]

---

[47] 'Labour's lost love' (Leader), *Scotland on Sunday*, 29 June 2008.

[48] Iain Macwhirter, 'Not great leader but she had the right idea about Scottish Labour', *Sunday Herald*, 29 June 2008.

[49] 'What now for Labour?' (Leader), *The Herald*, 30 June 2008.

Ian Swanson, while calling Alexander's period as leader 'effectively a wasted year for Labour,'[50] also highlighted at least one positive side of Alexander's short reign:

> Perhaps Ms Alexander's one notable success during her short reign as leader was to move Scottish Labour from its stance in last year's election against further devolution to acceptance of the 'more powers' case. Her St Andrew's Day lecture at Edinburgh University gave birth to the cross-party Calman Commission – though not without some resistance from Gordon Brown.[51]

Kenny Farquharson concurred and went even further: 'Her term as leader was flawed, but her vision for Scotland was sound. ... Wendy Alexander was right to resign. But her demise is a terrible setback for Scotland.'[52] By contrast, the most scathing farewell came from the *Sunday Times*: '... there will be many in the SNP sorry to see her go, for she has been a singularly ineffective leader of the opposition.'[53]

Compared to Wendy Alexander's resignation, the surprise resignation of Nicol Stephen – 'Mr Predictable surprises everyone'[54] – played second fiddle. Giving his 'low profile' leadership and his 'recognition problem' a cursory glance, Campbell Gunn summed it up perfectly:

> It's said that political journalists should never be cynical but always be sceptical. So when a politician resigns, often citing a desire 'to spend more time with my family', there's usually a flurry of speculation as to the real reason behind the departure. In the case of Nicol Stephen, who gave exactly that reason for standing down, it appears, disappointingly for the conspiracy theorists, to be true.[55]

---

[50] Ian Swanson, 'The battle begins...', *Edinburgh Evening News*, 31 July 2008.

[51] Ian Swanson, 'Leadership is not the only change needed', *Edinburgh Evening News*, 11 September 2008.

[52] Kenny Farquharson, 'How bad was she?', *Scotland on Sunday*, 29 June 2008.

[53] 'Let the party begin' (Leader), *The Sunday Times*, 29 June 2008.

[54] Douglas Fraser, 'Stephen faced ultimatum: choose family or leadership of the party', *The Herald*, 3 July 2008.

[55] Campbell Gunn, 'So, nothing much happens in recess!', *The Sunday Post*, 6 July 2008.

Stephen, despite his 'lack of charisma',[56] was credited to have been 'surprisingly nimble against Alex Salmond,' landing 'more blows on the nationalist's thick hide than anyone else on opposition benches.'[57]

Both Jenny Hjul and Murray Ritchie encouraged the Lib Dems and their new leader to be 'decisive' and 'radical'. Should they or, more likely, the SNP win Jack McConnell's seat when he steps down as an MSP to take up his role as High Commissioner for Malawi, the arithmetic at Holyrood would change and the relative importance of the Lib Dems would increase. Hjul discovered the Lib Dems' federalism as a 'firm proposal to maintain the United Kingdom based on a more federal state' which she called 'better than outright separatism and better than doing nothing about the shifting political landscape.' Murray Ritchie perhaps overegged the pudding by claiming that 'most Scottish Liberals would opt for a confederal UK containing an independent Scotland. I don't know any who would prefer reheated devolution.'[58]

The two leadership resignations crowned 'a charmed first year in power' for the SNP, Campbell Gunn commented: 'the task of challenging Alex Salmond seems to have been beyond two of the three opposition leaders, resulting in both of them throwing in the towel.'[59] That dramatic beginning of the recess set the tone for the summer, with two leadership contests. 'Alex Salmond must be wondering what he has done to scatter his enemies so successfully,' mused the Edinburgh Evening News: 'It's just a week since MSPs broke up for the summer recess, and suddenly both the Labour Party and the Liberal Democrats in the Scottish Parliament find themselves leaderless.'[60]

GLASGOW EAST BY-ELECTION

As soon as the by-election, triggered by the resignation on health grounds of David Marshall MP on 30 June, was called, it was seen as a nightmare in waiting for Gorden Brown. Glasgow East, held by Marshall with a majority of 13,500 votes in the 2005 general election, would have been seen, at any other time, as a safe Labour bastion, but not with a Labour government plummeting to a new all-time low in public opinion.

---

[56] Martin Williams, '"Safe" option who achieved helped credibility', The Herald, 3 July 2008.

[57] Jenny Hjul, 'Their role could be decisive, but are the Lib Dems up to it?', The Sunday Times, 10 August 2008.

[58] Murray Ritchie, 'It's time for the Lib Dems to get radical', Scotland on Sunday, 31 August 2008.

[59] Campbell Gunn, 'It's back to bread and butter politics', The Sunday Post, 31 August 2008.

[60] 'People deserve good opposition party leaders' (Leader), Edinburgh Evening News, 4 July 2008.

Alex Salmond predicted a 'political earthquake'.[61] Martin Kettle warned that 'to lose such a seat for the first time since 1922 would not just be a spectacular Labour disaster but also an unmissable sign of wider Labour disintegration in Scotland.'[62] The Labour-leaning *Daily Record* wrote: 'If Gordon Brown cannot hold on to the party's third safest seat in Scotland he will struggle to hold on as Prime Minister.'[63]

The Holyrood Labour leadership contest had been postponed till after the election. Most predictions were for a close by-election; some thought Labour would hold on to the seat, '... polls and pundits predicting Labour is likely to hold on to the seat, albeit by a wafer-thin majority;'[64] but some predicted defeat:

> With Gordon Brown a political liability, no leader at Holyrood, expenses rows that will not go away, and a dogged unwillingness to do anything to ease the credit crunch, there is no likelihood of Labour winning a raffle, never mind an election anywhere in the UK until at least 2015.[65]

Bordering on farce, the Labour campaign was off to a 'nightmare start', as 'their favoured candidate pulled out at the last minute, then others could not be persuaded to stand.'[66] Thus, the party missed out on the first weekend of the short campaign.

> Observing Scottish Labour over the past few months has been like watching a re-run of the Seventies slapstick comedy *Some Mothers Do 'Ave 'Em*, with pratfall followed by a slip on a banana skin, then stepping on a garden rake. You half expect the party to crash en masse through a shop window on a pair of roller skates.[67]

[61] Chris Watt, 'Salmond predicts voting "earthquake"', *The Herald*, 8 July 2008; see also: Ross Lydall, 'High risk for Salmond as he fronts bid to trigger "earthquake"', *The Scotsman*, 23 July 2008.

[62] Martin Kettle, 'This byelection could be the most important ever', *The Guardian*, 4 July 2008.

[63] 'Right Choice' (Leader), *Daily Record*, 7 July 2008.

[64] Ian Swanson, 'Win or lose, this vote will deliver verdict on Salmond', *Edinburgh Evening News*, 24 July 2008.

[65] 'Labour meltdown will start decades in the wilderness' (Leader), *Scottish Sunday Express*, 20 July 2008.

[66] 'Right Choice' (Leader), *Daily Record*, 7 July 2008.

[67] 'Slapstick Politics' (Leader), *Scotland on Sunday*, 6 July 2008.

The 'selection debacle',[68] satirised by Eddie Barnes as 'the strange tale of Labour and the missing candidate,'[69] made the campaign not easier for Labour. Increasingly, defeat became a real possibility.

And the predicted earthquake happened. After Dunfermline in February 2006, another 'safe' Labour seat changed hands, as the SNP's John Mason topped the poll. 'SNP storms to historic election victory by 365 votes,' shouted the front page of the *Scotsman* on the day after the by-election.[70] The SNP 'narrowly snatched a sensational victory... over Labour's Margaret Curran after recording a 22% swing.' Gordon Brown had been given 'a Glasgow kiss', as Jason Grove had it – 'a short, sharp headbutt designed to leave its victim dazed and bleeding in the gutter.'[71]

In the past, when the SNP won seats from Labour, it tended to lose them at the next general election, 'but in the current climate all bets are off.'[72] Kenny Farquharson offered this analysis of Salmond's triumph:

> The explanation for Salmond's abiding appeal, culminating in last week's triumph, is now clear: for the first time in British politics, someone can be in government and opposition at the same time. In one breath Salmond can be playing the statesman as First Minister of Scotland, and in the next he can be a niggling thorn in the side of Prime Minister Gordon Brown. Salmond can be both underdog and top dog, David as well as Goliath. He has rewritten the rule book.[73]

Glasgow East was the icing of the cake for the SNP, and in particular for Alex Salmond who – in stark contrast with Gordon Brown – had been a constant presence in Glasgow East during the campaign:

> Alex Salmond remains in clover, his honeymoon with the voters continuing. He has in the last 12 months established an unrivalled position of authority in Scottish politics;

---

[68] Hamish Macdonell, 'Selection debacle has piled on the woes for party', *The Scotsman*, 7 July 2008.

[69] Eddie Barnes, 'The strange tale of Labour and the missing candidate', Scotland on Sunday, 6 July 2008.

[70] Ross Lydall and David Maddox, 'SNP storm to historic election victory by 365 votes', *The Scotsman*, 25 July 2008.

[71] Jason Groves, 'Can Brown stay after Glasgow's kiss-off?', *Scottish Daily Express*, 27 July 2008.

[72] 'The SNP triumph' (Leader), *The Herald*, 26 July 2008.

[73] Kenny Farquharson, 'Salmond rewrites the rulebook', *Scotland on Sunday*, 27 July 2008.

indeed, it's hard to think of anyone who has exercised such supremacy. Is there anyone who can dent it?[74]

Moreover, Glasgow East stands for a deeper, perhaps seismic shift in the political landscape of Scotland. Salmond's 'is no longer a small, crabbit party of protest,' John MacLeod wrote in the *Scottish Mail on Sunday*:

> This SNP is today the most formidable political force in Scotland, fighting Glasgow East quite deliberately not as the principal opposition, but as a party of government – of a country, the Nationalists assert, increasingly fed up with being run by another country.[75]

On a wider scale, the *Independent* tried to assess the significance of the Glasgow East result:

> Ten years after the establishment of the Scottish parliament and the Welsh Assembly, it is not at all clear where devolution will lead; forecasts – wishful or otherwise – that it will spell the end of the Union may well be premature. The significance of Glasgow East is not that it brings closer the break-up of the United Kingdom, but it could presage the end of Labour as a party of British government. If it does, then the blame, for constitutional, as for electoral failure, will rest with the hapless Gordon Brown.[76]

LEADERSHIP CONTESTS

Glasgow East 'was the asteroid that threatens to wipe out the Labour dinosaur and the time has come for the great beast to evolve or risk political extinction.'[77] It raised the stakes for the Scottish leadership campaign of the party. According to the *Scotsman*, 'Labour needs a bold new direction and confidence if it is to take on Alex Salmond. On the current showing, its leadership contenders will have to work harder to

---

[74] *Ibid.*

[75] John MacLeod, 'Once again, Alex Salmond has rolled the dice and won – as a devastated Scottish Labour continues its remorseless decline', *The Mail on Sunday*, 27 July 2008.

[76] 'Labour's Glasgow East defeat is a portent of worse to come' (Leader), *The Independent*, 26 July 2008.

[77] 'Labour must evolve now or face extinction' (Leader), *Edinburgh Evening News*, 5 August 2008.

convince us they have a roadmap.'[78] One of the problems is that 'in the Labour Party rule book, the leader of the Scottish Labour Party remains Gordon Brown, or whoever happens to run the party at a UK level. The advent of devolution did nothing to change this.'[79] As Ian Macwhirter has tirelessly argued, 'some way has to be found to make the Scottish leader a real leader, otherwise Scottish Labour could end up going into the same political oblivion that obliterated the Scottish Tories.'[80]

After Glasgow East, Macwhirter had published a more extended analysis of the decline of Labour in Scotland:

> The strange death of Labour Scotland has been taking place for well over a year. In that time Labour have lost the Scottish government, two Scottish leaders and now the third safest Westminster seat in Scotland. If the Glasgow East result were to be reflected across Scotland at the next general election, Labour would be left with only one seat north of the border. ... The SNP fought a classic Labour campaign in Glasgow East, as the people's party against the establishment. ... Labour's abandonment of social democracy in England makes it a loser in Scotland .... Instead of allowing the SNP to take over their territory, Scotland's Labour MPs should be moving to merge with the Labour MSPs to form a new Scottish political organisation. The election of a replacement for Alexander should be turned into the election of a fully-fledged Scottish leadership with functional autonomy from Westminster. .... None of the candidates to replace Wendy Alexander seems interested, but it is the only sure way of persuading Scottish voters that the party they have supported for the last half century deserves to win their votes again. It is the only way Labour can emerge from the grave they have dug. There is life after Glasgow East, but not as Labour currently knows it.[81]

From a slightly different angle, Kenny Farquharson arrived at the following conclusion:

> If Scottish Labour wants a future, it must accept a truth wich might at first seem like an oxymoron – that you can

[78] 'No positives coming out of Labour' (Leader), *The Scotsman*, 11 August 2008.

[79] Eddie Barnes, 'Up to the job?', *Scotland on Sunday*, 3 August 2008.

[80] Iain Macwhirter, 'Time for Scottish Labour to find its own voice', *The Herald*, 1 September 2008.

[81] Iain Macwhirter, 'The Death of New Labour in Scotland', *Sunday Herald*, 27 July 2008.

be a nationalist and a unionist at the same time. You can believe in the United Kingdom and still put Scotland first. You can owe your allegiance to a Scottish leader first, and a UK leader second. Not for any wild woad-wearing reason. But simply because Scotland is where you live, and where you bring up your family. I'm not holding my breath. I suspect that Labour will squander this opportunity to renew itself, mainly because it has arrived too soon after the party's defeat in last year's Holyrood elections. Labour is still hurting. But the hurt it feels is the hurt of rejection, not the ache of wanting to regain power. The party is not yet hungry enough to make the radical changes required for a comeback.[82]

Arguably, the most important intervention during the leadership campaign came from Tom McCabe MSP, a former Holyrood minister, in an article for the *Sunday Herald*.[83] The paper's editorial summed it up:

McCabe's advice to whoever succeeds Alexander is ... sage. The leader must speak fort the Scottish party as a whole, not just the group in Edinburgh. He or she must get on to the front foot of the constitutional debate by supporting extra financial powers for the parliament. The new leader should also challenge the UK government, of whatever hue, when the need arises. ... Given Tom McCabe's article, it is a pity that four candidates are not going for the top job.[84]

While Paul Hutcheon piled scorn on the complex electoral college (involving MPs, MSPs, councillors, party members, trade unions and affiliated organisations) which the Scottish Labour Party uses to select its leader, claiming that 'the three-way battle between Iain Gray, Cathy Jamieson and Andy Kerr is perhaps the most anti-democratic farce you will witness in the UK this year,'[85] Iain Macwhirter contended that 'of the three leading candidates the only one the SNP worries about

[82] Kenny Farquharson, 'Labour doesn't look hungry for power', *The Sunday Times*, 10 August 2008.

[83] Tom McCabe, 'What do we in Scottish Labour need in our nation's new political landscape? A leader with the guts to stand up to Westminster', *Sunday Herald*, 3 August 2008.

[84] 'A ray of light for Labour, but is it too late?' (Leader), *Sunday Herald*, 3 August 2008.

[85] Paul Hutcheon, 'Labour's electoral charade', *Sunday Herald*, 24 August 2008. For a more measured, but no less incisive view, see Brian Taylor's 'Blether with Brian' blog, 'Not technical, but fundamental', *BBC News Scotland*, 28 July 2008, <www.bbc.co.uk/blogs/thereporters/briantaylor/2008/07/not_technical_but_fundamental.html>.

is Cathy Jamieson, who is much brighter than she is given credit for, and performed very ably at First Minister's Question time as a stand-in for Wendy Alexander,'[86] while Joan McAlpine found all three of them 'equally bland and unpalatable.'[87] Anyway, as Campbell Gunn summed up the summer, he seemed to offer a little ray of hope for embattled Labour:

> Whoever takes over as Labour leader ... will have his or her work cut out. Labour has campaigned hard over the summer, tackling the SNP Government on issues like school numbers and hospital cleanliness. But without strong leadership, these attacks have failed to hit home. All that could change... [88]

In the end, Iain Gray prevailed with a comfortable majority in a proper contest, 'which gives him a powerful mandate.'[89] He promised a 'fresh start' for the party, cautiously welcomed by the media.[90] 'It is time to close the manifesto on which we fought the 2007 Scottish election and time to write our programme for Scotland for 2011 and beyond,' he said. Margaret Curran, the defeated candidate in Glasgow East, was given the portfolio to develop 'policy which was in line with Labour values but in touch with the wider Scotland.' Gray said lessons from the by-election loss of Glasgow East to the SNP would be learnt and written into 'every line' of Labour's programme for winning in 2011. This would include reform of the council tax to make it fairer while still protecting local services. Gray made clear he would argue for Scotland to receive a share of the millions being invested in London for the 2012 Olympics. Some of the investment was in fact regeneration cash, and Scotland should get a share of this extra spending through the Barnett formula: 'I will make that argument – it's my intention to stand up for Scotland,' he said. He also argued for Scotland to receive more in council tax benefit: 'Scotland should be receiving more than £400 million because 48% of pensioners in Scotland who are entitled to council tax benefit don't receive it at the moment.' Rejecting the SNP's local income tax, he said he wanted to see a reformed council tax, but argued that since it would still be a property tax it would not mean losing the council tax benefit cash, as the

[86] Iain Macwhirter, 'Labour in Scotland is a body without a head', *The Herald*, 28 July 2008.

[87] Joan McAlpine, 'Pretenders to Labour throne lack vision', *The Sunday Times*, 7 September 2008.

[88] Campbell Gunn, 'Labour set for a new start', *The Sunday Post*, 7 September 2008.

[89] Lorraine Davidson, 'Labour's new leader could unsettle SNP', *The Sunday Post*, 14 September 2008.

[90] 'Gray to be applauded for taking a fresh approach' (Leader), *The* Scotsman, 15 September 2008.

UK government says will happen if the SNP goes ahead with its proposed local income tax.[91] As Brian Taylor blogged, 'this could be intriguing.'[92]

But Gray rowed back on the referendum commitment the party had made under Wendy Alexander. He ruled out Labour support for the SNP's planned referendum on independence. 'Wendy Alexander was right to challenge Alex Salmond to put the question to the public and get it out of the way,' he said, but Salmond had made clear he is not going to do that: 'He wants to bring forward a referendum bill with a question that's rigged and a timing that's rigged and we cannot support that.' Asked if he would support a referendum if the question was right, Gray said: 'There is no prospect of that.'[93] Clearly, he is alluding to the SNP's speculation that a Tory government at Westminster would boost a yes vote in a Scottish independence referendum, which is backed by a recent YouGov poll.[94] But will Labour really risk going into the 2011 election campaign as the party that has blocked a vote on Scotland's constitutional future? 'This is dangerous territory for Labour. If Gray denies Scots the opportunity to have their say, Labour will be punished even more. Who wants to back a party that doesn't trust the people?'[95]

Gray's inauguration as new Scottish leader was also overshadowed by news of MPs plotting against Brown – and, a few days later, by the resignation of David Cairns, the No.2 Minister in the Scotland Office (who had been responsible for Labours Glasgow East campaign), adding to the ominous signs that it was increasingly 'a question rather of when and how than if Gordon Brown steps down.'[96] The precarious situation of Labour at Westminster – and its leadership woes – ensured that the Labour contest dominated the summer, compared to the contest triggered by Nicol Stephen's resignation. Tavish Scott was the favourite to succeed him but, as the contest progressed, some media pundits saw the vote between him and Ross Finnie and Mike Rumbles as too close to call. They were wrong. Scott secured a 59% share of the turnout.

Seemingly ignoring the advice to be 'brave' and 'decisive', he reiterated in his first statements Nicol Stephen's position that he would do nothing

[91] 'Gray becomes Scots Labour leader', BBC News Scotland, 13 September 2008. <news.bbc.co.uk/go/pr/fr/-/1/hi/scotland/7614081.stm>.

[92] Brian Taylor, 'Fine words, noble sentiments' (Blether with Brian), BBC News Scotland, 13 September 2008, <www.bbc.co.uk/blogs/thereporters/briantaylor/2008/09/fine_words_noble_sentiments.html>.

[93] Ian Swanson, 'Gray assembles new shadow cabinet in bid for fresh start', Edinburgh Evening News, 15 September 2008.

[94] Robbie Dinwoodie, 'Conservative win would "fuel support for independence"', The Herald, 8 September 2008.

[95] Kenny Farquharson, 'Will Labour be glad to be Gray?', Scotland on Sunday, 14 September 2008.

[96] Gordon Brewer on BBC Newsnight Scotland, 16 September 2008.

which might bring about independence 'by the back door'.[97] Then, in sync with the Lib Dems' Bournemouth conference's turn towards becoming tax-cutting party, he called on Holyrood ministers to bring forward an emergency income tax cut to help struggling families. A 2p in the pound cut, he said in Bournemouth, would save the average Scot more than £300 a year, easing the pain of the current economic crisis.

To complete the summer of resignations, Robin Harper, the 'cheerful chieftain of the Scottish Greens', announced that he would leave the leading position 'under no pressure at all.'[98] He will remain an MSP, and has recommended to his party that his colleague Patrick Harvie should become his successor.

SNP FLAGSHIP POLICIES UNDER FIRE

Replacing the unpopular council tax with its brand of Local Income Tax is one of the flagship policies of the SNP. 'The new Lib Dem leader in Scotland must save us from LIT,' the *Scotsman* pleaded, 'be it the SNP's or something cobbled together in an SNP-Lib Dem committee.'[99] While popular in the polls, it 'may still be a high-risk strategy politically,[100] as the consultation produced an overwhelming wave of criticism of the proposed scheme. Business leaders voiced their opposition. 'In business and economic terms, the case against local income tax remains overwhelming,' wrote Peter Jones.[101] And Teresa Hunter added:

> A local income tax sounds attractive, and certainly would be to pensioners and other non-workers. But how fair is it on two-earner families killing themselves to keep food on the table and clothes on the backs of their growing families? Their bills, from food to fuel, have already rocketed. They need a local income tax to take a bigger chunk out of their salary like they need a hole in the head.[102]

---

[97] 'Scott plays down referendum issue', *BBC News Scotland*, 27 August 2008. <news.bbc. co.uk/go/pr/fr/-/1/hi/scotland/7584125.stm>.

[98] Douglas Fraser, '"I've done my 10 years. I think I'll have a wee bit of fun" – Interview', *The Herald*, 13 September 2008.

[99] 'Who'll save us from LIT?' (Leader), *The Scotsman*, 8 August 2008.

[100] Campbell Gunn, 'Local tax is a high-risk strategy by SNP', *The Sunday Post*, 7 September 2008.

[101] Peter Jones, 'The business case against local income tax stands', *The Scotsman*, 15 August 2008.

[102] Teresa Hunter, 'SNP's tax would increase burden on struggling families', *Scotland on Sunday*, 7 September 2008.

Liz Cameron, the Chief Executive of the Scottish Chamber of Commerce, made this intervention:

> The Scottish Government may well have a case that council tax requires serious reform, but, as with any tax reform, it is important t stick with the right principles. Call it what you want, ministers, but make sure your new local tax is locally set, relates to what it pays for, and does not hit something as mobile as skilled labour.[103]

Labour has painted LIT as the SNP's poll tax. And Tom Gordon and Jason Allardyce seem to hint at similar historical parallels:

> As Margaret Thatcher found to her cost, the introduction of a new tax can bring a swift end to even the most feted political career. Her replacement of rates with the community charge, or poll tax, in the late 1980s led to rioting in the streets and to a cabinet revolt. Salmond knows all this, but so far hasn't blinked, dismissing his growing ranks of critics as out-of-touch with the political mood of the country.[104]

Having variously declared 'dead in the water,'[105] 'a disgrace'[106] and 'ill-considered',[107] suggestions of a 'backroom deal over local income tax' between the SNP, the Liberal Democrats and the Greens 'send shivers down the spine of middle Scotland and the business community.'[108]

With the Glenrothes by-election in view, the *Edinburgh Evening News* spotted a potential trap for Labour:

> The principle of a tax levied on the ability to pay is almost impossible to counter, and in opposing it Labour will be going into its industrial heartland arguing against a tax

---

[103] Liz Cameron, 'Taxing times are justified for LIT', *Edinburgh Evening News*, 9 September 2009.

[104] Tom Gordon and Jason Allardyce, 'Spitting tax', *The Sunday Times*, 7 September 2008.

[105] 'Tax plan dead in the water' (Leader), *Daily Record*, 19 June 2008.

[106] 'Tax plans are a disgrace' (Leader), *Daily Record*, 4 September 2008

[107] 'Just Nat Fair' (Leader), *Daily Record*, 2 June 2008.

[108] Michael Tait, 'Lib Dems and SNP to strike backroom deal over local income tax', *The Mail on Sunday*, 7 September 2008.

which even its critics accept will see the least well-off paying less. At this time that seems suicidal.[109]

Another plank of the SNP policy platform, the Scottish Futures Trust, also came under fire. It was called a 'shambles' and a 'broken election promise',[110] and was roundly rejected by the Daily Record:

> The SNP came to power promising a radical new way of financing major public buildings such as schools and hospitals. They promised to create the Scottish Futures Trust. Under the scheme, the government would raise money by issuing bonds that would give investors a guaranteed return. It was to end the much-maligned system of public-private partnerships, in which private-sector developers built schools or hospitals and leased them back over 25 or 30 years, making a tidy profit in the process. Yesterday, Finance Minister John Swinney finally unveiled the Scottish Futures Trust. But his scheme is completely unrecognisable from what the Nats originally promised. The first problem came when it emerged the Scottish government had no powers to issue bonds. And when ministers suggested that local councils could, it turned out that town halls simply didn't want to. So the Scottish Futures Trust we've ended up with is nothing more than a £17million quango, headed by a merchant banker, overseeing another version of public-private partnerships. As critics said yesterday, it is a rebranding – and an expensive one at that. It is a face-saving exercise designed to conceal the fact the Nats have again failed to deliver.[111]

The Unions branded the Scottish Futures Trust a 'costly and unnecessary new quango,'[112] although the appointment of Sir Angus Grossart was seen as 'a major coup for the Scottish Government' which 'provides the one ray of hope that the Scottish Futures Trust may work.'[113]

---

[109] 'Local income tax: The issue will dominate the by-election' (Leader), Edinburgh Evening News, 9 September 2008.

[110] David Maddox, 'Big projects must wait as SNP funding plan remains in doubt', The Scotsman, 21 May 2008.

[111] 'Nats need to get a grip' (Leader), Daily Record, 11 September 2008.

[112] Cameron Brooks, 'Union delivers scathing verdict on new public financing scheme', Aberdeen Press and Journal, 9 September 2008.

[113] 'Grossart appointment offers hope' (Leader), The Scotsman, 11 September 2008.

Other points of criticism concerned the continuing litany of 'broken promises' and inactivity in the face of industrial and public service unrest:

> Days after the euphoria of the SNP's victory in Glasgow East, First Minister Alex Salmond finds himself confronted by a serious and far-reaching industrial relations crisis. There are currently fourteen industrial disputes raging across Scotland, involving some key public services workers including firemen, coastguards, passport office staff and driving examiners. Beyond that, 5,0000 civil servants will stage a one-day strike on Thursday, 160,000 council workers are threatening further action after rejecting a 2.5% pay offer and teachers will decide whether to strike in October. .... What s Alex Salmond's response? 'The majority of these issues relate to the Westminster Government's remit and responsibilities,' claims his spokesperson. Not good enough, Mr Salmond. In fact, potentially fatal for the SNP. Since taking office, this administration has constantly beaten the drum for an increase in powers to Holyrood, insisting it should be running things reserved to London. At the first sign of problems, however, the SNP's instinct is to pass the buck.[114]

Water off a duck's back. Despite this criticism, 'Mr Salmond is not only continuing to set the pace on legislative reform, he is also showing an impressive ability to force his opponents to play to his tune. ... the Salmond ascendancy continues as Labour slumps.'[115]

LEGISLATIVE PROGRAMME

After the summer recess, the Scottish Government set out its plans for the coming parliamentary year, containing 15 bills announced by the First Minister in Parliament on 3 September.[116] Apart from the annual Budget Bill, the focus will surely be on the Council Tax Abolition Bill – the SNP's plan to replace council tax with a 3p local (but centrally set) income tax. The council tax, often branded 'unfair' and 'regressive', is to be replaced by a new method to raise public cash based on ability to

---

[114] 'A tough test ahead' (Leader), *The Scottish Mail on Sunday*, 27 July 2008.

[115] 'Salmond makes another giant leap' (Leader), *The Scotsman*, 8 September 2008.

[116] 'Scottish legislation plans in full', *BBC News* Scotland, 3 September 2008, <news.bbc. co.uk/go/pr/fr/-/1/hi/scotland/7595583.stm>.

pay, saving the average Scottish family between £350 and £535 per year – according to Government claims. The proposals – as they currently stand – do, however, not have enough parliamentary backing to go through. But both the Greens and the Lib Dems have begun to talk to the SNP about a compromise. And Margo MacDonald, the independent Edinburgh MSP, has offered her backing in return for extra cash for the Capital.[117] The other controversial issue is that the UK Government has told Scottish ministers they cannot retain £400m a year in council tax benefits from Westminster if the council tax is scrapped.

The Rural Schools Bill is to introduce a presumption against the closure of rural schools, which make up 41% of Scottish primaries and 23% of secondaries. The SNP has already overruled the closure of three schools, preventing hardship on the residents and economies of rural communities. This bill would aim to improve the consultation process on proposed closures, but critics have questioned whether forcing councils to keep open schools with only a few pupils on the roll would be a justifiable cost.

Another Health Bill would ban the open display of tobacco products in shops and bring in a tobacco sales registration scheme. In order to tackle alcohol-fuelled violence, ministers said they wanted to ban under-21s from buying drink at off-licences and set a minimum price for alcoholic drinks in an attempt to stop cut-price booze deals. The age restriction plan has been branded an 'ill-thought-out, reflex reaction not based on evidence' that would not solve Scotland's drink problem.[118]

The Scottish Climate Change Bill is to introduce a target to achieve an 80% cut in emissions by 2050 (going beyond the UK target of 60%), along with a legal framework to ensure work towards achieving the goal was being carried out – but no annual reduction targets as promised in the SNP manifesto.

A Criminal Justice and Licensing Bill aims to reform community sentencing, while ensuring serious and violent offenders would still be sent to prison and dealt with 'firmly and effectively' in jail. Also, a Sentencing Council would be set up with the aim of improving public confidence in sentencing decisions, while the Bill would also reform criminal law and court procedures.

The Scottish Parliament and Local Government Elections Bill is to draw the lessons from last year's election fiasco (with 146,000 spoiled ballot papers). Its main focus is on separating the Scottish Parliament and the Local Council elections, but it cannot do what Alex Salmond really wants, i.e. transfer the power to run Scottish elections from Westminster to Holyrood.

---

[117] Ian Swanson, 'Margo ready to back local income tax in return for Capital cash', *Edinburgh Evening News*, 15 September 2008.

[118] Katrine Bussey, 'Fresh criticism of alcohol sales plan', *The Scotsman*, 7 September 2008.

After this year's wash-out of a summer, a Flood Risk Management (Scotland) Bill seems a very timely piece of legislation. The bill would create a single enforcement body to oversee the operation of reservoirs and strengthen flood risk co-ordination. It would also incorporate European flooding legislation into Scots law.

Under the Public Services Reform Bill, Scottish public bodies and scrutiny bodies would both be cut by 25% by 2011. The bill would also resurrect plans to incorporate Scotland's main arts bodies into a new organisation, Creative Scotland, which stumbled at the first hurdle in its passage through Parliament in mid-June. The plan to merge the Scottish Arts Council and Scottish Screen had cross-party backing, but was thrown out after MSPs refused to back the financial arrangements contained in the legislation.

A Children's Hearings Bill is to set up a unified children's hearing system to deal with youngsters in trouble or at risk, with its 33 separate organisations brought under one national body. The Additional Support for Learning (Amendment) Bill would allow parents and children to make requests to attend schools outside their catchment area under this bill. It would also set up mediation and dispute resolution services where requests are rejected. A Marine Bill aims to reconcile the marine industry (50,000 jobs and £2.2bn income generated from Scotland's seas, excluding oil and gas) with the protection of the tens of thousands of marine and plant species in Scots waters.

Three legal reform bills round of the legislative programme. The Legal Profession Bill would bring in the first significant reform of the legal profession since 1980; the Arbitration Bill is to modernise arbitration law in Scotland, making it easier for people and businesses to settle disputes out of court; and the Legislative Reform Bill aims to improve scrutiny of legislation, in tandem with the Scottish Parliament.

Yet before any of these Bills reach their decisive stages in the Parliament, the focus will be firmly on the by-election for the other Parliament, which could have far-reaching consequences, bringing a boost for Iain Gray or continuing the electoral rampage of the SNP, making or breaking Gordon Brown's fate as Prime Minister.[119]

---

119 Kevin Schofield, 'Lose Glenrothes by-election and you're out, Gordon Brown is warned', *Daily Record*, 16 September 2008.

GLENROTHES BY-ELECTION

As the *Scotsman* commented: 'If Gordon Brown needed the Glasgow East by-election like a hole in the head, he needs the forthcoming poll brought about by the untimely death of Glenrothes Labour MP John MacDougall like a full decapitation.'[120] The Glenrothes poll, expected to be held in November, 'may turn out to be do-or-die time for the Prime Minister. For Labour, in its present baleful state, either would be better than what they have at present.'[121]

Despite a majority of over 10,000 in 2005, Labour are perceived as outsiders in the race. 'No, it isn't looking good for Labour,' according to Iain Macwhirter: 'The SNP will have to mount a dreadful campaign to lose in Glenrothes. I'm afraid this could be Gordon's big red one.'[122] Again, the focus is firmly on Gordon Brown's political fate:

> Brown is heading for an epic defeat in the Glenrothes by-election – the third crushing reverse in a row. Even he must realise that it's all over – but in his present debilitated state [it] is too much to expect him to go quietly. Labour have a choice to make … as they prepare for their conference: do they take responsibility for the future and change, or do they stick to the bitter end with a lost leader. Their decision could decide the course of British politics for a generation.[123]

For a moment, it looked as if Labour could launch a surprise candidate in the person of former First Minister Henry McLeish. Selecting him would have been a 'fascinating choice',[124] but then McLeish made clear that he would not be available. And the consensus seems to be that 'everything … points to an SNP triumph in the nextdoor seat to Brown's own.'[125] Indeed, according a *Guardian* editorial, 'the surprise today would be a Labour win, not a loss.'[126]

---

[120] 'The longer-term prospects look grim for Labour' (Leader), *Edinburgh Evening News*, 14 August 2008.

[121] Eddie Barnes, 'Brown gives it one last shot', *Scotland on Sunday*, 7 September 2008.

[122] Iain Macwhirter, 'If Brown loses on home turf, he risks losing everything', *Sunday Herald*, 17 August 2008.

[123] Iain Macwhirter, 'If Brown won't call it a day, Labour must do it for him', *Sunday Herald*, 7 September 2008.

[124] Robbie Dinwoodie, 'Why McLeish could be the ideal candidate', *The Herald*, 15 August 2008.

[125] Martin Kettle, 'Go early and take the hit – or go late and risk a knockout?', *The Guardian*, 15 August 2008.

[126] 'Brown's backyard blues' (Leader), *The Guardian*, 14 August 2008.

OUTLOOK

So, how will the 'tale of two parties' continue? Will other parties get a word in edgeways? Will Iain Gray do any better than Wendy Alexander in repositioning Labour? Will Glenrothes be a new start for Labour or the seal on Gordon Brown's fate? If there were a change of Prime Minister, would that trigger a UK general election? Will the SNP honeymoon go on and on and on? Will John Swinney find partners for a compromise on LIT? When will we see a Holyrood by-election in Motherwell and Wishaw? And let us not forget the European Parliament elections next June – in their own right, with Lisbon in limbo after the Irish referendum vote, and as the last electoral test before the next UK general election...

The Calman Commission and the National Conversation will produce their reports – will Calman provide substantial proposals for increased powers of the Scottish Parliament? Would that bind a future Conservative government in Westminster?

> Let's spell out what's at stake. If Calman fails to come up with a renewed and reinvigorated form of devolution, with real power over the Scottish economy, then the Union is unlikely to survive. In fact, it won't deserve to survive. The devolution we have today was a historic first step away from London rule, but it simply isn't up to the job of delivering a Scotland that takes real responsibility for itself and its future. In a choice between independence and the status quo, many Scots – myself included – would be tempted to opt for full sovereignty. Calman's job is to ensure there's a credible third choice: a strong and grown-up Holyrood Parliament that governs in partnership with Westminster – but can no longer blame London for Scotland's many ills.[127]

And what then? Will pressure mount to put the recommendations of Calman and/or the National Conversation before the people, or will the SNP introduce a referendum bill next September without a chance of getting it through Parliament?

Or will all that party-politicking simply 'seem piffling' while banks collapse and 'tales of financial apocalypse' unfold?[128] Will, therefore, the

---

[127] Kenny Farquharson, 'All the commission's men must be heard', *Scotland on Sunday*, 7 September 2008.

[128] Brian Taylor, 'Sentiment and history' ('Blether with Brian'), *BBC News Scotland*, 17 September 2008, <www.bbc.co.uk/blogs/thereporters/briantaylor/2008/09/sentiment_and_history.html>.

next 'Annals' reflect on a quieter, perhaps less eventful year in Scottish politics? Don't bet your Lehman Brothers shares on it.

[September 2008]

Chapter VI

THE YEAR AT HOLYROOD
2008-2009

All change since September 2008. Lehmann Brothers; bail-out of the Scottish banks; demise of the Dunfermline Building Society; surprise at Glenrothes, Homecoming 2009; Calman, Westminster expenses row, Euro elections, Megrahi affair, cuts, cuts, cuts, the looming Glasgow North-East by-election, and the introduction of a Referendum Bill... Overall, Henry McLeish and Tom Brown have a point when they write: 'Since the dramatic developments in Scotland in the wake of he 2007 Holyrood election, Westminster has taken central stage.'[1]

All change? Not quite. Alex Salmond may have found 'his second year in charge harder than the first,'[2] with some more flagship policies ditched, like the local income tax or the class size target of 18 for Primary 1-3. And with defeat in Glenrothes. But not that much harder. The opposition parties still seem to fear nothing more than new elections, which protected Fiona Hyslop and Kenny MacAskill, two cabinet secretaries who repeatedly came under pressure. The opposition parties have, time and again, shied away from a confidence vote in the Parliament. A veritable safety net for Salmond's minority government.

The SNP could celebrate its 75th anniversary, 'from protest to power', as the most popular party in Scotland, while Scotland marked the tenth anniversary of devolution.[3] The celebrations were only marred by the sad deaths of Bashir Ahmad, the first Muslim MSP who died in February, aged 68, after representing Glasgow for the SNP since 2007, and Sir Neil MacCormick, the architect of a modern, social democratic SNP and internationally renowned law professor, who died in April, aged 67. Another sad loss, in this devolution anniversary year, was Bill Speirs, the charismatic trade union leader, committed internationalist and intrepid Labour campaigner for a Scottish Parliament, who died in September, aged 57, after a long illness.

---

[1] Tom Brown and Henry McLeish, *Scotland: A Suitable Case for Treatment*, Edinburgh: Luath Press, 2009, p.172.

[2] Hamish Macdonell, *Uncharted Territory: The story of Scottish devolution, 1999-2009*, London: Politico's, 2009, p.258.

[3] Gerry Hassan (ed.), *The Modern SNP: From Protest to Power*, Edinburgh: Edinburgh University Press, 2009.

BAILING OUT THE BANKS

Lehmann Brothers was not the start of it, but it was the most striking symptom of the world financial system coming close to the brink. The apocalypse was, just, avoided. If Lehmann was the heart attack, the global efforts at bailing out banks and stimulating the economy with billions of taxpayers' money have saved the patient. But are there signs of convalescence? Has there been a therapy with a chance of lasting success? Or are we, now that the worst of the recession seems over, lapsing back into the old ways of under-regulated financial speculation and unlimited bankers' bonuses? Adair Turner was heckled a few weeks ago when he said, at the Mansion House Dinner in London, that taxpayers would have to foot the bill for a banking crisis 'cooked up in trading rooms where not just a few but many people earned annual bonuses equal to a lifetime's earnings of some of those now suffering the consequences.'[4] Whether we will actually come out of the crisis with a firmer regulatory system that can prevent a repeat show seems, even after the G20 in Pittsburgh, in the balance.

Gordon Brown used the Labour conference in Brighton to reveal 'plans for tougher than expected legal action against bankers' bonuses.'[5] 'We won't allow greed and recklessness to ever again endanger the whole global economy and the lives of millions of people,' Alistair Darling told the Labour conference.[6] But as legislation would only come into force next year, the Chancellor said the banks had to show 'the party is over' for excessive banking incentivisation, which was a major factor in the subprime lending disaster.[7] The UK was first to implement the G20 agreement on bonuses, and Britain's top-five banks have pledged to 'crack down on the greed and irresponsible risk-taking.'[8] But will it work?

The crisis has humiliated two of Scotland's most high-profile institutions: Halifax Bank of Scotland (HBOS) was controversially swallowed by Lloyds to save it and, following part-nationalisation, seventy per cent of the Royal Bank of Scotland (RBS) now belong to the British taxpayer.[9] Gone,

---

[4] Peter Ranscombe, 'Brussels binds the banks', *Scotland on Sunday*, 27 September 2009.

[5] Patrick Wintour, 'Clampdown on bonuses to be "toughest in the world"', *The Guardian*, 28 September 2009.

[6] Nigel Morris and Michael Savage, 'Excessive bonuses to be banned in war on greed', *The Independent*, 28 September 2009.

[7] Martin Flanagan, 'Darling to meet banks over bonus culture', *The Scotsman*, 28 September 2009.

[8] Tom Peterkin, 'Banks pledge to curb "greedy" bosses' bonuses', *The Scotsman*, 1 October 2009.

[9] Graeme Wearden, 'British government unveils £37bn banking bail-out plan', *The Guardian*, 13 October 2008.

too, is the much-trumpeted 'arc of prosperity'– with Ireland in deep trouble, and Iceland seeking refuge in the EU after its total financial melt-down. All parties are now talking about cuts. Budgets are being trimmed. Capital investment projects like the Glasgow Airport Rail Link are being abandoned. And that it is not the end of it. Tough choices will lie ahead. And the blame game about 'Labour cuts', 'Tory cuts', or 'SNP cuts' (or, indeed, the Lib Dems' 'savage cuts') has already started. After all, a UK general election is not far off...

A LITTLE LIGHT LEGISLATION

Overall, there was a trickle rather than a stream of bills making their way through Parliament between September of last year and the summer of 2009. Most of them were non-controversial and were carried with cross-party support. On 25 September 2008, the Judiciary And Courts (Scotland) Bill was passed unanimously by the Scottish Parliament. It guarantees the independence of the Scottish judiciary, reforms the court structure and gives the country's leading judge, the Lord President, formal recognition as head of the Scottish judiciary.[10] In October, Conservative MSP Jamie McGrigor's pet project, the Scottish Register of Tartans Bill, was universally approved by Parliament. It establishes a Scottish Register of Tartans, a Keeper of the Register of Tartans to maintain and oversee the new registrations (maintained and administered by the Edinburgh-based National) Archives in Scotland, and the process for registering new tartan designs in the Register.

In January, the Scottish Parliamentary Pensions Bill got all-party support, as it gives MSPs bigger benefits but will not cost taxpayers any extra money. At the end of the month, the Budget Bill failed after the vote was tied at 64 votes for and 64 against, and the Presiding Officer, Alex Fergusson, used his casting vote to maintain the status quo. The Greens had demanded £100m for house insulation; Finance Secretary John Swinney had offered £22m. Patrick Harvie demanded at least £32m. When he did not get an unequivocal commitment from Swinney, the Greens voted against the Budget, along with Labour and the Lib Dems. What looked like a major crisis, and could have led to a vote of confidence, was quickly sorted when the First Minister actually threatened such consequences. So little appetite for a confidence vote (and new elections) had the Labour and Lib Dem parties that they U-turned on the spot, the Lib Dems dropping their 2 p tax cut demand, and Labour happy with the SNP's reassurances about apprenticeships. The Greens were the ultimate

---

[10] Stewart Paterson, 'Judicial independence is backed by MSPs', *The Herald*, 26 September 2008.

losers, as the final figure for home insulation was cut back in the Budget that was voted through by all the other parties on 4 February. Again, the Conservatives had been the SNP's constructive partners in the budget process.

In March, a bill concerning Asbestos-related illnesses was passed which allows people affected by wrongful exposure to asbestos to raise an action for damages. The Health Boards Bill, also passed that month, introduces, by way of pilots, elections to Health Boards in Scotland and provides for those pilot schemes to be evaluated before the changes are rolled-out to other areas.

In May, the Flood Risk Management Bill passed its third stage in Parliament – it creates a framework for improved coordination in case of flooding and aims at delivering sustainable approaches to managing all forms and consequences of flooding. The Education (Additional Support for Learning) Bill was deemed necessary to improve the 2004 legislation which had already intended to provide for any need that requires additional learning support for the child or young person.

The Sexual Offences Bill, passed in June, provides for a statutory framework for sexual offences in Scots law. It is largely based on the draft bill published by the Scottish Law Commission in their final report. These reforms of the law on rape and sexual offences aim at a higher conviction rate. The Scottish Local Government (Elections) Bill separates local government elections from elections to the Scottish Parliament and allows for the publication of, and access to, a greater level of information about votes cast in local government elections.

The last bill to be passed before the summer recess was the Climate Change (Scotland) Bill, which set the most ambitious climate change targets of any industrialised nation. There was unanimous agreement in the Chamber to cut the country's greenhouse gas emissions by 42% by 2020, and by at least 80% by 2050, following a huge push by Scottish campaigners of the Stop Climate Chaos Scotland coalition. This legislation takes the toughest stance yet to be adopted by any developed country in the bid to tackle climate change and could be an important signal to other world leaders in the run up to global climate talks in Copenhagen in December. Mike Robinson, Chair of Stop Climate Chaos Scotland, commented:

> This is a truly momentous day. The Scottish Parliament has voted for legislation that will be held up as an example to the world ahead of climate talks in Copenhagen in December. At a vital time ahead of the UN's talks to put in place an agreement to replace the Kyoto Protocol in Copenhagen, world governments have been set an example by Scotland which we would urge them to follow if we are to avoid

catastrophic climate change. In particular, this presents a challenge to the UK Government. By supporting this bill, Labour MSPs at Holyrood have been much more ambitious than their government colleagues at Westminster. If the Labour Party believe it is the right thing for Scotland, it must surely be the right thing for the UK as a whole.[11]

Alas, only a day after the climate change bill was passed, the Scottish government published its National Planning Framework, which fast-tracks fourteen large-scale developments. Some of them may cut pollution, but others are likely to increase it. Among the latter are the new Forth Road Bridge, a new coal-fired power station at Hunterston in North Ayrshire (to replace the aging nuclear power station there) and new coal or gas plants at Longannet in Fife, Cockenzie in East Lothian and Boddam in Aberdeenshire.

How can these projects be squared with the ambitious climate change targets? Could they be in danger? Could they now be deemed illegal because they might help bust the 42% target? Senior civil servants, Rob Edwards reported, 'are privately warning that major polluting projects will now be vulnerable to legal challenge and cancellation because they pose a threat to the new statutory target to cut greenhouse gas emissions by 42% by 2020.'[12] Or could those projects lead to a watering down of the targets?

Otherwise, the general lightness of legislation was compounded when, in February, one of the flagship policies of the SNP was unceremoniously dropped from the legislative programme. It sparked another round of accusations about broken manifesto promises and was called 'the most humiliating U-turn yet for Alex Salmond and his government.'[13] The SNP had pledged to replace the widely discredited council tax with a local income tax of 3% from 2011. No doubt, their promise to 'scrap the unfair council tax' was a vote-winner in 2007. But the SNP's version of a local income tax was criticised as unworkable and unfair by finance experts, business leaders, trade unions, students and the Army:

> Critics claimed Swinney's figures did not add up and the scheme would leave a £1billion black hole in council coffers. Some said the tax would have to be set at 5p to maintain

[11] Scottish Catholic International Aid Fund (SCIAF), 'SCIAF Welcomes 'World Leading' Climate Target', <www.sciaf.org.uk/news/2009_news/sciaf_welcomes_world_leading_climate_target>.

[12] Rob Edwards, 'New Forth road bridge "could be cancelled"', *The Herald*, 28 June 2009.

[13] Magnus Gardham, 'Humiliating U-turn for Alex Salmond as SNP ditch local income tax', *Daily Record*, 12 February 2009.

current service levels and protect jobs. Unions warned families with two earners in modestly paid jobs would be hit hard and business leaders warned firms could quit Scotland. The SNP also faced the possibility of having to set up a tax collection agency, costing tens of millions of pounds.[14]

Most importantly, there was simply no majority for it in the Parliament. John Swinney blamed Labour at Westminster, in particularly Alistair Darling's 'swingeing Westminster-imposed cuts' and announced that the SNP would fight the 2011 election on the same promise to scrap council tax.

For Labour leader Iain Gray, this was 'the biggest and most humiliating climbdown since devolution.' Lib Dem finance spokesman Jeremy Purvis called it 'a gross betrayal of the people who voted for the SNP.' Tory leader Annabel Goldie said: 'We have long argued local income tax was unfair, unworkable and totally discredited. If the SNP really believed in this policy it would have fought for it tooth and nail. Instead the SNP has been exposed as a party of cheap election slogans, with no intention of delivery.' And independent MSP Margo MacDonald commented: 'I think John Swinney has done the sensible, the right and the brave thing – but he should not go back to promising a daft policy.'[15]

At First Minister's Questions, Iain Gray asked if Alex Salmond would follow the bankers and 'say sorry to Scotland's voters for the way he conned them.' But Salmond retorted: 'I think apologies are required from the council tax cabal of Labour and the Tories, who have been voting to uphold the council tax in Scotland – a Valentine's Day love-in between Labour and the Conservative parties.'[16]

GLENROTHES –
END OF THE SNP HONEYMOON?

After the Glasgow East by-election success of the SNP in July 2008, the party had high hopes of landing another blow on Labour in the Westminster by-election in Glenrothes in November. Despite a lead of 10,000 votes for John MacDougall MP, whose death brought about the

---

[14] *Ibid.*

[15] *Ibid.*

[16] 'Apology call after tax decision', *BBC News Scotland*, 12 February 2009, <news.bbc.co.uk/1/hi/scotland/7885953.stm>.

by-election, Labour was seen as an outsider in the race. An 'epic defeat' was predicted, not just for the Labour candidate Lindsay Roy, but also for Gordon Brown himself who holds the seat in the neighbouring constituency of Kirkcaldy.[17]

But the mood had changed. Gordon Brown was now seen as 'the man who saved the world financial system'. At least, that was the formulation of economic Nobel Laureate Paul Krugman, even if he put it in question form. He heaped praise on the British prime minister:

> [T]he Brown government has shown itself willing to think clearly about the financial crisis, and act quickly on its conclusions. And this combination of clarity and decisiveness hasn't been matched by any other Western government, least of all our own.[18]

Against that backdrop, Brown had a good Labour conference, and bringing back Lord Mandelson into the Cabinet has proved a bold and rewarding step for him. Labour's ratings climbed, and the Conservatives' opinion poll lead was slashed, at least for the time being. In contrast to Glasgow, Brown did personally campaign in Glenrothes. More to the point, we saw his wife Sarah emerging as a campaigner and 'political spouse'. Alex Salmond and the SNP maintained that the seat was as good as theirs. Another by-election 'earthquake' was in the offing. And Labour had privately conceded that they were heading for defeat.[19] But when the votes were counted on 6 November, Lindsay Roy held the seat with a comfortable majority: 'In a result that seemed to take even party insiders by surprise, their candidate Lindsay Roy coasted to victory with a majority of 6,737.'[20] Nick Robinson, who recalled that at the Labour conference just a few weeks earlier all had agreed that Glenrothes was already lost, reflected on the reasons behind the astonishing 'Brown bounce':

> Gordon Brown isn't just the MP for the neighbouring constituency. He was born and bred a Fifer – a citizen of the Kingdom of Fife. Labour's candidate was the highly respected and well known head teacher of his old school. His wife Sarah regularly popped in to campaign from their home four miles down the road. The SNP were the

[17] Iain Macwhirter, 'If Brown won't call it a day, Labour must do it for him', *Sunday Herald*, 7 September 2008.

[18] Paul Krugman, 'Gordon Does Good', *The New York Times*, 12 October 2008.

[19] George Parker and Jim Pickard, 'Brown faces new by-election battle', *The Financial Times*, 13 August 2008

[20] '"Brown Bounce" aids Glenrothes win', *Metro*, 7 November 2008.

incumbents. They ran both the council and the Scottish government and, although this was a Westminster election, Labour successfully turned this into a referendum on the SNP's performance – their local spending squeeze and their national promise made in headier times that an independent Scotland could join an 'arc of prosperity' with, er, Iceland.[21]

Was the vote an endorsement for Gordon Brown? Had the SNP 'bubble well and truly burst?'[22] During that heady week in early November – which also saw the election of Barack Obama – it may have been tempting for commentators to strike that note. There was even talk of a snap general election. Iain Gray could be forgiven if he thought that Glenrothes was Labour's 'Yes we can' moment. But the Glenrothes defeat did not critically harm the popularity of Alex Salmond and his government. And the 'Brown bounce' was not to last.

MOATS, MANURE AND DUCK HOUSES

Never before did one national newspaper set the agenda for six consecutive sordid weeks like the *Daily Telegraph* did this spring, from early May to mid-June. It was the 'scoop of the century'. Day after day the paper revealed how MPs at Westminster had milked the system of expenses, from government ministers down to obscure backbenchers, affecting all parties.[23] The 'offences' ranged from Oliver Letwin's tennis court to Sir Peter Viggers' duck house, Bill Wiggin's phantom mortgage and Douglas Hogg's £2,200 bill for cleaning his moat; from house flipping and tax dodging to the suggestion of deliberate fraud.

The story began in the unlikely setting of a Chilean vineyard, when Robert Winnett, the *Daily Telegraph*'s deputy political editor, first learnt from Gordon Brown's infamous aide Damian McBride that a disc containing details of every MP's expense claims might have been obtained by a whistleblower. The paper got hold of it and, together with Gordon Rayner, Winnett ran a team of reporters who sifted through

[21] Nick Robinson, 'Extraordinary', (Nick Robinson's Newslog), *BBC News Scotland*, 7 November 2008.

[22] Hayley Jarvis, 'Has the SNP bubble finally burst?', *BBC News Scotland*, 7 November 2008, <news.bbc.co.uk/1/hi/scotland/edinburgh_and_east/7714699.stm>.

[23] Available also in book form: Robert Winnett and Gordon Rayner, *No Expenses Spared: The inside story of the scoop which changed the face of British politics – by the team that broke it*, London: Bantam, 2009. Martin Bell vents his anger in his *A Very British Revolution: The Expenses Scandal and How to Save Our Democracy*, London: Icon Books, 2009.

more than a million expenses documents.

The revelations shook the political establishment to its foundations; they cost several Cabinet ministers their jobs, dozens of MPs were deselected for the forthcoming general election,[24] a by-election in Norwich was triggered when the well-liked local Labour MP Ian Gibson resigned after the party's 'star chamber' had declared him unfit to stand in 2010. And it culminated on 19 May in the resignation of the Speaker, Glasgow North East MP Michael Martin, following fierce criticism over his handling of the expenses controversy – the first Commons Speaker in 300 years to be forced out of office – and the controversial election of Tory MP John Bercow to the post of Speaker. SNP and Plaid Cymru tabled a motion calling for a Commons dissolution and new elections,[25] backed by a majority of the British people – but not finding enough support in the Commons.[26]

MPs paid back more than £100,000,[27] and yet it looks likely to 'lead to one of the biggest clear-outs of the Commons in living memory.'[28] For a while it seemed as if the expenses saga had brought Gordon Brown to the brink of losing his grip on the government.[29] Following his short respite after the G20 summit in London at the beginning of April, a series of calamities befell the hapless Prime Minister – from the Damian McBride emails attempting to smear leading Tories to his initial clumsy responses to the expense revelations (among them his cringeworthy appearance on YouTube on 21 April), while Cameron, in his 'John Wayne moment',[30] managed to present himself as more decisive, promising radical reform.[31] The Budget on 22 April, which gave a glimpse of the dramatically mounting debt in the wake of the banking fiasco, was seen as the final nail in the coffin of Labour's general election hopes.[32] Then came the defeat on the Gurkhas in the Commons, following Joanna Lumley's campaign – all

---

[24] Michael Settle, 'Up to 50 Labour MPs face axe over expenses', *The Herald*, 21 May 2009.

[25] Michael Settle, 'Gordon Brown faces calls for parliament to be dissolved', *The Herald*, 3 June 2009.

[26] Andrew Sparrow, 'Two-thirds of voters demand early general election – poll', *The Guardian*, 23 May 2009.

[27] Ross Lydall, 'Expenses row: Worst offenders are exposed', *The Scotsman*, 14 May 2009.

[28] Ian Swanson, 'The MPs who'll pay for expenses', *Edinburgh Evening News*, 28 May 2009.

[29] Eddie Barnes, 'On the brink', *Scotland on Sunday*, 24 May 2009.

[30] Gordon Rayner, 'MPs' expenses scandal: David Cameron's reaction to the scandal was his "John Wayne moment"', *The Daily Telegraph*, 26 September 2009.

[31] Brian Currie, 'Cameron orders Tories to come clean on expenses', *The Herald*, 16 May 2009; Andrew Woodcock, 'Cameron promises political revolution', *The Scotsman*, 26 May 2009.

[32] Andrew Grice, 'The moment that finally cost Labour the general election', *The Independent*, 25 April 2009.

adding up to, in Lord Mandelson's understatement, 'a bit of a week' for Gordon Brown.[33]

In Ian Swanson's view, 'MPs' excessive and arrogant expense claims have rightly sparked unprecedented public anger,'[34] but as week segued into week of revelations, some voices warned of a loss of perspective. An *Independent* editorial questioned the way in which the *Daily Telegraph* presented its findings, day after day, stretched out over weeks, as 'in danger of doing more harm than good to our body politic'. It pointed out that there is a difference between actual fraud and 'the milking of a laxly policed expenses system' and diagnosed a sense of 'hysteria' and 'overreacting'.[35] The Glasgow law professor Hugh McLachlan went furthest, claiming that, morally, most MPs were in fact not to be blamed. 'Much criticism of MPs with regard to their claiming of allowances,' he wrote, 'has been hyperbolic and hypocritical.' If they had not broken rules, then 'there is a case for saying their behaviour is not only legally but also morally defensible.'[36]

And was the expenses scandal not perfectly timed to take the sting out of the debate about bankers' bonuses and golden handshakes? While Fred 'the Shred' got away with millions, people got all het up about bath plugs, chandeliers, trouser presses and garden trees purchased on MPs' expenses. 'Leading bankers must have betrayed the odd smirk of satisfaction this week,' commented Alf Young: 'For months they were pilloried for their role in the global; financial collapse and for their thickly-upholstered corporate lifestyles. (...) For some of the bankers' biggest critics, our MPs, the boot is now firmly on the other foot.'[37]

But the visceral outrage about the allegedly self-serving MPs was also an expression of the deep unease and alienation many people in Britain feel with the outdated institutions of Westminster, an expression of the contempt for politics and politicians and for the systemic inadequacies of the British constitution. Brown tried to respond with a package of constitutional reforms, from an elected House of Lords to a referendum on electoral reform. He repeated these proposals at the Labour conference in Bournemouth. But, as some of these reforms had been pledged since the 1997 manifesto, the reception was suitably sceptical.[38]

---

[33] Torcuil Crichton, 'Sad end to "a bit of a week" for Prime Minister', *The Herald*, 1 May 2009.

[34] Ian Swanson, 'The MPs who'll pay for expenses', *Edinburgh Evening News*, 28 May 2009.

[35] 'The pursuit of MPs is becoming a witch-hunt' (Leader), *The Independent*, 23 May 2009.

[36] Hugh McLachlan, 'Morally, most of our MPs are blameless', *The Scotsman*, 25 May 2009.

[37] Alf Young, 'Now it's the bankers who are grinning like Cheshire fat-cats', *The Herald*, 15 May 2009.

[38] James Mitchell, 'Brown's reform pitch is a last desperate bid to cling to power', *The Herald*, 2 October 2009.

The expenses farce also had the side effect of allowing Holyrood, just in time for the tenth anniversary of devolution, to shine by comparison with Westminster. Surveys show that the Scottish Parliament enjoys greater trust than Westminster among the electorate. 70% in Scotland think that devolution has been good for Scotland. 41%, the biggest group of respondents, favour enhanced powers for the Scottish Parliament.[39] Here, MSPs' expenses had been sorted, and Alex Salmond could recommend the transparent and accountable allowances system of the Scottish Parliament – where members' expenses are published every three months – as a model of reform for Westminster:

> When the Scottish Parliament moved to total transparency, two things happened: the scandals stopped because information was volunteered and, secondly, everybody behaved themselves because they knew it was going to be published every three months. (…) there's actually a working model of how to solve this issue in Scotland a the present moment and why doesn't everybody just adopt it?[40]

Scottish MPs got off relatively lightly.[41] Home furnishings and second home allowances, Michael Connarty's £250 alarm clock, Angus MacNeil's chocolate bars, John Reid's armchair and sofa, Angus Robertson's home cinema system and Alex Salmond's London food bills (while Westminster was not sitting) could simply not compete. Even for the *Daily Telegraph*, they were among the also rans. Except, of course, for Michael Martin. And for Jim Devine, the successor to Robin Cook. His was one of the more bizarre cases, involving heavy duty shelving in the basement of a local pub and wiring his London flat by non-taxpaying cowboys.[42] Deselected for next year's general election, Devine decided, in contrast to Ian Gibson in Norwich, to hang on to his mandate until polling day.

---

[39] Populus, 'The Times Scotland Poll – Anniversary of Devolution', *The Times*, May 2009 <www.populuslimited.com/the-times-the-times-scotland-poll-anniversary-of-devolution-may-2009-030509.html>.

[40] Angus MacLeod, 'Adopt Scottish expenses reform, Salmond urges', *The Times*, 29 April 2009.

[41] Torcuil Crichton, 'Dodgy deals have taken less of a toll north of the border', *The Herald*, 23 May 2009.

[42] Severin Carrell, 'Labour MP Jim Devine fights for career in expenses controversy', *The Guardian*, 3 June 2009.

DISASTER FOR LABOUR AT THE POLLS

The expenses fiasco cast a long shadow over the local elections in England and the Euro elections in early June.[43] The Tories gained a resounding victory; Labour was humiliated at the polls. The BNP made alarming gains and won two seats in the European Parliament; UKIP could claim a political breakthrough as it pushed Labour into third place. In Scotland, the picture was not quite as grim. UKIP and BNP did not make major inroads. But it was not an uplifting story for Labour there, either:

> The people have spoken, not with one voice, but in a grumbling cacophony of dissent and discontent which saw Labour with its lowest share of the vote since the end of the First World War, the SNP nine points above Labour in Scotland, the Conservatives beating Labour in Wales, the UK Independence Party pushing Labour into thirds place and the BNP talking two seats in the north of England.[44]

In Scotland, the SNP ended up with two seats, as did Labour (but their poll results had reversed), the Lib Dems won one seat, as did the Tories (who lost a seat – but could blame that on the fact that Scotland now returned only six instead of the previous seven MEPs to Strasbourg). The Nationalists claimed they were now on course to destroy Labour at the next general election. Alex Salmond hailed the 'historic' victory and said his party could send 27 MPs to Westminster – up from six at present. With 29.1% overall, the SNP came top in 22 of the 32 council regions. Labour managed 20.8% – with local results indicating potential defeats in the general election of Alistair Darling in Edinburgh South West and Jim Murphy, the Scottish Secretary, in East Renfrewshire. Labour pointed out that the low turn-out of 28.6% did not allow for a projection of the outcome of a general election, or a Scottish Parliament election.[45]

Again, there were calls for Brown's resignation, from (among others) Work and Pensions Secretary James Purnell (who himself resigned) but in the end, as on previous occasions, though 'pushed to the edge of collapse by cabinet resignations, a botched government reshuffle, disastrous election results and demands from people who were once his closest colleagues that he should quit to save the Labour party', Brown

---

[43] Andrew Grice, 'An election dominated by just one issue: expenses', *The Independent*, 4 June 2009.

[44] 'A party in tatters' (Leader), *The Herald*, 9 June 2009.

[45] Severin Carrell, 'Salmond celebrates as Labour points to turnout', *The Guardian*, 9 June 2009.

survived again, having 'fought off' the 'half- hearted attempted coup'[46] – another 'great escape'.[47]

On to the Norwich by-election in July. Won by Chloe Smith, a young Tory hopeful, with a swing of 16.4%, this was another 'calamitous' result for Brown – 'further evidence that Labour is staring general election defeat in the face.'[48] Unsurprisingly, the by-election defeat just before the summer holidays was not exactly a tonic for the Labour troops, and another round of infighting was on the cards, led by the former home secretary Charles Clarke's attack on the way Labour had dealt with the expenses issue. He had lambasted the party's disciplinary panel (or 'star chamber') as a 'kangaroo court' before; now, he said, this unfair treatment of MPs by the party had led to a 'corruscating verdict' by the voters.[49]

DEVOLUTION ANNIVERSARY

Against the backdrop of the recession and of the expenses shenanigans at Westminster, Holyrood could look back on ten years of devolution. It has been, overall, a success story. There may have been 'ups and downs', as Henry McLeish observed, but it has created a 'new sense of national purpose' and is an 'enormous achievement';[50] the Parliament has actually become so embedded and familiar that is sometimes difficult to remember a time when it was not there. It is also difficult, as Joyce McMillan said on the same BBC programme, to remember how 'extremely radical' the mere idea of a Scottish Parliament had been less than 20 years ago.

We were also reminded, as Holyrood's birthday coincided with the thirtieth anniversary of the first Devolution referendum and Margaret Thatcher's arrival at No 10 Downing Street, of the distance travelled since.[51] None more so than the Tories. In a BBC documentary, David Cameron admitted that they had been wrong to oppose devolution:

[46] Jonathan Oliver, Isabel Oakeshott and Marie Woolf, 'Night of the blunt knives', *The Sunday Times*, 7 June 2009.

[47] Patrick Wintour and Allegra Stratton, 'Brown's great escape', *The Guardian*, 9 June 2009.

[48] John Curtice, 'This is a calamitous result for Brown', *The Independent*, 25 July 2009.

[49] Charles Clarke, 'My party has been injured the most by expenses scandal', *The Independent*, 25 July 2009.

[50] Glenn Campbell (host), *The Big Debate – Devolution Ten Years On*, BBC One Scotland, 1 July 2009.

[51] See David Stewart, *The Path to Devolution and Change: A Political History of Scotland under Thatcher*, London: I.B. Tauris, 2009; David Torrance, *'We in Scotland': Thatcherism in a Cold Climate*, Edinburgh: Birlinn, 2009.

I think you can argue that the principled position, of arguing that devolution within a unitary state is extremely difficult and there are all sorts of problems it brings, and those problems are there. But I think where we went wrong was we should have spent more time in government thinking, how do we give legitimate help to those people within our United Kingdom who want to have a greater expression of self-government?[52]

He reaffirmed what he had already said at the Scottish Tory conference: that he would respect the right of the Scottish Parliament to rule on domestic matters in Scotland if he became prime minister.[53] And Annabel Goldie urged Scottish voters: 'Judge us on today, not perceived echoes of the past.'[54]

Hamish Macdonell chronicled, blow by blow, the 'evolution of devolution', from the heady days of 1999 to the frustrations of the building project, disappointment with the performance of the newly-elected parliamentarians, shock and sadness over the death of Donald Dewar and Enric Miralles, the architects of devolution, disillusionment when a First Minister and a party leader were forced to step down by scandals. But he also described the way the Parliament settled down and grew in stature, leading the way on legislation like free care for the elderly, student tuition fees and the ban of smoking in public places, overhauling criminal and civil justice, initiating land reform and introducing a new electoral system for local government.[55] Academic assessment was differentiated – the Holyrood experience was, on the whole, positive, but also characterised by shortcomings. It compared the divergence of public policy north and south of the border. Question marks were put behind the 'new politics' promised at the start of the new institutions and the degree of actual cross-party cooperation, even under a minority administration.[56]

Devolution has addressed the lack of legitimacy felt in the pre-devolution years. The transition was remarkably smooth, aided no doubt by economic growth and substantial increases, year on year, to the Scottish block grant. Also, for the first eight years of Devolution, the administations in Edinburgh and London were both led by the same

---

[52] Brian Taylor, *Holyrood and the Search for Scotland's Soul*, BBC One Scotland, 28 June 2009.

[53] Hamish Macdonell, 'Cameron: Tory party will respect Scots if it wins power', *The Scotsman*, 11 May 2009.

[54] Ian Swanson, 'Scottish Tory leader tries to lay ghost of Thatcher', *Edinburgh Evening News*, 14 May 2009.

[55] Hamish Macdonell, *Uncharted Territory: The story of Scottish devolution, 1999-2009*, London: Politico's, 2009.

[56] Charlie Jeffery and James Mitchell (eds), *The Scottish Parliament, 1999-2009: The First Decade*, Edinburgh: Luath Press/Hansard Society, 2009.

party. James Mitchell understands Scottish devolution 'as an important development in a continuous process of challenges to and defence of existing institutions. Its advocates,' he says:

> have, understandably, emphasised its novel features but, inevitably, many features reflect institutional arrangements before devolution. This is not to suggest that nothing has changed. Scottish devolution has transformed Scottish politics in significant ways. Changes affecting representation – the electoral system, number of parliamentarians and opportunities for greater participation – have been most significant. (…) Devolution's most significant impact has been in terms of representative democracy.[57]

An ICM poll for BBC Scotland, carried out to mark the first decade of devolution, broadly supported this picture. 41% responded that devolution was a good thing, only 9% said it was a bad thing, while 46% said they had not noticed a difference. When asked about policy areas, 33% thought that the health service in Scotland had improved, 9% found it had deteriorated, and 52% saw no change; 29% thought that standards in Scotland's schools had gone up, 12% believed that standards had slipped, and 41% thought standards had remained the same.[58]

On the question of Scotland's clout in the UK, 55% of Scots reckon devolution has given Scotland a stronger voice, while 9% saw Scotland's position weakened; for 34%, devolution has made no difference.[59] While 63% still want Westminster to retain control over defence and foreign policy matters, when asked who should make most of the decisions for Scotland about other reserved matters, the result is markedly different: asked on income tax, 62% said the Scottish Government, only 34% said the UK Government. The question of who should have responsibility for old age pensions received a similar response, with 65% saying it should be devolved to Holyrood, but only 32% wanting control retained at Westminster. When it came to devolved matters, the margins became even bigger. 78% backed the Scottish Government making the big decisions over the NHS in Scotland, with 19% believing health policy should be decided by Westminster.

Both the First Minister and the Secretary of State for Scotland welcomed the BBC poll. Alex Salmond claimed:

---

[57] James Mitchell, *Devolution in the UK*, Manchester: Manchester University Press, 2009, p.141.

[58] 'Devolution backed by 41% of Scots', *BBC News Scotland*, 28 June 2009, <news.bbc.co.uk/1/hi/scotland/8123114.stm>.

[59] Brian Taylor, 'Scotland "now has stronger voice"', *BBC News Scotland*, 29 June 2009, <news.bbc.co.uk/1/hi/scotland/8123346.stm>.

> The poll as a whole is extremely good news for those who believe in the parliament, and those who want to see the parliament grow in influence and regard. It is quite clear the parliament is regarded as a success by the people, and it is also clear that people are getting increasingly ambitious to see their parliament as a powerhouse parliament for the people and much less as a pocket money parliament for Westminster.[60]

As Jim Murphy also said that the Parliament should have more powers, this reflected the state of play.

With not just one, but two devolution review processes on the go – the SNP's 'National Conversation', and the Calman Commission, established by the Scottish Parliament with the votes of Labour, Tories and Lib Dems – the days of the present model of Devolution seem numbered.[61] The question now is whether an enhanced model of devolution or the SNP's aspiration of an independent Scotland will replace the present 'settlement'.

CALMAN REPORT

The Calman Commission into Scottish devolution, established by the Parliament in December 2007 to review devolution in Scotland, had begun its work under the chairmanship of Sir Kenneth Calman in April 2008. An interim report in December was dismissed by the SNP as a 'constitutional mouse'. It ruled out 'full fiscal autonomy' as it was, in Calman's words, 'inconsistent with the Union'.[62] At a seminar of the Institute of Governance at Edinburgh University, Calman defended the report, which had been widely criticised as too tame, saying that apart from full fiscal autonomy nothing was ruled out, and the final report could surprise critics with a range of radical proposals.

When the final report was published in June, it recommended handing Edinburgh greater control over income tax and other areas, including stamp duty, land tax, airgun legislation, powers over drink-driving and speed limits and the running of the Scottish elections. The Calman Commission called for a new Scottish-set tax, which would see the UK

---

[60] 'Backing for more Holyrood powers', *BBC News Scotland*, 29 June 2009, <news.bbc. co.uk/1/hi/scotland/8124129.stm>.

[61] Charlie Jeffery, 'Devolution: What's Wrong with the Status Quo?', *Scottish Affairs*, No.68 (Summer 2009), pp.21-35

[62] 'Full Scots fiscal power ruled out', *BBC News Scotland*, 2 December 2008, <news.bbc. co.uk/1/hi/scotland/7759382.stm>.

Treasury deduct 10p from standard and upper rates of income tax in Scotland, accompanied by a cut in the block grant Holyrood gets from the UK Government. Holyrood would then have to decide whether to levy the full 10p, allowing the amount of money Scotland received to stay the same, or to cut the tax rate, meaning a possible reduction in public services.

> The report's findings on finance and taxation are tentative and complex and the proposals on powers are hesitant and modest but that should not surprise anyone. It should not disguise the fact that Calman has moved the argument on and provided a more developed platform for the Unionist case: a new settlement founded on a new understanding of Britain's unwritten constitution. (…) Calman has broken the log jam, by proposing partial fiscal responsibility and by proposing the transfer of more powers from Westminster. A form of federalism is now taking shape.[63]

While the BBC devolution poll found that 56% of Scots wanted a referendum before Holyrood was handed any further tax powers, Jim Murphy said it would not be necessary as 'the tax power is already established at a variable rate within the Scottish Parliament.'[64]

Labour, the Liberal Democrats and the Tories welcomed the report, but none of the parties has made any firm commitment yet to implement its recommendations. Indeed, as John Cairney has noted:

> The irony is that the party most critical of the report is also the keenest to see some of it implemented immediately. The SNP is particularly opposed to its fiscal measures, but would like further devolution powers.[65]

MEGRAHI: A DIFFICULT DECISION

If the expenses scandal at Westminster dominated May and June, the one big story of this summer was Kenny MacAskill's decision to release the convicted Lockerbie bomber Abdelbaset Ali Mohmed al Megrahi

---

[63] Brown and McLeish, p.175.

[64] 'Backing for more Holyrood powers', *BBC News Scotland*, 29 June 2009, <news.bbc.co.uk/1/hi/scotland/8124129.stm>.

[65] John Cairney, 'Scotland', *Monitor*, 43 (London: Constitution Unit), September 2009, p.4.

from Greenock Prison on compassionate grounds.[66] Eight years into his 27-year sentence for blowing up Pan Am Flight 103 over Lockerbie on 21 December 1988, the worst terrorist atrocity ever in Scotland with 270 casualties (ten of them from Lockerbie, killed by the impact of the debris), Megrahi, diagnosed with terminal prostrate cancer, was given less than three months to live and was therefore set free by the Scottish Justice Secretary, and welcomed triumphantly in Tripoli, Saltires waving and all.[67]

Was MacAskill's the right decision? It caused immediate outrage. The tabloids ran riot. Polls indicated that only a minority in Scotland supported it. Hillary Clinton and Barack Obama had tried to influence the Scottish government to keep al Megrahi in Scotland. And Gordon Brown kept shtum. The American families of the victims felt deceived. Had MacAskill not assured them that there would be no prisoner transfer? They had interpreted that as an assurance that Megrahi would remain in Scotland. What he had not told them was that he would release Megrahi on compassionate grounds.

But the outrage, fuelled by the image of Saltires welcoming Megrahi and the media reports about it, faded after a few days, and more rational judgement seemed to prevail. Would it really have been a good idea to let Megrahi die in a Scottish prison and thus make him a martyr in the Arab world? The UK government certainly did not think so.[68] This left the opposition parties who had censured the decision at a specially convened meeting of the Parliament with a majority of 73 to 50, out of touch with a sizeable part of public opinion. When even Gordon Brown came out with his statement that he 'respected' the decision, respected that it was the Scottish justice secretary's quasi-judicial decision to make, and that he respected the motives behind the decision (and that there was 'no deal, no conspiracy' to exchange Megrahi for Libyan oil guarantees), Iain Gray's blunt opposition began to ring hollow. And, again, coordination between Labour in Edinburgh and London seemed totally absent. As was, obviously, consultation and cooperation between the London and Edinburgh governments – even in this serious decision with repercussions far beyond Scotland and the UK.

While the debate about whether the medical advise was correct and authoritative will be one of the issues on the agenda of the Scottish Parliament's justice committee inquiry into MacAskill's handling of the case, the discussions about Megrahi's life expectation and what would happen if he exceeded the three months given him by the doctors

---

[66] Under Scots law, any prisoner with a terminal illness can apply for compassionate release – it is then for the Justice Secretary to decide in a quasi-judicial role.

[67] David Maddox, 'Hero's welcome is nightmare for SNP', *The Scotsman*, 21 August 2009.

[68] Robbie Dinwoodie and Michael Settle, 'Brown: Don't let Megrahi die inside a Scots prison', *The Herald*, 2 September 2009.

has been, frankly, pretty unpleasant and ghoulish. But there remain important questions. Why compassionate release and not a prisoner transfer? Yes, the SNP government had always criticised the prisoner transfer agreement between the UK and Libya. But it would have meant that Megrahi would have gone home as a prisoner, not a free man. According to Sir Christopher Meyer, the UK ambassador to Washington at the time of the Lockerbie trial, the US had the 'clear political and diplomatic understanding' that Megrahi would serve his full sentence in a Scottish prison.[69]

Was it not astonishing that, while Justice Secretary Kenny MacAskill put his trust in the Scottish justice system on the record in Parliament and said that he is convinced that Megrahi was rightly convicted and guilty of the heinous crime he was accused of, MacAskill's party colleague Christine Grahame MSP, who had repeatedly visited Megrahi in prison, wrote that Megrahi was innocent and the victim of a politically-driven mis-trial?[70] And, finally, was there any link between compassionate release and the dropping of the appeal? May the US and the UK governments not have been quite happy, despite their public utterances, with this 'elegant' solution: the combination of compassionate release and the abandoned appeal? Christine Grahame MSP was adamant that Megrahi was 'pressured' to drop the appeal;[71] she repeated a few weeks later that she had the 'strong impression' that 'bigger political powers' had persuaded Megrahi to give up his appeal, ensuring that there would be no investigation into the trial.[72] After all, the truth about the Lockerbie bomb may be found closer to Damascus and Tehran than Tripoli.[73]

Given the doubts about the investigation, the prosecution and the conviction, is it enough for Kenny MacAskill to say the Scottish government would cooperate with any inquiry into the Megrahi trial? As the appeal was accepted, is there not sufficient suspicion that a miscarriage of justice could have taken place? Should a Scottish justice secretary not be more proactive in order to safeguard the integrity of Scottish justice? Should he not actually set up a public inquiry?[74] The

---

[69] Michael Settle, 'America had a "clear understanding" that Megrahi would stay in Scotland', The Herald, 4 September 2009.

[70] Christine Graham, 'Al-Megrahi is home. And he is innocent.', Independent on Sunday, 23 August 2009.

[71] Lucy Adams, 'Megrahi was pressured to drop appeal, claims MSP', The Herald, 15 August 2009.

[72] Martin Williams, 'Anger as MacAskill releases record number of killers early', The Herald, 28 September 2009.

[73] Robert Fisk, 'For the truth, look to Tehran and Damascus – not Tripoli', The Independent, 22 August 2009.

[74] 'Lockerbie inquiry more urgent than ever as Salmond clouds issue' (Leader), The Scotsman, 19 August 2009.

justice committee inquiry into the handling of the release will not be able to look at the big issues.[75] They will concentrate on MacAskill's role, e.g. why he thought it necessary to visit Megrahi in person – did he do the same when he released three Scottish murderers on compassionate grounds?[76]

Overall, though, the Scottish government, Kenny MacAskill and the SNP seemed to gain in respect as the days passed, for having made and staunchly defended a difficult decision. Even if there still are dissenting voices, this 'defining moment not just for Kenny MacAskill but for the SNP government'[77] has shown that the SNP is capable of making difficult decisions. James Mitchell explained the September poll results which saw the SNP comfortably in the lead both for Holyrood and for Westminster as partly caused by the Megrahi affair. Labour, he argued, had 'badly misjudged' public feeling on the Megrahi release:

> When reason and emotion clash reason will win so long as the rational response is articulated clearly, coolly and consistently and I think that's what the Scottish Government did and as this decision was explained, I think the public moved behind the SNP.[78]

LEGISLATIVE PROGRAMME

At the beginning of September, Alex Salmond introduced his government's draft legislative programme. It comprises thirteen bills, ranging from action on alcohol abuse to measures for wildlife protection. After the last round, the Budget Bill, against the background of looming cuts in public expenditure, will be a focal point. After all, it is

> [t]he government's most important piece of legislation, setting out overall spending priorities for the year ahead and pushing the SNP's main goal of economic recovery and

---

[75] Brian Currie, 'Megrahi inquiry will not question release', *The Herald*, 30 September 2009.

[76] Martin Williams, 'Anger as MacAskill releases record number of killers early', *The Herald*, 28 September 2009.

[77] Glenn Campbell, *BBC Newsnight Scotland*, 20 August 2009.

[78] 'New poll gives SNP strong lead in UK election', *Holyrood Magazine*, 14 September 2009.

growth. Unless this bill is passed, the government of the day cannot function.[79]

Passed only on the second go last February and triggering the possibility of the fall of the SNP government, will John Swinney try to avoid such parliamentary dramatics this time round?

A compromise seems possible on the proposed Alcohol Bill, as Labour has signalled agreement to its plans for minimum pricing,[80] although there could still be legal challenges. Health Secretary Nicola Sturgeon quotes the figure of £2.25bn – the annual cost of Scotland's alcohol problem in 'extra services and lost productivity'. Therefore, she argues, radical action is needed. Minimum pricing has the support of the UK chief medical officers, and a study by scientists at Sheffield University suggests that minimum pricing and a clampdown on 'irresponsible drinks promotions' would 'lead to a huge reduction in alcohol-related illnesses and a drop in deaths of up to 370 a year.'[81]

At an estimated cost of up to £2.3bn, the new Forth road bridge is easily the biggest single infrastructure project in Scotland for the present generation. It is to 'replace' the existing road bridge which, aged 45, has problems with deterioration which could lead, first, to weight restrictions and, ultimately, to closure. The bridge, as Andrew Black reminds us, 'is hugely important to Scotland's economy – the government says economic output could fall by about £1bn, and see a loss of about 3,200 jobs without an alternative crossing.'[82] But there is also the issue of financing the project. The British government has offered £1bn, but the Scottish government insists on the right to borrow cash from future budgets.

The new Housing Bill would protect all new-supply social housing from the right to buy. It is supposed to complement the government's plan to spend £1.5bn on house building over three years. An overhaul of the Children's Hearing system is to establish the Scottish Children's Hearings Tribunal, a new national body to oversee its operation. The bill was originally announced for last year's legislative programme, but some present members of Children's panels threatened to resign if the bill went through, and opposition parties criticised it as not fully thought

[79] Andrew Black, 'At a glance – legislative programme', BBC News Scotland, 3 September 2009, <news.bbc.co.uk/1/hi/scotland/8235604.stm>.

[80] Jason Allardyce, 'Labour supports SNP bid to call time on cheap booze', The Sunday Times, 22 March 2009.

[81] Iain Harrison, 'Study supports SNP booze plan', The Sunday Post, 27 September 2009.

[82] Andrew Black, 'At a glance – legislative programme', BBC News Scotland, 3 September 2009, <news.bbc.co.uk/1/hi/scotland/8235604.stm>.

through. The Patient's Rights Bill would give a 12-week waiting time guarantee for in-patients and those waiting to be treated as day-cases. The bill would also set up 'patients' rights officers' for health board areas. On the other hand, it would also clarify the patients' responsibilities (like keeping appointments). It remains to be seen whether the Lib Dems are still of the opinion, as voiced by their former leader Nicol Stephen when it was first mooted, that it could 'create a lawyer by every bedside'.[83]

Controversy can be expected when the Crofting Bill is introduced to Parliament. The main aim of the legislation is to reverse the population downturn in rural and island communities. Absenteeism, inactivity and neglect are at the core of the crofting problem. The legislation is supposed to toughen existing rules requiring crofters to live on or near the croft and work the land. And it wants to prevent crofts from being sold at market prices to outsiders (who might then turn it into a holiday home), while local people cannot afford to buy a croft (or its lease). Western Isles Council and the Scottish Crofting Foundation have articulated reservations about the bill. The Debt and Family Homes Bill is to balance out the interests of creditors and debtors and prevent bankrupt people from automatically becoming homeless. The Debtor Protection Bill would give increased protection to those facing repossession or bankruptcy.

The Wildlife and Environment Bill aims at modernising game laws, deer management, regulation on non-native species, badger protection, and a new accreditation scheme for those who set snares. The Historic Environment Bill would amend existing legislation, enabling ministers to declare a building immune from listing for five years, and would provide better partnership between councils and developers. And the Legal Services Bill would reform the regulatory framework for solicitors, allowing them to secure external investment and to enter business relationships with non-solicitors.

Last, but certainly not least, there is the Referendum Bill, supposed to set out the parameters for 'a fair and democratic referendum' on independence. Alex Salmond has repeatedly offered a multi-option referendum – the Lib Dems' favoured model – which could offer a choice between the status quo, the proposals following the recommendations of the Calman Commission for enhanced devolution, and Scottish independence.

---

[83] *Ibid.*

MAKING PROGRESS

In September, Education Secretary Fiona Hyslop announced legislaton to put a legal cap on Primary One class sizes of 25.[84] It was greeted with derision by the opposition parties. After all, the SNP had pledged to reduce class sizes for P1, 2 and 3 to 18 in the course of this Parliament. 'It all adds up to one thing – the SNP has misled parents and, as with the pledge to dump student debt, was only interested in conning the electorate,' was Tory education spokeswoman Liz Smith's verdict.[85] The SNP had admitted defeat over its flagship education policy, contended Lib Dem MSP Margaret Smith: 'SNP ministers have failed to deliver the legislation, the funding, or the teachers for councils to reduce class sizes across Scotland in line with this pledge. It is another example of the SNP centralising the policy but localising the blame.'[86]

Shortly after, Fiona Hyslop announced that 14 new schools would be built, at the cost of £1.25 bn. These were the first new schools to be built since the SNP came into office in 2007. And they would only be finished by 2013, well into the next parliamentary term. Also, there were doubts over he role which the controversial Scottish Futures Trust would play in the building of them. The government was only prepared to say that it would play a role in 'project management'. Was this really, as the cabinet secretary claimed at the launch, matching Labour's spending commitments on schools 'brick by brick'? Iain Gray pointed out that his party had pledged 100 new schools to be built, had it won the election in 2007. He called the announcement 'far too little and far too late'; it showed 'the complete failure of the Scottish Futures Trust'.[87] Or, as an editorial put it in July when the school building plans were first announced, another SNP promise the party 'has spectacularly failed to live up to.'[88]

Also in September, Lindsay Paterson challenged Fiona Hyslop over the new 'Curriculum for Excellence', which he called 'vague' and 'confused', and 'incapable of providing clear guidance'; he questioned the apparent belief that the new curriculum was 'the answer to almost everything – low attainment, misbehaving pupils, economic regeneration, the alleged

---

[84] Tom Peterkin, 'SNP to "abandon" key pledge on class sizes', *The Scotsman*, 23 September 2009.

[85] 'Primary 1 class size to be capped', *BBC News Scotland*, 23 September 2009, <news.bbc. co.uk/1/hi/scotland/8269996.stm>.

[86] *Ibid.*

[87] David Maddox, 'SNP chalk up 14 new schools – but they won't be finished until 2013', *The Scotsman*, 29 September 2009.

[88] 'The SNP has failed to live up to its promise' (Leader), *Edinburgh Evening News*, 18 June 2009.

need to make education more relevant to life.'[89] The curriculum was due to be introduced this autumn, but was delayed by twelve months over fears that it was not ready to be implemented.[90] Compared to England, Paterson had argued in a talk at a Scottish Tory party conference on education, also in September, that in mathematics, science and reading, Scotland's attainment rates, 'mediocre by international standards', had 'actually got worse' in the past decade or so.[91] In July, the Education Secretary had come under fire for 'failing to deliver on key promises to Scotland's pupils', when it became known that only three of Scotland's 32 councils had formally agreed to offer every pupil two hours per week of physical exercise.[92] Many of the SNP's education pledges were totally unrealistic in the first place, be it the cancelling of student debt or class-size targets. Fiona Hyslop was lumbered with them, so the blame about climb-downs and U-turns should not be hers alone to bear. But that will not stop the opposition to drive home the point that key manifesto pledges of he SNP have not been kept.

Throughout the year, Justice Secretary Kenny MacAskill has been under pressure. First, when he preferred a junket to Canada for a Burns Supper to being present at the Knife Crime Summit at Holyrood; then for ignoring a parliamentary vote to set up a community court in Glasgow. In March, he had to drop the blanket ban on under-21s buying drink at off-sales. Then his authority was challenged over absconded violent prisoners from open prisons. He only escaped a confidence vote because of Alex Salmond's threat to resign. Again, in the censure vote over the handling of the Megrahi release, the opposition eschewed a no confidence vote.

Health Secretary Nicola Sturgeon has been credited for her 'measured and cautious' handling of the swine flu epidemic, but the 'softly-softly' approach is, of course, only laudable, as long as it is seen as an adequate tackling of the problem;[93] and she has come under fire for the alarming rise of casualties among Scots from C Diff. In March, Environment Minister Roseanna Cunningham announced in Parliament that the proposal for the leasing of up to 25% of Scottish forests to raise £200m would be scrapped.

[89] Lindsay Paterson, 'Grand aims can't provide clear guidance', *The Scotsman*, 21 September 2009.

[90] Fiona MacLeod, 'Hyslop facing revolt over schools reform', *The Scotsman*, 21 September 2009; see also Fiona MacLeod, 'Confusion to reign in Scottish classrooms over radical reforms', *The Scotsman*, 29 May 2009.

[91] Lindsay Paterson, 'Literacy and Numeracy: What are they and what are they for?', 8 September 2009, <www.scottishconservatives.com/rts/conference/conference_speeches/lindsay_paterson.aspx>.

[92] Fiona MacLeod, 'Only three Scottish councils giving pupils two hours of PE every week', *The Scotsman*, 28 July 2009.

[93] Campbell Gunn, 'Clock is ticking on softly-softly flu plan', *The Sunday Post*, 26 July 2009.

At the same time, Cabinet Secretary Richard Lochhead was criticised by farmers for 'failing to deliver' on government pledges to the rural sector; they voiced concerns about the implementation of the Scottish Rural Development Programme.[94]

When John Swinney introduced the outline of his Budget in September, the biggest bombshell it contained was the scrapping of the Glasgow Airport Rail Link (GARL), despite the fact that Transport Minister Stewart Stevenson had stated only eight weeks earlier: 'Ministers are committed to the delivery of the Glasgow Airport Rail Link and any reports to the contrary are inaccurate.'[95] Given the government's priorities for economic growth, Bernard Ponsonby found the decision 'simply baffling'.[96] It is a further instance of the fact that the present (as the former) government seems to have no cohesive transport policy – or one for every day in the week... Apparently, the Borders rail line is still safe – even if suffering further delays.[97] Swinney was also criticised for axing the housing budget. Shelter Scotland called upon the MSPs to reverse the decision.[98] Culture Minister Michael Russell is under fire from the artistic community and from opposition parties for the £3.3 million costs involved in setting up Creative Scotland (the new arts body merging the Scottish Arts Council and Scottish Screen). Tory culture spokesman Ted Brocklebank MSP said: 'Despite the rhetoric the minister has yet to convince the creative sector that the botched delivery of Creative Scotland bodes well for the future of the arts in Scotland.'[99] And, of course, back in February, the plan to replace the council tax with a Local Income Tax had been shelved.

For the opposition parties, all this amounts to a litany of broken promises. In its defence, the government resorts to the rhetoric of 'making progress'; it also likes to roll out the concordat with the local authorities as a universal explanation and points at Westminster cuts. Moreover, a spokesman for the First Minister claimed his government had already delivered half their manifesto commitments, from the freezing of the council tax and cutting business rates to abolishing bridge tolls, saving A&E units, and scrapping tuition fees. He added that free prescriptions were being phased in and 1000 extra police officers were

[94] Dan Buglass, 'Farmers angry over broken SNP promises', *The Scotsman*, 27 March 2009.

[95] Brian Currie and Stewart Paterson, 'Stevenson vows ministers are committed to airport rail link', *The Herald*, 22 July 2009.

[96] 'Politics Now', STV, 17 September 2009.

[97] Alastair Dalton, 'Train to Borders is delayed – again', *The Scotsman*, 31 March 2009.

[98] Graeme Brown, 'Scottish Government is failing to give lead on social housing', *The Scotsman*, 19 September 2009.

[99] 'Creative Scotland formation criticised as £3.3m cost announced', *Holyrood Magazine*, 3 April 2009.

also being delivered.[100] 'Broken promises' vs 'making good progress' – this will clearly be one of the major battlegrounds for the election contests to come.

GLASGOW NORTH BY-ELECTION

When Michael Martin announced that he would step down as Speaker on 21 June and retire as MP for Glasgow North East, the by-election necessitated was widely seen as an opportunity for the SNP to snatch another traditional Labour stronghold, despite the lead of more than 10,000 votes Martin had in 2005 over his SNP competitor.[101] But then a Glasgow East in reverse scenario seemed to unfold. Instead of Labour, now the SNP had a chaotic selection process, ending up with their 'fourth choice' candidate David Kerr, who only a week before his nomination had been rejected by the constituency party.[102] Questions were also raised about his 'playing down' of sectarianism, his 'sneering' at Glasgow Caledonia University, his membership of Opus Dei, and about 'brandishing a gun' outside a supermarket in Springburn.[103] While, this time round, Labour managed to smoothly install its local candidate William Bain, a law lecturer and Constituency Labour Party secretary. There was no quick call of the election, despite efforts by the SNP to bring the contest forward. It is now expected for November.

SNP hopes to take the seat took another blow when Finance Secretary John Swinney announced in Parliament that the Glasgow Air Rail Link was to be scrapped. The Labour reaction, in Glasgow and in the Scottish Parliament, that this was 'a dagger in the heart of Glasgow'[104] may have been over the top, given all the other capital investment programmes for Glasgow and the west of Scotland, but the decision will certainly not enhance the SNP's chances of winning the by-election. The Nationalists will try to use the school closures across Glasgow as a weapon in the

---

[100] Mark Aitken, 'SNP claims to have delivered on more than half election manifesto', *Sunday Mail*, 3 May 2009.

[101] Hamish Macdonell and David Maddox, 'Nationalists poised to break Labour's grip on Glasgow North East seat', *The Scotsman*, 20 May 2009.

[102] David Maddox, '"Stitch-up" as fourth-choice candidate to fight for seat', *The Scotsman*, 17 July 2009.

[103] David Maddox, 'SNP poll candidate is attacked for "playing down" sectarianism', *The Scotsman*, 18 July 2009; Tom Gordon, 'SNP's Glasgow candidate derides city university', *Sunday Herald*, 19 July 2009; Eddie Barnes, 'SNP candidate a proud member of Opus Dei', *Scotland on Sunday*, 19 July 2009; Tom Gordon, 'Why the SNP's Glasgow candidate pulled a gun in a public carpark', *Sunday Herald*, 26 July 2009.

[104] Brian Currie, Robbie Dinwoodie, Damien Henderson and Gerry Braiden, 'Outrage as Swinney swings his budget axe on Glasgow', *The Herald*, 17 September 2009.

campaign, but Labour will try to divert that criticism from the Labour-led council to the SNP government at Holyrood.[105]

It remains to be seen whether the Glasgow hero John 'Smeato' Smeaton, the former airport baggage handler who tackled the suicide bombers in July 2007, can play the role of 'joker'. He has entered the race as an independent candidate supported by the Jury Team. He may have struggled to explain the policies of his backers (like leaving the EU) when he held his first press conference,[106] but he also impressed:

> His pitch is that he constituency in question has suffered from decades of neglect from subsequent Labour administrations, that its elected representatives have totally flunked the mandate given to them by the electors to get its problems sorted out. (...) For all that 'inward investment' and 'social inclusion' patter, Springburn is an infinitely worse place to live now than it was in the early 1960s, its heart ripped out by a motorway, municipal vandalism, sub-standard council housing and unemployment, all brought to you by the dead hand of Labour.[107]

'How refreshing it would be,' commented *Scotland on Sunday*, 'if a genuine working-class hero not only succeeded in taking a place in the corridors of power but also managed to maintain a strict adherence to his principles.'[108]

WILL THERE BE A REFERENDUM?

Apart from the general election, the story of 2010 could be an autumn referendum on independence. But will the SNP find a majority in the Scottish Parliament to hold it? Perhaps not.

Labour's position – about the fifth in the past few years – now seems to be: not now, in the middle of a recession, not with the question outlined in the National Conversation but, in principle, yes, there should and will be a referendum in due time. Iain Gray has said: 'I would favour a

---

[105] David Maddox, 'SNP to play "trump card" of school closures in battle for Martin's seat', *The Scotsman*, 23 May 2009.

[106] David Maddox, 'Tackling terror easier than fielding questions for wannabe MP Smeaton', *The Scotsman*, 26 September 2009.

[107] Joanna Blythman, 'Smeato MP represents the people politics forgot', *Sunday Herald*, 27 September 2009.

[108] 'Wha's like us... John Smeaton' (Leader), *Scotland on Sunday*, 27 September 2009.

referendum only with a straight question, a straight yes/no question.'[109] The party is still haunted by Wendy Alexander's 'Bring it on!' of May 2008, when it wanted to bring the referendum legislation forward so that it could be held in 2009, well clear of the next Scottish election in 2011.

The Liberal Democrats heard calls for a referendum at their Bournemouth conference. In March, Tavish Scott had not ruled out a referendum; now, in September, he stated categorically: the Lib Dems do not support independence, and they do not support an independence referendum. For Nick Clegg, the referendum is a 'monumental distraction'. But the newly-elected MEP George Lyon called on his party 'to take on the SNP and win the argument.' Eventually, the Lib Dems' chief whip told MSPs to stop talking about a referendum altogether.[110]

The Tories have clearly indicated that they will not consider agreeing to a referendum for 2010 – despite some voices among the party who are in favour of 'calling the SNP's bluff'. That was what Lord Forsyth, former Tory Secretary of State for Scotland, urged Gordon Brown to do: call a referendum on the same day as the general election. He also called on David Cameron to promise a Referendum Bill, adding that the UK Tory leader could 'win a yes vote and save the Union'.[111] Other Tory 'mavericks', like Brian Monteith, are on the same wavelength, most clearly expressed by the commentator Gerald Warner:

> Last week the First Minister solemnly unveiled 30 November, 2010 as the chosen date for Scotland's putative referendum on independence: he might as realistically have pencilled in 30 February. For the great plebiscite is not going to happen, due to the unanimous cowardice of the opposition parties. That will be a huge relief to Salmond. When Holyrood votes the proposal down, he will be able to blame his opponents for preventing the expression of the will of the Scottish people, while secretly relieved that he does not have to hold a referendum he would lose. (...) There has never been a better moment to call Salmond's bluff. The SNP is beginning to experience the public disillusionment that attaches to all political parties in government. (...) The SNP is governing with the mentality of an opposition – because it remains in opposition to the British state. That is hardly a sound basis for governance: this nihilist instinct

---

[109] 'Scots "want an independence vote"', *BBC News Scotland*, 30 June 2009, <news.bbc.co.uk/1/hi/8125041.stm>.

[110] *BBC Newsnight Scotland*, 22 September 2009.

[111] Dave King, 'SNP should concentrate on creating jobs not independence referendum, say Labour', *Daily Record*, 31 August 2009.

will destabilise the United Kingdom unless it is neutralised by a decisive expression of the public will. That can only be achieved by a referendum on independence. Bring it on.[112]

Would a Cameron victory at the general election be a boost for independence? With predictions that the Tories north of the border may fall even short of their aim at returning five or six MPs at the election,[113] would there not be a reprise of the democratic deficit? Or will a 'de-toxified' Tory party implementing at least parts of the Calman proposals finally shed the tag of the 'anti-Scottish party', as John Curtice has suggested? He also pointed out that an SNP minority government relying on the Tories to get their budget approved in the Scottish Parliament may not be hell-bent at destroying relations with a Tory government at Westminster.[114] Iain Macwhirter's vision may sound utopian. But it counters the scenario that a Tory victory next year would necessarily 'boost support for independence', as an SNP poll had found,[115] and it describes the perspective of 'independence in Britain':

> The SNP has recently been talking increasingly in terms of a new 'social union': a new relationship in which Scotland retains the Queen as head of state, shares the network of UK embassies abroad, retains the pound as the Scottish currency, and upholds the values of common UK institutions such as the integrated National Health Service. It could be argued that the SNP has given up on independence, in the old secessionist sense. Perhaps one day we might even see Alex Salmond and David Cameron meeting at Buckingham Palace to unveil to the Queen their blueprint for a new improved federal United Kingdom.[116]

Denying the people their say will be a difficult position for the 'unionist' parties to defend come the 2011 election. A clear majority of Scots want an independence referendum, as the ICM poll for the BBC found. 58% of respondents were in favour of the idea of holding a referendum in 2010 on whether Scotland should become independent, with only 37%

[112] Gerald Warner, 'Now is the time to call Salmond's bluff', *Scotland on Sunday*, 6 September 2009.

[113] Gerri Peev, 'Tories "will have only one new MP in Scotland next year', *The Scotsman*, 3 October 2009.

[114] *BBC Newsnight Scotland*, 22 September 2009.

[115] Tom Gordon, 'Tory victory "would boost support for independence"', *Sunday Herald*, 26 April 2009.

[116] Iain Macwhirter, 'Almost Blue', *Sunday Herald*, 4 October 2009.

against.[117] And that does not take into account that the SNP wants to cut the voting age for the referendum to 16 – a move which was immediately lambasted as 'manipulation' and 'opportunism'.[118]

As that poll further indicated, there is no majority among the Scots for independence. When asked, 'In a referendum on independence for Scotland, how would you vote?', 38% responded that they believed Scotland should become an independent country, with 54% saying they did not believe it should become independent. However, the pollsters also separately asked whether people agreed or disagreed that 'the Scottish Government should negotiate a settlement with the government of the United Kingdom so that Scotland becomes an independent state' – the preferred wording of the Scottish Government for a future referendum. In this case, 42% agreed with the statement, with 50% opposed. Given multiple options, only 28% backed independence, 47% were in favour of remaining in the UK, with the Scottish Parliament able to make some decisions about the level of taxation and government spending in Scotland. A further 22% said Scotland should remain part of the UK, with decisions about the level of taxation and spending in Scotland made by the UK Government.[119]

Clearly, the collapse of the 'arc of prosperity',[120] the £37 bn bail-out of the Scottish banks, and the demise of the Dunfermline Building Society have all had an effect on the debate about independence, a debate which, as Michael Keating argues in a new book, has been 'remarkably low key'. There has not been, he says, 'a serious intellectual analysis on the meaning and implications of independence' – a gap he goes a long way to fill with his book.[121] In the end, he argues that the future of the Union depends more on the politics at the centre than on Scottish nationalism:

> If English elites and English opinion insist that the central constitution remain essentially untouched by devolution then their only real option is to constitute themselves as a new nation state. The end of the United Kingdom is unlikely

[117] 'Scots "want an independence vote"', BBC News Scotland, 30 June 2009, <news.bbc.co.uk/1/hi/8125041.stm>.

[118] Michael Settle, 'Salmond under fire over plans for teenage vote in referendum', The Herald, 21 September 2009; 'Vote age opportunism' (Leader), Scotland on Sunday, 20 September 2009.

[119] 'Scots "want an independence vote"', BBC News Scotland, 30 June 2009, <news.bbc.co.uk/1/hi/8125041.stm>.

[120] For a chilling account of the Icelandic crash, see Roger Boyes, Meltdown Iceland, London: Bloomsbury, 2009. See also Iain Macwhirter, 'The arc of darkness', Sunday Herald, 7 June 2009.

[121] Michael Keating, The Independence of Scotland: Self-government and the Shifting Politics of Union, Oxford: Oxford University Press, 2009, p.vi.

to come about from the secession of Scotland as long as the Scots have other options.[122]

GENERAL ELECTION –
A FOREGONE CONCLUSION?

Gordon Brown and the Labour party wanted their Brighton conference to be the start of the 'fight-back'. A decent, well-received speech gave a flicker of hope. Was that instantly quashed by the *Sun*'s 'sabotage'? On 30 September, it titled 'Labour's lost it' – claiming that 'after 12 long years in power, this Government has lost its way. Now it's lost The Sun's support too.' But, interestingly, while its editorial in England called for a vote for David Cameron's Tories, the Scottish edition stated that 'we need to be convinced' that Cameron 'is serious about Scotland. That he really cares about what happens north of the border.' It was time, it concluded, 'for Cameron to come out from behind the rhetoric and show what he really will do for our nation.'[123]

Scotland is important: if Labour's 'fight-back' were to stand any chance of success, Labour would have to hold on to its Scottish seats. The party would also have to put up a real fight. At the Euro and the English local elections in June the party was, in many instances, not even at the races.[124] Iain Gray may have steadied the good ship Labour, but he has yet to make a lasting impression on the voters. A year after taking over as the leader of Labour in Holyrood, he admitted that many people in Scotland still do not know who he is.[125]

A recent Ipsos MORI poll put the SNP 13 points ahead of Labour for the Holyrood poll and six points ahead for Westminster. The Conservatives polled 15% for Holyrood and 18% for Westminster, and the Lib Dems 15% and 14% respectively.[126] Before its 1997 victory, Labour was way above 50% in the polls; David Cameron's Conservative party is nowhere near that kind of lead. A victory for Cameron is highly probable, but he has not sealed the deal yet. After the Irish Yes in the Lisbon referendum, the divisive question of a Euro-Referendum is back on the Tory agenda, and

---

[122] *Ibid.*, p.179.

[123] 'Labour's lost it... An historic announcement by The Sun' (Leader), *The Sun*, 20 September 2009.

[124] David Hencke, 'Prescott blasts Harriet Harman for Labour's election nightmare', *The Guardian*, 5 June 2009.

[125] David Maddox, 'Scots still don't know who I am, admits Gray', *The Scotsman*, 7 September 2009.

[126] 'New poll gives SNP strong lead in UK election', *Holyrood Magazine*, 14 September 2009.

the Tories' new allies in the European Parliament have already drawn severe criticism.

Ian Bell, no friend of Lord Mandelson's, grudgingly granted that 'his lordship has a point when he says that the next election is up for grabs, despite the public's apparent determination to have anyone-but-Brown.'[127] He points out that, although the Ipsos poll of 29 September had Labour trailing both Conservatives and the Liberal Democrats (maybe their Bournemouth conference was not quite so 'shambolic' as perceived by many media pundits), the Tories at 36% were down 7 points.

For many Scottish voters, it could be decisive how tight the race between Labour and the Tories is. If they thought that a Conservative victory was a given, they might feel more inclined to vote SNP, if they are their first preference. If Labour were in with a chance, voters wavering between Labour and SNP (or the Lib Dems) might come out for Labour to prevent a Tory prime minister. A YouGov poll after Brown's conference address had the Tories at 37%, Labour up six points on 30%, and the Liberal Democrats on 21%.[128] Peter Jones even felt an early election coming on, should Labour close the gap in the course of the autumn conference season.[129]

HOMECOMING 2009

So much has changed in that past year, and yet so much has stayed the same. A year of paradoxes, then.

In the wake of the banking crash we saw the return of Keynesianism, but at the same time, electorally, most of Europe seemed to swing to the right, often rewarding those freemarketeering and deregulating neoliberals whose very ideology had landed us in the mire. While the bulk of the banks now belong to the taxpayer, the 'fat cats' still get away with millions in bonuses, and small businesses are starved of credit.

While Holyrood celebrated its tenth anniversary, the focus was on the misdemeanors of Westminster. Despite ditching key policies, the SNP rides high in the polls, but the continuing *hausse* for the SNP goes hand in hand with a similarly stubborn *baisse* for the constitutional option of independence.

---

[127] Ian Bell, 'Brown sees red as he tries to come off the political ropes', *The Herald*, 30 September 2009.

[128] Andrew Grice, 'Brown fumes at Murdoch's sabotage of his big moment', *The Independent*, 1 October 2009.

[129] Peter Jones,. 'Labour's vital signs revived, election could come soon', *The Scotsman*, 30 September 2009.

People seem to be thoroughly fed up with Gordon Brown and Labour, but there seems to be no wide-spread enthusiasm for David Cameron and the Tories. The Lib Dems have a shambolic conference, making policies on the hoof, but get a boost in the opinion polls shortly after. We are set for an intriguing election year.

Oh yes, and it has been the Year of Homecoming, marking Robert Burns's 250th birthday. It culminated in the Gathering of the Clans in Edinburgh in July and draws to a close with a four-day St Andrew's Day extravaganza. But who would have thought that the abiding image of 'Homecoming 2009' would be Saltires in Tripoli?

Ah well, as the Bard would say, 'the best laid schemes o' mice and men / gang oft agley'.[130] A thought, maybe, that will come to be shared by many a campaigner in the forthcoming elections.

[October 2009]

---

[130] Robert Burns, 'To a Mouse, On Turning Her Up in Her Nest with the Plough', *The Canongate Burns: The Complete Poems and Songs of Robert Burns*, ed. by Andrew Noble and Patrick Scott Hogg, Edinburgh: Canongate, 2001, pp.95-96.

Chapter VII

THE YEAR AT HOLYROOD
2009-2010

The past political year has been full of surprises, and of all kinds of shambles. A Scottish Conservative became First Minister – no, not in Scotland, in Lower Saxony, where David McAllister inherited the job at the head of the Land government when the former incumbent, Christian Wulff, was promoted to the German Presidency. The biggest surprise, and closer to home, was the outcome of the General Election, not necessarily that he vote resulted in a hung parliament at Westminster, but the ease with which David Cameron and Nick Clegg managed to cobble together their coalition between the Liberal Democrats, who had campaigned on an anti-Tory platform, and the Conservatives, with their deep-seated suspicions of the Liberal Democrats. Nobody had expected huge changes in Scotland in the run-up to the Westminster election, but it did come as a surprise that, compared with the result of 2005, not a single seat did change hands. Then, of course, we expected progress on the Independence referendum in Parliament – surely some surprise that it has not even been at the races. And what about the 'wrong' Miliband getting the Labour leadership? Does he indeed 'get Scotland'?

Not as a total surprise came the death of the Scots Makar, Edwin Morgan – after all, he had been diagnosed with terminal prostate cancer back in 1999. Nobody who was there, or watched it on television, will ever forget that 'gallus moment', as Brian Taylor called it, when Liz Lochhead read out his poem at the opening of the Scottish Parliament building in October 2004:

> We give you our consent to govern well, don't say we
> have no mandate to be so bold.
> We give you this great building, don't let your work and hope
> be other than great when you enter and begin.
> So now begin. Open the doors and begin.[1]

With Jimmy Reid, one of the last of that species of self-educated working class and trade union leaders, bowed out, after a colourful

---

[1] Edwin Morgan, 'For the Opening of he Scottish Parliament, 9 October 2004', *The Book of Lives*, Manchester: Carcanet, 2007, p.10.

public life – a lifelong socialist, he stood as a Communist Party candidate Dunbartonshire Central in 1974 and polled more than 6,000 votes, joined Labour and stood in Dundee in 1979, and ended his political odyssey in the SNP, working also as a journalist and broadcaster before retiring to Bute. Reid rose to international prominence with his eloquence – 'There will be no hooliganism, there will be no vandalism, there will be no bevvying, because the world is watching us.' – during the famous 'work-in' of thousands of shipbuilders on the Clyde during 1971 and 1972, which thwarted government attempts to close the yards. At the height of his fame, he was elected rector of Glasgow University. His address to the students in 1971, rejecting the 'rat race' as being 'for rats', appeared in full in the *New York Times*. 'Man is a social being. Real fulfilment for any person lies in service to his fellow men and women,' could be taken as Jimmy Reid's credo. At the funeral, First Minister Alex Salmond made a commitment to make his famous 'rectorial address' available to every Scottish secondary pupil.[2]

'A BRAMMER OF A BY-ELECTION'

When he launched the SNP campaign for the contest in Glasgow North East, Alex Salmond predicted: 'We'll have a brammer of a by-election with a monster result.'[3] One is inclined to say: he never spoke a truer word. The Labour candidate, Willie Bain, indicated his party's strategy for retaining the seat vacated by Speaker Michael Martin: 'The SNP has been in power in Scotland for two years and I think people are thinking they have not delivered on their promises.'[4] Although competing for a Westminster seat, Labour would run the campaign as an opposition to the SNP-government at Holyrood, exploiting John Swinney's by-election suicide note of cancelling the Glasgow Airport Rail Link, hammering home the message that the SNP neglected Glasgow. Glasgow Council seemed outraged that they had 'plugged a government funding gap' to allow for the completion of the M74 'only to have the Glasgow Airport Rail Link (GARL) unilaterally axed.'[5] The decision, against the gloomy backdrop of Scotland being deeper in recession than the rest

[2] Stephen McGinty, 'Jimmy Reid address to be made available to all high school pupils', *The Scotsman*, 20 August 2010.

[3] David Maddox, '"We'll have a brammer of a by-election" says Salmond', *The Scotsman*, 15 October 2009.

[4] Mark Hughes and Kunal Dutta, 'SNP bids to unseat Labour – and Brown', *The Independent*, 15 October 2009.

[5] Alistair Dalton, 'Glasgow: We bailed out SNP and they axed our rail link in return', *The Scotsman*, 3 November 2009.

of the UK and, according to the Fraser of Allander Institute, slower to recover, showed, as Labour leader Iain Gray said, that the SNP 'get it wrong.' The cancellation 'of GARL alone will cost 1300 jobs,' he argued.[6] From the start, the SNP was on the defensive, and when the votes were counted, it became clear that 'Labour's Willie Bain didn't just win Glasgow North East, he scooped it into his pocket,'[7] with a majority of over 8,000 votes, widening the gap between Labour and the SNP in this constituency.

And yet, as Iain Macwhirter summed up after the event, the SNP should have stood a fair chance of winning:

> By rights, Labour should never have won this by-election. In Gordon Brown's darkest days, in the midst of an unpopular war, after an epic expenses scandal in which the local MP, Michael Martin, played a leading role, voters in one of the most deprived and neglected constituencies in the country still turned out to support the party that has apparently done so little for them. The SNP has no excuses here.[8]

And leader comments questioned, on the strength of the SNP's performance, Alex Salmond's predictions that his party would gain 20 MPs come the polling day for Westminster: 'Mr Salmond's forecast of 20 seats for the SNP now looks overambitious. As each month goes by, Scottish Labour is gaining more and more traction on the SNP's performance in St Andrew's House.'[9] The 'brammer' or 'monster result' had come true, but in form of a 'reality check'[10] for the SNP: the long Holyrood honeymoon was finally over. The lowest turnout ever in a Scottish Westminster by-election (just under 33%) showed a massive disaffection by voters, due to apathy or, as Joyce McMillan argued, anger 'at the irrelevance of modern politics,'[11] – whichever, not a healthy sign for Scottish democracy.

---

[6] Ian McConnell and Brian Currie, 'Scotland's recession far deeper than rest of the UK', *The Herald*, 18 November 2009.

[7] Joan McAlpine, 'SNP must learn to fight dirty', *The Sunday Times*, 15 November 2009.

[8] Iain Macwhirter, 'Struggling Nationalists could be staring into the electoral abyss', *The Herald*, 16 November 2009.

[9] 'Game on' (Leader), *Scotland on Sunday*, 15 November 2009.

[10] Eddie Barnes, 'Reality check', *Scotland on Sunday*, 15 November 2009.

[11] Joyce McMillan, 'Anger, not apathy, is to blame for lowest voter turnout', *The Scotsman*, 14 November 2009.

THE SCOTTISH BUDGET 2010

The £120m GARL cancellation had been part of John Swinney's outlining of the 2010 budget in which he claimed that the Scottish Government was forced to make cuts, due to a £500m reduction in the block grant as a result of Westminster efficiency savings.[12] But he assured Parliament that front line public services would be protected. In fact, health spending overall would rise by 2.4% to £11.35bn.

Of most concern, he said, were UK cuts to health spending, which would mean a shortfall of £129m for the Scottish health budget. He could use unspent Treasury money to ensure that Scottish health services would not suffer – but that would only cover one year. Another reason, according to the Finance Secretary, why GARL had to bite the dust.

A massive £253 cut was to be doled out to housing and regeneration, but overall spending on affordable housing would remain untouched at £1.65bn. Despite these assurances, Shelter Scotland claimed investment in housing was the 'main casualty' in the draft budget.[13] Swinney further announced administrative savings in the police force, but funding for the police would actually increase by £6m. £49m in cuts would affect the education budget, with teacher training particularly hit by savings. But there would be an increase in real terms of over £16m for education, including £10m for school building. And there would be £8m of cuts in the environment budget.

The Scottish Government's administration budget would be cut by £14m, while spending on advertising was to be more than halved. However, ministers would provide funding to councils to extend the council tax freeze to a third year. Efficiency savings across government agencies wold produce another £2.7m of cuts. But there was also good news for farmers: an extra £4.5m for farmers in fragile rural areas, increased investment of £7.9m in a new facility for the University of Aberdeen Rowett Institute of Nutrition and Health, and £700,000 more for the Scottish food industry.

Labour's main demands for supporting Swinney's budget were the reinstating of GARL, a reversal of the cuts in the housing budget, and an incrased number of apprenticeships.[14] The independent MSP Margo MacDonald said she would support the budget if extra money for training stonemasons 'to repair Edinburgh's crumbling tenements' was made

---

[12] Andrew Black, 'At-a-glance: Scottish budget plan', *BBC News Scotland*, 17 September 2009 <news.bbc.co.uk/go/pr/fr/-/1/hi/scotland/8255282.stm>.

[13] 'Warning over cuts to council cash', *BBC News Scotland*, 19. September 2009, <news.bbc.co.uk/go/pr/fr/-/1/hi/scotland/8263264.stm>.

[14] Tom Peterkin, 'Labour spells out budget demands', *Scotland on Sunday*, 22 November 2009.

available.[15] The Liberal Democrats pressed for a pay cut for highly-paid public sector bosses, using the saved money for the aid of manufacturing and for the funding of college places for young people. The Greens were once again trying to secure a comprehensive programme to insulate homes across Scotland. The Tories showed exasperation at the SNP 'living in denial over the inevitability of cuts' – Annabel Goldie labelling Alex Salmond as 'the King Canute of Scottish politics.'[16]

A number of late deals secured a majority in Parliament for the SNP budget. The Liberal Democrats got £20m for additional college places and £10m to support access to finance for firms. The SNP conceded to the Tories on their demand to open up the Goverment's accounts to the public, under which plan every item of spending worth £25,000 was to be publicly listed. The establishment of an 'Independent Budget Review', another key Tory demand, was set to identify savings – taking a look at, among other areas, free personal care for the elderly, prescription charges and school meals.[17] Further concessions concerned the Greens' insulation demands, so that Swinney 'succeeded in his goal of leaving Labour isolated as the only party ... to oppose the budget.'[18] Eventually, the SNP, the Tories, the Greens and Margo MacDonald voted in favour of the budget, the Liberal Democrats abstained, and Labour voted against it.

OTHER LEGISLATION

The Budget Bill, passed on 3 March 2010, turned out to be the most important bill of this Parliamentary year. It could have been topped by the SNP's Referendum Bill, but that was not to materialise. Here a short summary of the other bills that passed through Parliament.

The Arbitration (Scotland) Bill, passed on 18 November 2009, puts the vast majority of the general Scots law of arbitration into a single statute, replacing most of the few existing statutory provisions relative to arbitration in Scotland. The Schools Consultation (Scotland) Bill, passed the following day, aims at updating and strengthening the consultation practices and procedures that local authorities apply to all school closures and other school proposals.

---

[15] Ian Swanson, 'Margo: I'll back SNP budget if city gets masonic funding', *Edinburgh Evening News*, 12 January 2010.

[16] Ian Swanson, 'Parliament prepares for annual budget wrangle', *Edinburgh Evening News*, 15 January 2010.

[17] Tom Peterkin, '"Hatchet gang" to find cuts in Scots services', *The Scotsman*, 4 February 2010.

[18] David Maddox, 'Swinney's late deals seal new Scottish cash plan', *The Scotsman*, 3 February 2010.

On 27 January 2010, the Tobacco and Primary Medical Services (Scotland) Bill was passed which bans the display of cigarettes and other tobacco and smoking related products, bans the sale of cigarettes from vending machines, introduces a registration system for tobacco retailers, and introduces a new system of sanctions for breaches of the law, involving fixed penalty notices and banning orders for related offences. The bill also makes provision to amend and clarify the eligibility criteria for providers of primary medical services, including introducing a requirement that all parties to a contract for primary medical services must demonstrate a sufficient involvement in the provision of care and/or the day to day running of services.

The Marine (Scotland) Bill, voted through on 4 February 2010, creates a new legislative and management framework for the marine environment, including a new system of marine planning, to manage the competing demands of the use of the sea whilst protecting the marine environment. It also creates a system of licensing, with the aim of reducing the regulatory burden for key sectors, and includes powers to establish marine protected areas to protect natural and cultural marine features. Finally, the bill introduces a new regime for the conservation of seals and gives powers to Scottish marine enforcement officers to ensure compliance with these new licensing and conservation measures.

The Home Owner and Debtor Protection (Scotland) Bill of 11 February 2010 introduces amendments to primary legislation in order to protect home owners and debtors during a period of recession, and in particular to reduce the risk of homelessness as a result of insolvency. The Public Services Reform (Scotland) Bill of 25 March 2010 is to help simplify and improve the landscape of Scottish public bodies, to deliver more effective, co-ordinated government that can better achieve its core functions for the benefit of the people of Scotland.

Introduced by Christine Graham MSP and passed on 22 April 2010, the Control of Dogs (Scotland) Bill – also dubbed the 'Dog Asbo Bill' – modernises the law on control of dogs. It enables local authorities to impose penalties on the owner, or the person in charge, of a dog where that person has failed to keep the dog under control. Under the new legislation, more responsibility will be placed on the owners of badly-behaved dogs, with a focus on the 'deed and not the breed' of the dog.[19]

The Interpretation and Legislative Reform (Scotland) Bill of 28 April 2010 addresses four concerns: the publication, interpretation and operation of Acts of the Scottish Parliament and instruments made under them, the making and publication of subordinate legislation in the form of Scottish Statutory Instruments (SSIs) and the scrutiny procedures which apply to those instruments in the Parliament; the special procedure which applies

---

[19] '"Dog Asbo" legislation approved by MSPs', BBC News Scotland, 22 April 2010 <news.bbc. co.uk/go/pr/fr/-/1/hi/scotland/8636913.stm>.

to orders that are subject to special parliamentary procedure; and giving the Scottish Ministers a power, by order, to make certain amendments to enactments in order to facilitate their consolidation or codification. Rivetting stuff. And there is more. On 9 June 2010, the Scottish Parliamentary Commissions and Commissioners etc. Bill passed, which establishes a new standards body, a body corporate, to be known as the 'Commission for Ethical Standards in Public Life in Scotland' (CESPLS).

On 30 June 2010, the Criminal Justice and Licensing (Scotland) Bill was backed by Parliament. It includes a presumption against prison sentences of three months or less. It also institutes a new sentencing council, raises the criminal responsibility age from eight to 12, favours community payback orders as alternative to jail terms, and introduces new offences on stalking, slavery and 'extreme pornography' as well as tougher penalties for involvement in organised crime, but it rejects the Labour proposal of mandatory jail sentences for knife-carriers.

Finally, the Crofting Reform (Scotland) Bill passed on 1 July 2010, makes provision to reform and rename the Crofters Commission and to modify its statutory functions. It is to establish a new map-based Crofting Register that will be maintained by the Keeper of the Registers of Scotland, and which will be developed over time through regulatory trigger points that will require crofts to be registered.

The Bill defines a category of owner-occupiers known as 'owner-occupier crofters' and imposes duties on them and on tenant crofters in relation to residency, misuse and neglect of crofts. The bill also amends provisions in the Crofters (Scotland) Act 1993 on decrofting, resumption, re-letting of vacant crofts and on obtaining consent to certain regulatory matters.

The first bill to pass in autumn 2010 was the controversial Legal Services (Scotland) Bill, on 6 October, whose Alternative Business Structures element earned it the nickname 'Tesco Law', as it allows supermarkets and other commercial organisations to provide legal services to the public. The Bill split the legal profession, with many solicitors fiercely opposing it:

> It caused the biggest schism of modern times in the Scottish legal profession. The president of the Law Society admitted its members were 'split up the middle' over alternative business structures. The initial proposal was called Tesco Law because it held out the prospect of 100% ownership of law firms by supermarkets (hence Tesco law, which sounds better than Lidl law) and others. In the end, after internecine warfare, a compromise of sorts was reached

and ... Scottish law firms can bring in partners who are not legally qualified.[20]

GENERAL ELECTION:
GORDON BROWN'S LAST STAND

The most surprising thing at the start of the Westminster election campaign was that, despite the woes of Gordon Brown and the Labour party, David Cameron had not been able to seal the deal with the British electorate. Nobody really believed it would eventually come to it, but talk of a hung parliament was in the air from the beginning of the campaign. Before the last conference season, the Tories had a lead of 17% over Labour. That narrowed slightly in the aftermath of the conferences, but was re-established by November. Then, following the last Queen's Speech before the election, Labour seemed to close the gap again, down to 10% in December, and talk of a snap election in March made the round.

In that sense, the election promised to be exciting. The Tories needed 6.9% swing to achieve an outright majority. The Scottish Conservatives hoped to contribute by upping their representation at Westminster from one to eleven MPs. For Labour to achieve a historical fourth term, it was paramount to maintain its Scottish stronghold, an aim the SNP had promised to scupper, increasing its number of MPs von six to 20, hoping for a 'balanced parliament'. The Liberal Democrats had achieved their best ever Westminster election result in 2005 but were hopeful to build on it. They hoped to at least hold Dunfermline and West Fife, which Willie Rennie had sensationally won in the 2006 by-election.

For the three televised Leaders' Debates,[21] Gordon Brown and David Cameron had agreed to have the Liberal Democrats also represented, and Nick Clegg's performance, particularly in the first debate on 15 April, caused a media frenzy – 'Cleggmania' broke out; the poll ratings of the Liberal Democrats soared, and they seemed to challenge Labour for the No.2 spot, if not in seats, then at least in the popular vote. The SNP was 'furious' about its exclusion and complained of bias[22] and eventually went to court, trying to get Alex Salmond onto the panel, to no avail. While it would have been odd to have the SNP – which only stands in Scotland

[20] David Lee, 'Freedom – or squeeze on the small?', *The Scotsman*, 7 October 2010.

[21] For background and verdict on the TV debates, see Owen Dudley Edwards, 'The Prime Ministerial Debates 2010', *Scottish Affairs*, no.72 (Summer 2010), pp.9-27.

[22] Lindsay Moss, 'Leaders' television debates "rigged" says SNP', *The Scotsman*, 22 December 2009.

– widely broadcast in England (just think of the frustration of all those English voters who would be inspired to vote for Salmond but could not), there could of course have been a televised debate in Scotland with the UK party leaders sharing a platform with the SNP leader – and, likewise for Wales and Northern Ireland.

In the end, the media bubble created by the debates seems not to have had a huge effect on the way people voted – after all the hillaballoo of the campaign (including the media outrage about Brown's 'bigot' gaffe) and unprecedented peaks in the opinion polls, we were back on polling day roughly where the campaign had started, and duly got a hung parliament. The alleged surge in support for the Liberal Democrats 'appeared to evaporate in the polling booth.'[23]

What became abundantly apparent during the campaign was that no one was prepared to spell out where the cuts would fall, whether the intent was halving the deficit by 2015 and deferring cuts to begin in 2011, as laid out in the Labour Manifesto, or starting right away and cutting far deeper, as Cameron and Osborne promised. It was a phony war – cuts, but no one prepared to spell out where they would fall and who would be hit.

The Labour party, both UK-wide and in Scotland, had done the utmost to make itself unelectable. A series of inept attempts at palace revolution against the Prime Minister, the last one particularly ill-timed and shambolically organised, seemed to have all but sealed the fate of the Brown administration:

> What little chance Labour had of retaining its grip on power has this weekend all but disappeared. The attempted coup by former cabinet ministers Geoff Hoon and Patricia Hewitt was a farce, as ineptly executed as it was ill-conceived, and its effect has been to make Gordon Brown's leadership abilities – or their absence – the touchstone issue of the looming general election.[24]

Prime Minister Gordon Brown showed a glimpse of what he is capable of with an impassioned speech to the Citizen UK conference three days before the election,[25] but that 'last stand' came too late to be a game changer.

In Scotland, the Purcell affair in Glasgow, the standing down of 'shamed' MP Nigel Griffith, a close ally of Gordon Brown, in Edinburgh

[23] Kenneth Macdonald, 'The Same Again, But Different: Implications for Scotland of the 2010 UK General Election Result', *Scottish Affairs*, no.72 (Summer 2010), p.1.

[24] 'Labour at a loss' (Leader), *Scotland on Sunday*, 10 January 2010.

[25] Patrick Wintour, 'Battered PM finds his voice', *The Guardian*, 4 May 2010.

South,[26] dissatisfaction with candidate selection in South Lanarkshire and the 'battle of Prestonpans' (no, not the one on the new tapestry, the one about the deselecton of Anne Moffat MP) seemed to bode anything but well for Labour. And yet, their poll lead over the SNP in Westminster voting preferences held up. The SNP had hoped that the more likely a Tory victory at Westminster would become, the more their electoral chances would improve. But polls throughout the period showed that this was not the case.

The result in Scotland was close to a carbon copy of the 2005 result. In contrast with the rest of the UK, Labour actually gained 2.5%, and comfortably snatched back the two seats lost in by-elections. After a lacklustre campaign, the SNP had to make do with their six MPs, a far cry from the twenty promised by their leader. Not the springboard for the Holyrood elections next year the party had hoped for. The Liberal Democrats experienced no Clegg-bounce, perhaps, as Owen Dudley Edwards has argued, because of the shabby treatment Clegg's predecessors, Sir Menzies Campbell and Charles Kennedy, received from the UK party.[27] For the Scottish Conservatives, the result was depressing. They had dreamed of eleven MPs and, while pundits thought that perhaps slightly over-ambitious, experts thought they were at least on their way. 'They are certainly going to pick up seats,' James Mitchell predicted, 'and if they pick up four or five, they will be quite happy.'[28] In the end they returned just the one, David Mundell, and he has since come under scrutiny over the financing of his campaign.

Table 4: UK General Election Results (UK and Scotland) 2010

UK General Election Result 2010				
Conservative	36.5%	(+5%)	306 seats	(+97)
Labour	29%	(-6%)	258 seats	(-89)
LibDem	23%	(+1%)	57 seats	(-5)
Other	11.5%	(+2%)	28 seats	(-3)
UK General Election Scottish Result in Scotland 2010				
Labour	42%	(+2.5)	41 seats	
SNP	19.9%	(+2.3)	6 seats	
LibDem	18.9%	(-3.7)	11 seats	
Conservatve	16.7%	(+0.9)	1 seat	

---

[26] Susan Smith, 'Sex scandal MP set to stand down at election', *The Scotsman*, 1 February 2010.

[27] Owen Dudley Edwards, 'The Prime Ministerial Debates 2010', pp.23-24.

[28] Tom Peterkin, 'Cameron's Highland gains?', *Scotland on Sunday*, 13 December 2009.

It was not the most glorious hour for the pollsters – two (YouGov and Angus Reid) had the Lib Dems topping Labour in their final poll on 2 May, suggesting 'that a Tory majority was now more likely than a hung result'.[29] In Scotland, the final poll before the actual election correctly predicted that the Tories would be stuck with one MP, underestimated Labour (-2) and gave both the Lib Dems and the SNP a single gain.

It was noteworthy during the coalition-forming 'Five Days That Changed Britain'[30] that Alex Salmond, who had in the run-up to the campaign indicated he could support a Tory minority government at Westminster on an issue-to-issue basis,[31] and had seen the 'celtic bloc' as in a prime position to negotiate with either Tories or Labour in a hung parliament,[32] had by now changed his mind, calling on the Liberal Democrats to join a 'progressive alliance', an 'anti-Tory pact,' involving Labour, the SNP and Plaid Cymru.[33] Apart from the numerical and ideological difficulties, this proposal was shot down by Scottish Labour MPs like Douglas Alexander.[34]

As in the negotiations for the Labour/Lib Dem coalition at Holyrood in 1999, the Lib Dems again seemed better prepared for the task than their prospective partners. With a bit of bluff – about the alternative voting system allegedly having been offered by Labour without a Referendum – the deal between David Cameron and Nick Clegg was sealed, and they seemed to get on like old mates, the 'odd couple' or, indeed, the 'happy couple'.[35] The Lib Dems found the Tories surprisingly easy to deal with. 'The Tories are ditching policies faster than they can list them,' Danny Alexander was quoted. And a right-wing Tory MP, Philip Davies, complained: 'I get the distinct impression that David Cameron is happier with his Lib Dems than he is with some of the people in his own party.'[36]

---

[29] James Cusack, 'Britain in the balance', *Sunday Herald*, 2 May 2010. The four forecasts were: YouGov: Labour 27%, Lib Dem 28%, Conservative 35%; Angus Reid: Labour 23%, Lib Dem 29%, Conservative 35%; ComRes and ICM were closer, but still overestimated the Lib Dems – ComRes: Labour 28%, Lib Dem 25%, Conservative 38%; ICM: Labour 29%, Lib Dem 27%, Conservative 35%.

[30] Nick Robinson's BBC programme of that title on the formation of the Con-Dem coalition, broadcast by BBC 2 on 29 July 2010.

[31] Jason Allardyce, 'Salmond: I'd back Tories at Westminster', *The Sunday Times*, 11 October 2009.

[32] Michael Settle, 'Salmond: hung parliament is golden chance', *The Herald*, 1 April 2010.

[33] 'SNP calls for "progressive" Westminster alliance', *BBC News Scotland*, 8 May 2010 <news.bbc.co.uk/1/hi/uk_politics/election_2010/scotland/8669883.stm>

[34] David Gunn, 'Douglas Alexander "can't envisage" Labour working with SNP', *The Scotsman*, 11 May 2010.

[35] David Maddox, 'The odd couple', *The Scotsman*, 13 May 2010; Patrick Wintour, 'The happy couple at No 10', *The Guardian*, 13 May 2010.

[36] Simon Walters and Brendan Carlin, 'Tories ditched policies as fast as they listed them', *The Mail on Sunday*, 16 May 2010.

There were critical voices, from non-Orange Book Lib Dems like the former leaders Charles Kennedy and Sir Menzies Campbell. But the grassroots backlash failed to materialise.[37] On the face of it, it looked as if it had been a good deal for the Lib Dems – five cabinet posts and a firm promise on an AV referendum, the scrapping of the ID card scheme, and tax relief for the lowest paid earners. On the other hand, the cuts agenda remained a Tory domain, the Lib Dems had to swallow the VAT hike and the massive cut backs of the June emergency budget. Why did Clegg not reign in the coalition, Ian Bell asked, and predicted that selling the Tory cuts plan to the electorate as 'unavoidable' would invite voters in England to 'take the next step' and vote Tory and, in Scotland, where the party will have to face the electorate next May, when 'harsh but fair' is enacted, he foresaw '101 uses for a Dead party'.[38] Had the Lib Dems, rather than being triumphant in the coalition talks, been set up as the 'fall-guys' for the cut-and-slash Tories?[39] Some even predicted a quick divorce,[40] for some Clegg had signed his party's 'suicide note'.[41] There may have been cries of 'sell-out',[42] and the poll ratings of the Lib Dems may have plummeted[43] – not so in Scotland, incidentally – but, five months into the coalition, it still looked as if they were in this together.

Immediately after the election, following the resignation of Gordon Brown, Labour was plunged into a leadership campaign which they made last until the party conference in September, not the most riveting summer entertainment! But it finished in a surprise when the younger (Ed) Miliband pipped the favoured older (David) Miliband in the last round of the count, due to his greater support from the affiliated Union members. It was widely commented, from the *Daily Star* to the *Press and Journal*,[44] that this marked the end of New Labour, reinforced by Ed

[37] Eddie Barnes, 'Clegg faces grassroots backlash', *Scotland on Sunday*, 16 May 2010.

[38] Ian Bell, 'Why does Clegg refuse to reign in his coalition masters?', *The Herald*. 26 June 2010.

[39] Iain Macwhirter, 'The brilliant pact that turned Lib Dems into the fall guys', *Sunday Herald*, 27 June 2010.

[40] Eddie Barnes, 'Heading for divorce', *Scotland on Sunday*, 16 May 2010.

[41] Simon Jenkins, 'Clegg chose glory in death. And has condemned his party to oblivion', *The Guardian*, 17 September 2010.

[42] Brian Brady and Matt Chorley, 'Clegg sold out to get power, say voters', *The Independent on Sunday*, 19 September 2010.

[43] Nigel Morris, 'Survey puts Liberal Democrats' popularity at post-election low', *The Independent*, 29 June 2010.; Andrew Grice, 'Four in 10 Lib-Dem voters would not vote for party again, says poll', *The Independent*, 7 September 2010.

[44] 'Ed Miliband declares end of New Labour', *Daily Star*, 28 September 2010; David Perry, 'RIP New Labour as Miliband promises to make fresh start', *The Press and Journal*, 29 September 2010.

Miliband's acknowledgement of Labour failures and, in particular, his declaration that the Iraq war was wrong. The Scottish Labour leader, Iain Gray, enthused that 'Ed Miliband gets Scotland', that he appreciated the need to underline the status of the Scottish party; and that Scotland would provide the first test of his leadership, with the Holyrood elections in May.[45] But, the prolonged internal Labour contest also meant that the coalition had a relatively free ride for its first four months in office.

One of the first visits of the new Prime Minister after his election was to the Scottish Parliament, where he promised to govern with respect to the devolved institutions. How this tallies with the planning of the Alternative Vote referendum on the same day as the Holyrood elections, and the brusk way of proposing to shift the following Holyrood elections as they would clash with the next UK general election after the agreed five-year term of the coalition, has raised questions.[46]

With 11 Lib Dem MPs (in addition to the lone Tory), Cameron has at least some legitimacy, although no more than Margaret Thatcher and John Major had in the late 1980s and up to the 1997 election. David Cameron may have made progress in de-toxifying the Tory brand south of the Border – in Scotland the shadow of Mrs Thatcher and the perception of the Scottish Tories as an essentially English party seem more difficult to banish. As the recriminations within the party started, it was also argued that Cameron was unpopular in Scotland, and that his prominence in the campaign had been counterproductive.[47] Tory is still a four-letter word in Scotland. To keep the Tories out, Scots tend to vote Labour in Westminster elections – but will they do so for Holyrood as well, come May 2011?

ALL ON BOARD THE AUSTERITY EXPRESS?

What is the difference between the Scottish administration's Draft Budget and a work of art?,' Bill Jamieson had asked. 'None,' was his answer: 'It is creative. It is bold. It radiates technique. And it defies imagination. But is it a budget?' He called it 'surreal' – 'just months ahead

[45] Brian Taylor, 'Getting Scotland' (Blether with Brian), *BBC News Scotland*, 27 September 2010, <www.bbc.co.uk/blogs/thereporters/briantaylor/2010/09/getting_scotland.html>.

[46] David Maddox, 'Anger as voting reform poll clashes with Scottish elections', *The Scotsman*, 6 July 2010.

[47] David Torrance and Tom Peterkin, 'Cameron blamed for scaring off Scottish voters', *Scotland on Sunday*, 9 May 2010.

of a general election and what is set to be the toughest austerity budget in a generation.'[48]

The Scottish budget was only the preliminary battle, the prelude, as it were; after all, none of the cuts had actually taken effect yet. And it had a 'surreal' quality to it, as figures of £270m of cuts at local government level were discussed, with the loss of 3,000 jobs, even before the real cuts will arrive in 2011. As the UK general election drew closer, the debate about the proper recipe for recovery from the recession became the dominant issue. While Alistair Darling and Labour accepted that the state deficit needed to be reduced and that cuts were therefore inevitable, their plan was halving the deficit in the lifetime of the next Parliament, and to defer cuts until 2011 to allow economic recovery to take root before the cuts would kick in. David Cameron and George Osborne had unveiled their plans of an emergency budget within 50 days of coming into power,[49] announced a public sector pay freeze and a rise in the state pension age, outlined plans to target Whitehall costs and axe child trust funds for the better off. Osborne told the Tory conference in autumn 2009 that 'we're all in this together', and that the measures would save £7bn a year.[50]

The pace and the depth of the cuts became the prime battleground during the general election campaign, and that was reinforced by the emergency budget George Osborne revealed on 22 June: VAT up to 20% from January 2011; a two-year pay-freeze for public sector workers earning over £21,000 a year; welfare and universal benefit cuts totalling £11bn. Instead of £73bn, in Labour's plans, there would be £113bn cuts by 2014-15.[51] The Chancellor called the budget 'unavoidable' as otherwise the UK 'would have been at the mercy of the financial markets and the rating agencies, its sovereign debt levels regarded as unsustainable as those of Greece, Spain....' – but, as critics pointed out, it ran the risk 'that it gold plates Britain's AAA credit rating but snuffs out the fragile recovery before it manages to take proper hold.'[52] A 'radical, even a revolutionary Budget', with a 25% real-terms cut across non-protected government departments in four years – 'Margaret Thatcher never tried anything so ambitious.'[53] Macwhirter called it 'a huge gamble', Bill Jamieson, despite

---

[48] Bill Jamieson, 'Swinney and Co hooked on surreal financial dream', *The Scotsman*, 22 January 2010.

[49] Campbell Gunn, 'Tough times ahead as spending cuts bite', *The Sunday Post*, 20 December 2009.

[50] Deborah Summers, 'Osborne pledges public sector pay freeze for those on more than £18,000', *The Guardian*, 6 October 2009.

[51] Bill Jamieson, 'Osborne doesn't miss in £113bn battering', *The Scotsman*, 23 June 2010.

[52] Alf Young. 'Scotland must find a path to gain amid the pain', *The Scotsman*, 25 June 2010.

[53] Iain Macwhirter, 'A huge gamble for him ... and us', *The Herald*, 23 June 2010.

coming from a different ideological position, saw 'not one breathtaking gamble, but four':

> There is the gamble with his Liberal Democrat partners. They face outrage from their constituency parties over collaboration with what they will see as a classic Tory, anti-public sector budget. It turns Nick Clegg into a poor man's Vichy.
> There is a huge gamble with he voters, whose support he coalition must keep if it is to survive...
> There is also a huge gamble with the markets...
> And, most fateful of all, there is a gamble with the British economy. The Office of Budget Responsibility has shaded down its forecast for economic growth next year to take account of the budget measures.[54]

George Osborne claimed it was a 'progressive Budget' – for Iain Macwhirter 'a novel definition of the word,'[55] a view backed by the Institute for Fiscal Studies (IFS) which found the Budget neither 'tough but fair' nor 'progressive'.[56] A Budget to have William Beveridge and John Maynard Keynes birling in their graves.[57]

Was it the only option? Are we now all on board the austerity express? Or is Osborne 'trying to close the deficit too soon and too fast'?[58] The Princeton economics professor Paul Krugman pointed at Greece and Ireland as counter examples:

> Anyone who doubts the suffering caused by slashing spending in a weak economy should look at the catastrophic effects of austerity programmes in Greece and Ireland.[59]

In his *New Statesman* columns, David Blanchflower has tirelessly warned that the Government's budgetary policies would lead to a double-dip recession in the UK:

> For many months in this column, I have made clear the dangers of falling back into recession. I have never believed

---

[54] Bill Jamieson, 'Osborne ushers in year zero of the age of austerity', *The Scotsman*, 23 June 2010.

[55] Iain Macwhirter, 'A huge gamble for him ... and us', *The Herald*, 23 June 2010.

[56] Sean O'Grady, 'Budget is not progressive, declares IFS', *The Independent*, 24 June 2010.

[57] Larry Elliott, 'A brand of austerity about as progressive as Thatcher's', *The Guardian*, 26 August 2010.

[58] 'Cuts and common sense' (Leader), *The Independent on Sunday*, 22 August 2010.

[59] Paul Krugman, 'The cruel bonds cult', *The Guardian*, 21 August 2010.

it was appropriate to set out a plan to reduce the deficit by a certain date, principally because of the high levels of uncertainty we face. Economic policy in these circumstances has to be path-dependent.[60]

His verdict is clear: 'The British government's austerity package is based entirely on ideology, not on any economic rationale.'[61]

Robert Skidelsky attacked the Budget because it was 'deflationary'. He asked, 'how does the Government suppose that taking money out of the economy is going to help recovery?' As a Keynesian, Skidelsky said: 'I don't understand how you help growth by reducing spending.'[62] And Joseph Stieglitz predicted that the Budget 'will make Britain's recovery from recession longer, slower and harder than it needs to be.' He also warned that 'the rise in VAT could even tip us into a double-dip recession.'[63]

The debate continues. It has heated up in view of the Spending Review due on 20 October 2010. While he OECD and the IMF had applauded the brisk course of cutting after the election, they now seem to have second thoughts about the UK's pace (although, this autumn came another ringing endorsement from the IMF for Osborne's 'strong and credible plan' for deficit reduction[64]). Borrowing has already come down, before the imposition of any cuts – the UK may have choices, according to the IMF, which it did not have earlier in the year.[65] Even the *Daily Telegraph*, which celebrated austerity as 'the new cool' back in May,[66] changed its tune, urging the Tories to go beyond the strategy of debt reduction 'by outlining a Tory programme for economic growth.'[67] Obviously, the lobby against harsh cuts is growing: 'Suddenly austerity is no longer cool – it is now politically dangerous.'[68] And the suspicion grows that the 'difference

---

[60] David Blanchflower, 'Balls and Bernanke have got it right', *New Statesman*, 6 September 2010.

[61] David Blanchflower, 'Why Robert Chote gets my vote', *New Statesman*, 20 September 2010.

[62] Robert Skidelsky, 'By George, he hasn't got it', *The Independent*, 25 June 2010.

[63] Paul Vallely, 'Wrong!', *The Independent*, 27 June 2010.

[64] Mark Smith, 'IMF hails Osborne's "strong and credible" austerity package', *The Scotsman*, 28 September 2010.

[65] 'Are cuts still the right medicine for a sick economy?' (Leader), *Sunday Herald*, 12 September 2010.

[66] Jeremy Warner, 'Austerity is the new cool as Europe turns its back on Keynes', *The Daily Telegraph*, 24 May 2010.

[67] 'The Tories must offer a blueprint for growth' (Leader), *The Daily Telegraph*, 2 October 2010.

[68] James Cusick, 'The Cuts: Is there an alternative?', *Sunday Herald*, 12 September 2010.

between being in a hurry to reduce the size of the state, and being in a hurry to bring down Britain's debt.... have ... converged inside Cameron and Osborne's circles.'[69]

The outcry over George Osborne's announcement at the Tory Conference that child benefits would be scrapped for higher rate taxpayers may be a foretaste of what is to come in the Spending Review. It, and the 'tactically inept', 'appallingly managed' way of announcing it,[70] caused fears even inside the Conservative party that Osborne's 'shock and awe' strategy could backfire and that it 'may have triggered a row to rival the debacle over Gordon Brown's 10p tax rate.'[71] On the other hand, polls indicate that a majority of voters backs the austerity programme and the cuts to universal benefits. 73% in a YouGov poll for the *Sunday Times* said abolishing child benefit for families with a higher-rate taxpayer was right. But 75% thought it unfair that households with two earners of less than £44,000 each will continue to receive the benefit.[72]

With the agreement of the new coalition government in London, the SNP administration at Holyrood opted to defer the cuts until next year, as it said implementing them any sooner would risk throwing the country back into recession. The exact level of expenditure cuts Scottish ministers will have to deal with will be known after the UK government's Comprehensive Spending Review on 20 October.

The Fraser of Allander Institute predicted 120,000 job losses in Scotland over the coming five years, and warned of an increased risk that Osborne's Budget would plunge Scotland back into recession.[73] According to the Independent Budget Review (which was installed by the SNP government to get its Budget through Parliament), the choices for Scotland are stark. Published by Crawford Beveridge, Sir Neil McIntosh and Robert Wilson in late July, it laid out that the council tax freeze and free services (free eye tests, free bus passes for pensioners) are no longer tenable, that NHS ringfencing will not work, as that would leave other departments in Scotland facing budget cuts of more than 20% by 2014-15. It also recommended a fall in public sector employment of between 5.7 and 10% by 2014-15, which would mean the loss of up to 60,000 public sector jobs. It also called for a review of public sector pensions and a reduction in the number of public bodies. It further recommended reconsidering tuition

---

[69] 'Cameron's big on society ... but not on detail' (Leader), *Sunday Herald*, 10 October 2010.

[70] Alan Cochrane and Bernard Ponsonby, respectively, on *Politics Now*, STV, 7 October 2010.

[71] Nicholas Watt. 'Osborne cuts to the core – but is this the Torius' 10p tax moment?', *The Guardian*, 5 October 2010.

[72] Isabel Oakeshott, 'Britain backs bonfire of benefits for higher-paid', *The Sunday Times*, 10 October 2010.

[73] Ian McConnell, Robbie Dinwoodie and Michael Settle, 'Spending cuts could mean loss of 120,000 Scots jobs', *The Herald*, 1 July 2010.

fees for students. And it said the status of Scottish Water – currently publicly owned – may have to be reconsidered, although it stopped short of demanding its privatisation. Beveridge also warned the parties not to make spending pledges in their 2011 election manifestos.[74]

In welcoming the Report, John Swinney reaffirmed that the SNP government was committed to retaining free concessionary bus travel and free care for the elderly. 'There are many options,' he said, 'but clearly there is no need to pursue all of these as they would generate far more savings than is actually required.'[75]

MISFORTUNES, MISHAPS AND MISBEHAVIOURS

This past Parliamentary session proved once more that we rarely do big scandals in Scotland, but we are very good at producing some small fry. Labour, the SNP and the Tories had their share of minor embarrassments. But the more serious case first. The failures in fulfilling promises in the education sector – class sizes, the 'shambolic' introduction of the Curriculum of Excellence, and her tendency to blame everything and everyone in what Edwin Morgan would have called 'the droopy mantra of "it wizny me"' – cost Fiona Hyslop her job as Education Secretary in November. Alex Salmond threatened a vote of confidence but, in a sign that the opposition parties now no longer feared the potential collapse of the minority government, they did not back down – and the First Minister sacked her from his Cabinet.[76] She had to swap with Culture Minister Michael Russell, and became the eleventh incumbent in as many years of Devolution in the culture portfolio, which is a comment in itself.

Said Michael Russell ran into some trouble over a 'cybernat' aide who had blogged anonymously, casting doubts on the sexuality of a Labour MSP and had called a QC a liar. Russell announced that the blogger, Mark MacLachlan, had resigned; he had been sacked, MacLachlan stated (and took legal action against the SNP for 'unfair sacking'[77]), and he also then claimed that Russell had not only known about the blog but had

---

[74] Crawford W Beveridge, Sir Neil McIntosh and Robert Wilson, *Independent Budget Revue* (July 2010), <www.scotland.gov.uk/Resource/Doc/919/0102410.pdf>.

[75] 'Budget review recommends up to 60,000 public jobs cut', *BBC News Scotland*, 29 July 2010, <www.bbc.co.uk/news/uk-scotland-scotland-politics-10794298?print=true>.

[76] Brian Currie, 'Cornered Salmond sacks Hyslop from his Cabinet', *The Herald*, 2 December 2010.

[77] Jason Allardyce, 'Nationalist blogger sues SNP over "unfair sacking"', *The Sunday Times*, 13 December 2009.

suggested ideas for it.[78] Rob Davidson, the SNP group leader on Dumfries and Galloway Council, admitted his involvement in a smearing website, after having denied it before.[79] Citing Labour's infamous Damien McBride case, the *Herald* called for more 'accountability' in the blogosphere.[80]

In February, Deputy First Minister Nicola Sturgeon was at the centre of a storm in a teacup, when it surfaced that she had asked a court not to jail a constituent of hers who was a serial fraudster.[81] Her resignation was demanded, and loudly dismissed by Alex Salmond.[82] In stunning contrast to the bluster of the First Minister, his Deputy 'fully and frankly' apologised after the February recess to the Parliament for the way she had dealt with the case.[83]

At the same time, Salmond himself came under fire for auctioning off meals at the Scottish Parliament's Members' Restauraunt for thousands of pounds in aid of his party's finances. Holyrood as 'a state-funded cash machine for politicians who find their coffers empty at election time'?[84]Again, not a big issue, but taken together with the other cases, it seemed to 'call into serious question the judgement of those heading the Scottish Government.'[85]

If the SNP can do 'Lunchgate', Labour managed to get into trouble over a barbecue – Iain Gray's 'Marqueegate', as it was dubbed. The Prestonpans Labour Club had hosted the launch of Gray's Labour leadership campaign in a council-owned marquee. It also transpired that the Labour Club's annual fundraising barbecue over the past 14 years had been subsidised by council taxpayers.[86] More serious was the demise under a cloud of scandal of the Glasgow council leader Steven Purcell, one of the great hopes of the Labour party. The 37-year-old cited stress and exhaustion but was at the centre of 'lurid claims about his drug use;'

---

[78] Brian Currie, 'Row over blog deepens with "Liar Liar" post', *The Herald*, 19 December 2010.

[79] Tom Peterkin, 'SNP politician admits lying over e-mail "black ops" to smear rivals', *The Scotsman*, 19 December 2010.

[80] 'We can do without these online smear campaigns' (Leader), *The Herald*, 17 December 2009.

[81] Brian Currie, 'Sturgeo in storm over support for fraudster', *The Herald*, 11 February 2010.

[82] 'Loudness of attempt to defend Sturgeon speaks volumes', *The Scotsman*, 12 February 2010.

[83] Hamish Macdonell, 'Sturgeon apologises over support for benefit cheat' (Leader), *Caledonian Mercury*, 24 February 2010, <caledonianmercury.com/?s=Sturgeon+apologises+over+support+for+benefit+cheat>.

[84] Tom Gordon, 'For sale: lunch at Holyrood with first Minister – £9,000', *The Herald*, 4 February 2010.

[85] 'Sturgeon's error is latest blow for SNP' (Leader), *The Herald*, 12 February 2010.

[86] Campbell Gunn, 'Red face and black mark for Iain Gray', *The Sunday Post*, 6 December 2010.

it had also emerged 'that the gay former councillor had been warned by police last year about an underworld plot to blackmail him.'[87] And the whole way he used to run the council administration came under scrutiny.[88] Compared to that, Frank McAveety's latest gaffe was a spot of 'the politics of the kindergarten'.[89] The Labour MSP and convener of the petitions Commmitee had, in a break while the microphones were still 'live', made 'lurid' remarks over a 'dark and dusky' girl in the audience who, it turned out, was just 15 years of age. He had to resign his committee convenership.[90]

And finally, as already mentioned, the Scotland Office Minister and only Tory MP in Scotland, David Mundell, admitted to breaking the law by overspending on the last leg of his general election campaign which, he claimed, was an 'innocent mistake'. Nonetheless, he was reported to the Crown Office, which confirmed that it was investigating – prompting Labour to demand that the Member for Dumfriesshire, Clydesdale and Tweeddale be stripped of his ministerial post.[91]

RUNNING OUT OF PUFF?

While the first two-and-a-half years of the SNP minority government radiated activity and saw the party soaring in the polls, the tide seems to have turned. Not only the defeats in two successive by-elections and in the General Election indicate this, their poll ratings concerning Westminster, where the Nationalists had led over Labour in 2007 and 2008, began to decline in 2009, and from the autumn of last year, Labour has been clearly in front on that count. While in October 2009 Labour was still trailing the SNP by eight points on both constituency and regional list votes for Holyrood, this turned into a lead of two and seven points

[87] Graham Grant, 'Labour "visionary" quits politics amid drugs blackmail scandal', *Daily Mail*, 8 March 2010.

[88] Gerry Braiden, 'A tangled web: how Purcell ran Glasgow', *The Herald*, 1 April 2010.

[89] Angus MacLeod on *Politics Now*, STV, 17 June 2010.

[90] Andrew Picken and Sarah Bruce, 'Top Scots politician quits after lecherous comments about 'dark, dusky' girl, 15, in public gallery are picked up on parliament microphones', *Daily Mail*, 17 June 2010.

[91] Tom Gordon, 'Tory MP reported to the Crown for breaking electoral law', *Sunday Herald*, 10 October 2010.

respectively by February 2010.[92] By August, Labour had opened up a 10-point lead, which seems to have since solidified.[93]

> For a time, after smashing Labour's hegemony north of the Border and winning the Holyrood elections, Alex Salmond, leader of the Scottish National Party, really did bestride the narrow world of Scottish politics. (...) That, however, was then. Today, ... the picture is completely different. Not to put too fine a point on it, Alex Salmond looks like a busted flush – though I must, having offered that hostage to fortune, enter a couple of caveats: he is a formidable campaigner and can never be written off for next May's Holyrood elections; and he still has a reasonably able team around him. It's just that nothing is going right either for him or them.[94]

Indeed, the past year and a half have seen the segueing of the opposition's chipping away at the 'boken promises' of the SNP manifesto into mounting troubles about making policy and implementing it. The range of calamities is impressive or, as some in the SNP may well say, depressive. The policy of lowering class sizes in primaries one to three 'in ruins', with the percentage of classes with more than 18 pupils risen since 2007. 'Nor has the SNP delivered on its pledge to write off student debt, increase teacher numbers or improve the standard of school buildings.'[95] The class size pledge was dropped in January,[96] teacher numbers fell to their lowest level in eight years,[97] students' hopes for increased financial support was ruled out in December,[98] of the 236 schools the SNP claimed to have built since coming into office, Labour claimed that nearly 70%

---

[92] Robbie Dinwoodie, 'Labour takes poll lead over SNP', *The Herald*, 8 February 2010.

[93] Hamish Macdonell, 'Poll suggests Holyrood win for Labour in 2011 election', *Caledonian Mercury*, 9 August 2010, <politics.caledonianmercury.com/2010/08/09/poll-suggests-holyrood-win-for-labour-in-2011-election/>; Robbie Dinwoodie, 'SNP trails Labour by 10 points', *The Herald*, 6 September 2010.

[94] Alan Cochrane, 'SNP Party Conference 2010: Alex Salmond now frightens no one', *The Daily Telegraph*, 11 October 2010.

[95] Gillian Harris, 'Schools scandal', *The Sunday Times*, 24 January 2010.

[96] Michael Tait, 'SNP backtracks on "nightmare" class size pledge', *The Mail on Sunday*, 17 January 2010.

[97] Tom Peterkin, 'Broken promises' claim as teacher numbers drop to lowest in 8 years', *The Scotsman*, 26 September 2010.

[98] Fiona MacLeod and Oliver Tree, 'SNP rules out extra cash for Scots students', *Scotland on Sunday*, 13 December 2009.

were started under the previous government,[99] some 600 schools – nearly a quarter of all mainstream schools in Scotland – are, according to a Scottish Government report, 'unsuitable for the delivery of education,'[100] and this summer the SNP was 'under fire over its decision to slash more that 1,000 university places.'[101]

The introduction of the Curriculum of Excellence was, despite having been delayed by a year, called a 'shambles', lacking clarity and guidance, and funding. Iain Gray had made that accusation during First Minister's Questions on 11 March. And the Liberal Democrats, while they supported the curriculum, also called Michael Russell's handling of the situation 'shambolic'.[102] If the new curriculum has caused the government headaches, the teething problems, if not structural faults, of the new arts body Creative Scotland have proved a nightmare, even more so for the artistic community. Kenneth Roy summed it up perfectly:

> The abject performance of Creative Scotland would be hilarious were it not so potentially disastrous for the arts in Scotland and for the thousands of creative people – some of the best people in this country – whose livelihoods depend on public funding of their work. It seems that the present Holyrood administration, intelligent and honourable in so many other ways, is content to surrender the arts, a central part of our national life, to inexcusable chaos.[103]

Then, Alex Salmond was forced into an embarrassing U-turn about yet another 'shambolic' occasion – the handling of the 'Gathering', the flagship event of Homecoming 2009. That centrepiece event in Edinburgh made a £600,000 loss, and left hundreds of small businesses out of pocket, with the First Minister sanctioning the use of taxpayers' money to bail it out, and offering more money to stage a second clan gathering, despite admitting that it would probably also not cover its costs.[104] Salmond first refused to be questioned by the Scottish

[99] David Maddox, 'SNP: We've built 236 schools, Labour: 70% started under us', *The Scotsman*, 19 November 2009.

[100] Andrew Denholm, '170,000 Scots pupils being taught in schools "not fit for purpose"', *The Herald*, 30 September 2010.

[101] Nicholas Christian, 'SNP under fire over cuts to universities', *Scotland on Sunday*, 29 August 2010.

[102] 'New Scottish Curriculum for Excellence takes effect', *BBC News Scotland*, 16 August 2010 <www.bbc.co.uk/news/uk-scotland-10951893>.

[103] Kenneth Roy, 'The final curtain?', *Scottish Review*, 9 September 2010, <www.scottishreview.net/KRoy18.shtml>.

[104] David McCann, 'Pressure on Salmond as gathering links revealed', *Edinburgh Evening News*, 30 September 2010.

Parliament committee investigating the use of public money for this loss-making event, but eventually bowed to mounting pressure and agreed to appear before the inquiry.[105]

All the while, the Edinburgh trams project was heading further into chaos. The SNP government had not wanted the trams, but was defeated in Parliament in June 2007. It capped the revenue at £500m, and then let the Lib Dem/SNP council in Edinburgh get on with it – in stark contrast to the Trump golfing enterprise in the North-East, which the Scottish Government called in when it hit the first hurdle in the planning committee of Aberdeen County Council. Is it really proper for the Scottish government to stand by and let the capital become 'a laughing stock' over – and here is that word again – the 'shambolic' trams project?[106] Or, worse, just to say: 'we told you so'? Why were funds made available, although milestones in the building process were clearly missed?[107] The trams have, as The Scotsman commented, 'moved in short order from a capital city embarrassment to a national debacle.' And it called for 'high-level intervention.'[108]

While police numbers reached record highs and crime fell to its lowest level in 30 years – resounding good news for Justice Secretary Kenny MacAskill – even that bright success is clouded by the fear that massive cuts could cost thousands of police jobs and wipe out all the progress made in the past years.[109] In health, Labour counted hospital beds and found that there were 1148 fewer, compared to when they were in power in 2007,[110] this autumn, the SNP was denied its 'Smoking Ban moment', when the opposition parties voted down minimum pricing for alcohol. It had become a political football between the SNP and the opposition, particularly Labour which installed its own Alcohol Commission – whose report rejected minimum pricing in favour of UK-wide 'floor price' (the basic cost of production plus VAT and duty).[111]

[105] Robbie Dinwoodie, 'First Ministers refuses to talk to audit probe', The Herald, 25 September 2010; Simon Johnson, 'Alex Salmond performs U-turn on Gathering inquiry', The Daily Telegraph, 1 October 2010.

[106] Chris Marshall, '"Shambolic" tram project is up to two years behind', Edinburgh Evening News, 25 January 2010.

[107] Colin Donald, 'SNP under pressure to accept blame for spiralling tram costs', Sunday Herald, 12 September 2010.

[108] 'Tram debacle has made the capital into a laughing stock' (Leader), The Scotsman, 9 October 2010.

[109] Brian Donnelly, 'MacAskill: Scotland is winning war on crime', The Herald, 8 September 2010; Paul Hutcheon, 'Fears for 2800 police jobs', Sunday Herald, 29 August 2010.

[110] Hillary Duncanson, '1148 hospital beds cut since SNP took power', The Herald, 23 August 2010.

[111] Brian Currie, 'Calls for standard price limit on alcohol across UK', The Herald, 1 September 2010.

Jim Mather, the energy minister, 'has been dogged by criticism' since he gave the green light for the building of the 137 mile Beauly to Denny power line, with 600 pylons, up to 217 ft tall – without forcing it under ground, at least where it passes through the Cairngorms National Park. Were National Parks not created by the Scottish Parliament to prevent such developments?

> Throughout the sorry saga, the minister has left the public confused and unclear – even though the Beauly to Denny power line is an issue of such dramatic public concern that the SNP government surely should have taken extra pains to be as clear as possible. Why this has happened is difficult gauge. [112]

Mather had ignored recommendations by experts to bury the line in two sectors, one in Stirlingshire, the other in Perthshire and approved the entire line, despite 18,000 objections from the public. [113]

This summer, Kenny MacAskill had to answer further questions about the man who stubbornly refuses to die. After having been criticised by the Scottish Parliament's justice committee in February about his handling of the release of convicted Lockerbie bomber Abdelbaset Ali Mohmed al-Megrahi, [114] the first anniversary of his release in August brought new revelations and recriminations. While his survival, despite the prognosis of his death within three months of his release, was celebrated in Libya, [115] four cancer specialists who had previously been involved in al-Megrahi's treatment, claimed they had not been consulted before MacAskill's decision. [116] President Obama and Secretary of State Hillary Clinton both condemned MacAskill's decision, and the US Senate Committee on Foreign Relations was 'furious at the refusal of any British politicians to appear before its inquiry into the release' of al-Megrahi. [117]

Notwithstanding the rightness or wrongness of MacAskill's decision, the Megrahi affair has become a problem in US-Scottish relations, countering all the good efforts put into trade sessions and Tartan Days.

[112] Jenny Fyall, 'Mather's tactics appear to have backfired', *The Scotsman*, 19 January 2010.

[113] Jenny Fyall, 'Energy minister ignored expert advice before giving power line the go-ahead', *The Scotsman*, 14 January 2010.

[114] Eddie Barnes, 'MacAskill should have sought second opinion before freeing Lockerbie bomber, says inquiry', *The Scotsman*, 5 February 2010.

[115] Eddie Barnes, 'Libyans quietly hail "big victory" as Megrahi marks a year of freedom', *The Scotsman*, 21 August 2010.

[116] David Maddox, 'Doctors cast fresh doubt on case for freeing Megrahi', *The Scotsman*, 16 August 2010.

[117] Brian Brady, 'The Megrahi mysteries', *The Independent on Sunday*, 15 August 2010.

But it is also a problem for the Scottish government. An Ipsos/Mori poll this summer saw a rise of the number of Scots opposing the release from 46 to 54%, compared to last year, 'It's easy to see,' wrote Kenny Farquharson, 'how this could become a key issue of confidence in the SNP's competence in government.'[118] If Megrahi still lives when the Scots go to the polls next May, MacAskill's decision – 'a ruling that will define the SNP's first ever period in government,' as Eddie Barnes claimed – could become costly for the SNP's re-election prospects.[119]

Add to all of that the troubles in getting the Scottish Futures Trust off he ground,[120] which was lambasted by the economists Jim and Margaret Cuthbert as no improvement on the Private Finance Initiative it has replaced,[121] the open question about how the new £2.3 bn Forth road bridge will be paid for,[122] the fact that the local income tax was unceremoniously shelved in February 2009, and a gloomy picture emerges: 'The past is strewn with manifesto wreckage and the future holds little but grief.'[123]

LAST LEGISLATIVE PROGRAMME

What life has been left in the SNP government could perhaps be glimpsed from this parliamentary session's last legislative programme, which was unveiled by Alex Salmond on 8 September 2010. It includes, besides the Budget Bill, plans to scrap the 'double jeopardy' rule which prevents a person standing trial twice for the same crime (which has already been dispensed with in England and Wales), a 'surprise announcement' to 'evolve' Scottish Water 'from a utility to an agency which would play a key role in driving the economy and protecting the environment.'[124] It would remain in public ownership, but would gain powers to make money and be able to sell expertise or generate renewable energy. Selling off Scottish Water or mutualising it

---

[118] Kenny Farquharson, 'Scotland itself is in the dock', *Scotland on Sunday*, 22 August 2010.

[119] Eddie Barnes, 'Freeing Megrahi "will cost SNP the election"', *The Scotsman*, 20 August 2010.

[120] Andrew Whitaker, '£111m Futures Trust savings claim attacked as laughable', *The Scotsman*, 2 September 2010.

[121] Eddie Barnes, 'Flagship economic policy "a disaster"', *Scotland on Sunday*, 24 January 2010.

[122] Eddie Barnes, 'New bridge in all its glory – but who'll pay?', *The Scotsman*, 18 November 2009.

[123] Bill Jamieson, 'Alex Salmond is down but not out', *The Scotsman*, 23 September 2010.

[124] Andrew Black, 'At-a-glance: Scottish government bills', *BBC News Scotland*, 8 September 2010, <www.bbc.co.uk/news/uk-scotland-11233248>.

are not on the agenda.

A Private Rented Housing Bill is to give councils more powers to deal with unscrupulous landlords who operate outwith the law and make tenants' lives a misery. A Long Leases Bill is to implement recommendations of the Scottish Law Commission by simplifying property law, converting ultra-long housing leases into ownership, matched by compensation paid to landlords by the tenants. An Electoral Administrations Bill aims at establishing an electoral management board to improve the administration of council elections and further reforms to ensure that the fiasco of the 2007 election will not be repeated.

A Public Records Bill is to improve record keeping in public bodies like the NHS and local councils. A Health (Certification of Death) Bill will bring in a new, single system of certifying death and cut out paperwork and abolish fees – although there will be a 'modest' fee to cover the cost of the new death certification system. A Forced Marriage Bill will bring in measures to protect people from being forced to enter into marriage. And a Reservoir Safety in Scotland Bill aims at protecting the public from the risk of flooding from reservoirs without over-burdening owners with red tape.

Pretty small beer – introduced in a strangely lacklustre fashion. In the absence of an Independence Referendum Bill – the big hole in the legislative programme – the Budget Bill features as the main event in the run-up to the Holyrood elections. Until the UK Government presents its Comprehensive Spending Review on 20 October, the Scottish Government will not know how big exactly the scale of the cuts will be, and how the Barnett consequentials will affect the Scottish budget. Despite pressure from the opposition parties and from CoSLA, both Alex Salmond and John Swinney have resisted to bring forward a 'back-of-the-envelope budget' before that date. But the SNP has warned that Scotland faces £3.7bn of cuts over the next four years.[125]

NO REFERENDUM BILL

When Wendy Alexander in May 2008 offered the SNP the possibility to have an independence referendum, the famous 'Bring it on!' moment – Alex Salmond and the SNP rejected the offer: they would stick to their time table – first the National Conversation in 2007 and 2008, then the White Paper on St Andrew's Day 2009, then the Referendum Bill in January 2010 and, finally, if a majority for a referendum could be found

---

[125] Andrew Whitaker, 'Swinney warns of £3.7bn cuts in next four years', *The Scotsman*, 6 September 2010.

in the Scottish Parliament, the referendum itself in the autumn of 2010 – in other words, about now.

It clearly has not happened. The SNP stuck to its time table until last November, when the White Paper – *Your Scotland, Your Voice* – was duly published, even if the fanfares were muted.[126] An Ipsos/Mori poll had support for independence as low as 20 percent, the second lowest figure recorded since 2007, and only 25% of Scots wanted the chance to have an early say on the country's constitutional future, i.e. a referendum.[127] In place of a simple Yes or No question, the White Paper indicated a multiple-choice offer of (a) maintaining the status quo; (b) introducing the Calman reforms; (c) full fiscal powers – 'devolution max' – but still within the UK; and (d) independence.[128] *The Times* dismissed it as 'an academic exercise.'[129]

Then, at the beginning of 2010, it became obvious that the SNP plan had begun to unravel. Instead of introducing a bill in January, only a Draft bill saw the light of day, allowing for another three-month consultation. That period petered out nearly unnoticed but, when reminded, Alex Salmond reassured everybody that a Referendum Bill would be tabled at Holyrood in time for a vote to take place before the next election.[130] Yet, at the beginning of September, Alex Salmond announced a change in tactics: a Referendum Bill would be published but not introduced in Parliament.[131] It was not a total surprise. Even before the White Paper had been launched in November 2009, there had been reports that the SNP had all but given up on a referendum in 2010.[132]

Instead, Alex Salmond announced, the independence question would become the central issue of the next election, thus going to the electorate over the heads of opposition MSPs hell-bent to vote it down in Parliament.[133] Does it make sense? Not to put the Bill before

[126] Brian Currie, 'Salmond faces mounting opposition to referendum', *The Herald*, 30 November 2009.

[127] Jason Allardyce, 'Support for referendum at new low', *The Sunday Times*, 29 November 2009.

[128] Ben Borland, 'Independence vote descends into shambles', *Scottish Sunday Express*, 29 November 2009.

[129] Angus MacLeod and Lindsay McIntosh, '"It's time for the people of Scotland to have their say on Scotland's future"', *The Times*, 1 December 2009.

[130] Brian Currie, 'Salmond promises vote will take place', *The Herald*, 28 June 2010.

[131] Lorraine Davidson, 'Salmond drops flagship referendum bill plans', *The Times*, 6 September 2010.

[132] David Maddox, 'Nationalists "give up" on 2010 referendum', *The Scotsman*, 31 October 2009.

[133] Andrew Whitaker, 'SNP to shelve plans for vote on independence', *The Scotsman*, 6 September 2010.

Parliament does not only bin another manifesto pledge,[134] it let the opposition MSPs off the hook – quite a few of them might have been very uncomfortable about voting No, as their parties were, at the same time, backing plebiscites in Wales on increased powers of the National Assembly and, UK-wide, on the introduction of the Alternative Voting system for Westminster elections. Had the opposition parties blocked a Scottish referendum, the SNP would have been in a strong position: We wanted to give you, the Scottish people, a say in your constitutional future, the others don't trust you and vetoed it. Now, the SNP goes to the country on the assumption that the opposition parties would have rejected a referendum, but it is conjecture. Moreover, putting the bill before Parliament would have triggered a real national conversation.

Making independence the centrepiece of the Holyrood election campaign is a risky strategy. Was it not the decoupling of the constitutional issue from issues of good devolved governance that secured the win for the SNP last time round? Moreover, using it as a panacea in the campaign – as vital to the present spending cuts – is problematic. The sheer time scale means that independence is not a realistic answer to deal with the present woes. Even if the SNP had stuck to its time table, even if the Parliament had voted through a referendum bill, even if the Scots had voted for independence, by the time it was negotiated, the present set of economic circumstances would long be in the past. Even after the SNP government's White Paper, the Herald had warned: 'If the SNP chooses to make Scottish independence the main plank of its campaign when so many other vital issues dominate the political agenda, it could rebound on them.'[135] As Iain Macwhirter observed, 'formal independence is becoming increasingly marginal to Scottish constitutional politics. The debate is now all about extending home rule: how far and how fast.'[136] As only less than a third of the Scottish electorate favour independence, but around two thirds agree that Holyrood should get more powers – is the SNP not handing advantage over to the opposition parties?

Even if the Nationalists held all their seats in 2011 – or, if their strategy worked and they made gains – they would still be in a minority at Holyrood, and the other parties would still be likely to oppose a referendum. Back to square one, then? And keep the bill on the shelves until 2015? The question may be asked: what is the point of an SNP government at Holyrood if it does not use the opportunity to put an independence referendum to the vote?

The last Queen's Speech penned by Gordon Brown's government endorsed the recommendations of the Calman Commission, including

---

[134] 'Salmond abandons manifesto pledge' (Leader), The Herald, 7 September 2010.

[135] 'Salmond's gamble' (Leader), The Herald, 1 December 2009.

[136] Iain Macwhirter, 'The real question is: does independence matter?', The Herald, 30 November 2009.

greater tax powers for the Scottish Parliament. A White Paper – *Scotland's Place in the United Kingdom* – on 26 November 2009 outlined the changes planned. The former Labour spin doctor Lorraine Davidson gushed:

> The Scottish Secretary Jim Murphy is playing a tactical blinder by embracing the ideas contained in the Calman report to pass control over a portion of income tax, along with the likely transfer of laws on speed limits and airguns from Westminster to Holyrood. By publishing a white paper outlining the changes … Labour will kill off nationalist claims that the Calman investigation into Holyrood's powers was a waste of time.

While David Cameron was hesitant to give a full commitment to Calman,[137] the coalition government fully endorsed the Calman package in its first Queen's Speech in May and has promised to have a Scotland Bill introduced at Westminster before the end of this year.[138] The SNP agrees that most of Calman is perfectly acceptable – only the fiscal arrangements are deemed 'flawed and unworkable'.[139]

TOWARDS THE HOLYROOD ELECTIONS

Every year since Donald Dewar formed the first devolved government, the Parliament has had more money to spend than in the previous year, the only 'problem' was how to spend it; now the very real problem is how to manage declining budgets. Was the last election a competition in numbers – who would promise more policemen on the beat, more nurses in our hospitals, more teachers in our schools, this time round the public is aware of the dire financial circumstances and 'will not settle for unrealistic or uncosted promises and are in no mood for a toxic blame game.'[140] The voters will want answers – about the future of free personal care for the elderly, about the financing of further education and, above all, how and to which degree the Scottish Parliament can protect Scottish public services from the hatchet of the coalition government.

[137] Gerri Peev, 'Tories silent over greater tax powers for Scotland', *The Scotsman*, 19 November 2009.

[138] Michael Settle, 'The new devolution', *The Herald*, 26 May 2010.

[139] David Maddox, 'Westminister reviews devolution plans after tax power confusion', *The Scotsman*, 27 May 2010.

[140] 'Salmond abandons manifesto pledge' (Leader), *The Herald*, 7 September 2010.

That is the biggest challenge yet for devolution. Both Alex Salmond and Iain Gray have acknowledged this. Alex Salmond said, when he introduced the legislative programme for the final Parliamentary session before the elections that 'looming spending cuts mean the first age of devolution is over.' Similarly, Iain Gray spoke of the 'third phase' of devolution, where the focus was no longer on extending public services, but on 'jobs and the economy'.[141]

With rising unemployment – 8.6% in October[142] – it is commendable that all the Holyrood parties got together to defend the jobs in the shipyards on the Clyde and in Rosyth endangered by cuts to the defence budget.[143] It is also a good sign that the devolved administrations formed a rainbow alliance to stand their ground against the sweeping cuts, arguing that they are going too far, too fast.[144]

What are the prospects of the parties for the Holyrood election? The odds seem to be stacked against the SNP at the moment:

> The patchy SNP record on policy delivery over the past two years (the perils of minority government) after an energetic start, the Lockerbie bomber saga, the passing of the New Labour era that had pushed many left-leaning Scots into the SNP camp, and a re-energised Labour party under an new UK leader are all expected to be factors in play.[145]

A lack of élan, a lack of ideas, some disquiet about the list rankings for the regional vote, which could cost up to 12 SNP MSPs their job[146] – but it would be wrong to write Alex Salmond off. His personal ratings are still way ahead of anything Iain Gray or any other of the Scottish party leaders can hope for. If the election is, as Nicola Sturgeon hopes, simply a personality contest between the leaders, Salmond may yet come out tops.[147] Also, the SNP minority government has lasted for four years, an

---

[141] Brian Currie, 'Salmond: Cuts mark new era of devolution'. *The Herald*, 9 September 2010; Lucinda Cameron, 'Gray calls for devolution to move into "third phase"', *The Scotsman*, 28 May 2010.

[142] Eddie Barnes, '140 a day join dole queue as Scotland sees UK's fastest-growing jobless toll', *The Scotsman*, 14 October 2010.

[143] Brian Currie, 'SNP and Labour truce puts shipyard fight first', *The Herald*, 10 September 2010.

[144] Robbie Dinwoodie, 'A common cause against cuts', *The Herald*, 25 May 2010

[145] 'Tough questions for the SNP' (Leader), *Scotland on Sunday*, 10 October 2010.

[146] Andrew Whitaker, 'Dozen SNP MSPs "effectively deselected"', *The Scotsman*, 28 September 2010.

[147] Andrew Whitaker, 'Holyrood election will be battle of leaders', *The Scotsman*, 14 October 2010.

achievement in itself, as Ian Swanson has pointed out: 'The party has a credibility it did not have before 2007.'[148] And the Nationalists have made inroads into the media – two prominent journalist have been selected as candidates, Joan McAlpine and George Kerevan. As Tom Gallagher has argued,

> After four years in which it has shelved most of its 'flagship policies' it could hurt the SNP if it is seen to be bound up with style and contemptuous of substance. But what if none of its rivals can devise appealing policies due to financial constraints or having lost touch with most non-elite Scots? Then a party's skills in the dark arts of media warfare may come into their own.[149]

Should the SNP lose the election, would Alex Salmond stay? Doubtful, to say the least. And how would a defeat affect the SNP? The years since 2007 have been characterised by an astonishing loyalty inside the SNP, not a sign of dissent. Was it perhaps too becalmed? But there 'have recently been rumblings inside the Nationalist movement that there is too much emphasis on 'governing well' and not enough on the *raison d'etre* of independence.[150] That formidable pair of critics of the present tendency in the SNP, Margo MacDonald and Jim Sillars, have been scathing in their verdict: the SNP has lost its way, it has 'right now... about as much intellectual weight as a burst balloon has air,' and it has failed to build the case for independence.[151] The SNP's former leader Gordon Wilson, in a slightly less adversarial way, made similar points at an SNP conference fringe meeting in Perth.[152]

Labour, by contrast, has the most reason to look confidently towards the May poll, 10 points ahead of the SNP,[153] with the wind of the General Election in Scotland at their back, they even feel the need to warn against complacency. Will they be back in the driving seat by default, as it were? Or have they done their homework? It is fine, if not exactly popular, to

---

[148] Ian Swanson, 'The border at the margins?, *Edinburgh Evening News*, 14 October 2010.

[149] Tom Gallagher, 'Breaking free of the pack?', *Scottish Review*, 14 October 2010 <www.scottishreview.net/TomGallagher33.shtml>.

[150] Joan McAlpine, 'SNP's independence gambit has downsides', *The Scotsman*, 8 September 2010.

[151] Jim Sillars, 'The SNP is rapidly and vapidly losing its way', *The Scotsman*, 10 May 2010; Margo MacDonald, 'SNP forgot to sell us independence', *Edinburgh Evening News*, 11 November 2009.

[152] Eddie Barnes, 'Wilson to push independence', *Scotland on Sunday*, 10 October 2010.

[153] Laura Cummings, 'Blow to SNP as Labour takes ten-point lead', *Scotland on Sunday*, 5 September 2010.

say that he council tax freeze cannot go on forever – it is regressive, anyway.[154] Even if the SNP promises another two years of the same, with reduced funding for councils.[155] But where is the workable alternative to a tax that is widely perceived as unfair? Has Labour a strategy to reform local government, clearly in its present form unfit for purpose? Iain Gray's promise of a 'living wage' for the 20,000 lowest paid workers in the public sector in Scotland is attractive,[156] but is it fully costed? In marked contrast to the SNP's attack out of opposition, when they pummelled the public with policy initiatives throughout the summer of 2006 and thus took the initiative into the election campaign, there was very little in terms of new policies coming from Labour this summer.

Ed Miliband's acknowledgement that Scots Labour must make its own policy is refreshing.[157] In an odd way, Labour had remained the least devolved party under devolution. Maybe that is about to change. Miliband's stance on Iraq and his understanding that the Scottish elections could be a milestone in reviving Labour's electoral fortunes will certainly do no harm,[158] but there are questions about leadership in Scottish Labour that have to be answered. Otherwise, a lacklustre Labour administration, without new ideas, returned without enthusiasm, might very quickly run out of public favour.[159]

The Liberal Democrats have not suffered the same slump in the polls as south of the Border, and their constituency MSPs have solid majorities. Tavish Scott said at their party conference that, contrary to public perceptions, they had gained substantially in membership this year,[160] perhaps less so, it may be assumed – although the Scottish Lib Dem leader tried to sell it as a result of the coalition – after the election than before, when Nick Clegg bestrode the TV airwaves. And yet, the most awkward critics of the Con-Dem coalition are the former Lib Dem leaders Sir Menzies Campbell and Charles Kennedy – both, of course, Scots. And when the cuts really start to hurt, will the Lib Dems be punished

[154] Michael Kelly, 'If Salmond won't stop this council tax con, then Labour will', *The Scotsman*, 6 July 2010; Tom Gordon, 'Revealed: Labour's council tax bombshell', *Sunday Herald*, 3 October 2010.

[155] Eddie Barnes and Tom Peterkin, 'SNP to freeze council tax for two years', *The Scotsman*, 15 October 2010.

[156] David Maddox, 'Gray to pledge "living wage"', *The Scotsman*, 27 September 2010.

[157] Robbie Dinwoodie, 'Miliband says Scots Labour must make own policy', *The Herald*, 1 July 2010.

[158] David Maddox, 'Labour: "Red Ed" will help us defeat the SNP', *The Scotsman*, 27 September 2010.

[159] See Tom Gallagher, 'A Dash for Safety: Scottish Voters, Gordon Brown, and Labour', *Scottish Affairs*, no,72 (Summer 2010), pp.43-55.

[160] Robbie Dinwoodie, 'Coalition has boosted party membership, Scott tells Lib Dems', *The Herald*, 11 October 2010.

for propping up the Tories as they gleefully roll back the state? Will they have to pay at the ballot box for the acrobatic U-turns of their party in coalition, from VAT to tuition fees, and for being the most visible part of the Westminister government in Scotland?

The Scottish Tories are in a desperate situation. Their Scottish leader Annabel Goldie is popular and well-liked across party divides, but while the Tories in Wales have seen a remarkable revival, her party remains unelectable. Should it go its own way, declare independence from the Tories south of the border, as a Tory think tank recommended?[161] Has not David Cameron all but abandoned them anyway, as a hopeless case?[162] He seems to have signed Scotland over to the 11 Liberal Democrat MPs, as far as his government is concerned. Another flat-lining result may be one too many for Annnabel Goldie, but whether the party can do any better under a new leader – Murdo Fraser? – is doubtful. Fraser has argued that only a Tory premier acting in Scotland's favour can banish the shadow of Mrs Thatcher.[163] A think tank oracled that it could take 25 years before the Tories revive in Scotland[164] – but will by then perhaps the austerity shadow of Cameron and Osborne have eclipsed that of the Iron Lady?

Constituency boundary changes may give them a helping hand in 2011, as Professor David Denver suggests.[165] But their case has not exactly been helped by gaffe-prone candidates for the forthcoming election: one of them calling children's carers 'the great unwashed', another declaring the Scots 'so thick' that they 'swallowed' Labour's demonisation of Margaret Thatcher 'as if she was an evil force.'[166]

And what about the smaller parties and the Independents? Robin Harper, the most prominent Green and first-ever British Green parliamentarian, is stepping down. If, as it looks, the elections will again be a two-horse race between the SNP and Labour, it is hard to see the Greens picking up any extra seats. Although some SNP voters, disaffected over Trump or the Beauly to Denny power line, might consider switching their vote. The Scottish Socialists, presently all assembled in the High Court in Edinburgh in Tommy and Gail Sheridan's perjury trial,[167] have made sure by pushing

---

[161] Michael Settle, 'Why Tories should split from UK party', *The Herald*, 5 July 2010.

[162] Hamish Macdonell, 'Scots Tories "cast adrift" by Cameron', *Scotland on Sunday*, 5 September 2010.

[163] *BBC Newsnight Scotland*, 18 May 2010.

[164] Michael Settle, 'It could take 25 years to revive Scottish Tories', *The Herald*, 30 August 2010.

[165] 'Boundary changes may help Tories at Holyrood', *The Herald*, 9 September 2010.

[166] Brian Currie, 'Scots Tory election candidates under fire for insults', *The Herald*, 7 October 2010; Andrew Whitaker, 'Scots are "so thick" says Tory Holyrood hopeful', *The Scotsman*, 5 October 2010.

[167] Alison Campsie, 'Sex, lies and politics as the Sheridans' perjury trial opens', *The Herald*, 4 October 2010.

the self destruct button that there is not the slightest chance of them showing up at Holyrood. Margo MacDonald, whose Private Member's Bill on assisted dying was scrutinised by a specially convened Scottish Parliament committee and is to be given a free vote in Parliament, is a favourite to be re-elected, and it remains to be seen if the cuts may trigger independents to stand in defence of local services.

The Tories said they would be willing to enter into coalition talks with the SNP and the Lib Dems to keep Labour out of office, but would the other parties be interested?[168] They confirmed their conversion in October, with the SNP as their favoured partner to share power with.[169] The problem seems to be that no party at Holyrood wants to form a coalition with any of the other parties. During the silly season there were stories about the SNP having put feelers out to Labour about he possibility of an alliance after the election – one should never say never, but that looks like a non-starter.[170] 'If Scotland's two leading parties are serious about defending Scottish jobs,' Iain Macwhirter remarked, 'might they not at least consider the possibility of uniting in defence of them?'[171] Well, they and all the other Holyrood parties did so to defend the aircraft carrier programme against looming defence cuts. Pity it had to be about defence dinosaurs intended to uphold 'Britain's illusion of grandeur',[172] rather than forward-looking jobs in renewables that could give the shipyard workers a more solid and long-term future. But Iain Macwhirter's plea will probably go unheard: 'If only Labour and the SNP could shelve their tribal animosities, they could perform a very useful function in the coming age of austerity: fashioning a Scottish economic alternative.'[173]

So, will it be minority government again? The SNP minority government was protected by soaring poll results in its first two years of office – the other parties feared to bring down the government as they knew the SNP would be returned even stronger if elections were called. Could Labour bank on similar circumstances?

When John Osborne allowed the SNP government to defer until next year cuts he had announced in June, it was seen as if he had handed them

[168] Jason Allardyce, 'Tories look at SNP pact to stop Labour', *The Sunday Times*, 27 June 2010.

[169] Eddie Barnes and Tom Peterkin, 'Sots Tories in U-turn on coalition', *Scotland on Sunday*, 3 October 2010.

[170] David Maddox, 'Row flares over claim of SNP-Lab coalition talks', *The Scotsman*, 23 August 2010.

[171] Iain Macwhirter. 'I think the time has come to think the unthinkable', *The Herald*, 9 September 2010.

[172] Gerard DeGroot, 'What cost Britain's illusions of grandeur?', *The Scotsman*, 7 October 2010.

[173] Iain Macwhirter. 'I think the time has come to think the unthinkable', *The Herald*, 9 September 2010.

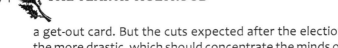

a get-out card. But the cuts expected after the election are therefore all the more drastic, which should concentrate the minds of the campaigning parties. Or will we have yet another phony war, where nobody is prepared to give full disclosure of their plans to manage the declining budget?

As of now, Labour seems most likely to regain the position of strongest party at Holyrood – but who, and in what combination, will be able to form a government, will only emerge when the ballot boxes are emptied and the votes are counted (hopefully in a less, er, shambolic manner than in 2007). It would appear that there is only one clear bet: that we will not wake up to a Conservative government in Scotland on 6 May. Now, here's a thought – what if the Tories lured that David McAllister chap over from Lower Saxony? A Hanoverian with a British passport and a track record of electoral success – what more could the Tories ask for?

[October 2010]

Chapter VIII

THE YEAR AT HOLYROOD
2010-2011

WHAT A DIFFERENCE A YEAR MAKES

The last instalment of the Annals finished on a downbeat note – the SNP, having started so well into its term as a minority government, seemed to have run out of puff, the opposition's relentless tune about the broken promises of the 2007 SNP manifesto seemed to dominate the political discourse and, after the good performance in the 2010 Westminster elections, Labour enjoyed a solid lead in the polls. But there were worries, too, that Labour had not done its homework in opposition, that it was lacking in ideas and policies. The Tories were flat-lining, and the Liberal Democrats were feeling the scorn of the Scottish public for entering into coalition with the 'toxic' Tories at Westminster.

At the turn of the year, and well into 2011, Labour felt that a victory in the May Holyrood election was not much more than a formality, and even SNP commentators began to give a gloss on a prospective SNP defeat, arguing that it would then be Labour's task to implement the cuts agenda and, after another spell of Labour-led government, there would surely come the chance for the SNP to bounce back.

But was it all a foregone conclusion? What about the ebullient personality of Alex Salmond, by far the most clever and popular politician in Scotland? 'There are any number of reasons for writing off Salmond's chances this May,' Iain Macwhirter contended at the beginning of the year: 'All except one: Salmond himself. So, in spite of all the odds, I believe he may still be in Bute House this time next year.'[1] And so he was. Moreover, according to an Ipsos/MORI poll, the SNP ended the year 2011 on a high of 51 per cent![2]

Nearly forgotten already – we did have a UK-wide referendum on the Alternative vote for Westminster: the Lib Dems' prize for entering

---

[1] Iain Macwhirter, '2011: The Holyrood Election', *Sunday Herald*, 2 January 2011.

[2] 26% for Labour, Conservatives 12%, and Lib Dems 8%. See Brian Currie, 'Nationalists' popularity at record levels', *The Herald*, 10 December 2011.

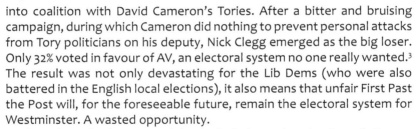

into coalition with David Cameron's Tories. After a bitter and bruising campaign, during which Cameron did nothing to prevent personal attacks from Tory politicians on his deputy, Nick Clegg emerged as the big loser. Only 32% voted in favour of AV, an electoral system no one really wanted.[3] The result was not only devastating for the Lib Dems (who were also battered in the English local elections), it also means that unfair First Past the Post will, for the foreseeable future, remain the electoral system for Westminster. A wasted opportunity.

The phone-hacking scandal which led to the demise of Rupert Murdoch's not-at-all missed *News of the World*, had only a glancing effect in Scotland, revealing slightly embarrassing overtures on Alex Salmond's side to the media mogul,[4] and throwing up a few questions about the Tommy Sheridan trial which had put the ex-MSP for three years in jail in January of last year.[5]

The intensifying Euro-crisis provided the dramatic backdrop to Scottish politics. From the Irish bail-out in November 2010 the Eurozone limbered on to the Greek bail-out in October, the viability of which seemed, at the beginning of 2012, threatened by Greece's deteriorating economy. David Cameron's 'veto' to the Euro rescue package including closer fiscal union in Europe at the EU summit in December may have far-reaching consequences for the UK and for Scotland. The UK's austerity policies brought the people out in protest, from 'Occupy' tents to big demonstrations. On 26 March, 400,000 protesters from all parts of the UK marched in London against the cuts in public spending, and on 30 November most public sector trade unions called a one-day strike which saw thousands out in the street against cuts in public-service pensions, pay freezes and privatisation,

On 28 October Campbell Christie, the former general secretary of the Scottish Trades Union Congress, died at the age of 74. He had been STUC general secretary from 1986 to 1998, was active in the struggle against the poll tax and a staunch supporter of Scottish devolution, a founder and key member of the Scottish Constitutional Convention which prepared the 'blueprint' for the Holyrood Parliament. In June 2011, the Commission bearing his name and investigating the future of public services in Scotland warned in its final report that, with spending not expected to return to 2010 levels for 16 years, major reforms were needed: 'Unless Scotland embraces a radical, new, collaborative culture throughout our public services, both budgets and provision will buckle under the strain.'[6]

---

[3] Ian Bell, 'Going into battle for a cause that nobody loves', *The Herald*, 2 April 2011.

[4] Andrew Whitaker, 'Salmond's TV offer to tycoon Murdoch', *The Scotsman*, 5 August 2011.

[5] Severin Carrell, 'Sheridan given three years of jail for perjury', *The Guardian*, 27 January 2011.

[6] Commission on the Future Delivery of Public Services, *Final Report*, Edinburgh: June 2011, <www.scotland.gov.uk/Resource/Doc/352649/0118638.pdf>.

Campbell Christie urged the Scottish government to begin moving ahead with the reforms. While the government promised to look closely at the findings with a view to taking them forward, the local authorities umbrella group CoSLA said it was moving immediately to implement the recommendations, regardless of the SNP's timescale. This report is the final legacy of Campbell Christie – 'a giant of the trade union movement and public life."[7]

The Japanese tsunami, and the Fukushima nuclear disaster in its wake, boosted anti-nuclear Green policies and caused the German government to end its nuclear energy programme, a move welcomed by the Scottish government as a confirmation of its own policy of no new nuclear power plants in Scotland.[8] And the convicted Lockerbie bomber Abdelbaset al-Megrahi, released by Kenny MacAskill in August 2009 'to die', survived even the demise of Muammar Gaddafi!

2011 was also, lest we forget, the year the Pandas came to Edinburgh Zoo. For 'giant pandas', Tian Tian and Yang Guang (or Sweeetie and Sunshine) are rather small and cuddly, as the first visitors observed. For 'a present from the Chinese government', they are also rather expensive. But Alex Salmond, who was visiting China in early December, praised 'the great gift of these giant pandas' which 'symbolises the great and growing relationship between Scotland and China.'[9] The Zoo hopes that visitor numbers will be significantly up and, as Martin Hannan quibbed, 'for once, tram was not the first word that people associated with Edinburgh.'[10] Moreover, the pandas gave SNP politicians the perfect Tory put-down: 'Scotland now has more giant pandas than Conservative MPs.'[11]

A LITTLE LIGHT LEGISLATION

The legislative programme of the final months of the Scottish Parliament's third session was distinctly on the 'lite' side, and overshadowed by the looming election campaign. As the Independence Referendum Bill was not introduced by the Government, the Budget Bill was the biggest, and the Alcohol Bill the most controversial among the

[7] Andrew Black, 'Commission says public services need "prevention" focus', BBC News Scotland, 29 June 2011, <www.bbc.co.uk/news/uk-scotland-13945938>.

[8] Brian Currie, 'SNP's green vision boosted by German nuclear exit', The Herald, 31 May 2011.

[9] Hilary Duncanson, 'Panda-mania as furry pair arrive in Scotland', Irish Examiner, 5 December 2011.

[10] Martin Hannan, 'A bitter taste to panda politics', Edinburgh Evening News, 10 January 2012.

[11] Alex Salmond, 'Why Cameron's petulance comes at a high price', Sunday Herald, 18 December 2012.

twenty Bills that were passed between October 2010 and the dissolution of Parliament in March.

The Legal Services Bill, passed on 6 October, made some regulatory changes; the Criminal Procedures Bill of 27 October was emergency legislation following the Supreme Court's ruling in the Cadder case that the Scottish practice of allowing suspects to be held and questioned for six hours without access to a lawyer was in breach of the European Convention of Human Rights. The debate in Parliament was at times vitriolic, the Lib Dems and the Greens opposing the extension of police detention powers. The new law preserves a right to legal advice for suspects being questioned by the police, but also extends the existing six-hour period for police detention to 12 and potentially 24 hours; it also was feared that it could lead to thousands of new appeals. Alex Salmond voiced his concern that the Supreme Court was undermining Scots law.[12]

The Housing Scotland Bill of 3 November is to improve the value that social housing delivers for tenants and taxpayers, to safeguard the supply of that housing for the benefit of future generations of tenants and to improve conditions in private sector housing. It ended the right-to-buy, a 'truly historic day for social housing,' as Housing and Communities Minister Alex Neil claimed.[13]

The Alcohol Bill, and particularly its minimum pricing proposal to protect and improve public health by reducing alcohol consumption, was challenged by the opposition parties. There was agreement on further restrictions on off-sales promotions and promotional activity and the requirement for an age verification policy, but the minimum unit pricing ran into opposition. The main objection was that the additional revenue generated by minimum pricing would end up in the retailers' tills rather than with the state, as would be the case if the price was driven up through taxation. Taxation, though, would have to happen at the UK level. The SNP government even offered a 'sunset clause' (i.e. a limited testing phase after which the legislation could be reconsidered) in order to tackle the scourge of alcoholism now. But the other parties declined – perhaps also because they wanted to deny the SNP a flagship policy before the elections. As passed on 10 October, the bill banned quantity discounts such as 'three for two' or '25 per cent off when you buy six', restricted alcohol promotions in off-sales, introduced a Challenge 25 age verification scheme for all licensed premises and paved the way for the introduction of a social responsibility levy to ensure those who profit from the sale of alcohol also put something back into the community.

---

[12] Robin Dinwoodie, 'Salmond: Scotland's legal system undermined', *The Herald*, 27 October 2010.

[13] Brian Currie, 'MSPs call time on right-to buy housing scheme in "historic" move', *The Herald*, 4 November 2010.

There was widespread disappointment about the opposition parties' blocking of minimum pricing. 'Just as the 2005 smoking ban showed Holyrood at its best, this was Holyrood at its worst,' complained Iain Macwhirter: 'Sheer mindless oppositionism. The kind of politics that would shame a local council.'[14] Health Secretary Nicola Sturgeon commented:

> I am disappointed that the legislation we have passed today is not as strong as we would have liked or as it could have been. It has, undoubtedly, been diluted through the absence of minimum pricing, which would save lives and reduce crime (...). I believe this bill is an important milestone towards changing Scotland's relationship with alcohol. But I am also clear that the journey is not over. There is more work to be done and we will not shirk from leading the way in addressing this challenge.[15]

The Children Hearings Bill, which finished its Stage 3 hearing on 25 October, provides for a dedicated national body, Children's Hearings Scotland, which is involved in the recruitment, selection, training, retention and support of panel members and in monitoring hearings and processes, provides independent advice to children's hearings, monitors panel members and acts as advocate for the Children's Panel. The reform was thrown into disarray after the suspension of its national convener, only ten months after her appointment.[16]

At the end of November, symbolically on St Andrew's Day 2010 (the day Salmond had originally earmarked for the independence referendum), the Scotland Bill was introduced at Westminster, based on the findings of the Calman Commission, and giving Holyrood the power to levy 10p of each income rate band – which would raise Scottish tax responsibility from 14% (council tax and business rates) to 35%. It also would allow the Parliament (going beyond Calman) to borrow £2.2b for capital projects like the Forth road bridge and £500m for day-to-day spending.[17] Although two tax powers – Air Passenger Duty and the Aggregates Levy (worth £150m a year) – were excluded, Scottish Secretary Michael Moore claimed:

---

[14] Iain Macwhirter, 'Killing the alcohol bill will cost lives – and Labour votes', Sunday Herald, 14 November 2010.

[15] Scottish Government News Release, 10 October 2010, <www.scotland.gov.uk/News/Releases/2010/11/10083013>.

[16] Stephen Naysmith, 'Children's Panel boss is suspended', The Herald, 14 December 2011.

[17] Peter Jones, 'New powers to borrow – but will they buy Scotland a better deal?', The Times, 1 December 2010; see also: Eddie Barnes, 'Devolution 2.0', Scotland on Sunday, 28 November 2010.

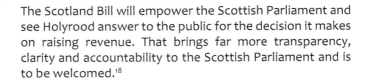

> The Scotland Bill will empower the Scottish Parliament and see Holyrood answer to the public for the decision it makes on raising revenue. That brings far more transparency, clarity and accountability to the Scottish Parliament and is to be welcomed.[18]

The SNP called the plans 'extraordinary modest', half-baked and potentially damaging for the Scottish economy,[19] while Wendy Alexander saw them as modernising the devolution settlement and conferring 'real financial accountability on the Scottish Parliament.'[20] Unusually, the Westminster Bill was to be scrutinised at Holyrood first. It would also need the consent of the Scottish Parliament before becoming law.

Consent was withheld by the Parliament in early December for Margo MacDonald's End of Life Assistance Bill. It was defeated in a free vote by 85 to 16 votes, after a 'thoughtful, mature, humane and even moving political debate.'[21] Margo's bid to change the law on assisted dying received support from Jeremy Purvis, Robin Harper, Patrick Harvie and Richard Lochhead (who was the only Cabinet Secretary voting in favour of the bill). Margo MacDonald pledged that she would try again if she was re-elected in May.[22]

The Forth Crossing Bill of 15 December is to give the Scottish Ministers power to construct a new bridge over the Firth of Forth and to build and improve associated roads and structures and to authorise the acquisition, or temporary possession and use, of land for construction and improvement works. The main three opposition parties backed the bill, only the Greens and Edinburgh West MSP Margaret Smith (Lib Dems) opposed it, calling this 'biggest infrastructure project in Scotland's history' a 'gamble with Scotland's economy'.[23] They were backed by a ream of environmental organisations. An amendment to the Historic Environment Bill, passed on 20 January, should improve the management and protection of Scotland's historic environment.

After the cliffhanger of the Budget in February 2010, the question was: would the final budget of the SNP minority government take its

---

[18] Eddie Barnes, '"Retreat" on new Scots tax powers', *Scotland on Sunday*, 28 November 2010.

[19] Severin Carrell, 'Scotland embarks on devolution phase 2', *The Guardian*, 1 December 2010.

[20] Wendy Alexander, 'New Bill gives Holyrood more responsibility over how our taxes are spent. We should embrace it', *The Times*, 1 December 2010.

[21] Joyce McMillan, 'Mature debate did parliament proud', *The Scotsman*, 3 December 2010.

[22] Brian Currie, 'MSPs reject legalising the right to die', *The Herald*, 2 December 2010.

[23] Alastair Dalton, 'New Forth bridge gets go-ahead as MSPs reject fears of a giant gamble', *The Scotsman*, 16 December 2010.

Parliamentary hurdle? Or could a failure of the bill even trigger an early election? In the end, on 9 February, the SNP minority government 'won comfortable support for its £34bn budget … having successfully wooed the Conservatives and Liberal Democrats with concessions.'[24] Only Labour voted against the budget and the £1.3bn cuts entailed, including a 2.6% cut to the funding of local authorities and a freeze of public service pay, but delaying any really tough decisions until after the election.[25] *The Scotsman* called the budget

> A ploy, a feint, an exercise in obfuscation, designed to avoid difficult decisions. The SNP clearly believes it can somehow continue to fool enough of the people enough of the time to win re-election. It is a foolish strategy. The people are no fools, as the SNP is likely to find out in May.[26]

Given the electoral cycle, it was perhaps to be expected that John Swinney would not give any figures beyond 2012, but that did not mean that the opposition parties did not denounce the budget as an exercise of 'shameless electioneering'.[27] Alex Salmond's response was the announcement of the Christie Commission on the Future Delivery of Public Services which would report in June 2011 – after the election.[28]

The Patient Rights Bill of 24 February established a patient advice and support service and Patient Rights Officers who are to safeguard that the health care that patients receive meets certain criteria, according to a set of health care principles. It also provides a treatment time guarantee and establishes a right to make complaints.

The Wildlife and Natural Environment Bill, which was approved by Parliament on 2 March, contains a package of measures intended to ensure hat the legislation which protects wildlife and regulates the management of the natural environment and natural resources is fit for purpose. On 3 March, the Property Factors Bill was passed, establishing a register of property factors and requiring property factors to be registered. On the same day, the Damages Bill also was voted through, making further provision as regards rights to damages in respect of personal injuries and death. The Reservoirs Bill, approved on 9 March,

---

[24] Andrew Bolger, 'Battle lines drawn for Scottish election', *Financial Times*, 13 February 2011.

[25] Brian Currie, Robbie Dinwoodie and Gerry Braiden, 'Swinney delivers a Budget sidestep', *The Herald*. 18 November 2010.

[26] 'Swinney's stop-gap solutions are no answer to the problem' (Leader), *The Scotsman*, 18 November 2010.

[27] 'Budget questions remain unanswered' (Leader), *The Herald*, 18 November 2010.

[28] 'Passing the budget parcel' (Leader), *The Guardian*, 18 November 2010.

makes provision about the regulation of the construction, alteration and management of certain reservoirs, in particular in relation to the risk of flooding from such reservoirs, for the repeal and replacement of the Reservoirs Act 1975, about offences to facilitate the achievement of the environmental objectives set out in river basin management plans.

Meanwhile, the Scotland Bill Committee under Wendy Alexander backed the proposals of the Calman-based bill – after acrimonious clashes with academics Drew Scott and Andrew Hughes-Hallett over the economic benefits of fiscal autonomy[29] and with reservations from the SNP MSPs on the Committee regarding the fiscal arrangements envisaged by the bill.[30]

Four bills were passed on 16 March. The Local Electoral Administration (Scotland) Bill continues the process of improving electoral administration following the difficulties faced in the 2007 joint local government and Scottish Parliamentary elections. The bill establishes the Electoral Management Board for Scotland on a statutory basis for its work in relation to local government elections in Scotland, provides for the convener of the Board to be appointed by Scottish Ministers and creates a power of direction for the convener over local returning officers and electoral registration officers. The bill provides that the Board must prepare and submit to Parliament an annual report on the carrying out of its functions.

The Certification of Death Bill introduces a new system of scrutiny of medical certificates of cause of death. It creates the post of medical reviewer and senior medical reviewer whose functions are to review for accuracy the certificates referred to them from a variety of sources. A number of certificates will be referred at random by district registrars. The Registrar General will be responsible for ensuring that certificates are referred according to the chosen selection scheme. Persons with some connection to the deceased can now apply for a review and certificates may also be selected by the medical reviewers themselves for scrutiny. The Public Records Bill amends the Public Records (Scotland) Act 1937 (c.43) in relation to court records.

The Domestic Abuse Bill amends the Protection from Harassment Act 1997 by making provision in relation to harassment amounting to domestic abuse, and the Legal Aid (Scotland) Act 1986 by making provision in relation to eligibility for, and the making of contributions towards, civil legal aid in certain proceedings arising from domestic abuse.

The Private Rented Housing Bill, passed on 17 March, strengthens the regulation of the private rented sector, in order to support responsible

---

[29] 'What some defended as robust questioning, others recognised as plain rudeness,' commented James Mitchell, 'Holyroood on display as new politics is laid to rest', *The Herald*, 24 January 2011.

[30] Robbie Dinwoodie, 'Committee backs Calman', *The Herald*, 2 March 2011.

landlords and address more effectively the problems caused by landlords who act unlawfully. This involves changes to the operation of the systems for registration of private landlords and licensing of houses in multiple occupation. The bill also includes provisions intended to deal with problems caused by overcrowding in the private rented sector and to improve the working of the private sector tenancy regime.

Just before the dissolution of the Parliament on 22 March, the two final bills were passed: the Forced Marriage Etc (Protection and Jurisdiction) (Scotland) Bill aims at protecting persons from being forced into marriage without their free and full consent and at protecting persons who have been forced into marriage without such consent. And the Double Jeopardy Bill is a response to advanced technology, making provision as to the circumstances in which a person convicted or acquitted of an offence may be prosecuted anew.

THE 2011 HOLYROOD ELECTION

The run-up to the election campaign was fraught with set backs for all parties. In the autumn, the SNP seemed to be on the back foot. Apologising became a bit of a habit for Alex Salmond and his ministerial team. First, Finance Secretary John Swinney got himself into a pickle over his decision (not disclosed to the Parliament at the time) to allow the tax-varying power of the Scottish Parliament to lapse.[31] He was obliged to apologise to Parliament. Then came an apology from the First Minister himself about the financial handling of the 'Gathering' during the 2009 Year of Homecoming (which led to the write-off of a £180,000 loan). Next in line was Transport Secretary Stewart Stevenson. He got caught out by the snow and had to take responsibility for his inept handling of the travel chaos during the 'big freeze' in early December which paralysed the travel network, with thousands stuck in cars and trains, as the M8 was blocked for nearly three days and train journeys were severely disrupted. He had maintained that here had been a 'first-class response,' but regretted that remark a few days later and resigned.[32] Keith Brown took over.

Education Secretary Mike Russell faced accusations of 'duplicity' about 'meddling' in a council's school closure plan – not in his constituency, but in the one he was selected to stand in come the May elections.[33] All that

---

[31] Robbie Dinwoodie, 'Fury as Scotland loses its tax-raising powers', *The Herald*, 19 November 2010.

[32] Tom Peterkin, 'Stevenson quits over snow chaos', *Scotland on Sunday*, 12 December 2010.

[33] Robbie Dinwoodie, 'Russell is accused of meddling in schools closure bid', *The Herald*, 4 January 2011.

against a backdrop of policy failures stacking up – failing to meet the PE target in primary schools, falling teacher numbers, more primary 1-3 kids in large classes.[34]

The SNP came also under fire for letting the trams fiasco in Edinburgh unfold without taking control, despite having intervened immediately when the controversial Trump project of a luxury golf course in the dunes on Aberdeenshire's coast ran into a little local difficulty. While the party claimed it had kept 84 of the 94 pledges it had made in 2007,[35] some critics close to the party were scathing in their verdict: 'The stark truth of the matter is that, sadly, the SNP administration has actually achieved very little during its four years in power.'[36] Others saw the Nationalists' record in a more positive light:

> This has I think been a decent Scottish Government, and one that for all its limitations marks an important watershed not just for the SNP, but our democracy, politics and nation.[37]

The SNP managed to defuse a potential pitfall over Salmond's refusal to publish ministerial advice on their proposed Local Income Tax by shelving any replacement of the Council Tax until after the next elections in 2016. And their manifesto boasted a number of populist policies like free university education for Scots, the five-year council tax freeze and the protection of NHS spending. In the end, the council tax freeze and the SNP's 'green vision' – a renewable energy target of 100%, coupled with the creation of 130,000 jobs in the 'low-carbon economy', all by 2020 – were the cornerstones on which the SNP staked its success.

As the campaign gathered momentum, opposition parties seemed, oddly enough, to let the SNP off on its record in government. After having won a series of Westminster by-elections by attacking the SNP on Holyrood themes Labour, for whatever reasons, thought that they could win at Holyrood with a Westminster campaign. It is interesting to compare the Labour campaign in Wales, which always put Wales first and the effect on Westminster second, with Scottish Labour's campaign, which saw Ed Miliband come to Glasgow to tell the Scots they should vote Labour to give the Tory-led coalition in London a bloody nose and help the Labour

---

[34] Brian Currie, 'SNP fails to deliver PE target', *The Herald*, 29 November 2010; Andrew Denholm, 'Number of Scots teachers plunges by 3000', *The Herald*, 2 December 2010.

[35] Robbie Dinwoodie, 'SNP claim to have fulfilled 84 of 94 pledges in last four years', *The Herald*, 16 April 2011.

[36] Ewan Crawford, 'High water mark for the SNP?', *Caledonian Mercury*, 31 January 2011 <politics.caledonianmercury.com/2011/01/31/opinion-high-water-mark-for-the-snp/>.

[37] Gerry Hassan, 'Time for next step on SNP's journey', *The Scotsman*, 14 January 2011.

Party in the UK to get back in power. Some would call that an insult to Scottish voters. 'Maybe deciding to fight Thatcher not Salmond wasn't such a good idea,' was *Scotland on Sunday*'s dry comment.[38] And when that campaign did not manage to get any traction, they panicked and reverted to scaremongering about independence, an issue the SNP had long since successfully managed to separate from elections for Holyrood.

Labour was also criticised for its £90m spending plans, revealed during their party conference in Glasgow in October, while not mentioning any cuts.[39] Iain Gray announced a 2% council tax rise, only to revert the plan in an embarrassing U-turn, agreeing to the SNP's two-year freeze (promptly upped by the SNP to five years). Otherwise Labour did not say too much, relying on the polls which saw them firmly ahead of the SNP. There were worries about the 'unknown' leader Iain Gray – ten weeks before the election, only 20% of Scots recognised him when shown his photo.[40] Earlier, he had become embroiled in an embarrassing diplomatic row after linking Montenegro with ethnic cleansing when he picked on parallels alluded to by the SNP between Scotland's and Montenegro's paths to independence. The dismal Labour campaign found its surreal metaphor with Iain Gray dodging into a Glasgow sandwich shop when he was confronted by anti-cuts activist Sean Clerkin.[41]

The Tories were the only party planning to make students pay tuition fees of up to £16,000 for a four-year degree. But their campaign had a 'terrible start', beginning with the sacking of one Glasgow candidate over allegedly undisclosed previous financial difficulties, then the resignation of another Glasgow candidate who accused the party not to have investigated allegations of vote-rigging in the city. And a third one declined the offer of a list position.[42] But Annabel Goldie had another good campaign, standing her ground in debates with Alex Salmond, winning praise for her blunt speaking and no-nonsense manner. She produced the best line of the campaign when she promised during the BBC leaders' debate that she would have Alex Salmond and Iain Gray 'by the short and curlies' if they were up to any nonsense.[43] But all to no avail.

---

[38] 'Salmond turns the Leader tide', *Scotland on Sunday*, 17 April 2011.

[39] Eddie Barnes, 'Labour faces questions over spending pledges', *The Scotsman*, 1 November 2010.

[40] Andrew Whitaker, 'Does anyone know who this man is?', *The Scotsman*, 18 February 2011.

[41] Alastair Dalton,' From station to Subway – the flight of a politician', *The Scotsman*, 8 April 2011.

[42] 'Goldie's star turn but Scottish Tories must up their game' (Leader), *Sunday Herald*, 3 April 2011; see also Scott Macnab, 'Tories deny collapse after third blow to campaign', *The Scotsman*, 29 March 2011.

[43] Andrew Black, 'Scottish election: Talking nearly over for politicians', *BBC News Scotland*, 4 May 2011 <www.bbc.co.uk/news/uk-scotland-scotland-politics-13271161>.

The media and many Scots may have loved her, the electorate showed her party the cold shoulder.

Losing two candidates before he campaign proper had even started did not augur well for the Liberal Democrats. One stood down being charged with soliciting prostitutes,[44] and former MSP Hugh O'Donnell quit the party in protest of its role in the Westminster coalition.[45] Then, adding to the party's woes, their long-serving former MSP John Farquhar Munro called Alex Salmond 'the only one' to lead Scotland in the years ahead.[46] Their manifesto launch, revealing their flagship policy of selling off the debt from publicly owned water utilities, got immediately into troubled water when it transpired that the UK government might cash in the £1.5bn the Lib Dems hoped would be freed up.[47] The Liberal Democrats tried their utmost to distance themselves from 'that lot down south', but Tavish Scott fought a losing battle. The Scots were, quite obviously, not happy with Nick Clegg's U-turns, particularly on tuition fees and, more generally, with the Lib Dem-Tory Westminster love-in, and they seemed determined to make them pay at the election.

The SNP ran a professional, slick campaign, well-oiled by donations like Brian Souter's £500,000 for the campaign coffers,[48] allowing them to outspend the other parties,[49] and making good use of new technology, their superior voter data base, and social media. It cannot have harmed the SNP's prospect that prescription charges, already reduced over the previous three years, were abolished as from the beginning of April. Moreover, the party gained the public backing for Alex Salmond's bid to win a historic second term as Scotland's First Minister from more than 200 of the country's top business figures, including the 'committed Unionist' and Rangers FC owner Sir David Murray.[50] Oil bosses, entrepreneurs, an aristocrat chef and the heads of some of the nation's biggest companies signed a document that hailed the SNP leader's achievements over the

---

[44] Frank Urquhart, 'Lib Dem Holyrood hopeful quits over prostitution charges', The Scotsman, 23 February 2011.

[45] Andrew Whitakler, 'Lib Dem plans suffer blow as key candidate quits the party', The Scotsman, 28 March 2011.

[46] Andrew Whitaker, 'Senior Lib Dem gives backing to Samond', The Scotsman, 5 April 2011.

[47] Andrew Whitaker, 'Lukewarm minister adds to Lib Dem water torture', The Scotsman, 9 April 2011.

[48] Eddie Barnes, '£500,000 war chest for Salmond', Scotland on Sunday, 13 February 2011.

[49] Eddie Barnes, 'Scottish Labour struggled to match SNP's £2.1m war chest, figures show', The Scotsman, 29 July 2011.

[50] Andrew Whitaker, '"Big Business trying to swing election" as Murray backs SNP', The Scotsman, 28 February 2011.

past four years and said he and his team have been good for the nation.[51] The businessman Jim McColl stated: 'Alex Salmond has run a competent government for the past four years. He deserves a second term in office.'[52] That was echoed by some of the leading newspapers who recommended a second term for Salmond, without endorsing the SNP's goal of Scottish independence.[53]

A first inkling of a wobble in the polls had come in February, when an Ipsos/MORI poll registered a narrow SNP lead over Labour. The Budget – where Labour had asked for additional apprenticeships for young people, was given it, and still voted against it, and Wendy Alexander's surprise announcement that she would stand down at the election, may have contributed to that. It was widely regarded as a rogue poll. But in March, the swing was definitely on. At the start of the campaign 10 to 16 points ahead, Labour's lead was whittled away by the start of the campaign proper, and completely turned around by polling day, when the SNP romped home with a massive victory, securing what the Holyrood electoral system was supposed to make nigh impossible: an absolute majority. 'An apparent winter of despair for the SNP had,' David Torrance commented, 'quickly become a spring of hope.'[54]

James Robertson called the campaign 'lacking in excitement'.[55] The verdict of the media about the campaign was also negative. *The Herald* ran a Steven Camley cartoon with two guys gazing at a gorse fire in the distance. The caption read: 'We don't know what set the heather on fire – but it wasn't the election campaign.'[56] Others, like Pat Watters, talked about the parties having 'offered little more than junk food.'[57] The manifestos – 'none of them wholly honest, one verging on fantasy' – ignored the difficult decisions, were 'uncosted', 'financially unworkable' and deemed an 'insult to voters'.[58]

---

[51] Cameron Brooks, 'Top 200 back Salmond bid for second Holyrood term', *The Press and Journal*, 4 May 2011.

[52] Jim McColl, 'Scottish parties must fight for financial power', *The Sunday Times*, 17 April 2011.

[53] 'Salmond deserves a second term' (Leader), *The Scotsman* 4 May 2011; 'Scottish National Party deserves a second term' (Leader), *Sunday Herald*, 1 May 2011; 'Salmond is best choice' (Leader), *Scotland on Sunday*, 1 May 2011

[54] David Torrance, 'A Tale of Two Elections', *Scottish Affairs*, No.76 (Summer 2011), p.32.

[55] James Robertson, 'The 2011 Scottish Election: Are We All Nationalists Now?' *Scottish Affairs*, No.76 (Summer 2011), p.1.

[56] *The Herald*, 4 May 2011.

[57] 'Public not served by a poor standard of debate' (Leader), *The Herald*, 11 April 2011.

[58] Eddie Barnes, 'SNP and Labour "ignore the difficult decisions"', *The Scotsman*, 21 April 2011; Brian Currie, 'Voters told to be sceptical of manifestos', *The Herald*, 21 April 2011; Jason Allardyce, 'Grand pledges don't come for free', *The Sunday Times*, 17 April 2011; 'Party manifestos are insult to voters' (Leader), *Sunday Herald*, 10 April 2011.

Graph 1   Salmond's Extraordinary Reversal

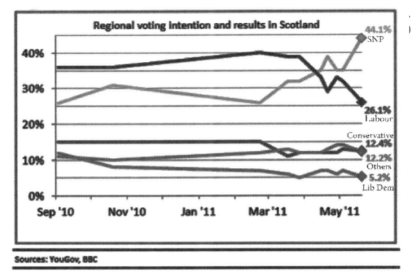

The Spectator, 6 May 2011, <http://twitpic.com/4u6ku2>

and a full session with minority government (again, a novelty in the UK), now the election outcome of 2011 provided the first single-party majority government for Holyrood,[59] with 69 SNP seats. The Greens who had hoped to make gains, on a manifesto pledging tax increases to defend public services,[60] kept their two seats in Glasgow and Edinburgh, and Margo MacDonald is still the only Independent at Holyrood.

According to the Scottish Election Study, it was the competence of the SNP which won the day. The SNP gained where it used to be weak, 43% of support from Catholics, 47% of the working-class vote, and 43% of the women's vote. 71% held the SNP capable of strong government, 85% saw the party as united, 75% in touch with ordinary people and, despite the broken pledges, 50 credited them with keeping their promises.[61]

---

[59] For an analysis of the election result, see David Denver, 'Another "Historic Moment": The Scottish Parliament Elections 2011', *Scottish Affairs*, No.76 (Summer 2011), pp.33-50; and John Curtice, 'The 2011 Scottish Elections: Records Tumble, Barriers Breached', *Scottish Affairs*, No.76 (Summer 2011), pp.51-73.

[60] Scott Macnab, 'Greens go it alone with taxing plans to combat the cuts', *The Scotsman*, 20 April 2011.

[61] <www.scottishelectionstudy.org.uk>; See Eddie Barnes, 'Competence not constitution won it for SNP', *The Scotsman*, 22 June 2011.

Table 5: Scottish Parliament Election Results 2011

| | Constituency / Regional List / **Seats** | | | |
| | % | % | | |
	1999	2003	2007	2011
Labour	38.8 / 33.6 / **56**	34.6 / 29.3 /**50**	32.1 / 29.2 /**46**	31,7 / 26,3 / **37**
SNP	28.7 / 27.3 / **35**	23.8 / 20.9 / **27**	32.9 / 31.0 / **47**	45,4 / 44,0 / **69**
Lib Dem	14.2 / 12.4 / **17**	15.4 / 11.4 /**17**	16.2 / 11.3 / **16**	7,9 / 5,2 / **5**
Con	15.6 / 15.4 / **18**	16.6 / 15.5 /**18**	16.6 / 13.9 / **17**	13,9 / 12,4 / **15**
Green	----- / 3.6 / **1**	----- / 6.9 /**7**	0.1 / 4.0 / **2**	---- / 4,4 / **2**
Others	2.7 / 7.7 / **2**	9.6 / 15.6 /**10**	2.1 / 10.6 / **1**	1,1 / 6,8 / **1**

In the wake of the landslide, Alex Salmond showed an admirable degree of humility, when he made his victory speech at Prestonfield: 'I welcome the declarations from the opposition parties about constructive opposition because, although the SNP has a majority of the seats, we don't have a monopoly of wisdom.'[62] The first couple of months after the election triumph could be seen as revealing the janus face of Alex Salmond.

SUPREME COURT STUSHIE

First came an epsiode which did not quite live up to the 'Prestonfield Principle'. A row over the 'interference' of the UK Supreme Court in the Scottish justice system had been rumbling on, but it developed into a major stushie over an interview with Alex Salmond in *Holyrood* magazine on his salvo of personal attacks on Lord Hope, one of Scotland's most senior judges, accusing him of 'routinely interfering in criminal appeals in Scotland,' and on Scotland's top human rights lawyer Tom Kelly.[63] If that was not offensive enough, Justice Secretary Kenny MacAskill questioned the competence of the English judges on the Court, suggesting their knowledge of the Scottish justice system was picked up on trips to the Edinburgh Festival, and threatened that he would cut Scottish funding for the UK Supreme Court.[64]

The Cadder and Nat Fraser cases, appeals in criminal cases based on human rights issues, raised the question who has the last say in Scottish criminal law cases: the High Court in Scotland or the UK Supreme Court? Thus, there is a real issue about Scots law being undermined by a UK legal body. What made the outbursts of Salmond and MacAskill so unpalatable was that, in both cases, the UK court was right. Six hours

---

[62] Alex Salmond, 6 May 2011; see 'Scottish election: Salmond offers olive branch to rivals', *BBC News Scotland*, 6 May 2011, <www.bbc.co.uk/news/uk-scotland-13317382>.

[63] Mandy Rhodes, 'Interview: Alex Salmond', *Holyrood*, 13 June 2011; See also Robbie Dinwoodie, 'Leading lawyer to sue First Minister', *The Herald*, 16 June 2011.

[64] David Leak, 'MacAskill; threat to end Supreme Court funding', *The Herald*, 1 June 2011.

police questioning without access to a lawyer (Cadder) and neglect of evidence (Fraser) were blatant offenses committed by Scots law and Scots courts, respectively. Kenneth Roy summed it up brilliantly:

> Our proud justice system, whose independence must be saved at all costs from southern interference, was responsible in the Fraser case for a disgraceful failure to disclose a vital piece of evidence, as a result of which the accused could not and did not receive a fair trial. So wonderful is this justice system that, had it not been for the appeals procedure which led in the end to the UK Supreme Court, the evidence in question would probably never have come to light. Had it, however, been produced at the trial, as it should have been, the Crown case would have collapsed at once, as the Crown itself has been big enough to admit. There are two ways of looking at last week's judgement. We can either huff and puff about an English court meddling in Scottish affairs that are none of its business, and run off with the ba' like wee laddies; or we can be grateful to Lord Hope for sorting out a mess entirely of our own making and preparing the way for a re-trial. Motivated mainly, it seems, by some misguided patriotism, we have chosen to look at it the first way rather than the second.[65]

Justice must prevail – where it comes from should be of secondary importance. Or is Alex Salmond's 'sanctity of Scots Law' more important than justice?[66] Topmost principle has to the independence of the courts from government. Lord McCluskey, a former Solicitor General, said Kenny MacAskill ought to be 'ashamed' of his claim that the 'ambulance-chasing' UK Supreme Court's judges know nothing of Scotland other than visits to the Edinburgh Festival, endorsed by the First Minister. He called his comments of 'he who pays the piper calls the tune' egregious and unsuitable for a man holding his office.[67] 'The SNP threatened a court not because of what it does but because of where it is – in England,'

---

[65] Kenneth Roy, 'The shameful treatment of Lord Hope augurs ill', *Scottish Review*, 1 June 2011 <www.scottishreview.net/KRoy131.shtml>.

[66] Alex Salmond, 'Why the sanctity of Scots Law remains an important cause and one that is well worth fighting for', *The Scotsman*, 1 June 2011.

[67] Simon Johnson, 'Lord McCluskey says Kenny MacAskill's conduct is "unsuitable" for a Justice Minister', *The Daily Telegraph*, 3 June 2011.

the *Scotsman* concluded: 'Such narrow nationalism is not worthy of the modern, outward-looking SNP Mr Salmond claims to lead.'[68]

THE 'PRESTONFIELD PRINCIPLE' AT WORK

The humble side of Alex Salmond, it could be argued, came to the fore when he bowed to the storm of opposition facing his rushed Offensive Behaviour at Football and Threatening Communications Bill, which he had wanted to push through Parliament to become law in time for the new football season in the summer.[69] There was consensus, not just between the parties at Holyrood, that the series of 'ugly and sinister events' that had blighted the 'beautiful game' during the last season had to be stopped.[70]

> Scottish football rarely seems far from a new low, but last season was something special. Hundreds of arrests at a Rangers vs Celtic match in February were followed by ugly touchline scenes involving the clubs' management teams. (…) Things got worse, with bullets, parcel bombs and death threats sent to Celtic manager Neil Lennon and others linked t the club in April, putting the issue of sectarianism front and centre in the Scottish election campaign.[71]

The bill proposed two new offences, each carrying a maximum of five years in prison: first, offensive and abusive behaviour at football matches; second, threatening communications (emails, blogs, twitter, etc) inciting to violence or 'religious hatred'. Would it mean that singing the national anthem or crossing yourself could put you in jail? Roseanna Cunningham, Community and Safety Minister, had an unfortunate appearance before the justice committee – which only added to the confusion. Opposition mounted against the haste with which the legislation had been pulled together. Aidan O'Neill, QC, who wrote the legal opinion on the bill, said: 'It was one of the worst drafted bills I have ever seen from the Scottish Parliament.'[72] Even the Old Firm united in opposition to the Bill.

---

[68] 'Narrow nationalism is not worthy of Leader modern SNP', *The Scotsman*, 2 June 2011.

[69] Eddie Barnes, 'U-turn on football hate bill – in 90 minutes', *The Scotsman*, 24 June 2011.

[70] 'Don't kill anti-sectarian bill' (Leader), *Sunday Herald*, 26 June 2011; for background, see John Kelly, 'Scotland's shame is alive and kicking', *The Scotsman*, 13 May 2011.

[71] Tom Gordon, 'Kicked into extra time', *Sunday Herald*, 26 June 2011.

[72] *Ibid.*

Was the unseemly haste perhaps also triggered by a degree of bad consciousness over having neglected the problem for most of the four years of SNP minority rule? Jack McConnell repeatedly voiced his frustration over those four years of watching 'others take their eye off the ball.'[73] Anyway, Salmond changed his mind, granting a six-month reprieve to give more time for consensus building. The SNP spin doctors hailed that as a demonstration of the 'Prestonfield Principle', but 'there was no disguising that the first bill set out by the SNP majority government had come an embarrassing cropper.'[74]

HUBRIS?

Alex Salmond also used the momentum of the election victory to demand further powers for the Scottish Parliament. In a speech on 18 May he, as he summed it up himself, 'outlined six areas of potential common ground where there is agreement across the parliament to a greater or lesser extent: borrowing powers, corporation tax, the Crown Estate, excise duties, digital broadcasting; and a stronger say in European policy.'[75] Only one of the demands was met by the Westminster government – borrowing powers were increased from £2bn to £5bn and brought forward to 2012 – the others were rejected. London then angered the SNP by giving part of the Crown Estate profits directly to local councils in Scotland.

Using its absolute majority and defying convention, the SNP installed Tricia Marwick MSP as the new Presiding Officer and, sticking with d'Hondt, all the Holyrood committees now have an inbuilt SNP majority, and two-thirds of them have an SNP convener. This is new territory for the Scottish Parliament. Will scrutiny of legislation still work in a unicameral parliament, with one-party rule? John Curtice said that the attitude taken by SNP committee members was crucial. They needed to be 'critical friends' of the government.[76] In the autumn, he went so far as to suggest a change in the Scottish electoral system to prevent majority rule on a minority vote.[77]

---

[73] Jack McConnell, 'All sections of society must act to end Scotland's national shame', *The Herald*, 21 April 2011.

[74] Tom Gordon, 'Kicked into extra time', *Sunday Herald*, 26 June 2011.

[75] Alex Salmond, 'Time to seize the moment', 18 May 2011, <www.heraldscotland.com/politics/political-news/time-to-seize-the-moment-alex-salmond-s-speech-in-full.13729407>

[76] Brian Currie, 'Salmond warned over number of committees dominated by SNP', *The Herald*, 2 June 2011.

[77] Andrew Whitaker, 'Scottish election system is branded a failure', *The Scotsman*, 16 November 2011.

The question of sufficient checks and balances were raised. The former Presiding Officer George Reid spoke in favour of more 'post-legislative scrutiny', and his predecessor Lord Steel called for a second chamber. Kenyon Wright, who convened the Constitutional Convention, also urged a rethink, as the monocameral parliament was designed with a view that civic Scotland would provide additional scrutiny through bodies like the Civic Forum – but that has not really happened.[78]

Concerns about 'hubris', 'arrogance', even 'elected dictatorship',[79] were raised, fuelled by the Supreme Court stushie, the unholy rush to legislate against sectarianism, Salmond's refusal to publish the economic advise about the costs of a local income tax, ignoring the advise of the information commissioner, and the apology the First Minister was forced to offer to the Parliament for his false claim that a letter he had read out in Parliament had been written by the academic Matt Qvortrup when, in fact, it had been the SNP's press spokesman's draft which the academic had declined to endorse.[80]

The First Minister also got some flak for insisting that the so-called 'UK riots' were, 'until such time we do have a riot in Scotland, … riots in London and across English cities' and claiming that Scotland had 'a different society',[81] which earned him accusations of gloating and scoring cheap political points. But, objectively, he was only stating the obvious – there had been no riots in Scotland. Whether Scotland is so much different as a society may be more debatable. And then Salmond claimed his part in the downfall of Margaret Thatcher,[82] sadly missed by the Meryl Streep biopic. But it led the *Scotsman* to speculation as to who could have played our First Minister – 'only one actor could do justice to the roly-poly chutzpah: Danny DeVito.'[83]

BY-ELECTION SUCCESS FOR LABOUR

After the tragic death of Labour MP David Cairns in May, aged just 44, a Westminster by-election was called for the Inverclyde constituency on 30 June, not quite two months after the SNP triumph at Holyrood.

---

[78] 'Holyrood: power and scrutiny' (Leader), *The Herald*, 16 December 2011.

[79] Scott Macnab, 'Scotland heading for "elected dictatorship"', *The Scotsman*, 4 June 2011.

[80] Robbie Dinwoodie, 'Salmond apology over poll expert's remarks', *The Herald*, 28 October 2011.

[81] Ian Swanson, 'Riot-free Scots are unequal too', *Edinburgh Evening News*, 17 August 2011.

[82] Andrew Whitaker, 'Day I tamed Maggie, by Alex Salmond', *The Scotsman*, 3 January 2012.

[83] Leader, 'From Holyrood to Hollywood? Perhaps not, Leader Alex', *The Sotsman*, 3 January 2012.

Would the SNP take another Labour bastion?[84] Or would voting patterns revert towards those of the 2010 UK election? Labour selected Inverclyde Council leader Iain McKenzie to defend the seat, while former Glasgow MSP Anne McLaughlin contested it for the SNP. Both campaigned vigorously on new 'high quality' jobs and investment for Inverclyde, but it was one of those by-elections which 'fail to catch fire, failing to excite the interest of the press, the public or the voters – and which disappear without trace.'[85]

Alex Salmond visited the constituency five times during the short campaign: 'I think this is earthquake proportions if we win this seat,' he said. 'I think that the political impact of a victory for the SNP in Inverclyde would be absolutely huge.'[86] That did not sound as if he was fully convinced his party would take another scalp. And, indeed, Labour held the seat comfortably, with a reduced majority of just under 6,000 votes.

The result for the Lib Dems was, in the words of Ross Finnie, a former Scottish Lib Dem MSP who was environment minister for eight years, a 'humiliation'. [87] Their candidate limped home with 627 votes in fourth place, having lost the deposit. Finnie warned that voters north of the Border had lost trust in the Deputy Prime Minister.

EDINBURGH TRAMS FIASCO

The never-ending saga of the Edinburgh tram kept on agitating folk way beyond Edinburgh. What was striking was the passivity of the Scottish government in the face of a mounting crisis, Of course, the SNP had tried to kill the project off in 2007 and was only forced by the other parties to give the go-ahead for the scheme then capped at £500m. But since then it has never been out of the headlines. 'I do not understand,' wrote an exasperated Iain Gray,

> how a First Minister, whose self-proclaimed belief in
> Scotland knows no bounds, can stand back for four years

---

[84] David Cairns had won in 2010 with a majority of over 14,000 votes.

[85] Hamish Macdonell, 'Inverclyde by-election can only get better', *Caledonian Mercury*, 15 June 2011 <politics.caledonianmercury.com/2011/06/15/inverclyde-by-election-campaign-can-only-get-better/>.

[86] Severin Carrell, 'Inverclyde byelection race goes to the wire', *The Guardian*, 30 June 2011

[87] Daniel Martin, 'Clegg blamed as Lib Dems sink to poll humiliation in by-election', *Daily Mail*, 2 July 2011.

and watch the shambles of our capital's major infrastructure
project with nothing more to say than 'I told you so'.[88]

When the trams crisis reached its climax in September, with a real
possibility of the project being abandoned, and then the Edinburgh
Council decision to run the line only from the Airport to Haymarket, at
long last, the Government stepped in and took control of the £776m
project.[89]

There remain questions. Why, for example, did the Government
agency Transport Scotland continue to pay out money for a project that
was being constantly delayed and reduced in size? Edinburgh Council
leader Jenny Dawe said:

> I'm sure there will be a public inquiry at some stage. I would
> hope that it goes back into the roots of what went wrong,
> for no other reason than to make sure it doesn't happen
> again, not to witch hunt or to cast blame but to find out
> what went wrong.[90]

The First Minister was accused of 'dragging his feet', as that inquiry will,
in all likelihood, only happen after the local elections in May.[91]

LACKLUSTRE LEGISLATIVE PROGRAMME

On 6 September, back from the summer recess, Alex Salmond
introduced 15 bills in his programme for government for the current
Parliamentary year. Legislation to create a single police force and a single
fire service in Scotland was at the core of the programme. Further, and
also controversial, were plans to revisit minimum alcohol pricing and for
picking up the bill tackling sectarianism postponed in June.[92] The absence
of an early bill for a referendum on independence was, as Brian Taylor

---

[88] Iain Gray, 'SNP should get off he sidelines and help Edinburgh deliver a modern tram
system we can all be proud of', *The Scotsman*, 1 September 2011.

[89] Brian Ferguson, 'SNP takes charge of stricken city tram project', *The Scotsman*, 15
September 2011.

[90] Kate Shannon, 'Tram project "a nightmare" says Edinburgh Council leader', *Holyrood*, 17
October 2011.

[91] Michael Blackley, 'Salmond 'has "ducked out" of public probe into tram farce', *Edinburgh
Evening News*, 26 November 2011.

[92] Alex Salmond, 'Programme for Government 2011-12', Scottish Parliament, 6 September
2011, <www.scotland.gov.uk/News/Speeches/ProgrammeforGov-2011-12>.

blogged, 'the dog which didn't bark during Mr Salmond's address.'[93] Overall, the legislative programme was seen as strong on rhetoric – coining the phrase of the 'independence generation' – but 'hardly ambitious'.[94]

Creating a single police force and a single fire service, Salmond claimed, would save money without hitting frontline services. He said that single services would 'sustain and improve the delivery of local services,' create a 'national expertise' in both and ensure 'clear separation from ministers' and their 'continued operational independence.'[95] The proposed changes would see Scotland's eight police forces and eight fire services merged into national bodies. A single police and fire service for Scotland would, according to Justice Secretary Kenny MacAskill, save an estimated £130m a year and £1.7bn over 15 years. 'There is broad support across parliament for single services,' he claimed, 'and there is strong consensus that we need to reform to safeguard the hard-fought gains the services have made.'[96]

Indeed, the Tories and Labour have given their backing to the plan in principle. But the Scottish Liberal Democrats are against the idea. Their justice spokeswoman, Alison McInnes MSP, did not only question the costs, she argued that the proposal was 'disingenuous on the views of senior officers,' that it 'contradicts the Christie Commission report,' and was 'hypocritical on the independence of the justice system.' She called it 'downright misleading on the consultation that was carried out.'[97] Backed by the Liberal Democrats, Scottish council leaders have remained the heaviest critics of the proposals for a single force and single fire service because they believe Alex Salmond's government is diluting local democracy. Pat Watters, the president of the Convention of Scottish Local Authorities (CoSLA), accused the SNP government of a 'centralising agenda' and of 'ignoring the opposition in consultations.'[98]

Alex Salmond also argued that Scotland's historic drink-related problems necessitated bringing back the proposals to set a minimum price per unit of alcohol, which were defeated in the last Parliament. The legislation, he said, would 'tackle the scourge of alcoholism on Scottish

[93] Brian Taylor, 'Salmond outlines Scottish vision', *BBC News Scotland*, 7 September 2011, <bbc.co.uk/news/uk-scotland-14826009>.

[94] 'Salmond's keeping his legislative powder dry' (Leader), *The Scotsman*, 8 September 2011.

[95] 'Scots ministers to reform police, jobs and alcohol laws', *BBC News Scotland*, 7 September 2011, <www.bbc.co.uk/news/uk-scotland-14804184>.

[96] 'Single police and fire service to save £130m per year' *BBC News Scotland*, 8 September 2011, <www.bbc.co.uk/news/uk-scotland-14841802>.

[97] *Ibid.*

[98] David Maddox, 'SNP ministers accused of railroading police plan', *The Scotsman*, 22 August 2011.

society and families.'[99] The Lib Dems have since changed their mind, and are now in favour of minimum pricing.

The First Minister pledged that a 'jobs agenda would be at the heart of the programme for government,' including a guarantee to give every young person a training opportunity: 'No young person should go through school only to become an unemployment statistic at the age of 16. We will not allow that in Scotland.'[100] He repeated that when he announced in December that a dedicated Minister for Youth Employment would be established and an extra £30 million would be invested in helping Scotland's young people into training, work or education to secure a stronger workforce of the future, after Labour had claimed Scotland was in the midst of a 'national crisis', with 100,000 16 to 24-year-olds out of work.[101]

By the end of the year, 229,000 Scots were out of work. In three months, the unemployment rate had risen from 7.5 to 8.5% (against 8,3% in the UK) – the unemployment level for 16-24 year-olds rose by 27%, from 89,000 in May-July, to 113,000 in October-December.[102] While the First Minister had hailed the earlier figures, when Scottish unemployment was lower than in the UK, as a result of his government's policies, (and had urged George Osborne to reverse his austerity cuts), he now had to take the flak as Scotland trailed the UK.

John Swinney had tried to preempt this by again demanding from George Osborne an injection of £20bn into the ailing economy to head off another recession, and by announcing a £60bn 20-year investment plan, including a high-speed rail link in Scotland, and nearly 80 more construction projects. But Infrastructure Secretary Alex Neil had hardly finished detailing the spending plan in Parliament, when it came under fire as a 'Christmas wish list', containing projects that had already been announced, projects that would not be realised in decades, and questions about how it would all be funded. Only 12.8bn, it transpired, were to be spent before the next Scottish election in 2016, with much of it 'reliant on risky private finance funding schemes.'[103]

---

[99] 'Scots ministers to reform police, jobs and alcohol laws', *BBC News Scotland*, 7 September 2011, <www.bbc.co.uk/news/uk-scotland-14804184>.

[100] *Ibid.*

[101] 'Salmond announces youth jobs minister portfolio', *BBC News Scotland*, 1 December 2011, <www.bbc.co.uk/news/uk-scotland-scotland-politics-15984120>.

[102] Tom Peterkin,'Salmond under fire as 25,000 more Scots out of work', *The Scotsman*, 15 December 2011.

[103] Scott Macnab, 'SNP comes under fire for £60bn spending "wish list"', *The Scotsman*, 7 December 2011.

OWN GOAL?

The First Minister announced that the government would also bring forward the Offensive Behaviour at Football and Threatening Communications (Scotland) Bill, delayed in June, to crack down on violent and bigoted behaviour. This legislation aims at tougher penalties for football-related behaviour and violence. The bill passed its final stage in December (to become law in late January 2012), but all opposition parties rejected it, as did churches, human rights activists and football fans. Patrick Harvie, the leader of the Green Party, accused the SNP at the end of the Stage 2 debate at Holyroiod of having 'steam-rollered' the measures through Parliament, ignoring 'the growing chorus of objections.'[104]

The government may have tagged a freedom of speech clause to the Bill,[105] but Iain Macwhirter was scathing in his verdict, as the bill cleared its last hurdle at Holyrood:

> MSPs in Holyrood passed a law that could make the singing of the national anthem punishable by a five-year sentence if it is associated with 'offensive or threatening behavior' in any context that involves football. No one knows exactly what 'offensive and threatening behavior' is, and anyway, because of the Catch-22 drafting, the very singing of 'sectarian' songs is itself deemed offensive. (...) This dumb law could also make the carrying of flags, colours or religious symbols illegal at football matches, in the trains going to football matches or in pubs or in any public place where football is being shown. It could make singing The Sash illegal in a pub, but not in the street outside. This is utter madness. (...) This legislation is otiose, contradictory, subjective, illiberal, anti-democratic and contrary to internationally accepted definitions of basic human rights. It is threatening and offensive to freedom of speech, freedom of association, freedom of thought and to personal liberty. (...) It has been frog-marched through Parliament by an act of elective dictatorship. This is Alex Salmond's first own goal, if you'll excuse the pun. He should have listened to Parliament and dumped it last summer when he had the chance. The only hope now is that courts and juries will

---

[104] Scott Macnab, 'Crackdown on sectarian chants to be law by spring', *The Scotsman*, 23 November 2011.

[105] Scott Macnab, 'Salmond's freedom of speech concession', *The Scotsman*, 8 October 2011.

treat it with the contempt it deserves.[106]

And he was not alone. The anti-sectarian group Nil By Mouth was as critical of he new legislation as the Law Society of Scotland. Bill McVicar of the latter's criminal law committee said: 'We recognise something needs to be done about these issues, but not new legislation – rather better enforcement of existing laws.'[107] Back in June, the *Herald* had argued that, ultimately

> the police are right to maintain that Scotland cannot arrest its way out of sectarianism. Rather we must challenge the mindset that creates this unacceptable behavior. That is why no amount of well-intentioned legislation will make up for properly-resourced community-based initiatives involving schools, churches, voluntary groups and the clubs themselves.[108]

Was the Sectarianism Bill another instance of an SNP with absolute power 'trampling the opposition and using their political muscle to bulldoze legislation through Holyrood'?[109]

FROM GREEN POWER TO GAY MARRIAGE

Other government projects and plans ran into difficulties and drew critical comment. The hope of burying at least some sections of the controversial Beauly-Denny power line were – well, buried when ScottishPower ruled this option out because of the costs and because it would lead to a three-year delay in its construction. The Conservative MEP Struan Strevenson captured the outrage felt by the campaigners: 'I think it's a great tragedy. ScottishPower should be forced to pay more attention to our landscape and underground the most sensitive sections of he power line.'[110]

The green energy plans – to generate 100% of the country's needs from green sources by 2020 – were branded 'unrealistic, unachievable

[106] Iain Macwhirter, 'This dumb, unjust law is Salmond's first own goal', *The Herald*, 15 December 2011.

[107] Bill McVicar, 'Why are we creating new laws to criminalise things that are already criminal?', *The Scotsman*, 16 September 2011.

[108] 'Let us challenge sectarian mindset' (Leader), *The Herald*, 18 June 2011.

[109] 'Holyrood: power and scrutiny' (Leader), *The Herald*, 16 December 2011.

[110] Jenny Fyall, 'Energy giant sparks anger as it says no to burying power line', *The Scotsman*, 30 august 2011.

and not in the best interest of energy consumers' by Inverness-based Mackay Consultants who warned that by 2020 only 39% of Scotland's energy generation would be from renewable sources.[111]

The think tank IPPR (Institute for Public Policy Research) criticised the SNP policy of cutting corporation tax as insufficient to guarantee stronger economic growth.[112] John Swinney was criticised by business organisations because of his 'arrogant' decision not to follow standard practice by allowing for an official impact assessment for his proposed levy on large retailers of alcohol and tobacco, dubbed the 'Tesco Tax', which is supposed to raise £110m over the next three years.[113]

After five years of iron party discipline, with hardly any dissent within the SNP Parliamentary group, the proposed idea of legislating to allow 'same-sex marriages' caused the first major rift between socially conservative and socially liberal SNP representatives. John Mason and Bill Walker were on the side of the former SNP leader Gordon Wilson who demanded a referendum on the issue, as gay marriages posed 'a danger' to Scotland.[114] Mason had put in a Parliamentary motion that 'no person or organisation should be forced to be involved in or to approve same-sex marriages.' SNP MP Pete Wishart hit back by calling 'John Mason's nasty little anti-gay marriage motion ... just wrong.' [115] The Catholic Church, already enraged because of the sectarianism legislation, also attacked the policy. Cardinal Keith O'Brien declared it was 'not in the best interest of our society,'[116] and Muslim leaders in Scotland have warned the SNP that plans to legalise gay marriages 'could turn many of their community away from the party as the Iraq war turned them off Labour.'[117] The SNP government seemed determined to stick to its guns, perhaps offering a compromise of allowing same-sex marriages in Scotland but ban same-sex weddings from being held in churches. So, it may perhaps not turn out quite 'the SNP's Section 28 moment', as David Torrance surmised.[118]

---

[111] David Ross, 'Experts warn 100% green energy plan is unrealistic', The Herald, 10 June 2011.

[112] 'Less rhetoric and more reality would serve the SNP better' (Leader), The Scotsman, 14 September 2011.

[113] Colin Donald, 'Swinney under fire over lack of scrutiny for "supermarket tax"', Sunday Herald, 30 November 2011.

[114] David Ross, 'Former SNP leader calls for gay marriage referendum', The Herald, 12 October 2011.

[115] Craig Brown, 'Bitter row erupts within SNP ranks over gay and lesbian marriages', The Scotsman, 5 August 2011.

[116] Eddie Barnes, 'SNP set to move on gay weddings', Scotland on Sunday, 18 December 2011.

[117] Eddie Barnes, 'Muslims warn SNP over gay marriage plan', Scotland on Sunday, 11 December 2011.

[118] David Torrance, 'This is the SNP's Section 28 moment, and it is proving just as unmanageable', The Scotsman, 12 october 2011.

POLITICAL LIMBO?

Bad news were drowned out by the intensifying referendum debate: funding cuts meant that a thousand jobs at Scottish colleges were being slashed, teacher numbers have fallen by 4,000 since the SNP came to power, house building hit its lowest level for 30 years, slashing spending on environmentally-friendly travel runs counter to anti-pollution targets...

Lesley Riddoch worried that politics became more concerned with the hypothetical issues of post-independence Scotland than with the 'here and now' issues facing Scottish society. Bemoaning 'political limbo land,' she criticised that those who opposed the referendum were now the ones always talking about it: 'We need Scotland's opposition leaders to focus relentlessly on the here and now – not the hypothetical problems of independence or the largely redundant policy solutions of the past.'[119]

Two-and-a-half years of politics of the subjunctive – what if Scotland were independent? – will not suffice. If proof was needed that there is work for our politicians in the here and now, and not just in preparing the nation for the referendum in a few years' time, then the shocking care home crisis has been a case in point. Private companies like Southern Cross 'piled in when there was money to be made from looking after the elderly,' reported Steven Vass, 'now that the cash has dried up, it is the most vulnerable who are most at risk.'[120] Questions galore for the Parliament – about regulation, about the quality of carers being recruited, about training levels and supervision and, above all, on funding.

REFERENDUM POKER

After the SNP's landslide victory, some expected, feared or hoped that the referendum would be held now, using the winning momentum. After all, as Ian Bell contended, 'it may not get any better than this.'[121] There is no doubt that 2011 was a game changer – the referendum has become a live issue. Just going by column space in the papers, one cannot but realise that the debate about the independence referendum has taken on a greater urgency. Although polls in 2011 showed that still only between 28 and 38% of Scots support the SNP's favoured option,

---

[119] Lesley Riddoch, 'Politicians failing to focus on now', *The Scotsman*, 19 September 2011.

[120] Steven Vass, 'From boom to bust ... how the care home gravy train hit the buffers', *Sunday Herald*, 5 June 2011.

[121] Ian Bell, 'Now is the time for Salmond to call independence referendum', *The Herald*, 7 May 2011.

there is a sense that the momentum is with the independence argument – and a growing lament among unionist-minded media pundits that the opposition has been slow to mount any meaningful counter attack.

The Scottish Social Attitudes Survey found a 9% increase of support for independence, up to 32% – but that is still lower than the 2005 figure of 35 per cent.[122] A YouGov survey in January found 33% in favour of independence (up 4% since May 2011), and 53% against (down from 58%). An Ipsos MORI poll for *The Times* in December 2011 had support for independence at 38 per cent.[123] While a TNS-BMRB poll, published in September 2011 by *The Herald*, showed those who would vote Yes for independence ahead by 39% to 38%,[124] it is still amazing how relatively stable the constitutional preferences of the Scots have remained in the past fifteen years.

Without doubt, the Scots are now more relaxed about the perspective of independence. Slogans like 'Divorce is expensive' have lost their power to instill fear in the Scots. When the Scottish Social Attitudes Survey asked whether they would support independence if every Scot was £500 better off per year, 29% said they were 'strongly in favour' and 36% said they would be 'in favour'.[125] That seems to indicate that public support for independence is heavily dependent on whether Scots can be persuaded that it would improve prosperity and economic success, 'suggesting that for many Scots independence is not based on a principled belief in national sovereignty for its own sake.'[126] But it also seems that, in terms of economic perspective, 'the policies that a country adopts post-separation are much more important than the act of separation itself.'[127]

Hardly a week, hardly a day has passed since the last election without some contribution to the debate. There was the intervention from Scottish Secretary Michael Moore, suggesting that one referendum might not be enough – that two were needed: one enabling the Scottish government to enter negotiations with the Westminster government about independence, and one on the actual package eventually negotiated.[128] While it may sound logical, politically it would open a can

---

[122] <www.scotcen.org.uk/study/scottish-social-attitudes-2011>.

[123] 'Poll finds rise in support for independence', *Edinburgh Evening News*, 12 January 2012.

[124] The Yes-vote had been ahead before, in 2008, but a year before and a year after it was 15 points behind. Robin Dinwoodie, 'Yes voters take lead in new independence poll', *The Herald*, 4 September 2011.

[125] See Severin Carrell, 'Scots back independence – but at a price', *The Guardian*, 5 December 2011.

[126] *Ibid.*

[127] Hamish McRae, 'Of course Scotland can stand on its own two feet. And here's how', *The Independent*, 14 January 2012.

[128] David Clegg, 'Scottish secretary says two referendums would be needed for independence', *The Courier*, 7 June 2011.

of worms. What if the Scots said yes in the first referendum but not in the second? Would the verdict the second time round cancel out the first vote? Or would we be in limbo – the Scots, in principle, in favour, but rejecting the conditions? Which would mean that the debate could continue unabated, with demands to get the conditions the Scots want. Also, having two referendums would lower the bar significantly for a first referendum – after all, there would be a second chance to get it right...

Then, there was the question of timing. The SNP had stated in its manifesto that it would bring forward a referendum bill during the lifetime of the present Parliament. But Alex Salmond qualified that in the campaign to having it in the 'latter part' of this Parliamentary term, as putting pressure on the Westminster government to increase the economic powers in the Scotland Bill would have priority and push the referendum to a later date. There was speculation that it might be in 2014, cashing in on the feel-good factor of the Bannockburn anniversary and the Commonwealth Games in Glasgow,[129] or in 2015, hoping that an outright Tory victory in the UK-elections would further alienate the Scots from Westminster.

Then, in January 2012, Prime Minister David Cameron intervened, offering the Scottish Parliament a temporary transfer of powers to allow for a referendum – 'fair, decisive and clear' – run by the Scottish Parliament which could not be legally challenged.[130] Scottish Secretary Michael Moore offered in the House of Commons 'to empower the Scots to participate in a legal referendum.'[131] In response, Alex Salmond announced, not a date, but a season: Autumn 2014 was 'the date we're moving towards.'[132] Not exactly Scotland's date with destiny – but at least its season...

While that timing seems now accepted, the opposition parties – the same parties which in the last Parliament opposed a Referendum Bill (with the exception of Wendy Alexander's 'Bring it on' moment in 2008) – still would like it to happen 'sooner rather than later' – mainly because all opinion polls indicate that the Scots are not (yet?) ready to ditch the UK or, as Brian Taylor put it,

---

[129] Not to forget the Ryder Cup at Gleneagles, and the Scottish Government's plans for another Year of Homecoming for 2014. Plus the European Parliament elections. And the centenary of the outbreak of the First World War (a 'British' anniversary?). Also, the bicentenary of Scott's *Waverley*. Maybe, just maybe, Scotland makes it to the FIFA World Cup in Brazil (hoping, of course, to avoid a rerun of Argentina 1978!).

[130] Nigel Morris and Hamish Macdonell, 'Downing Street plays poker with Salmond over fate of the Union', *The Independent*, 9 January 2012; Severin Carrell, 'Salmond sets poll date – and defies London', *The Guardian*, 11 January 2012.

[131] *BBC News at Ten*, 10 January 2012.

[132] *Ibid.*

> Because, right now, Mr Salmond is not confident he would win. Because he prefers to wait, to build the case. Because, right now, he wants to focus upon the economy and public services. Because he hopes that public anger over impending cuts in public spending will turn ultimately upon the Treasury and the UK government, not his own team.[133]

While welcoming the transfer of the legal power to hold a 'binding' referendum, the SNP rejects the 'strings attached' to the UK government's offer. The power transfer would only allow for a straight Yes/No question, no second question on 'Devo Max' (i.e. fiscal autonomy); the Electoral Commission would have to supervise it (not a new body formed by the Scottish Parliament), and the voting age would have to remain at 18 (rather than the SNP's intention of lowering it to 16).

Salmond introduced the possibility of 'Devo Max' on the ballot paper at the SNP conference in Inverness. Unionists reject this 'third way' option, somewhere between the status quo and independence, as a 'consolation prize' for Alex Salmond – it would allow him to claim a win whatever the outcome of the referendum. He could, if he loses the straight Yes/No vote, claim 'Devo Max' as a further step on the path towards full independence, the Union, as the Tories would have it, 'being sliced up salami-style until the final step to independence is small.'[134]

The official Labour position, as stated by Shadow Scottish Secretary Margaret Curran MP and the new Scottish Labour leader Johann Lamont, is that 'Devo Max' is a different issue – that the referendum should be on the fundamental decision of Scotland staying in the UK or going it alone.[135] While Alex Salmond argues that 'Devo Max', sometimes dubbed 'independence lite' by commentators – is on the same continuum, Douglas Alexander (who had argued for greater devolution in his Glasgow speech in November) and Sarah Boyack have been at pains to put a dividing line between devolution (in any shape or form) and independence as two 'completely different constitutional routes.'[136] An increasing number of Labour politicians, from Henry McLeish and Lord Foulkes to Malcolm Chisholm MSP have urged their party to promote 'Devo Max' to bolster its credentials as a devolution party for Scotland.[137] Will they grasp the

---

[133] Brian Taylor, 'Salmond outlines Scottish vision', *BBC News Scotland*, 7 September 2011, <www.bbc.co.uk/news/uk-scotland-14826009>.

[134] Allan Massie, 'Why the Scots want independence from the English', *The Daily Telegraph*, 22 December 2011.

[135] *BBC Newsnight Scotland*, 10 January 2012.

[136] *BBC Newsnight Scoitland*, 12 January 2012.

[137] Malcolm Chisholm, 'Flying the flag for greatest possible devolution', *The Scotsman*, 24 November 2011.

thistle? Or will they feel comfortable standing shoulder to shoulder in the 'No' camp with Michael Forsyth and George Osborne?

The Lib Dems have their own commission under Sir Menzies Campbell looking into Home Rule for Scotland beyond the ill-fated Scotland Bill.[138] The Tory leadership is not prepared to go beyond the Scotland Bill. But Alex Fergusson, Tory MSP and former Presiding Officer, has called for an increase of the Scottish Parliament's fiscal powers,[139] as have former Prime Minister John Major[140] and former Conservative cabinet minister Michael Portillo.[141]

As John Curtice has repeatedly pointed out, it is the 'Devo Max' option that would be most likely to enjoy a majority (a recent Ipsos-MORI poll found that 68% would vote for it), and denying the voters that option might lead those dissatisfied with the status quo to plumb for independence.[142] There seemed to be a new civic campaign emerging in January, involving trade unions, churches, business leaders, parts of the voluntary sector, academics, think tanks and politicians to press for the 'Devo Max' – or, as Kenyon Wright prefers, 'secure autonomy' – option on the ballot paper.[143]

On the other hand, as *The Economist* argued in a leader comment,

> anything other than a straight in-or-out question may result in a damaging wrangle. What if, in a three-part question, independence wins – but with only 35% of the vote? What if 51% of Scots vote for independence, but, in a second question, 80% vote for more powers? Nationalists would interpret that as a mandate for independence. But Westminster could fairly argue that Scots apparently prefer further devolution to outright independence.[144]

Arthur Midwinter, for eight years an adviser to Holyrood's finance committee, has warned that 'full fiscal autonomy' (aka 'Devo Max')

---

[138] 'Sir Menzies to lead new home rule commission', *The Herald*, 1 November 2011.

[139] Fergusson is one of the three opposition MSPs (besides Malcolm Chisholm of Labour and Tavish Scott of the Lib Dems) who has been asked by the think tank Reform Scotland to be part of a group looking into far greater fiscal powers for Holyrood.

[140] Ian Swanson. 'Major shift in power struggle', *Edinburgh Evening News*, 13 July 2011.

[141] David Lee and David Maddox, 'Scots should control fair share of oil, says Portillo', *The Scotsman*, 14 November 2011.

[142] John Curtice, '"Devolution max" could be the best way forward', *The Times*, 13 December 2011; and John Curtice, 'A gamble on Scotland', *The Guardian*, 10 January 2012.

[143] Robbie Dinwoodie and Michael Settle, '"Straight choice between independence and status quo disenfranchises a large number of Scots"', *The Herald*, 13 January 2012.

[144] 'Clarity, please' (Leader), *The Economist*, 14 January 2012.

was 'theoretically driven, rather than evidence based,' and would result in a 'policy mess' – he even compared it to the 'notorious poll tax,' and that including the option in a referendum would be 'inappropriate and irrational,' as it would lead to 'major spending cuts.'[145]

The UK government's intervention may have the law on its side. It acts according to Section 30 of the Scotland Act of 1998,

> Yet the moral argument that Westminster should have the upper hand in deciding the future of the Scottish people – particularly when there is only one Conservative MP in Scotland – is at best shaky.[146]

Andrew Grice called George Osborne 'the secret weapon of the SNP', warning that Osborne and Cameron, 'the two posh boys,' were 'certainly not the right ones to lead the crucial fight to save the Union.'[147] Even the conservative commentator Andrew McKie conceded that 'it would be foolish to deny that a pro-Union campaign seen as driven primarily by the Conservative Party would be counter-productive.' For him, the 'most forceful' argument for retaining the Union is that most Scots do not want to abandon it.'[148]

The former Labour MSP Brian Fitzpatrick warned against a figure like Michael Forsyth 'running' the campaign to preserve the Union – 'A successful Scotland in Britain campaign will need a Scot of progressive values at its fore…'[149] He put the Labour case for the Union like this:

> We view the Britain we cherish as a multicultural, tolerant and democratic place, and we celebrate shared achievements such as the NHS and the minimum wage, and look forward to our country's continuing tolerance and diversity.[150]

But is this a Britain as many Scots would see it, after Thatcher, Blair, Brown and Cameron? Or is David Cameron's European 'veto' reinforcing the arguments for independence? Philip Stephens put it in a nutshell:

---

[145] Arthur Midwinter, 'Poverty of analysis on devo-max', *The Scotsman*, 16 December 2011.

[146] Polly Curtis, 'PM has law on his side', *The Guardian*, 10 January 2012.

[147] Andrew Grice, 'Osborne: the SNP's secret weapon', *The Independent*, 14 January 2012.

[148] Andrew McKie, 'A positive reason for the Union? Most Scots want it', *The Herald*, 9 January 2012.

[149] *Ibid.*

[150] Brian Fitzpatrrick, Letter to the Editor, *The Guardian*, 10 January 2012

> Much of the Conservative party now speaks the language of English nationalism – driven to fury by Europe and increasingly driven out by the voters from Britain's Celtic fringes. (…) English nationalism feeds Scottish nationalism. The more a Tory-led government in London detaches Britain from Europe, the more easily the pro-European SNP points to a divergence of English and Scottish national interests.[151]

Most experts agree that an independent Scotland would remain an EU member state if it so wished, but there are dissenting voices who argue Scotland would have to apply for membership and would have to accept the *acquis communautaire*, i.e. Schengen and the Euro, not immediately, but at least in principle.[152] That would stand in the way of the SNP's preferred option to stick with the pound – until joining the Euro could be put to the Scottish people in a referendum. And Schengen would emphasise the Anglo-Scottish border, as would a markedly different immigration policy north of the Border.

With Cameron's appeasement of his Eurosceptic backbenchers, are we now perhaps facing a race – which Union can be dissolved fastest? Will Scotland still be part of the UK when the Tories take it out of the European Union? Or will Scotland end the UK Union before that can happen? Scots would, in their majority, agree with Alex Salmond's assessment that Cameron's isolationism is harmful to Scottish interests. But there are also ambiguous messages coming from the SNP about EU membership – could an independent Scotland opt for EFTA rather than the EU?[153] The SNP has long held aspirations to work more closely with the Nordic countries.[154] The architect of the SNP's 'Independence in Europe', Jim Sillars, is now advocating the Norwegian option of association with, rather than membership of, the European Union.[155]

Another question is whether the 'Constitution for Scotland' which the SNP produced in 2002 (and which was supposed to be submitted to a referendum after independence) is still valid. W Elliot Bulmer warns that

---

[151] Philip Stephens, 'Was this the moment UK stumbled out of Europe?', *Financial Times*, 12 December 2011.

[152] The SNP refuses to publish legal advice it received on the issue of EU membership in case of independence. See Tom Gordon, 'Labour to challenge SNP block on revealing legal advice over Scotland joining Europe', *Sunday Herald*, 13. November 2011.

[153] Michael Settle, 'Hyslop "blunder" in EU role debate', *Sunday Herald*, 8 September 2011.

[154] Hamish Macdonell, 'Bye, bye England? SNP plans closer Scandinavian ties after independence', *The independent*, 5 December 2011. See also Angus Robertson, 'High time to join our friends in the north and face the Arctic challenge', *The Scotsman*, 29 November 2011; and Lesley Riddoch, 'Look north, Scotland', *The Guardian*, 6 December 2011.

[155] Andrew Whitaker, 'Sillars in call for Scotland to switch to "dollar"', *The Scotsman*, 20 December 2011.

postponing the design of a Scottish Constitution until after independence would be a 'risky business' and make it 'easy for Unionists to say that the implications of independence have not been properly thought through.'[156] What kind of Scotland does the SNP envisage – a high or a low tax Scotland? Ireland used to be the model, when it was part of that 'arc of prosperity'– are Norway or Canada the new yardsticks for an independent Scotland?

'It's really quite simple,' says Neal Ascherson:

> The Scots want to run their own country as other small nations do. Most of them want to stay in the Union. They want a Scottish government that is not bossed about by London, and especially not by English politicians in parties most Scots did not vote for.[157]

Whether nationalist, unionist or devolutionist, there should be agreement, based on the Claim of Rights of 1989, that whatever the decision of the Scots will be, it is in exercise of their right to self-determination. It was insulting nonsense, spoken 'rashly, even stupidly,' for Labour MP Ian Davidson to call the SNP 'neo-fascist'.[158] Likewise, branding the Scottish opposition as 'anti-Scottish',[159] questioning the patriotism of Unionists, devolutionists and federalists, is as bad as scaremongering about independence. And comparing the Scottish situation with Ireland before a war of independence and a civil war, as Alex Salmond did during the British-Irish summit in Dublin, is not only disingenuous but outright dangerous.[160] 'Patriotism is not restricted to one side in the argument,' to quote Allan Massie: 'One can be both Scottish and British. Millions of us are, and remain therefore committed to support for the continuation of

---

[156] W Elliot Bulmer, 'Our future is waiting to be written', *Sunday Herald*, 11 December 2011; see also his 'An Analysis of the Scottish National Party's Draft Constitution for Scotland', *Parliamentary Affairs*, vol.52, issue 4, 2011, pp.674-93. Elliot Bulmer has since published *A Model Constitution for Scotland: Making Democracy Work* (Edinburgh: Luath Press, 2011), envisioning 'a new and more democratic political system constructed in an independent state'.

[157] Neal Ascherson, 'Let Scotland be a sovereign, mature nation and England profits too', *The Observer*, 15 January 2012.

[158] Allan Massie, 'False patriotism is the last refuge of the scoundrel', *The Scotsman*, 29 June 2011.

[159] See Brian Taylor, 'Displays of tone in referendum debate', *BBC News Scotland*, 12 January 2012 <www.bbc.co.uk/news/uk-scotland-16537271>.

[160] Tom Peterkin, 'Salmond claims link to Irish freedom struggle', *The Scotsman*, 14 January 2012.

the Union.'[161] The SNP's historic victory last year may have transformed it from a merely 'nationalist' to a truly 'national' party, but it must, Massie warns, resist the temptation of conflating itself with the nation.

To make an informed, democratic decision, a vigorous debate is needed, without any suspicion of 'rigging' from any side. Increasingly, commentators complain that the debate is bogged down by questions of process rather than the real issues. It is to be hoped that the debate is now moving beyond these quibbles. The onus is on the SNP to 'put some meat on the bone' and explain what independence for Scotland in the twenty-first century entails, whether holding on to Sterling (then a foreign currency) would really mean independence,[162] whether Scotland would be a high-tax or low-tax economy, what kind of armed forces an independent Scotland would have, and would it be part of NATO, would it get rid of Trident immediately,[163] and how the UK national assets and liabilities would be divided,[164] how pension rights would be guaranteed, how much oil and gas revenue would come into the Scottish coffers, etc. The onus on the opposition parties is to make a cogent argument about why Scotland should remain in the Union.

NEW OPPOSITION LEADERS

This is, particularly, the challenge for the new party leaders. When Tavish Scott resigned as Lib Dem leader, the former MP and newly-elected MSP Willie Rennie was quickly put in his place to lead the party north of the Border and the sad rump of his four fellow Lib Dem MSPs at Holyrood. The Lib Dems also installed a commission under their former

---

[161] Allan Massie, 'False patriotism is the last refuge of the scoundrel', *The Scotsman*, 29 June 2011.

[162] The SNP keeps the option to join the Euro (if it still exists whenever independence were to come), but only following a referendum – with the unlikely result of the Scots actually opting for it. George Osborne warned that London might not allow Scotland to use the pound (i.e. issue sterling) – see David Maddox, 'Treasury threat to future of Scottish bank notes', *The Scotsman*, 13 January 2012; George Parker and Andrew Bolger, 'Osborne queries currency for independent Scotland', *Financial Times*, 12 January 2012. The Chief Secretary to the Treasury Danny Alexander also raised 'the spectre of economic disaster 'over the problem of what currency Scotland would adopt. See David Maddox, 'Independence "risks currency catastrophe"', *The Scotsman*, 9 December 2011; Jim Sillars is in favour of a new Scottish currency; for a review of the different options, see Alan Trench, 'Four options – and none of them easy', *The Scotsman*, 9 December 2011.

[163] See William Walker, 'Nuclear deadlock', *Scotland on Sunday*, 8 January 2012.

[164] The SNP puts Scotland's share of the UK debt at around £40bn, sources close to the UK government talk of £100bn, Danny Alexander even of over £200bn. See Hamish Macdonell, 'How would the division work? It's complicated...', *The Independent*, 13 January 2012; Jason Allardyce, 'Breakaway costs Scots £43.5bn', *The Sunday Times*, 8 January 2012.

leader Menzies Campbell to look into the future of devolution, beyond Calman and the Scotland Bill, but explicitly excluding independence. Would the 'federalist' Lib Dems support 'Devo Max'?

Annabel Goldie and Iain Gray also announced their intention to step down after a new leader was elected. The leadership campaign of the Scottish Conservatives proved surprisingly interesting, but was also very divisive in the party. Murdo Fraser MSP, hitherto Annabel Goldie's Deputy, proposed to dissolve the Tories in Scotland and found a new centre-right party – the most radical de-toxifying programme suggested yet. But it opened up a deep rift between supporters of this radical rebranding exercise, including the break-away from the UK Tory party, and those who called it 'reckless' and 'destabilising'.[165] But Fraser's proposal catapulted the future of the Scottish Tories centre-stage at the Conservative Party Conference in October. Against Fraser's radical rebranding, which had the support of a majority of Scottish Tory MSPs, and was endorsed by grandees like Sir Malcolm Rifkind, stood Ruth Davidson, protegé of Annabel Goldie – a 32-year old openly lesbian kickboxer and former BBC journalist just elected to Holyrood, Jackson Carlaw MSP, and Margaret Mitchell. There was no love lost between the candidates. Jackson Carlaw called Ruth Davidson 'someone who has been parachuted in from absolutely nowhere, who we know nothing about, who has no political agenda that we know about, who has fought no campaign.'[166]

When the votes were counted, it became clear that the Tories had shied away from Murdo Fraser's revolution, going for the self-styled 'candidate of change' Ruth Davidson. But it was remarkable, and indicative of the despair within the Scottish Conservative Party about its continuous decline, that 47% of the membership were prepared to dismantle their party and start from scratch. Unfortunately, Ruth Davidson who, after her election, had difficulties stamping her authority on her parliamentary group and has since not landed too many punches on Alex Salmond in First Minister's Questions, has also not set the heather ablaze with her first speeches.[167] Her first big test will be the May local elections.

That test also awaits Johann Lamont who emerged victorious from the Scottish Labour Party's leadership contest. Ken Macintosh MSP, who had been seen as an early frontrunner, suffered a set-back when Ed Miliband failed to remember his name in an interview during the UK

---

[165] Andrew Whitaker, 'Tories at war over move to kill off party in Scotland', *The Scotsman*, 5 September 2011.

[166] Eddie Barnes, 'Voice of experience has harsh words for new kid on the block', *The Scotsman*, 19 October 2011.

[167] 'A damp squip more appropriate for a dreich November bonfire night than a snap, crackle and pop of a firecracker she should have kicked the new year off with,' was Ex-Tory Brian Monteith's verdict on her first keynote speech, 'Cold comfort food fails to tickle the taste buds', *The Scotsman*, 9 January 2012.

Labour Conference in September. And Tom Harris MP was always an outsider in the race.

A commission under Jim Murphy and Sarah Boyack, installed to draw the lessons from the May defeat, came to the conclusion that the party that had brought about devolution had failed to devolve itself. The Labour Party conference signed off the changes proposed by the Commission. So, the new party leader is no longer just the leader of the Parliamentary Labour group, but of Labour in Scotland.

For some commentators, though, the fact that, after the shock defeat last May, none of the so-called big-hitters among the Scots in Westminster put his hat into the ring – Jim Murphy or Douglas Alexander or even Alistair Darling, with a pledge to stand for Holyrood at the earliest opportunity – was a sign that the party, having 'lost a sinecure and seeking a role,'[168] had still not understood the impact of the SNP victory. When Douglas Alexander repositioned Labour and redefined Labour's role in Scotland and its 'open-minded approach as to how the architecture of devolution can be improved,' it was noted that none of the leadership contenders made any such far-reaching statements during the campaign – which was seen as highlighting 'the error the party has made in not having one of its big guns in situ.'[169] For too many, Harry Reid's observation rings true that, after the demise of Donald Dewar, Henry McLeish, Jack McConnell and Wendy Alexander, 'the big boys [of Labour] strutted their stuff in Westminster. The minnows swam around the wee Scottish pool.'[170]

Has the SNP stolen the mantle of social democracy from Labour? Paradoxically, Neal Ascherson observed, the SNP

> can be seen as the most 'British' of parties. Its social programme is to preserve and fortify what's left of the old British welfare state consensus, building a new Hadrian's Wall against the neoliberal tsunami that has weakened social justice and cohesion in England from Thatcher through Blair and Brown to Cameron. Ironically, this resistance is also the programme of the Scottish Labour party, brutally traumatised by the experience of Blairism and New Labour. On almost all policy save constitutional matters, the two parties agree. But they hate each other too much to say so.[171]

---

[168] John McTernan, 'Independence still a distant dream', *The Scotsman*, 2 November 2011.

[169] 'Labour in Scotland needs to follow Alexander's leader lead', *The Scotsman*, 19 November 2011.

[170] Harry Reid, 'Labour's minnows in a stagnant Scots pool', *The Herald*, 1 March 2011.

[171] Neal Ascherson, 'Let Scotland be a sovereign, mature nation and England profits too', *The Observer*, 15 January 2012.

Joyce McMillan saw a huge mountain to climb for Labour who

> must somehow strive to reinvent social democracy in an age
> when the nation-states that nurtured it are in meltdown,
> and to defend a politics of solidarity at a time when all the
> forces in play are explosively centrifugal, placing a premium
> on the assertion of difference, and on drawing of borders
> both on the map, and in the mind.[172]

But a letter writer to the *Independent* put it perfectly:

> Unless Labour is willing to present itself as a party dedicated
> to the pursuit of social justice for all and to follow that vision
> wherever it may lead, it has no reason to exist. Unless it can
> communicate that vision to young people, it won't.[173]

To what it boils down in Scotland, for Labour as for the Tories and the
Lib Dems, is standing up for Scotland, and being seen to stand up for
Scotland, developing a positive vision for Scotland, and being perceived
as truly Scottish, rather than extensions of Westminster, parties.

LOCAL ELECTIONS 2012

In 2011 we had revolution, radiation and riots, a permanent Eurocrisis,
Royal weddings in London and Edinburgh, earthquakes and tsunamis,
pandas at Edinburgh Zoo, the Scottish elections – and the end of a
metaphor, as the painting of the Forth Bridge – the proverbial job
without end – came to a close. What lies ahead? The Olympic Games in
London (controversial north of the Border because of the costs involved
and the low expectations that they bring adequate benefits to Scotland),
the Queen's Diamond Jubilee, the Ken and BoJo show in London, and
UEFA Euro finals, this time in Poland and the Ukraine, and again without
Scotland.

While the referendum debate will continue, even if 'more heat than
light is being generated in a debate calling out for clarity,'[174] it remains to
be seen how much attention the forthcoming local government elections
in May will be able to command.

---

[172] Joyce McMillan, 'Addressing the state of the Unionist', *The Scotsman*, 11 November 2011.

[173] Les May, 'Labour must find its vision' (Letter to the Editor), *The Independent*, 28 July 2011.

[174] 'Clarity and poll on nation's future' (Leader), *The Herald*, 7 January 2012.

> Local government contests are usually pretty low-key affairs but this year's will be slightly different. All the main parties will go into them knowing that they represent the only real test of public opinion this year and the only real indication of how well the SNP Government is doing – and that will be crucial ahead of the independence referendum.[175]

The SNP has won a series of council by-elections in recent months, from Aberdeen to Edinburgh and Glasgow, and took over Clackmannanshire Council after a vote of no confidence ousted the Labour administration there. Now leading 11 out of the 32 councils (and sharing power in two more), the SNP claims it can conquer Glasgow on 3 May. So, will the SNP juggernaut roll on? Or can Labour shore up support in Glasgow? If Labour fails to hold on to its power base in Glasgow, many will be writing the party's obituary.'[176] And what impact will the trams saga have on the council elections in Edinburgh?

Beyond May 2012, though, there are serious and far-reaching questions concerning Scottish local democracy. Does it even deserve the name 'local', given its remoteness from the citizens in many parts of Scotland? The present system of local government, introduced in 1994/96, three years before Devolution, by the UK government's Scottish Office, gives Scotland 'the largest average population per basic unit of local government of any developed country.'[177]

Highland Council, to take the most striking example, covers an area the size of Belgium with a population the size of Belfast. Councillors need to drive hundreds of thousands of miles a year to connect with fellow councillors and citizens in their council area. Despite such herculean efforts, many remote communities feel neglected and disenfranchised. That is 'damaging democracy and economic development in Scotland,' says Rob Gibson MSP in the introduction to 'Small Works.' His consultation document proposes a major shake-up of Highland Council, and he has made the task his 'personal priority' for this parliamentary session. '

> We have a situation in my constituency, where councillors can decide planning applications for projects hundreds of miles away and where spending decisions are made by officials with little or no knowledge of the places they are

[175] Hamish Macdonell, 'Scottish spring will reveal political fortunes for 2012 and beyond', *Caledonian Mercury*, 6 January 2012, <politics.caledonianmercury.com/2012/01/06/scottish-spring-will-reveal-political-fortunes-for-2012-and-beyond/>.

[176] 'Huge challenge for Scottish Labour' (Leader), *The Herald*, 17 December 2011.

[177] Michael Keating, *The Government of Scotland: Public Policy Making after Devolution*, Edinburgh: Edinburgh University Press, 2005, p.12.

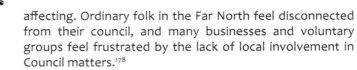

affecting. Ordinary folk in the Far North feel disconnected from their council, and many businesses and voluntary groups feel frustrated by the lack of local involvement in Council matters.[178]

When the SNP minority government took office in 2007, it promised to liberate and empower local communities. But instead, the former BBC journalist John Knox has argued, the councils were 'tied into "single outcome agreements" covering all sorts of central government targets, including a council tax freeze.'[179]

> Local government is dying in Scotland, as turnout falls and central government increasingly diverts the local revenue and tells councils what to do. The only thing that will keep local government alive is democratic engagement – the active support of the people.[180]

Now that a further transfer of powers is in prospect for the Scottish Parliament, including substantial fiscal and borrowing powers, it is precisely the right time for us and the Parliament to remember that Devolution was never meant to stop at Holyrood. It is also encouraging to hear just those sentiments included by Johann Lamont in her victory speech as new Scottish Labour leader. Rolling out Rob Gibson's consultation across Scotland would be a good start. Let us be optimistic – after all, is 2012 not the Year of Creative Scotland?

[January 2012]

---

[178] Rob Gibson, *Small Works: Decentralising Services in Local Government* (A consultation paper), 2011, <www.robgibson.org/2011/12/06/gibson-on-decentralisation-this-is-my-personal-priority/>.

[179] John Knox, 'Analysis: mayors the way to combat cuts?', *Caledonian Mercury*, 22 February 2010, <politics.caledonianmercury.com/2010/02/22/mayors-the-way-to-combat-cuts/>.

[180] Iain Macwhirter, 'Let's bring councils into line with elected mayors', *The Herald*, 1 September 2011.

Chapter IX

THE YEAR AT HOLYROOD
2012

Against the backdrop of big UK and London events – the Queen's Diamond Jubilee, the Olympics and Paralympics in London, the Government's austerity budget – the Scottish domestic political scene was dominated by the referendum debate, from the Prime Ministerial visit in January and the announcement of the date of the referendum on Scottish independence to the 'Edinburgh Agreement'. It feels increasingly as if we lived in two parallel worlds here in Scotland. There is the everyday business of Holyrood and local government, the budget, the cuts, policies (the 'real world') – and then there is the constitutional debate, full of what-ifs, staggering from one hypothetical question to another assertion. That, in the parlance of Bill Jamieson, is 'Planet Indyref'.[1]

Questions about the referendum process – when and how? – have increasingly been superseded, as the 'Yes Scotland' and the 'Better Together' campaigns got under way, by more substantial issues about the potential shape an independent Scotland would take. Would it continue to be a part of the European Union? Would it remain in Nato? What about army bases and defence-related jobs in Scotland? What about the removal of nuclear weapons from Faslane? Would independence boost Scotland's economy or harm it? Which currency would Scotland use? What about welfare and state pensions? How much of the UK national debt would burden an independent Scotland? Would it need a written constitution? All that did threaten to eclipse the Local Government Elections in May, and the day-to-day 'bread and butter' issues at Holyrood.

GRIM ECONOMIC REALITIES

The year 2012 began with warnings about Scotland's 'flagging economy' slipping back into recession;[2] in the middle of the year

---

[1] Bill Jamieson, 'Planet Indyref versus the real world', *The Scotsman*, 1 March 2012.

[2] Jane Bradley, 'Recession fears haunt fragile Scots economy', *The Scotsman*, 18 January 2012.

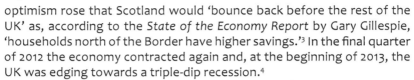

optimism rose that Scotland would 'bounce back before the rest of the UK' as, according to the *State of the Economy Report* by Gary Gillespie, 'households north of the Border have higher savings.'[3] In the final quarter of 2012 the economy contracted again and, at the beginning of 2013, the UK was edging towards a triple-dip recession.[4]

Notwithstanding its catastrophic performance, the Con-Dem coalition at Westminster survived, although it was repeatedly seen on the brink of collapse (failed House of Lords reform and, as a Lib Dem retaliation, no agreement on Westminster boundary reform). The Euro, though written off by many UK commentators, has also survived – thanks in no small measure to three words from the mouth of Mario Draghi, the president of the European Central Bank, spoken in July: 'whatever it takes' – a commitment by the ECB to buy, if needs be, unlimited quantities of troubled Eurozone countries' bonds.[5] 2012 was also the year Abdelbaset Ali Mohamed al Megrahi eventually died in Tripoli, the man convicted of the Lockerbie bombing of 1988, released in August 2009 by Justice Secretary Kenny MacAskill 'to die', and it was the year Barack Obama was elected for a second term as US president.

Closer to home, Scottish politics lost one of its finest activists, political thinkers and commentators: the lifelong Nationalist Stephen Maxwell who managed to finish his final contribution to the independence debate just before his passing, aged 69, on 24 April 2012.[6] Bob MacLean, convener of the pro-devolution Scottish Labour Action from 1988-1998 and one of the key figures in the Campaign for a Scottish Parliament, passed away on 14 July, at the untimely age of 55. The Liberal Democrat Donald Gorrie, also a long-standing and passionate advocate of devolution, died on 25 August 2012. He was an Edinburgh councillor for 26 years, and elected to Westminster in 1997, but swapped that seat for Holyrood in 1999. Reelected in 2003, he served as an MSP until his retirement in 2007. A former leader of the Scottish National Party, Jimmy Halliday, who had kept the party alive in the late 1950s, then became chairman, director and columnist for the *Scots Independent* and published an insightful memoir in 2011,[7] died aged 84 on 3 January 2013.

In the art world, the demise of George Wyllie, aged 90, and of Michael Marra, just 60, robbed Scotland of two very different geniuses – one a quirky sculptor who, with works like the 'Straw Locomotive', hung

---

[3] Scott Macnab, 'Good times to return sooner to Scotland than England", *The Scotsman*, 27 July 2012.

[4] Ian McConnell, 'Triple-dip fears as manufacturing falls', *The Herald*, 12 January 2013.

[5] James Wilson, Robin Wigglesworth and Brian Groom, 'ECB "ready to do whatever it takes"', *Financial Times*, 26 July 2012.

[6] Stephen Maxwell, *Arguing for Independence: Evidence, Risk and the Wicked Issues*, Edinburgh: Luath Press, 2012.

[7] James Halliday, *Yours for Scotland: A Memoir*, Stirling: Scots Independent, 2011.

from the Finnieston Crane in Glasgow, the 'Running Clock' at Glasgow's Buchanan Bus Station, and the 'Paper Boat', launched from the Clyde, helped his country to reimagine itself;[8] the other a marvellously idiosyncratic songwriter and singer, the 'Bard of Dundee' and the author of 'Hermless', a fine, if ever so slightly tongue-in-cheek, alternative national anthem:

> Wi' ma hand on ma hert and ma hert in ma mooth
> Wi' erms that could reach ower the sea
> Ma feet micht be big but the insects are safe
> They'll never get stood on by me
>
> Hermless, hermless,
> There's never nae bother fae me
> I ging to the libry, I tak' oot a book
> And then I go hame for ma tea

Just imagine Hampden or Murrayfield getting into the swing of it...

LOCAL ELECTIONS

Postponed by a year to avoid a clash with the Holyrood elections, the 2012 local government elections were the first stand-alone council elections since 1995. The election campaigns never really got going. Predictions of a low turnout were paramount. In the event, the figures were slightly better than feared, but still pretty dismal. Just under 40% made it to the polling stations on 3 May. It took 19 weeks before the final turnout figure was released – 39.8% – a fact that was criticised by the Electoral Commission.[9]

Decades of hollowing out local government, centralising powers and reducing councils to be not much more than the extended arms of the national executive, delivering public services according to the priorities of central government, have taken their toll. 'Local government has been deprived of much of the autonomy it used to enjoy.'[10] Why vote for a body with such little power? Even the council tax, one of the few real

[8] Joyce McMillan, 'His art was an expression of freedom', *The Scotsman*, 18 May 2012.

[9] Severin Carrell, 'Electoral watchdog criticises slow Scottish elections turnout figure', *The Guardian* (The Scotland Blog), <www.guardian.co.uk/uk/scotland-blog/2012/sep/11/scotland-council-turnout >.

[10] Allan Massie, 'Provosts can reverse the erosion of democracy', *The Scotsman*, 29 February 2012.

powers of local councils, has been centrally frozen for six years now – a regressive measure, delivering 'massive reductions in bills for those at the top.'[11]

> Though the SNP talked the talk of local democracy, they didn't seem to walk the walk. On the whole, the Scottish Government was more interested in powers and budgets being devolved from Westminster to Holyrood than from Holyrood to local communities.[12]

The SNP message during the election campaign seemed to be: vote for our candidates and, as councillors, they then can implement the wonderful policies we decide at Holyrood. Why connect with a body that is, in most parts in Scotland, too far removed and distant to be perceived or, even more important, experienced as 'local'?[13] Is this 'local' government? Is this 'local democracy'? 'Scottish democracy is like a ladder,' as a letter writer put it, 'that is missing the bottom rung that reaches down into the grass roots of community life.'[14] Both the Jimmy Reid Foundation and Reform Scotland published detailed reports arguing for reform of local democracy in Scotland.[15]

After all, what sense is there in asking the Scots to vote for independence, if they are not even trusted with running their own local affairs? Johann Lamont told the Labour conference in Dundee:

> Devolution can't just mean powers going from London to Edinburgh... If we believe in devolution we must be more radical than that and ask at which level should power lie if we are to serve the people. That means a radical look at not just what powers should the Scottish government have, but what powers does local government need and which should be devolved further to local communities to allow them to shape their lives.[16]

---

[11] Tom Gordon, 'Council tax freeze rewards richest Scots', *Sunday Herald*, 4 March 2012.

[12] 'Local communities have a chance to shape their future' (Leader), *The Herald*, 14 September 2012.

[13] See Eberhard Bort, 'Remote and Scanty: Scotland's Local Democracy Deficit', *Scottish Affairs*, no.81 (Autumn 2012), pp.68-97.

[14] Michael Gallagher, 'We should boost local democracy by empowering our community councils', Letter to the Editor, *The Herald*, 14 November 2012.

[15] Eberhard Bort, Robin McAlpine and Gordon Morgan, *The Silent Crisis: Failure and Revival in Local Democracy in Scotland*, Biggar: The Jimmy Reid Foundation, 2012 <reidfoundation. org/portfolio/the-silent-crisis-failure-and-revival-in-local-democracy-in-scotland/>; Reform Scotland, *Renewing Local Government*, Edinburgh, May 2012, <reformscotland.com/public/ publications/Renewing_Local_Government.pdf>.

[16] Quoted in Jason Allardyce, 'Kennedy leads Lib Dem drive to save the union', *The Sunday*

Table 6: Scottish Local Government Election Results 2012[17]

Parties	Share of Votes (%)	+/-	Councilors	Net Gain/Loss
SNP	32.32	+4.46	424	+61
Scottish Labour	31.39	+3.24	394	+46
Scottish Conservatives	13.31	- 2.26	115	- 28
Scottish Lib Dems	6.59	- 6.1	71	- 95
Scottish Green Party	2.2	+0.16	14	+ 6
Independents	11.86	+0.98	194	+ 2
Other	2.32	+0.9	11	+ 1

And yet, the dominant discourse points at even more centralisation. Lord Sutherland, in his report of free care for the elderly, urged a reduction of the number of councils;[18] following on from the centralisation of the police and fire services, Kenny MacAskill called a cut in the number of councils 'inevitable'.[19]

THE BATTLE(S) OF GEORGE SQUARE

As polling day loomed, the question was: would the SNP success story continue? The Centre for Scottish Public Policy predicted another landslide, with the SNP seizing power in all seven Scottish cities.[20] In the end, the SNP could claim an overall victory. It took the most seats nationally. But none of the cities.

The most important battle was about who would win Glasgow. At the SNP spring conference in Glasgow, Nicola Sturgeon had told delegates that the party would 'seize control of the city' where Labour was 'discredited' and 'losing councillors hand over fist.'[21] Indeed, Glasgow's Labour council had been through stormy waters in the run-up to the election: from the resignation of council leader Steven Purcell 'and the dark underbelly of the city it exposed, the dodgy property deals and the explosion of ALEOs (arms-length agencies) and the scale of councillor remuneration,'[22] to the six Labour councillors who, after being

Times (Scotland), 4 March 2012.

[17] For detailed results, see *Scottish Affairs*, no.80 (Summer 2012).

[18] Jason Allardyce, 'Scots "can't afford free care"', *The Sunday Times* (Scotland), 1 September 2012.

[19] Gareth Rose, 'Scots local councils face the axe', *Scotland on Sunday*, 25 November 2012.

[20] Alan Roden, 'SNP "set for council vote landslide"', *Daily Mail*, 16 April 2012.

[21] Paul Wilson, 'Sturgeon's call to arms sparks Glasgow row', *Scotland on Sunday*, 11 March 2012.

[22] Gerry Hassan, 'Civic pride may sometimes lead to civic hubris', *The Scotsman*, 14 April 2012.

deselected by their party for the May vote, turned against the council's budget and even stood as 'Glasgow First,' their own list, in the elections. 'Labour deserves to lose the City Chambers,' a *Sunday Herald* editorial commented, but it also warned that 'the SNP have not yet shown why they deserve to win.'[23] A few days before the election, the SNP called their canvass returns in Glasgow 'sensational', and the media were expecting, if not an outright win by the SNP, then certainly that Labour would lose.[24] In the end, Labour triumphed in Glasgow. Not only could it fend of the SNP challenge, it regained its absolute majority.

Scotland-wide, the SNP gained overall control of two councils (Angus and Dundee), Labour doubled the number of councils it controls – Renfrewshire and West Dunbartonshire, in addition to Glasgow and North Lanarkshire). Elsewhere in the country, all kinds of coalitions were formed, including a Labour-SNP pact in Edinburgh, where council Leader Jenny Dawe had lost her seat – as the Lib Dems were decimated across the board.

Hardly had the battle for the city chambers in Glasgow been decided, when another battle of George Square loomed. Following in the footsteps of Aberdeen, the Council wanted to give George Square a radical facelift in view of the coming Commonwealth Games – most controversial, as the 14 statues on the square (including Sir Walter Scott and Robert Burns) were under threat of being removed.

In Aberdeen, a referendum had narrowly endorsed the plans, supported by the oil magnate Sir Ian Wood, of transforming the Union Terrace Gardens beyond recognition.[25] Labour had campaigned in the local elections to overturn that decision. And, indeed, in August the now Labour-led council decided to ignore the referendum result and abandon the £155 million project. Perhaps a bad day for democracy – definitely a good day for the Gardens.

Now, people in Glasgow demanded a referendum on the future of George Square. Accompanied by protests, the plans were presented in mid-January 2013, but did not impress. And George Matheson, the Council Leader, much criticised for his handling of the matter, engineered a U-turn. The battle was called off. Back to square one for George Square. What next? Concreting over Princes Street Gardens?

---

[23] 'Labour deserve to lose Glasgow ... but do SNP deserve to win?' (Leader), *Sunday Herald*, 12 February 2012.

[24] Campbell Gunn, 'Gloves are off in the battle for Glasgow', *The Sunday Post*, 29 April 2012.

[25] Frank Urquhart, 'Aberdeen votes for biggest overhaul since Victorian era', *The Scotsman*, 3 March 2012.

HOLYROOD LEGISLATION: ALCOHOL, ANTI-SECTARIANISM AND GAY MARRIAGE

A trickle of legislation passed through Holyrood – if we include the Offensive Behaviour and Threatening Communications Bill, which was agreed on 14 December 2011, the tally for the first half of 2012 amounted to ten bills. The new anti-sectarian law, as the *Daily Mail* applauded, 'puts thugs in jail.' From the introduction in March to the end of September, 34 people were convicted of 'offensive behaviour' – nearly 5 per month, at a conviction rate of 83 per cent.[26]

The Budget Bill (8 February) which, for the first time, due to the SNP's absolute majority, did not involve prolonged haggling and knife-edge votes, authorised approximately £31bn of cash expenditure by the Scottish Government and its associated bodies in the financial year 2012-13. The only surprise was Finance Secretary John Swinney's concession, bowing to public pressure, of reversing a cut for college funding, pledging nearly £20 million in extra cash for the college sector – which secured the support of the Lib Dems for his budget. Eddie Barnes summed it up:

> Despite failing to win the backing of Labour, the Tories and the Greens, the SNP pushed through its spending plans for the next financial year, enforcing a pay freeze for all public sector workers, cutbacks to local government, but also offering a council tax freeze and free tuition for students. In the final round of negotiations, Mr Swinney sought to reduce a round of controversial cutbacks he had planned for further education colleges across Scotland, offering more money to support students. He also watered down a proposed multi-million pound a year tax grab on stores which sell alcohol and tobacco, cash which Mr Swinney wants to put towards improving the country's poor health.[27]

You may see that either as a government listening to the Scots and acting on their behalf, or as a giveaway that avoids radical measures in response to the financial crisis and does not rock the boat, because the SNP does not 'want to scare the voters before referendum day dawns.'[28]

---

[26] Graham Grant, 'New sectarian law puts thugs in jail', *Daily Mail*, 6 November 2012.

[27] Eddie Barnes, 'Swinney softens stance over Tesco tax and college cash', *The Scotsman*, 9 February 2012.

[28] 'Swinney's cash giveaway buys the SNP some extra approval' (Leader), *The Scotsman*, 9 February 2012.

On 22 March, the Welfare Reform (Further Provisions) Bill was passed – the result of the Scottish Parliament's withholding of consent to the UK Welfare Reform Bill in December 2011, it maintains devolved, passported benefits like free school meals and blue badge parking permits.

The controversial Alcohol (Minimum Pricing) Bill took its final hurdle on 24 May, with an 86:1 vote (32 abstentions). An amendment by Labour's Richard Simpson MSP to claw back windfall from the retailers was rejected, and Nicola Sturgeon, the Cabinet Secretary for Health, announced that the minimum price per unit would be set at 50 pence. Already there are indications that he UK and Ireland will follow Scotland's example.

A bill on the National Library of Scotland passed on 16 May; Land Registration, etc followed on 31 May; on 7 June the Agricultural Holdings (Amendment) Bill was agreed, a Criminal Cases (Punishment and Review) Bill on 20 June; and a Long Leases Bill on 28 June. These were minor adjustments. A bigger, and more controversial, affair was the Police and Fire Reform Bill, passed on 27 June by 101:6 votes (14 abstentions). The Liberal Democrats had fought to the last ditch to fell the bill, which creates a single police force and fire service for the whole of Scotland, as a centralisation too far, with dangers for local accountability.

On 4 September, Alex Salmond announced the legislative programme of his Government for the coming Parliamentary session. In included 15 bills. The headlines were grabbed, as expected, by the Referendum Bill, which will clarify the procedural specifics of the 2014 plebiscite. Next in profile came the delayed Marriage and Civil Partnership Bill, allowing same sex couples to marry – hailed beforehand as 'a bold – but correct – move for equality and liberty,'[29] but also triggering a furious response from the Catholic Church and other church groups, although the proposed legislation ensures that no religious institution would be forced to conduct same sex marriages in churches. The bill, which will be subject to a free vote in the Parliament, also allows for civil partnerships to be registered through a religious ceremony.

Three other bills 'stand out as potential statements of SNP intent':

> The Post-16 Education Reform Bill may become associated with Scottish Government plans to introduce grants for university students in low income families, perhaps marking further distance from the system in England; the Children and Young People Bill introduces a 'minimum of 600 hours free early learning and childcare provision'; and the Adult Health & Social Care Integration Bill seeks to integrate

---

[29] 'A bold move for equality and liberty' (Leader), *Sunday Herald*, 29 July 2012.

further some joint services between local authorities and health boards.[30]

The rest of the legislative programme induced little excitement, perhaps with the exception of the Forth Estuary Transport Authority Bill – which may revisit the issue of the cost and source of funding of the new Forth bridge. A big disappointment was that the Community Empowerment and Renewal Bill, consulted upon since June, did not make it onto the legislative list – instead, Derek Mackay, the Local Government Minister, stepped up a public consultation on the bill, which is supposed to include compulsory purchase powers for community groups to buy land or buildings that are unused. There will, on the other hand, be a return to Margo MacDonald's assisted suicide bill, after it got the backing of nearly 20 MSPs.

Between September 2012 and January '13, four bills concluded their passage through Holyrood. On 31 October, the Local Government Finance (Unoccupied Properties, etc) Bill met with approval. It is supposed to help regenerate town centres by allowing councils to vary council tax where a property is unoccupied, and it amends powers in respect of the ability of councils to require provision of information.

The Social Care (Self-directed Support) Bill, enabling local authorities to provide support to certain carers and to make provision about the way in which certain social care services are provided by local authorities, was passed on 28 November 2012. On 16 January 2013 the Freedom of Information (Amendment) Bill was agreed; and the Scottish Civil Justice Council and Criminal Legal Assistance Bill followed on 29 January, establishing a Scottish Civil Justice Council and introducing, controversially and for the first time, financial contributions for criminal legal aid, which will see some accused people having to pay criminal court defence costs. 'The legislation, which would also see lawyers being responsible for collecting money from clients, provoked anger from the legal profession,'[31] even threatening a split between the Edinburgh and Glasgow Bar Associations and the Law Society of Scotland out of anger that the latter had backed down on these reforms.

The Scottish Parliament also passed secondary legislation on housing support regulations. These accompany the statutory housing support duty to commence on 1 June 2013, requiring local authorities to house all involuntary homeless people in settled accommodation.

---

[30] Paul Cairney, 'Scotland', *Monitor: Constitution Unit Newsletter*, 52 (October 2012), <www.ucl.ac.uk/constitution-unit/publications/tabs/monitor/edit/monitor-newsletter/monitor52.pdf>.

[31] 'Scottish legal aid reform passed', *BBC News Scotland*, 29 January 2013, <www.bbc.co.uk/news/uk-scotland-21245700>.

When Finance Secretary John Swinney introduced his spending plans at Holyrood in September, they entailed another year of real term pay-cuts for civil servants and NHS staff and a package of £200 million to boost economic growth – deemed 'timid'[32] by the opposition. The Unions accused Swinney of being 'Osborne in a kilt'.[33] There was, as the economist Professor David Bell found, 'no evidence' that it was aimed at boosting growth.[34] And this January, the SNP lost its first vote in this Parliamentary session, when newly-independent Jean Urquhart joined Labour and Conservative MSPs in voting against a committee motion calling on Members to agree that John Swinney had 'produced a budget which encourages sustainable growth.'[35]

NURSES, TEACHERS, AND CREATIVE SCOTLAND

A success story was the location in Edinburgh of the UK's new Green Investment Bank in Edinburgh. Politics – and particularly the implications of that decision on the independence debate – certainly plaid a part in the decision, although the coalition at Westminster denied it was all about bolstering the Union. But there were other policy areas where the Government came under pressure.

The number of nurses in Scotland, which peaked in 2009, has since declined, so that now 2,000 fewer nurses are working in the NHS than when the SNP came to power.[36] On the same day that these figures came out, it was also revealed that only two of Scotland's health boards met Accident and Emergency waiting time targets. Labour's Jackie Baillie said: 'The SNP target for emergency waiting times now has not been met since 2009. Alex Neil has to get a grip on what is happening in the NHS.'[37] In December, internal health board audits suggested that NHS Lothian was not alone fiddling waiting time targets. Now, NHS Grampian had been added, and there was a suspicion that the practice of falsely declaring

---

[32] Magnus Gardham, 'Critics round on Swinney over "timid": Scots budget', *The Herald*, 21 September 2012.

[33] Eddie Barnes, 'Swinney branded "Osborne in a kilt" by unions', *The Scotsman*, 21 September 2012.

[34] Scott Macnab, 'Reverse college cuts and pour cash into creating growth, Swinney told', *The Scotsman*, 22 January 2013.

[35] Andrew Whitaker, 'SNP suffers defeat after MSPs reject call to back its budget', *The Scotsman*, 10 December 2012.

[36] Natalie Walker, '2,000 fewer nurses since SNP came to power', *The Scotsman*, 28 November 2012.

[37] Natalie Walker, 'A&E waiting time targets missed by all but two Scottish health boards', *The Scotsman*, 28 November 2012.

patients as unavailable in order to massage the figures was wide-spread across the country.

> When Nicola Sturgeon was moved from the health portfolio last year to take charge of the Government's referendum campaign she was instantly dubbed the 'Yes Minister'. Now her successor as Health Secretary, Alex Neil, has been given a new nickname of his own: the 'clean Up the Mess Minister'.[38]

Problems continued with the implementation of 'Curriculum for Excellence', the Educational Institute of Scotland (EIS) reporting abut 'unhappy classrooms' and one big local authority – Labour-led East Renfrewshire – delaying the introduction of the new national exams system by a year.[39] The bestselling children's book author (and Children's Laureate) Julia Donaldson said 'the laudable aims' of the Curriculum 'sometimes got in the way of good teaching.'[40] But there was praise, too:

> The Scottish Curriculum for Excellence, with all its well-rehearsed problems over lead in times and teaching resources, is nevertheless a product that recognises the stated current and future needs of most employers.[41]

Ruth Wishart also cited Professor Ken Robinson who 'made a point praising the Curriculum for Excellence as being "ahead of the curve".' In March came the U-turn. Michael Russell allowed councils to delay the introduction of the new national exams for a year. In January of this year, a study among Glasgow's secondary teachers found that half of them felt not secure in the delivery of the Curriculum for Excellence, about the same number was unhappy about the resources provided for the introduction of the new curriculum, and 60% complained that they had not enough time to prepare courses. The feedback underlines the level of concern and frustration with the present situation,' Hugh Donnelly of the Glasgow branch of the EIS commented, 'and the lack of consistency and cohesion in taking forward the new curriculum.'[42]

---

[38] Magnus Gardham, 'Neil has to be up for the fight on NHS', *The Herald*, 12 January 2013.

[39] Andrew Denholm, 'Curriculum crisis warning as council ignores advice', *The Herald*, 1 February 2012.

[40] Andrew Denholm, 'Teachers thwarted by new curriculum, claims author', *The Herald*, 28 January 2013.

[41] Ruth Wishart, 'Let the nation speak', *The Herald*, 7 February 2012.

[42] Andrew Denholm, 'Teachers raise fears about delivery of new curriculum', *The Herald*, 3 January 2013.

Teacher numbers have fallen by 3,690 since the SNP came to power in 2007, according to official statistics – a fact that led to opposition attacks. Labour's Hugh Henry MSP claimed that 'the figures show the shocking reality of the SNP's broken promise on teacher numbers.'[43]

In September, the SNP came under fire for a 'stealth' cut in student bursaries, affecting poorer students, by nearly £1,000 form April 2013, sold by Michael Russell, perhaps with a nod to George Orwell, as 'enhanced support'.[44] In October, the overall decline of learners, and the dramatic decline in women learners (-26% since 2006/2007), at Scottish colleges led to further attacks on the Education Secretary.[45]

'It is wrong of the government to reduce the number of places at colleges and the number of courses they offer,' wrote Allan Massie:

> Doing so will condemn many young people to unemployment or trap others in jobs that offer few prospects of a better life. (...) The burden of cuts is being placed on those most in need of the training that can make for a better life. Is this what the SNP calls a social democratic programme?[46]

Justice Secretary Kenny MacAskill announced in June that Scotland's crime rate had reached a 37-year low.[47] The Police Federation had accused the SNP government of 'manipulating' crime figures by downgrading or reclassifying crimes as less serious.[48] More worrying, perhaps, were the setting-up problems of the single police force, sliding into a turf war between the new Chief Constable of the new Police Service of Scotland, and the chairman of the overseeing Scottish Police Authority. The setting-up process was called a 'shambles' by the former senior police officer turned Labour MSP, Graeme Pearson.[49]

Two reports into the state of Scotland's infrastructure came up with worrying figures: while budgets fall, the 'repair bill to fix ... crumbling

---

[43] Chris Marshall, '"We have been conned" says Labour as teacher numbers fall 3,690 under SNP', The Scotsman, 12 December 2012.

[44] Eddie Barnes, 'SNP cuts bursaries for poor students by 1,000', The Scotsman, 5 October 2012.

[45] Andrew Denholm, 'Thousands of women hit by college cutbacks', The Herald, 3 November 2012.

[46] Allan Massie, 'Russell's tantrum distracts from the real issue', The Scotsman, 15 November 2012.

[47] 'Violent crime down by 17% in Scotland', BBC News Scotland, 26 June 2012, <www.bbc.co.uk/news/uk-scotland-18592130>.

[48] Andrew Whitaker, 'SNP accused by police of "manipulating" crime figures', The Scotsman, 14 April 2012.

[49] Magnus Gardham, '"Shambles" of new single police force', The Herald, 28 November 2012.

hospitals and roads now tops £2 billion.'[50] The Scottish Government has also come under pressure to explain how it is planning to meet its climate change and renewables targets. 'Appalling' was the verdict of Patrick Harvie MSP on the SNP Government's progress report on anti-climate change measures which was outlined in Parliament by Climate Change Minister Paul Wheelhouse who claimed that the report proved that Scotland remained 'at the forefront of climate change action.'[51] The Greens, Labour and Stop Climate Change Chaos Scotland doubted whether the three new measures announced in the report would suffice to meet Scotland's target of cutting harmful emissions by 42% (compared with 1990 levels) by 2020.

In the last quarter of 2012, the Scottish Government's controversial arts funding body Creative Scotland came under unprecedented attack from inside Scotland's artistic community. That it had to come to he boil in Scotland's official 'Year of Creative Scotland' may be regarded as the ultimate irony. But the stushie did not come unexpected. The market-driven 'investment', 'art as a branch economy of the tourist industry,'[52] expressed in atrocious management-speak, had alienated a growing section of the Scottish arts world from the inception of Creative Scotland, when it replaced the Scottish Arts Council and Scottish Screen in 2010.

A change in the funding structure, from fixed-term to project funding, the funding of an STV celebrity cookery programme (derided by Irvine Welsh as a 'joke'[53]), and the way the arts body dealt with criticism from practitioners led to an Open Letter, initially signed by 100 – eventually by over 400 – artists and art organisers, among them some of the finest artists, writers, playwrights, musicians and composers of the nation. At an artists' Tramway Theatre meeting in Glasgow, it was claimed that artists were made to feel like 'benefit scroungers' by Creative Scotland.[54] The poet Don Paterson referred to it as a 'dysfunctional ant-heap'; while the damning artists' letter, signed by figures such as John Byrne, Sir Peter Maxwell Davies, Alasdair Gray, James Kelman, A L Kennedy, Liz Lochhead and Ian Rankin, criticised its 'ill-conceived decision-making; unclear language and lack of empathy and regard for Scottish culture.'[55] As if that were not enough, Creative Scotland threw a gala awards ceremony at

---

[50] Scott Macnab, 'Hospital and road repair bill at billions', *The Scotsman*, 11 February 2012.

[51] Magnus Gardham, 'Government measures on climate are condemned', *The Herald*, 30 January 2013.

[52] Ian Bell, 'Arts body has lost the trust of our creative community', *The Herald*, 15 September 2012.

[53] Phil Miller, 'Arts body under fire for funding cookery series', *The Herald*, 30 August 2012.

[54] Brian Ferguson, 'Artists 'made to feel like benefit scroungers', *The Scotsman*, 1 November 2012.

[55] Phil Miller, 'Creative Scotland chief quits after artists' revolt', *The Herald*, 4 December 2012.

the Kelvingrove Museum and Art Gallery – without a single woman on the seven-strong judging panel.

Both the chief executive, Andrew Dixon, and one of the deputy directors, Venu Dupha, resigned. 'I have been disappointed,' said Dixon, 'given my track record, not to gain the respect and support of some of the more established voices in Scottish culture and I hope that my resignation will clear the way for a new phase of collaboration between artists and Creative Scotland.'[56] Venu Dhupa, the creative director, quit just before Christmas, days after the publication of a damning internal report into the running of the quango, which had revealed widespread problems due to 'fractured' relationships with artists and a 'gulf' between staff and senior management.[57]

This car crash of Scotland's arts organisation – responsible for dispensing £80 million a year in funding – can, of course, not be blamed solely on the SNP Government, but it happened on the watch of Culture Secretary Fiona Hyslop. While the present government inherited the unwieldy concept of Creative Scotland from the previous Labour-Lib Dem Holyrood coalition and implemented it, it could as easily 'have dropped it.'[58] The signs of dissatisfaction and discomfort should have led to much earlier intervention. Now, Creative Scotland has promised reform, but a lot of rebuilding of trust will be necessary in 2013, if the arts body wants 'to win back the support of a sector it spent the last year alienating.'[59]

Andrew Dixon, of course, hails from south of the Border, as did Vicky Featherstone who oversaw the first six years of the Scottish National Theatre (and so is her incoming replacement, Laurie Sansom). In the middle of the Creative Scotland debacle, Word Power published a book containing a piece by Scotland's finest writer, Alasdair Gray, on the role English people play in the arts in Scotland.[60] Gray's contribution was marred by 'ill-judged and old-fashioned'[61] categorising of them as either 'colonists' or 'settlers' but, after the storm about the loaded terminology had somewhat died down, a more serious debate could be had about leadership in arts administration, openness in the arts, cultural boundaries, about nationalism and internationalism in the arts. Are the

[56] *Ibid.*

[57] Brian Ferguson, 'Creative Scotland director Venu Dhupa stands down', *The Scotsman*, 21 December 2012.

[58] Gerry Hassan, 'Creative Scotland crisis is canvas for new vision', *The Scotsman*, 10 November 2012.

[59] Andrew Eaton-Lewis, 'the diary', *The Scotsman*, 6 December 2012.

[60] Scott Hames (ed.), *Unstated: Writers on Scottish Independence*, Edinburgh: Word Power, 2012.

[61] Joyce McMillan, 'Political nit-picking serves no-one', *The Scotsman*, 4 January 2013.

English 'colonising' Scottish arts? Is it 'an almost impossible task' for Scots 'to win the top creative and cultural jobs in Scotland'?[62]

Is that the message of the new, 'confident, outward-looking' Scotland? Or does it reveal 'a rich seem of insecurity and anti-Englishness within a section of the nationalist movement'?[63] Another manifestation of the 'Scottish cringe'?[64] The painter and playwright John Byrne praised the contribution that Vicky Featherstone had made to the National Theatre of Scotland and insisted that such jobs should simply go to the best and ablest candidate, regardless of their nationality.[65]

> Culturally, Scotland punches way above its weight. (...) Scotland was, for a long time, a country that people left – not just for England, but for Canada, America and Australia. The work of such as Gray and Byrne started a cultural renaissance that had people heading for Scotland in search of inspiration, rather than having to leave it in order to find it. That's a fantastic achievement, in a few short decades, and it's pathetic that Gray sees it as a problem to be decried, not a success to be celebrated.[66]

UNDER THE RADAR: THE SCOTLAND ACT 2012

Without great fanfare, the Scotland Bill was passed by the Westminster parliament on 26 April 2012, after the Scottish Parliament had approved the bill a week before. Based on the Calman Commission's findings and recommendations, it gives the Scottish Parliament the power to introduce a new 'Scottish rate of income tax', increasing its responsibility for raising revenue to up to £6 billion (replacing c.35% of the block grant from Westminster), and the power to borrow up to £3 billion annually. It also contains a flexible clause which will allow more taxation powers to be transferred to Holyrood without reopening the Scotland

---

[62] Pete Martin, 'Doing ourselves down', The Scotsman, 7 November 2012.

[63] Dani Garavelli, 'Settler Watch', Scotland on Sunday, 23 December 2012.

[64] Andrew Eaton-Lewis, 'The Year of Creative Scotland – a branding exercise overshadowed by controversy', The Scotsman, 20 December 2012.

[65] Brian Ferguson, 'Byrne wades into English "settlers" row and insists Gray is wrong', The Scotsman, 20 December 2012.

[66] Deborah Orr, 'Like many Scots, I came south seeking opportunity. Now the traffic's the other way', The Guardian, 22 December 2012.

Act at Westminster.[67] Other powers transferred include stamp duty, air weapons, drink-driving and speed limits legislation, and the landfill levy.

Scottish Secretary Michael Moore called it 'the largest ever transfer of financial powers to Scotland since the creation of the United Kingdom,' the SNP, which had given up five of its six key demands (control over corporation tax, excise duty, broadcasting, Scottish representation in Europe, devolution of the Crown Estate),[68] called it 'a missed opportunity'.[69] Bruce Crawford, the Cabinet Secretary for Government Strategy, said the bill had already been 'bypassed by history and events', meaning the planned referendum on independence and the evolving plans for further devolution most parties are working on.[70] Thus, an Act not fully implemented yet has become the status quo that is already outdated. Nonetheless, MSPs have already used the new powers transferred to Holyrood for new legislation on lowering the drink-drive limits.[71]

THE REFERENDUM

When David Cameron came to Edinburgh in January 2012, his visit marked the acceptance by the UK government of the facts created by the Scottish electorate in May 2011, that the SNP has a mandate for an independence referendum. There were still questions about the timing of that referendum (nearly everyone except the SNP wanting it to happen sooner rather than later), the wording of the question, the franchise, the role of the Electoral Commission in supervising the campaign and running of the referendum, and the spending limits imposed on the campaigns pro and con.

In his well-balanced speech – perhaps 'the strongest explicitly Unionist speech made in Britain since the 1950s'– Cameron also said: 'When the referendum on independence is over, I am open to looking at how the devolved settlement can be improved further. And yes, that means considering what further powers could be devolved.'[72] As Iain Macwhirter

---

[67] Adam Tomkins, 'A vital stepping stone which will aid devolution', *The Scotsman*, 19 April 2012.

[68] Robbie Dinwoodie, 'First Minister relents over Scotland Bill key demands', *The Herald*, 22 March 2012.

[69] Scott Macnab, 'Scotland steps into the future with new powers for Holyrood', *The Scotsman*, 19 April 2012.

[70] *Ibid.*

[71] Alastair Dalton, 'MSPs vote to lower limit for drink driving', *The Scotsman*, 2 November 2012.

[72] Joyce McMillan, 'Cameron grasps the thistle at last', *The Scotsman*, 17 February 2012.

commented, reflecting on Alec Douglas-Home's promise of 'something better' after a No vote in 1979: 'History weighs heavily on any Tory prime minister offering Scotland jam tomorrow.'[73] Nicola Sturgeon categorically ruled out the possibility of any power concessions after a No-vote: 'A No-vote would relegate Scotland to the bottom of the Westminster agenda – the idea that Holyrood would gain new powers in these circumstances is fanciful.'[74]

And, indeed, to have any credibility, the opponents to independence will have to put their cards on the table well before a referendum to show what kind of a devolved Scotland they would offer in case of a No-vote. That all three parties, Labour, the Lib Dems and the Tories, ruled out a third option on the ballot, may rebound on them. Iain Macwhirter echoed Nicola Sturgeon: 'Everyone knows that if the referendum returns a No to independence in 2014, then the unionist parties' enthusiasm for more devolution would rapidly evaporate.'[75]

DEVO MAX – DEVO PLUS – DEVO MORE

The year 2012 began with a YouGov poll in which 61% of the respondents rejected independence; 39% were in favour. But 58% wanted Holyrood to have all the powers over its finances. 46% wanted more than just the Yes-No options on the ballot paper – favoured by 43%. A second question on something like Devo Max seemed very much on the cards. In an Ipsos MORI poll published at the beginning of March, a majority of 59% of Scots wanted a 'Devo-max question on the ballot paper.'[76]

In January, Martin Sime of the Scottish Council for Voluntary Organisations, had announced a campaign to give Civic Scotland a say in the referendum debate, making the case for some form of Devo-Max,[77] anticipated in a *Herald* editorial which warmly welcomed 'the emergence of a third force advocating the inclusion in the referendum of a question on extending the powers devolved to the Scottish Parliament but stopping short of full-scale independence.'[78]

---

[73] Iain Macwhirter, 'The power and the Tory', *Sunday Herald*, 19 February 2012.

[74] Nicola Sturgeon, 'No more "what ifs"', *Scotland on Sunday*, 27 January 2013.

[75] Iain Macwhirter, 'Everyone loves Devo Plus .. or Max .. or even Minus', *Sunday Herald*, 4 March 2012.

[76] Angus Macleod, 'Majority of Scots want second question on referendum paper', *The Times*, 1 March 2012.

[77] Robbie Dinwoodie, 'Campaign aims to open up debate on referendum', *The Herald*, 30 January 2012.

[78] 'A question of civil society's role' (Leader), *The Herald*, 27 January 2012.

At the end of February, the Devo Plus Group presented its blueprint, prepared by the right-of-centre think tank Reform Scotland, with political representatives from the three unionist opposition parties – Duncan McNeil MSP (Labour), Alex Fergusson MSP (Conservatives), and ex-MSP Jeremy Purvis (Lib Dems). The Devo Plus plan entails the transfer of income and corporation taxes to Holyrood, a geographic share of the oil revenue, the devolution of welfare benefits to Scotland, while National Insurance and VAT would remain at Westminster, as would a number of smaller taxes and TV licensing, and state pensions, sickness and maternity pay. It would give Holyrood 'full control over raising much of what it spends'.[79] It was reported back in March that the UK Chancellor and a number of Tory MPs were turning towards 'Devo-plus'.[80]

The proposal differs from Devo Max, which would have all taxes devolved to Scotland, which would then pay Westminster a negotiated rate for reserved services such as defence and foreign affairs. Tavish Scott gave Devo Plus an enthusiastic welcome,[81] and Iain Macwhirter went even further: 'Devolution plus could offer the best of both worlds – independence within the United Kingdom.' And then he made an important point. Devo Plus 'could even give Scotland more control over its affairs than formal independence.'

> How so? Because there would still be a Scottish presence – albeit reduced – in Westminster, allowing Scotland's voice to be heard on the many nominally English issues that would have a bearing on Scotland. Not just defence and foreign affairs, but immigration, maritime law, the national grid, the NHS, interest rates and English employment law. Indeed, if the Coalition had any imagination, they would use the forthcoming reform of the House of Lords to turn it into an elected senate with a federal representation from the constituent nations of NUK – the New United Kingdom.[82]

Of course, House of Lords reform foundered in 2012, and making it a second chamber with regional representation should have been part of the devolution blueprint from the start, but is still not seriously considered.

[79] 'Maximising debate on independence' (Leader), *The Herald*, 29 February 2012.

[80] Jason Allardyce, 'Osborne leans to devo-plus policy', *The Sunday Times* (Scotland), 18 March 2012.

[81] Tavish Scott, 'Looking on the plus side, devo max is dead', *The Scotsman*, 1 March 2012.

[82] Iain Macwhirter, 'There are many plus points in independence within the UK', *The Herald*, 1 March 2012.

A poll published in early July found that 34% of SNP voters would prefer either the status quo (6%) or Devo Plus (28%) to independence. [83]

'A single-question referendum may be justifiable in the name of clarity and practicality,' wrote Alan Trench in April, 'but it cannot be a way of denying Scottish voters the constitutional settlement they want: more devolution within the union.'[84] That was the basis for Devo More, which Alan Trench wrote for the Institute for Public Policy Research (IPPR), published this January.

The proposals would see all personal income tax devolved, a share of VAT assigned and handed over to Holyrood, devolution of air passenger duty and 'sin' taxes (alcohol and tobacco) and, perhaps, employers' National Insurance contributions.

> Taken together, the package would put more than 60 per cent of devolved spending into the hands of the Scottish Parliament. But in contrast to devo-max – a model of full fiscal autonomy – there would continue to be a grant from the UK government to underpin cohesion and fairness across the UK.[85]

The IPPR being close to the Labour Party, this is the most likely blueprint that Labour might consider to offer as an alternative to independence. 'A fresh Scottish Labour initiative on the constitution is sorely needed,' Scotland on Sunday commented, 'if the pro-UK campaign in the referendum is to prove capable of countering the Yes campaign's arguments come the autumn of 2014.'[86]

The crux is that none of the schemes supported by the unionist parties, can be voted on, as Ian Bell pointed out:

> If each of the Unionist parties accepts the SNP won a mandate for a referendum, how can they reject the holding of a vote on something that is actually less than independence? How can they reject a vote on the very ideas they seem, all of a sudden, to espouse? (...) Who solicits an

---

[83] Scott Macnab, 'SNP has failed to open any UK talks on independence', *The Scotsman*, 4 July 2012.

[84] Alan Trench, '"Devo More" needs flesh on it for Union's sake', *The Scotsman*, 5 April 2012.

[85] Guy Lodge and Alan Trench, 'What about Scots who want powerhouse parliament in UK', *Scotland on Sunday*, 20 January 2013.

[86] '"Devo More" widens debate' (Leader), *Scotland on Sunday*, 20 January 2013.

informed electorate and says, 'I have a better offer, but you can't vote on it'?[87]

68% supported a second question in a Future of Scotland poll, conducted by MORI.[88] But Alex Salmond, when he launched the Consultation on the running of the referendum, showed an uncanny unity with the UK government by advocating a 'straightforward' and 'clear' choice, i.e. one question. After all, as he pointed out:

> Independence, in essence, is based on a simple idea: the people who care most about Scotland, that is the people who live, work, and bring up their families in Scotland, should be the ones taking the decisions about our nation's future.[89]

And yet, in his speech at the Consultation launch at Edinburgh Castle he left the option of a second question open: 'If there is an alternative of maximum devolution,' he said, 'which would command wide support in Scotland then it is only fair and democratic that option should be among the choices open to the people.'[90] He reiterated that in even stronger form, in June in America, when he not only praised Devo Max as a 'very attractive argument,' but spoke of he Scots' fundamental 'right to decide' whether Holyrood should have full taxation powers.[91]

But, in the view of Scottish Labour, a third option on the ballot paper would only 'muddy the water'; the Lib Dems feared more than one question would 'create turmoil, confusion and ambiguity' – in Lesley Riddoch's words, 'clarity, not democracy, had become the holy grail.' She went further: 'Party politics is failing to represent a sizeable chunk of Scottish opinion.'[92] Joyce McMillan chimed in: keeping Devo Max, Devo Plus or a federal UK 'off the table…, while we focus exclusively on debating complete independence, seems at best ridiculous, and at worst downright undemocratic.'[93] And Guy Lodge (IPPR) and Alan Trench have

---

[87] Ian Bell, 'By my reckoning, devo plus makes zero sense', *The Herald*, 3 March 2012.

[88] Tom Peterkin and Eddie Barnes, 'Row over support for second question', *Scotland on Sunday*, 24 June 2012.

[89] Oliver Wright, 'Referendum to ask Scots one thing: should we be independent?', *The Independent*, 26 January 2012.

[90] Eddie Barnes, 'One question, ten words, you choose', *The Scotsman*, 26 January 2012.

[91] Tom Gordon, 'Salmond Scots have a right to second question on devo max', *Sunday Herald*, 1 July 2012.

[92] Lesley Riddoch, 'Popular options struck off agenda', *The Scotsman*, 30 January 2012.

[93] Joyce McMillan, '"It won't work" is not good enough', *The Scotsman*, 27 January 2012.

warned that 'leaving the framing of a greater devolution option until after a referendum carries real risks for those who want Scotland to remain a part of the United Kingdom.'[94]

On 1 March, the Future of Scotland campaign, announced by Martin Sime, got under way at the SECC in Glasgow, with the declared intent that it would try to wrestle the ownership of the referendum back from 'party politics and Yes/No campaigns.'[95] Yet, despite the interventions of Canon Kenyon Wright,[96] the erstwhile convener of the Executive Committee of the Scottish Constitutional Convention, and of former First Minister Henry McLeish,[97] both in the media and in his latest book,[98] the campaign never got real traction, and any hope that a third option might appear on the ballot seemed buried with the 'Edinburgh Agreement'.

The SNP may hope that this will drive advocates of further devolution into the Yes camp. And there are indications that this could work – business tycoon Jim McColl, who had, like Tom Farmer, repeatedly spoke out against independence, preferring Devo Max, declared he would vote Yes, if the third option did not appear on the ballot.[99] But not all Devo-Max supporters will follow that example.

Very much will depend on the credibility of the blueprint of Better Together for a post-referendum devolved Scotland, and how that is backed by parties likely to form a Scottish or a UK government to implement that blueprint. Jeremy Purvis, the leader of the Devo Plus Group, put it this way: 'The aim is a clear one for me. When I vote in the referendum – and I will vote "No" – I want that no vote to be a positive vote for change, for reform along devo-plus principles.'[100]

Likewise Alan Trench: 'Getting devo-more agreed and out there before the poll ... would ... make a No vote in the referendum a positive one.'[101] If that message does not get across, if it is not backed by a strong coalition between and beyond anti-independence parties, then, so Ian Macwhirter, 'come the referendum, if all the unionists offer is jam tomorrow, I

---

[94] Guy Lodge and Alan Trench, 'What about Sots who want powerhouse parliament in UK', *Scotland on Sunday*, 20 January 2013.

[95] Martin Sime, 'Speak up now and shape Scotland's future', *The Scotsman*, 1 March 2012.

[96] Conon Kenyon Wright, 'Not enough to choose just between independence and the status quo', Letter to the Editor, *The Herald*, 12 May 2012.

[97] Brian Currie, 'Former FM: Lobby for second question on ballot', *The Herald*, 4 May 2012.

[98] Henry McLeish, *Scotland: The Growing Divide: Old Nation, New Ideas*, Edinburgh: Luath Press, 2012.

[99] Eddie Barnes, 'Business billionaire backs independence', *The Scotsman*, 7 September 2012.

[100] Jeremy Purvis, 'The plus factor must be taken into account', *The Scotsman*, 28 February 2012.

[101] Alan Trench, '"Devo-more" needs flesh on it for Union's sake', *The Scotsman*, 5 April 2012.

wouldn't put it past the Scottish voters to back independence in order to be sure that they get a better devolution.'[102]

THE EDINBURGH AGREEMENT

Official talks between the UK and Scottish governments about the referendum process, with the aim of reaching an agreement that would allow Westminster to transfer the powers to hold a referendum to the Scottish Parliament, were opened in February when Scottish Secretary of State Michael Moore met with Alex Salmond. Moore called on the Scottish Government to hold the poll a year earlier, in autumn 2013 which, predictably, was rejected by the SNP as an attempt by Westminster to 'dictate' the terms of the ballot.[103]

These talks continued throughout the summer and, when Alex Salmond introduced his legislative programme in the Scottish Parliament in early September, it seemed clear that an agreement could be reached which would allow him to introduce a Referendum Bill by early 2013. The question about the date and the franchise, allowing 16- and 17-year-olds to vote, if they are on the electoral register, had been conceded, much to the chagrin of the Scottish Tories. The Scottish Government was prepared to allow the Electoral Commission a consultative role in the wording of the referendum question, and accepted its role as a supervisory body. An expert group, led by Lord Sutherland, had recommended one 'clear, decisive' question for the referendum.[104]

A day after detailing his legislative programme on 4 September, the First Minister announced a cabinet reshuffle. Making Alex Neil the new Cabinet Secretary for Health, Alex Salmond gave Nicola Sturgeon the new title of Deputy First Minister (Government Strategy and the Constitution) and Cabinet Secretary for Infrastructure, Investment and Cities, a clear indication that Nicola Sturgeon would henceforth take the lead in negotiating the referendum with the UK government, and also be responsible for the Scottish economy – 'identified by Salmond as key to referendum success.'[105]

---

[102] Iain Macwhirter, 'Everyone loves Devo Plus ... or Max .. or even Minus', *Sunday Herald*, 4 March 2012.

[103] Kate Devlin, 'Moore wants referendum to be held in autumn 2013', *The Herald*, 23 February 2012.

[104] Eddie Barnes, 'Voting experts say just one question', *The Scotsman*, 23 August 2012.

[105] Michael Settle, 'First step in choreography of referendum agreement', *The Herald*, 13 February 2012.

Grandiosely titled 'The Edinburgh Agreement' (the occasion itself was 'distinctly underwhelming,'[106], and St Andrews House was not exactly besieged by interested punters), a document was signed by Alex Salmond and David Cameron on 15 October which binds both the UK and the Scottish government to respect the outcome of the referendum. The window in which Holyrood can hold the referendum is limited to the end of 2014. There was no mention of a possible second question.

And certainly no second referendum – as advocated by the Constitution Unit's Robert Hazell, who had argued that 'the reason for a second referendum ... is the principle of consent; but it must be informed consent' – meaning that it had to be based on 'knowing the terms [of independence] that have been negotiated.'[107] Although, as Iain Macwhirter observed, that 'would lower the stakes in the first ballot and allow Scots to vote in principle for independence, with a backstop if they didn't like the reality of it.'[108] The downside would be that we could end up with a principled Yes, followed by a No to the negotiated package – and what then? Limbo? Would the negotiations just continue until a better deal was struck? And if that was rejected? Would we get the dreaded 'Neverendum'? SNP MSP Sandra White has already rejected the provision in the 'Edinburgh Agreement' that binds both the UK and Scotland to respecting the outcome of the referendum ballot. 'If we don't get enough votes,' she said, 'then I believe we would go for another referendum, especially if it is close. It would be unfair to the people of Scotland, it it's close, to tell them that it's finished.'[109]

Odd, to say the least, that the result of the SNP Government's consultation (26,000, compared to the 2,875 respondents of the UK Government's consultation earlier in the year[110]) was published only after the Agreement was signed – it makes no reference to the consultation; although Salmond had said, back in April, 'that he will use the results of the consultation ... to decide whether to back a single question or two

[106] Peter Jones, 'Grey day, but there's a long way to go', *The Scotsman*, 16 October 2012.

[107] Robert Hazell, 'Britishness and the Future of the Union', in Andrew Gamble and Tony Wright (eds), *Britishness: Perspectives on the British Question'*, Oxford: Blackwell-Wiley (Political Quarterly), 2009, pp.101-111; p.103.

[108] Iain Macwhirter, 'Can the Unionist campaign coalesce round one leader?', *The Herald*, 23 February 2012.

[109] Scott Macnab, 'SNP rejects talk of "neverendum" gridlock', *The Scotsman*, 24 December 2012.

[110] Andrew Black, 'Scottish independence: UK consultation supports single question', *BBC News Scotland*, 4 April 2012, <www.bbc.co.uk/news/uk-scotland-scotland-politics-17600791>; Andrew Whitaker, 'SNP has tossed aside 26,000 views on independence, claims Labour', *The Scotsman*, 12 October 2012.

questions.'[111] So much for a listening government? The Liberal Democrats promptly accused the SNP of being 'disrespectful'.[112]

EUROPE

Moving from process to more substantial issues, one of the major debating points throughout the past year has been the prospect of an independent Scotland in Europe. Alex Salmond and the SNP tried to present the case as done and dusted. Scotland – and there was legal advice to back that up – would continue to be a member of he European Union and inherit the UK conditions of membership, including the opt-outs and the rebate. The opposition parties doubted these assertions, and asked for Salmond's legal advice to be published.

In the autumn, the Government's position unravelled spectacularly. Nicola Sturgeon admitted in October that no legal advice had been sought (although the Government had spent a hundred thousand pounds in court to keep advice they did not have secret).[113] You could not make it up.

Then, in a letter to the House of Lords Economic Affairs Committee, José Manuel Barroso, the President of the European Commission, expressed the opinion that 'a new independent state would, by the fact of its independence, become a third country with respect to the EU and the [EU's founding] Treaties would no longer apply on its territory'.[114] He did not comment directly on the Scottish case but, to the discomfort of the SNP Government, the message was clear: Scotland, as a new state, would have to apply for EU membership.[115] The SNP retreated to a position where it claimed hat the negotiations about Scotland's EU membership would be held from within the UK, and thus from within the EU, in the two years following a Yes-vote. But whether that tight time table can be deemed feasible has since been doubted, among others, by

---

[111] 'Referendum rules must be clear' (Leader), *The Herald*, 2 April 2012.

[112] 'SNP hails poll showing higher voter support following party conference', *STV News Scotland*, 23 October 2012, <news.stv.tv/scotland/196295-snp-hails-poll-showing-higher-voter-support-following-party-conference/>.

[113] Tom Peterkin, 'SNP reveal no legal advice sought on EU entry', *The Scotsman*, 24 October 2012.

[114] Paul Cairney, 'Independence referendum', *Monitor: Constitution Unit Newsletter*, 53 (February 2013), <www.ucl.ac.uk/constitution-unit/publications/tabs/monitor-newsletter/monitor53.pdf>.

[115] David Maddox, 'Brussels: separate Scotland must apply to join EU', *The* Scotsman, 6 December 2012.

the Irish Minister for Europe, Lucinda Creighton. She made clear that an independent Scotland would be welcomed into the EU, but would need to apply and go through a lengthy process: 'If Scotland were to become independent, Scotland would have to apply for membership and that can be a lengthy process, as we see even with the very advanced and well-integrated countries like Iceland.'[116]

Scots may be a lot less Europhobic but, as all surveys show, they are only marginally less Eurosceptic than their neighbours south of the Border.[117] And there are voices inside and outside the SNP, particularly Jim Sillars and Margo MacDonald, who advocate Scottish membership of Efta rather than the EU, come independence.[118]

Every now and then, the 'spectre of border controls' raises its ugly head. Would an independent Scotland, applying for EU membership, have to negotiate a Schengen opt-out? Or would it simply inherit the UK opt-out?[119] The threat of a Schengen external border at Berwick is certainly one of the remoter scenarios. On the other hand, if an independent Scotland were to pursue a markedly different immigration policy, might not then London consider border controls?

CURRENCY UNION

Apart from issues concerning what the negotiated share of UK assets and debts would be, the question which currency an independent Scotland would use is crucial for the economic future of Scotland. And, as polls and surveys have shown, if Scots can be persuaded that the economy would fare better under independence, they could be persuaded to vote Yes. It is by far the most important among the decisive factors that determinate how Scots will vote in 2014.[120]

The SNP's preferred option is to keep the pound 'for the foreseeable future',[121] in a currency union with the rest of the UK (rUK) – 'better

[116] Raymond Buchanan, 'Scottish independence: Irish minister says EU application "would take time"', *BBC News Scotland*, 25 January 2013, <www.bbc.co.uk/news/uk-scotland-scotland-politics-21195630>.

[117] Eddie Barnes, 'David Cameron's tale of two referendums', *Scotland on Sunday*, 27 January 2013.

[118] Jim Sillars, 'Collision Course', *Holyrood*, 5 November 2012; Ben Borland and Paula Murray, 'Scotland "Could Join" EU Mark II', *The Sunday Express*, 11 November 2012.

[119] Andrew Whitaker, 'Spectre of border controls raised by top Tory', *The Scotsman*, 21 February 2012.

[120] John Curtice, 'For sceptical Scots one victory will make all the difference – on the battlefield of economics', *The Times*, 29 February 2012.

[121] Eddie Barnes, 'Independent Scotland to stick with sterling', *The Scotsman*, 2 February 2012.

together', to coin a phrase, in that aspect, at least. But the plan is fraught with problems. First and foremost: how to sell it to the Scots? Does it make sense to become independent, only for your monetary policy to be determined by a foreign central bank, and using the Bank of England (BoE) as lender of last resort?

> If Scotland was to keep the pound, the BoE and the rUK government would require the Scottish Government to observe an agreed set of fiscal rules which would probably limit the scale of borrowing, the size of the primary budget deficit in relation to Scottish GDP and the level of Scottish debt to GDP.[122]

The National Institute of Economic and Social Research (NIEC) came to the conclusion that 'Scotland would have less economic freedom after independence than it does now.'[123] Moreover, gaining fiscal autonomy while staying in a currency union – is that not the exact opposite of what the Eurozone currently tries to achieve, because a currency union seems not to work without a fiscal and, eventually, political union? 'An independent Scotland within a sterling monetary union would face exactly the same issues.'[124] The former Prime Minister Gordon Brown went further: an independent Scotland under the SNP's plans to let London retain key economic powers would be 'a form of self-imposed colonialism more reminiscent of the old Empire than of the modern world;' Scotland would be governed like 'a British colony,'[125] and Alistair Darling said Scotland would be using sterling in the same way a country like Panama uses the US Dollar:

> That means you have to make whatever changes are suitable to keep up with the rest. Your interest rates are set by a foreign country, the value of your currency is set by a foreign country. It makes no sense – that's not freedom, it's serfdom.[126]

In January, the SNP seemed to move away from the 'euro-style currency union', towards a 'less formal set-up'. 'A stability pact based around debt

[122] Brian Ashcroft, 'Debate is only just starting', *The Scotsman*, 8 February 2012.

[123] Kate Devlin and Brian Currie, 'Separation "would mean less economic freedom"', *The Herald*, 3 February 2012.

[124] Gavin McCrone, 'Matter of no small change', *The Scotsman*, 28 February 2012.

[125] Eddie Barnes, 'Independent Scotland "a British colony"', *Scotland on Sunday*, 4 November 2012.

[126] Scott Macnab, 'Darling warning on SNP plan for sterling', *The Scotsman*, 19 June 2012.

and deficit levels,' the party's Treasury spokesman Stewart Hosie MP said in the House of Commons, 'is perfectly sensible but can in no way be portrayed as a foreign currency running Scotland's economy.'[127]

DEFENCE

Other disputed areas include defence, where Alex Salmond outlined his plan for Scottish defence forces in January 2012, insisting that the three Scottish regiments – the Scots Guards, the Royal Regiment of Scotland and the Royal Scots Dragoon Guards – would remain as the backbone of a Scottish army. He said the set-up emerging from the UK Government's Strategic Defence Review of one naval base, one air base and one mobile armed brigade would be 'exactly the configuration' needed for an independent Scotland. And he reiterated that the UK's Trident nuclear missiles would have to be removed from the naval base at Faslane. The SNP called the £1.1bn investment in nuclear-powered submarines announced by the UK government in June an 'obscene waste of money.'[128] While the UK Defence Secretary Philip Hammond called Salmon's plan to break off bits of the UK armed forces and establish them as a Scottish defence force 'laughable' and claimed Scotland would have to pay part of the massive bill of relocating Trident, Shadow Defence Secretary Jim Murphy attacked Salmond on his apparent conversion to UK spending cuts:

> After denouncing Tory defence policies, the SNP have suddenly announced it is the best they can threaten if Scotland was independent. This raises huge questions about separation. Scotland knows that leaving the UK would be a huge blow to Scottish defence communities.[129]

Westminster set up an inquiry by the House of Commons Defence Committee on the impact of independence on defence jobs and contracts. After all, defence contracts are worth in excess of £1.8bn a year to the Scottish economy; the Ministry of Defence alone employs 20,000 people in Scotland.[130] But both Labour and Tories were criticised

---

[127] Scott Macnab, 'Nationalists may consider "less formal" UK currency union', *The Scotsman*, 10 January 2013.

[128] Michael Stettle, 'SNP attacks spending on submarines', *The Herald*, 19 June 2012.

[129] Eddie Barnes, 'Salmond reveals vision for Scots armed forces', *The Scotsman*, 20 January 2012.

[130] Michael Settle, 'Defence inquiry into the impact of independence', *The Herald*, 13 February 2012.

for grossly exaggerating potential job losses if Trident were scrapped. A study by Paisley professor John Foster came to the conclusion that closing the nuclear base at Faslane would cost less than 1,000 jobs – not the inflated figure of 6,000 to 11.000 peddled by Tory and Labour politicians. 'Trident is, in reality, a jobs-destroyer,' said SNP MSP Bill Kidd, 'and attempts to justify the presence of weapons of mass destruction on the Clyde in terms of jobs is the worst kind of nonsense.'[131]

The Scottish Government was warned by Francis Tusa of the journal *Defence Analysis* that, given the SNP's pronouncements on a future Scottish Defence Force, that force would look more like that of Belgium or Ireland than that of Norway or Denmark. Thousands of jobs would be lost in the defence industries, including shipbuilding.[132]

Of course, all that was before the SNP announced its change of mind anent Nato. A Scotland in Nato may well help establishing military cooperation with the rest of the UK. An in-depth study of the SNP, published at the end of 2011,[133] found that a grassroots majority in the party actually supported Scottish Nato membership. More importantly, the SNP reckoned that giving up the anti-Nato stance would assuage security fears and gain some votes come 2014. The policy U-turn was then mooted in early March.[134] In contrast to the EU debate, the SNP had of course never anticipated continuing membership of Nato after independence. And even now, joining would be subject to negotiations and conditions, particularly the removal of nuclear weapons from the Clyde. Trevor Royle predicted that making the policy change would 'open a whole can of worms about the SNP's attitude towards the possession and possible use of nuclear weapons.'[135]

When it came to the crunch, at the October SNP conference in Perth, it made for a fierce, passionate and dramatic debate which the leadership around Angus Robertson MP won, but with a much narrower margin than they had expected.[136] And in the aftermath, the party at Holyrood lost two members – John Finnie and Jean Urquhart who accused the SNP of hypocrisy, wanting to join a defence pact which had a nuclear first-

---

[131] Rob Edwards, 'Labour and Tories under fire for inflating Trident job losses', *Sunday Herald*, 28 October 2012.

[132] Kate Devlin, 'SNP warned on defence jobs', *The Herald*, 16 March 2012.

[133] James Mitchell, Lynn Bennie and Rob Johns, *The Scottish National Party: Transition to Power*, Oxford: Oxford University Press, 2011.

[134] Severin Carrell, 'Independent Scotland could join Nato', *The Guardian*, 2 March 2012.

[135] Trevor Royle, 'Joining Nato will embroil Scotland in nuclear dialogue', *The Herald*, 21 July 2012.

[136] Robbie Dinwoodie, 'Close call as SNP scraps historic anti-Nato stance', *The Herald*, 20 October 2012.

strike option, but insisting at the same time that it was still adamantly opposed to nuclear weapons.

While Defence Secretary Philip Hammond visited Rosyth in October, defiantly – brazenly? provocatively? – announcing £350 million to design a replacement to the Trident missile programme in what he claimed was a demonstration of the government's 'very clear' commitment to Britain's nuclear deterrent,[137] Nick Clegg, the Deputy Prime Minister, warned 'that the Tories had promised there would be no decision on whether to build a new generation of submarines to carry nuclear weapons until 2016,'[138] and Danny Alexander, the Chief Secretary to the Treasury, recently argued in a *Guardian* interview that the replacement did not have to be 'like for like', as that would be 'not financially realistic'.[139] What effect would a non-replacement have on the referendum campaign? Give the SNP a boost as it shows they had been right all along that these weapons of mass destruction are not only morally reprehensible, but also unnecessary? Or deprive the Yes campaign of one of its most potent arguments – that you have to vote Yes in 2014 to get rid of Trident?

THE 'BRITISHNESS' OF INDEPENDENCE

Throughout the year, the SNP leadership tried to promote independence 'as a natural and painless extension of Holyrood's power,' with praise for continuing Britishness, the monarchy, and 'Scotland's intense neighbourly love of England.'

> What, many old SNP hands must wonder, happened to the passion? How did the most enormous, extraordinary decision in Scotland's modern history become a relentless exercise in triangulation and message management? Therein lies Salmon's central conundrum. Independence would mean seismic change for Scotland, a decisive break with the past and the cornerstone, for good or ill, of a wholly new future. The First Minister knows it – and desires it. But to get there, he has chosen to downplay its magnitude to avoid alarming swing voters. And in so doing he may leave

---

[137] Scott Macnab, 'UK minister lays down gauntlet over Trident', *The Scotsman*, 29 October 2012.

[138] Tim Ross, 'Nick Clegg warns Philip Hammond over Trident nuclear missile plan', *The Daily Telegraph*, 29 October 2012.

[139] Nick Hopkins, 'Trident: no need for like-for-like replacement, says Danny Alexander', *The Guardian*, 22 January 2013.

some in his party – and the country – unsure of what he stands for.[140]

Added to the list of continuities in case of independence was the power over subsidies for Scotland's renewables. According to the Energy Bill at Westminster, an independent Scotland would only have a consultative role in the joint administration of renewable energy subsidies. Apparently, the Scottish Government's aim is to assuage worries that energy bills in Scotland might rise drastically after independence.[141]

> The move by the SNP Government will be seen as echoing other post-independence policies that have attracted criticism for subordinating the country to rule by the remainder of the UK, such as keeping the pound and letting the Bank of England set interest rates.[142]

While Ewan Crawford stressed 'the co-operative nature of modern Scottish nationalism and the links that will necessarily endure within the British Isles',[143] and the SNP, *en route* to 'indy-lite', was busy enhancing 'its inner Britishness',[144] Patrick Harvie, the leader of the Scottish Greens, has warned: 'A strategy which pretends that independence can be all things to all people will end up delivering nothing.'[145] And Colin Fox agreed: 'Winning the independence referendum will be achieved by stressing how much will change not how little.'[146]

In November, over 600 activists from the political left gathered in Glasgow at the Radical Independence Conference – including representatives from the Scottish Greens, the Scottish Socialists, Solidarity, some trade unions, anti-nuclear campaigners and anti-monarchist republicans, united in their support for independence but rejecting the SNP's softly-softly approach. 'They see independence as an opportunity to create a radical, left-leaning society rather than the

---

[140] 'Will Scotland buy SNP's soft sell?' (Leader), *Sunday Herald*, 11 March 2012.

[141] Eddie Barnes, 'Independent Scotland "would see energy bills increase significantly"', *The Scotsman*, 12 December 2012.

[142] Steven Vass, 'UK to control green subsidies in an independent Scotland', *Sunday Herald*, 27 January 2013.

[143] Ewan Crawford, 'So who wants separation?', *The Scotsman*, 7 February 2012.

[144] Kenny Farquharson, 'Cultural revolution as SNP learns to love the Brits', *Scotland on Sunday*, 18 March 20123.

[145] Patrick Harvie, 'The Yes campaign launches', 25 May 2012, <www.patrickharviemsp.com/2012/05/the-yes-campaign-launches/>.

[146] Colin Fox, 'Let's revisit Maclean's vision of a free nation', *The Scotsman*, 1 December 2012.

watered-down version they believe Mr Salmond wants to offer Scots.'[147] The referendum, as Gregor Gall argued, is not 'merely about Scotland's constitutional future' but 'also about Scotland's economic and social future.'[148]

YES SCOTLAND V. BETTER TOGETHER

The Yes campaign was first out of he starting block. At a Fountainbridge cinema in Edinburgh, at the celebrity-studded launch of Yes Scotland on 25 May,[149] Alex Salmond pledged to sign up a million supporters for a 'Declaration of Independence'.[150] With him on stage, making the point that it is not just the SNP running the campaign, were the ex-Labour MP and independent MSP Dennis Canavan, the Scots Makar Liz Lochhead, the Green MSP and co-covener of his party Patrick Harvie, the actors Brian Cox and Alex Cumming, the writer and cultural activist Pat Kane, the Yes campaign leader Blair Jenkins, the singer and songwriter Dougie MacLean, the trade unionist Tommy Brennan and the SSP leader and former MSP Colin Fox. In a slight echo of 1776, Alex Salmond stated:

> We unite behind a declaration of self-evident truth: the people who live in Scotland are best placed to make the decisions that affect Scotland. We don't start from scratch. We have a parliament which has earned its spurs for more than a decade. If the parliament can run education, then why can't it run the economy? If it can be trusted to run the health service, then why can't it represent Scotland internationally? If it can be trusted to protect our old people, then why can't we protect the country, and do so without the obscenity of nuclear weapons?[151]

The launch itself got mixed reviews: 'the whole thing smacked of preaching to the converted.... a policy free zone .... the launch played to all things the SNP claims the independence debate is not about:

---

[147] Hamish Macdonell, 'Radicals threaten Salmond and Scottish independence campaign', *The Independent*, 24 November 2012.

[148] Gregor Gall, 'Look to the Left for a radical new vision', *The Scotsman*, 24 November 2012.

[149] Tom Peterkin, 'Stars on the bill at "Yes Scotland" launch', *Scotland on Sunday*, 20 May, 2012.

[150] Andrew Whitaker, 'Salmond's pledge to sign up 1m voters', *The Scotsman*, 26 May 2012.

[151] Quoted in Brian Currie, '"Scotland's future will be in Scotland's hands"', *The Herald*, 26 May 2012.

sentiment, national identity and nostalgia... it was a damp squib.'[152] On top of it all, it was ambushed by Alastair Darling who published a YouGov poll showing support for independence at 33%, opposition at 57 per cent.[153] The celebrity endorsement also came under flak, even from within the campaign. Elaine C Smith called the likes of Cox and Cumming 'politically naïve', and she added: 'they don't even live here.'[154]

The Better Together campaign eschewed celebrity and went instead for the plain people of Scotland. They launched at the Craiglockhart campus of Napier University, a month after Yes Scotland, 'with one political heavyweight, no celebrities, and a surfeit of ordinary citizens who were proud to call themselves British.'[155] Alastair Darling MP, the former Chancellor of the Exchequer, who was joined by Labour leader Johann Lamont, Conservative leader Ruth Davidson and Lib Dem chief Willie Rennie (who stood in for the indisposed Charles Kennedy), said

> The most important political campaign of my life has started and I had to get involved. This decision will be the biggest we have ever taken in Scotland. This is not about saving the Union, this is about providing the best possible future for the generations of Scots who will follow us.[156]

In style, the two launches could not have been further apart, but they had in common that each was in pains to emphasise a positive message – and that neither of them set the heather ablaze. On the day of the launch, the Future of Scotland group published a poll, according to which 59% of Labour voters and 57% of Lib Dem voters wanted a second question on further devolution on the ballot.[157]

On 22 September, the Meadows looked like 'a sea of saltire and lion rampant flags as people from across the country gathered for the march supporting a Yes vote in the 2014 referendum.'[158] Among the 20 speakers

---

[152] David Torrance, 'Amateur hour at Yes campaign launch', *The Scotsman*, 26 May 2012.

[153] Robbie Dinwoodie, 'First blow to Darling as Yes campaign launched', *The Herald*, 25 May 2012.

[154] Paul Hutcheon, 'Indy supporter Elaine C Smith hits out: "Yes Campaigns Hollywood stars are politically naïve and don't even live here"', *Sunday Herald*, 24 June 2012.

[155] Robbie Dinwoodie, 'No vote campaign launch gives citizens centre stage', *The Herald*, 26 June 2012.

[156] Scott Macnab, '"Make your mind up time for Scotland's biggest decision"', *The Scotsman*, 26 June 2012.

[157] Robbie Dinwoodie, 'No vote campaign launch gives citizens centre stage', *The Herald*, 26 June 2012.

[158] Ray Philip, 'Edinburgh independence rally: As it happened', *Scotland on Sunday*, 23 September 2012.

were Alex Salmond, Dennis Canavan, a Labour for Independence group, and Margo MacDonald – who encouraged the crowd: 'If a third of Scots believe in independence and want independence now, every one of us has got two years to persuade another Scot, and then we're home and dry. That's not fanciful, that's just practical.'[159]

The organisers spoke of 10,000 participants, the police of 5,000. Impressive. But, as Labour's Patricia Ferguson pointed out, more than three times that number turned out in the 1990s to demonstrate for devolution, and a rally in Barcelona saw 1.5 million Catalans demonstrate for independence. [160] The former Conservative leader David McLetchie said: 'Last week, one-and-a-half million people in Catalonia demonstrated for independence. Today, in stark contrast, Alex Salmond's march attracted less people than a struggling third division football team.'[161]

A LOST YEAR FOR THE YES CAMPAIGN

The Panelbase *Sunday Times* poll, which had the paper's alarm bells ringing in February 2012, when 47% supported a Yes vote,[162] one year later shows support for independence down to 34% – a further 3 points down since October – with voters particularly sceptical about the SNP's assurances about Europe and the economic benefits of independence.[163]

While a *New Statesman*/ICD poll in January 2012 had support for and against independence neck and neck, at 44% for and 45% against independence,[164] a TBS-BMRB survey showed that support for independence was already diminishing in the early months of 2012. Compared to an identical poll five months earlier, the February result showed support for the Union up by 6% at 44% and support for independence 4 points down at 35 per cent.[165]

---

[159] 'Thousands at Scottish independence rally in Edinburgh', *BBC News Scotland*, 22 September 2012 <www.bbc.co.uk/news/uk-scotland-19685144>.

[160] Stephen Burgen, 'More than 1.5m Catalans join rally for independence', *The Guardian*, 12 September 2012.

[161] Eddie Barnes and Tom Peterkin, 'Salmond hails independence on the march', *Scotland on Sunday*, 23 September 2012.

[162] Jason Allardyce, 'Poll shows union is on knife edge', *The Sunday Times* (Scotland), 5 February 2012.

[163] Jason Allardyce, 'Support for solo Scotland waning', *The Sunday Times* (Scotland), 27 January 2013.

[164] George Eaton, 'Exclusive poll: Scotland close to backing independence', *New Statesman*, 25 January 2012.

[165] Robbie Dinwoodie, 'Blow for SNP as support for independence slips', *The Herald*, 6 February 2012.

Despite all the sound and fury of the referendum debate – not a day without a contribution to the debate, either in the political arena or in the media – the people of Scotland seem strangely unmoved by it all. The Social Attitudes Survey recorded – between August and November 2012 – the lowest support for independence since devolution began – a mere 23% opted for independence.[166]

As they give respondents more choices than the Yes-No referendum will, this result may well be underestimating support for the Yes-side. But a *Sunday Times* poll published on 27 January 2013 had independence down 3 points since October, at 34%. And the latest three TNS-BMRB monthly polls recorded 28 (Oct '12), 27 (Dec '12) and 28% (Jan '13) in favour of independence,[167] a clear decline since earlier in the year, when it had been 30% (July) and 35% (Jan '12).[168] A YouGov poll published on 1 August showed, two months after the Yes Scotland campaign had started, a three per cent drop to 30% in support for independence, compared to an identical poll at the beginning of the year.[169] And an Ipsos-MORI poll in June showed a similar trend, compared with an identical poll in January, the number saying Yes to independence slipped from 39 to 35%, the No vote rose by five points to 55 per cent.[170] Even a poll among 2,500 seventeen-year-olds across Scotland found that only 26% favoured independence, 59% were against – which was interpreted as 'a blow to Alex Salmond', as the SNP may have hoped their plan of lowering the voting age would boost the Yes side.[171]

The Scottish Centre for Social Research summed up its findings on Scottish independence in the 2012 Scottish Social Attitudes Survey in five bullet points:

- Yes camp have, at best, lost a year
- We've become a little less optimistic about independence
- And rather more worried about it

---

[166] Markus Gardham, 'Support for Yes vote at post-devolution low', *The Herald*, 24 January 2013.

[167] Mike Settle, 'Independence blow as support for Union soars', *The Herald*, 8 October 2012.

[168] Michael Settle, 'Scottish support for the Union hits five-year high', *The Herald*, 9 July 2012.

[169] Eddie Barnes, 'Poll shows support for UK split has dropped', *The Scotsman*, 1 August 2012.

[170] Robbie Dinwoodie and Michael Settle, 'Labour hails poll blow for Yes campaign', *The Herald*, 20 June 2012.

[171] Stephen McGinty, 'Only one in four pupils wants independence', *The Scotsman*, 24 September 2012.

- Economics is key to gathering support, not just identity, and certainly not equality
- Yet task made more difficult by changed views of the economics of the Union since 2007?[172]

2012 was a UK year – the Olympics and Paralympics, the Royal Jubilee. The support for British institutions like the monarchy grew over the last year,[173] and the Scottish Social Attitudes Survey also bore that out by emphasising the UK's importance for Scotland. Both questions – Which of the following do you think has most influence over the way Scotland is run? And which do you think ought to have most influence over the way Scotland is run? – registered an increase for the UK government at Westminster and a decrease for the Scottish Government.[174]

Were the Royal Jubilee celebrations, the Olympics and the Paralympics game changers? It was not just a question of love, or at least respect for the monarch.[175] 'Just as Alex Salmond and the SNP are telling Scots that Britain is a clapped-out political relic to be left behind, along comes the diamond jubilee which, at a subliminal level at least, is saying the exact opposite.'[176]

The London Olympics, with Danny Boyle's presentation of Britain in the stunning opening ceremony – full of humour and eccentricity and striking a perfect balance between irony, nostalgia and vision – and the delirious medal haul of 'Team GB', had some SNP followers in near-despair. 'That was a £9 billion advert for the Union,' one said to me, 'now we'll never win that referendum.' That opinion was shared by Boris Johnston: 'The Scots are never going to vote for independence. These Games have done for Salmond. Vote Hoy.'[177]

The SNP, initially very critical of the Olympics, changed their tune. Now they were hailed as the perfect launch pad for the 2014 Commonwealth Games in Glasgow. Sports Minister Shona Robison now called the London Games a 'huge opportunity to showcase the best of Scotland.'[178] But it remains to be seen how long the afterglow of these events will last. And, as Joyce McMillan wondered, are we really 'to bet our futures on a Danny

[172] Ibid.

[173] Eddie Barnes, 'Scottish support for UK insitutions grows', The Scotsman, 7 March 2012.

[174] <www.scotcen.org.uk/media/1021487/ssa12tables.pdf>.

[175] Judith Duffy, 'Has Scotland learned to love the jubilee?', Sunday Herald, 27 May 2012.

[176] Peter Jones, 'Jubilee may make Scots think again', The Scotsman, 7 February 2012.

[177] Michael Settle, 'Olympics "have cost Salmond his dream of independence"', The Herald, 31 August 2012.

[178] Alison Campsie, 'Olympics boost for Glasgow 2014', The Herald, 8 August 2012.

Boyle vision of Britain that is no longer really represented by any major UK political party, and that now seems incapable of winning victory in a UK general election'?[179]

THE STATE OF THE HOLYROOD PARTIES

A Panelbase *Sunday Times* poll in February saw the SNP at 50% in the constituency vote, and at 48% in the regional vote, higher than at its landslide victory in May 2011, while the other parties were stagnating or losing ground: Labour at 29% in both constituency and regional votes, the Tories on 14% and 13%, respectively. Alex Salmond stood head and shoulders above any rival, in Scotland or in the UK – with 44% of voters satisfied with his leadership and 27% dissatisfied. This personal approval rating of +17 contrasts glaringly with David Cameron (-43), Ed Miliband (-41), Nick Clegg (-54), Johann Lamont (-18), Ruth Davidson (-32) and Willie Rennie (-27).[180]

An Ipsos-MORI poll in June saw a narrowing of the gap between Labour and the SNP, with Labour at 32% (up 9% since January), the SNP at 45% (down 4%). The Scottish Conservatives remaned in third place, with 12% (down 1%) and the Lib Dems on 6% (down 4%).[181]

THE SNP

At the beginning of 2013, the SNP continued to be top-dog in Scottish politics. In recent polls, the SNP was enjoying 45% support for both the constituency and regional votes at the Scottish Parliament.[182] The latest Angus Reid poll, in January 2013, showed the SNP leading Labour in Scotland by 39% to 35% for a Westminster general election.[183]

Winning the local elections, with 425 seats, 46 councillors more than in 2007, was another sign of strength for the SNP. Although they failed to hit their most prized target: to take Glasgow from Labour – which

[179] Joyce McMillan, 'Boyle's Britain is a vision we mourn', *The Scotsman*, 17 August 2012.

[180] Jason Allardyce, 'Union at risk as support for SNP hits 50%', *The Sunday Times* (Scotland), 5 February 2012.

[181] Robbie Dinwoodie, 'Labour improves in polls for he first time', *The Herald*, 27 June 2012.

[182] 'SNP hails poll showing higher voter support following party conference', *STV News Scotland*, 24 October 2012, <news.stv.tv/scotland/196295-snp-hails-poll-showing-higher-voter-support-following-party-conference/>.

[183] <www.angus-reid.com/polls/48604/britons-see-eu-membership-row-as-distraction-from-economic-crisis/>.

was interpreted as a slowing down, perhaps even a derailing of the SNP juggernaut.[184]

When Alex Salmond said, in early February, that he regretted his advice given to Fred Goodwin in 2007 on the acquisition of ABN AMRO, which led to the downfall of the Royal Bank of Scotland,[185] he did not know yet that apologising would become something of a theme tune for him in 2012. Not only had he, Mike Russell, and Nicola Sturgeon repeatedly to stand up at Holyrood and apologise for misleading Parliament[186] – on the impression that legal advise had been sought on Scotland's EU membership (it was, after all, only 'in terms of the debate'), on college funding (which was down, not up), and on overstating the number of Green jobs – the SNP also ended the year 2012 with three fewer MSPs than at the start of the year. First, the party's Dunfermline MSP Bill Walker was kicked out of the party after it emerged that he had a 'history of violence against three ex-wives.'[187] Then, after the party conference debate on Scotland's Nato membership, which was the undisputed highlight of he conference season, full of drama and passion, John Finnie and Jean Urquhart left the party.

The Leveson Inquiry into the culture and practices and ethics of the press in Britain did not incriminate Alex Salmond. Although he had offered to lobby on behalf of media mogul Rupert Murdoch and his BSkyB bid, he had not acted on it and thus was not culpable,[188] despite the lingering aftertaste of his 'worship at the tawdry court of The Sun king', just after having 'leaked the date of the Scottish independence referendum – October 18 – to give the supersoaraway *Sunday Sun* a front-page splash for its first edition.'[189] What was puzzling, given the SNP's insistence that their first loyalty is to Holyrood, not to Westminster, was that the First Minister repeatedly refused to answer questions in Parliament about whether his phone had been hacked into, always referring the questioners to the Leveson Inquiry in London, where he would answer all questions. His view that, following on from Leveson, Scotland would need its own law on press regulation, perhaps modelled on the Press Council of Ireland, was also controversial.

---

[184] John Curtice, 'SNP juggernaut slowed ... for time being at least', *The Herald*, 4 May 2012.

[185] Tom Peterkin, 'Salmond admits he was wrong to encourage Goodwin deal', *The Scotsman*, 2 February 2012.

[186] Andrew Whitaker and Eddie Barnes, 'Even Russell's apology was misleading, says Labour', *The Scotsman*. 21 November 2012.

[187] Paul Hutcheon, 'Revealed: MSP's history of violence against three ex-wives', *Sunday Herald*, 4 March 2012.

[188] Michael Settle, 'Salmond criticised over reaction to Leveson report', *The Herald*, 3 December 2012.

[189] Iain Macwhirter, 'Salmond and Murdoch: this friendship is bad for Scotland', *Sunday Herald*, 4 March 2012.

What was damaging for the First Minister and the SNP was the apparent close relationship with Rupert Murdoch (tea at Bute House), which gave rise to critical comments. Had not another pal of his made headlines by turning on him? Donald Trump had once hailed Alex Salmond as the greatest politician, but then the plan of an offshore windfarm within view of his fancy £750m golf course on the Aberdeenshire coast destroyed the bosom friendship – and now Salmond was not just 'misguided' and 'reckless' – he had become the devil incarnate who wold destroy Scottish tourism. Having fed the anti-windfarm lobby £10 million, he was asked to appear before the Economy, Energy and Tourism Committee – asked to back up his accusation with evidence, he memorably declared 'I am the evidence!'[190]

While 'I am the Evidence' vented his fury, Murdoch killed with kindness. He spoke before Leveson of his 'warm' relationship with Scotland's First Minister – 'an attractive person' and 'an amusing guy'.[191] Why schmooze with these moguls and tycoons? It 'leaves many of us with a nasty taste'[192] or, as Campbell Gunn put it: 'big spenders also bring big trouble.'[193] By sharp contrast, giving the 'snub' to the Dalai Lama on his Scottish visit landed Salmond with accusations of having conceded to Chinese pressure.[194]

SCOTTISH LABOUR

On a visit in Glasgow at the beginning of 2012, Ed Miliband challenged Alex Salmond's claim, an independent Scotland would be 'a beacon for progressive opinion', by putting egalitarianism and social justice, in the tradition of Keir Hardie, Clement Attlee and Aneurin Bevan, at the core of his argument for the Union. He got a cautious thumbs-up from the *Herald*, which called his intervention

> A thoughtful speech, which, in stark contrast to most contributions to date from the Unionist side, attempted

[190] Simon Johnson, 'Donald Trump accuses Alex Salmond of wind farm "betrayal"', *The Daily Telegraph*, 25 April 2012.

[191] Robbie Dinwoodie and Kate Devlin, 'With friends like these…', *The Herald*, 26 April 2012.

[192] Joyce McMillan, 'Civic Scotland has gone to sleep', *The Scotsman*, 27 April 2012.

[193] Campbell Gunn, 'Salmond learns big spenders also bring big trouble', *The Sunday Post*, 29 April 2012.

[194] Robbie Dinwoodie, 'Snub claims overshadow Dalai Lama's Scottish tour', *The Herald*, 22 June 2012.

> to focus less on the dangers of separatism than a positive
> vision for a future Scotland within the UK. That is what
> Labour must do if it is to win this argument.[195]

Douglas Alexander warned the party north of the border at its annual conference in Dundee that it had 'to change and change radically' and be 'open-minded' on how to improve devolution.[196]

'Labour gave Scotland devolution,' as a *Herald* editorial put it in a nutshell, 'but then failed to adjust to the new political world created by it.'[197] The party is now in the slow process of implementing the changes deemed necessary after the 2011 defeat and outlined in the review undertaken by Jim Murphy and Sarah Boyack. But it has a lot of persuasive work to do. Johann Lamont said she wanted 'no bidding war' concerning more powers for Holyrood.[198] When she announced the party's Commission on Extending Devolution,[199] the lack of 'genuine enthusiasm' was noted: 'Make no mistake, Labour has been dragged to this point. Its commission is about regaining power for itself, not delivering more power to Holyrood.'[200] Eventually, Lamont launched Labour's Devolution Commission, including Duncan McNeil (of the Devo Plus Group), Scottish Labour deputy Anas Sarwar MP, Ken Macintosh MSP, Margaret Curran MP and Gregg McClymont MP.[201]

At First Minister's Questions, Johann Lamont has surprised quite a few commentators with her performances. A palpable hit on Alex Salmond was a question on 22 March about missing blankets for old age pensioners in hospitals. Salmond rebuffed and dismissed it robustly, only to be presented by the Labour leader with a pair of pensioners in the Parliament's visitor gallery who had suffered the plight of missing blankets. The First Minister had 'walked into a political ambush,' and Salmond and his Health Secretary were forced to apologise to the two

[195] 'Labour puts a thoughtful case for the Union' (Leader), *The Herald*, 31 January 2012.

[196] Simon Johnson, 'Douglas Alexander: Labour candidates not good enough to beat SNP', *The Daily Telegraph*, 2 March 2012.

[197] 'All change at Scottish Labour' (Leader), *The Herald*, 19 September 2012.

[198] Eddie Barnes, 'Lamont says no powers "bidding war"', *Scotland on Sunday*, 4 March 2012.

[199] Michael Settle and Brian Currie, 'Lamont plans commission on devolution', *The Herald*, 3 March 2012.

[200] 'SNP conviction or Labour calculation? Not a hard choice' (Leader), *Sunday Herald*, 4 March 2012.

[201] Andrew Whitaker and Tom Peterkin, 'Labour seeks more powers for Holyrood', *Scotland on Sunday*, 30 September 2012.

pensioners.[202] 'The wee woman is a bit bigger than the First Minister realises.'[203]

Winning Glasgow in the Local Government elections in May and gaining 46 additional seats across Scotland, increasing the number of Labour councillors to 394, was widely seen as an astonishing performance and a feather in the cap of he new leader – and at least a part recovery from the devastating defeat at the Scottish elections of May 2011.

In a speech for party members in Edinburgh on 25 September, Johann Lamont, daringly – or foolishly – launched her plans for a 'cuts commission' to examine which popular universal services could be cut, removed or means tested in Scotland, challenging the SNP on universal benefits and arguing that in times of straightened budgets it was not feasible that the rich do not have to pay for tuition or prescriptions

> Well, I have to ask what is progressive about a banker on more than 100,000 a year benefiting more than a customer on average incomes from the council tax freeze?
>
> What is progressive about a chief executive on more than 100,000 a year not paying for his prescriptions, while a pensioner needing care has their care help cut?
>
> What is progressive about judges and lawyers earning more than 100,000 a year, not paying tuition fees for their child to follow in their footsteps at university, while one in four unemployed young people in Scotland can't get a job or a place at college? [204]

But she also used the unfortunate phrase that it was time to end a 'something for nothing' culture. The Tories were delighted. Nicola Sturgeon, on the other hand, latched on to the Labour Party's new departure, accusing Lamont of 'embarking on a disastrous approach':

> At a time when people are facing serious wage restraint and rising living costs, the council-tax freeze, the abolition of charges for prescriptions, support for higher education,

---

[202] Robbie Dinwoodie, 'Personal apology to pensioners left without blankets', *The Herald*, 23 March 2012.

[203] Ian Bell, 'At last, a Scottish Labour leader who grasps the thistle', *The Herald*, 24 March 2012.

[204] Andrew Whitaker, 'Labour in radical shift away from free services', *The Scotsman*, 26 September 2012.

apprenticeships and the elderly are all part of the support we in society give to each other.[205]

Richard Seymour asked, 'Why is the Scottish Labour leadership so abysmal? Why has it struggled to adapt to post-devolution Scottish politics, and why does it keep having rings run around it by the SNP?' He called Lamont's policy announcement a 'train wreck': 'The policy implications of Lamont's speech – ending universal benefits, raising tuition fees, cutting free prescriptions – were bad enough. The atrocious, reactionary soundbites, demanding an end to "something for nothing" culture, were worse.'[206]

In January, Ed Miliband went on the Andrew Marr Show and said, 'I think that universal benefits which go across the population are an important bedrock of our society.' Johann Lamont looked like having been 'publicly humiliated', Bob Duncan commented.[207] Only a month earlier, she had marked her first anniversary as leader with a speech in Glasgow in which she had claimed that free tuition for university students in Scotland was 'not sustainable' and that a return to the graduate endowment scheme had to be considered.[208] Is the whole episode another step towards the 'strange death of Scottish Labour'?[209] That particular policy shift is a huge gamble. Joyce McMillan called it 'ill-judged' – while it is not *per se* wrong to ask questions, Lamont failed 'to set that discussion in a clearly progressive context.'[210] An immediate vote winner it is certainly not.

Maybe the best advice for Scottish Labour came from south of the Border – a Christmas present, as it were. 'If anyone was to grab the Scottish Labour leadership by the lapels,' Owen Jones wrote, 'this is what they should tell them:

> That the SNP has positioned itself to the left gives Labour political space to be radical. Working-class and young voters who have deserted the party need to be inspired again.

[205] 'Labour's Johann Lamont questions free-for-all policy approach', *BBC News Scotland*, 25 September 2012, <www.bbc.co.uk/news/uk-scotland-scotland-politics-19711805>.

[206] Richard Seymour, 'Scottish Labour is blinded by hostility to the SNP', *The Guardian* (Comment is free), 28 September 2012, <www.guardian.co.uk/commentisfree/2012/sep/28/scottish-labour-hostility-snp>.

[207] Bob Duncan, 'Lamont "humiliated" as Miliband backs universal benefits', *newsnetscotland.com*, 14 January 2013, <newsnetscotland.com/index.php/scottish-news/6561-lamont-humiliated-as-miliband-backs-universal-benefits>.

[208] Scott Macnab, 'Scotland's free university education "no longer sustainable" says Lamont', *The Scotsman*, 18 December 2012.

[209] See Gerry Hassan and Eric Shaw, *The Strange Death of Labour in Scotland*, Edinburgh: Edinburgh University Press, 2012.

[210] Joyce McMillan, 'Austerity could cost Lamont dearly', *The Scotsman*, 28 September 2012.

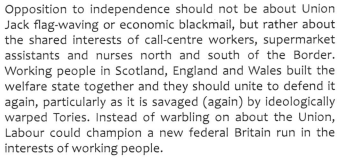

Opposition to independence should not be about Union Jack flag-waving or economic blackmail, but rather about the shared interests of call-centre workers, supermarket assistants and nurses north and south of the Border. Working people in Scotland, England and Wales built the welfare state together and they should unite to defend it again, particularly as it is savaged (again) by ideologically warped Tories. Instead of warbling on about the Union, Labour could champion a new federal Britain run in the interests of working people.

If Scottish Labour continues as it is – devoid of any coherent vision and unable to inspire those who have deserted it – then Salmond has little to fear. Scottish nationalism will not want for recruits. This will not be the Strange Death of Scottish Labour: it will be its Entirely Explainable Suicide. But it is not just the party's future at stake. Its failures could lead to Britain as we know it being dismantled.[211]

THE SCOTTISH CONSERVATIVES

Like Labour, the Scottish Tories began the year 2012 with a new leader, Ruth Davidson – after their rejection of the much more radical vision of Murdo Fraser. So far, the fortunes of the party north of the Border have not been turned around. Stagnation in the polls, no joy in the local elections: the Tories lost 28 seats but, at least, with a total of 115 councillors they came third.

In Scotland, the Conservatives are still a toxic brand (that is why Murdo Fraser had wanted to disband them and start anew).[212] The austerity policies emanating from London do not help, from the 'omnishambles' of George Osborne's March budget[213] to the welfare cuts of the Chancellor's autumn statement. And when Ruth Davidson waded into the debate branding Scotland a 'gangmaster state', claiming that just 12% of Scots households make a contribution to the economy at a fringe meeting of

[211] Owen Jones, 'The strange death of Labour Scotland (... or was it suicide?), *The Independent*, 24 December 2012.

[212] See David Torrance (ed.), *Whatever Happened to Tory Scotland?*, Edinburgh: Edinburgh University Press, 2012.

[213] David Maddox, 'Osborne raids the aged to aid the waged', *The Scotsman*, 22 March 2012.

the UK Conservative Party conference, that did not exactly help to de-toxify the Scottish Tory brand. The SNP was quick to liken her remarks to Mitt Romney's dismissal of 47% of the electorate because they did not pay income tax.[214] Those who pay income tax, she hinted in a speech marking her first anniversary in the job as leader, could expect a 1 per cent tax cut her party would campaign for when the new powers under the Scotland Act 2012 come to Holyrood.[215]

Seen from the South, the Scottish Tories are a problem, if not an embarrassment, for David Cameron. With just one Westminster seat, he has to rely on his coalition partners for a veil of legitimacy to pronounce on Scotland. Steven Camley, the *Herald*'s unsurpassed cartoonist, perfectly captured 'Cameron's problem' in two frames: one shows a perplexed Cameron with the caption 'One Nation Tory'; the other a map of Scotland, and the caption reads 'One Tory Nation'.[216]

Ruth Davidson, 'an effective performer within the hothouse of Holyrood,' but with 'little impact in the wider Scotland,'[217] began 2013 with the first of a series of speeches which are supposed to reposition her party and give it a new image (the logo was already changed in 2012). While she had drawn lines in the sand during the leadership contest, refusing to go beyond the powers outlined in the Scotland Bill, she now acknowledged that

> The debate has moved a great deal in the last year. We now know what the parameters are for a referendum on independence. But the conversation on the constitutional future of Scotland doesn't begin and end with that referendum. It will continue and the Scottish Conservatives must have a voice, a strong and positive voice, in that conversation.[218]

Murdo Fraser, who had argued for greater powers for Holyrood in 2011, tweeted, somewhat sardonically: 'Looks like a very good speech from Ruth Davidson. Could almost have written it myself.' Andy Maciver, who had run Murdo Fraser's leadership campaign, added that, while Ruth Davidson's 'U-turn' was 'extremely welcome', it did not go far enough,

---

[214] David Maddox, 'Tories: Just 12% of homes contribute to economy', *The Scotsman*, 8 October 2012.

[215] Andrew Whitaker, 'Scots Tory leader marks first year in job with pledge to cut income tax', *The Scotsman*, 6 November 2012.

[216] *The Herald*, 17 February 2012.

[217] Harry Reid, 'Same old Tories, a host of new troubles', *The Herald*, 18 September 2012.

[218] Quoted in Robbie Dinwoodie, 'Davidson in move to give Tories fresh Scots image', *The Herald*, 26 January 2013.

as her analysis stopped short acknowledging that the party has become unelectable in Scotland.[219]

Davidson had to act. The pressure came as much from London as from within Scotland. David Cameron's offer for more powers if Scots reject independence, ex-MSP Ted Brocklebank sniped, had 'destroyed any remaining shreds of her credibility.'[220] Osborne's support for giving Holyrood fiscal responsibility and Cameron's pragmatic dealings with the SNP government, and the involvement of Scottish Tories in further devolution undermined her lines in the sand. Back in February, Tory MSPs had joined the Devo Plus camp, and Alex Fergusson MSP was one of the cross-party group who presented their proposals. Thus, the evolution from 'lines in the sand' to Devo Plus. Jason Allardyce quotes a 'senior party source' as saying: 'This is exactly where the Conservative party needs to be. It's a boat we have missed for over 30 years since Margaret Thatcher turned around Ted Heath's policy on devolution.'[221]

Tim Montgomery, the editor of *ConservativeHome*, called Devo-Plus a 'palatable' blueprint for more Holyrood powers which Cameron should grasp, to 'save the union, enhance his party's electoral prospects and end outdated centralisation.'[222]

THE SCOTTISH LIBERAL DEMOCRATS

A sad story. The 2007 election had been bad enough – when Nicol Stephen had, against all the polling evidence, maintained up to election day that the Lib Dems would have an electoral breakthrough. They lost a seat. They then refused to even talk to the SNP about a partnership government, and never got to grips with opposition. In 2011, they were slaughtered at the polls, punished for jumping into bed with the Tories at Westminster. A rump of five MSPs returned to the Parliament, shell-shocked as if Holyrood had been moved to Caiglockhart over night.

Willie Rennie, elected as their new leader after the disastrous 2011 election, does not even feature in every First Minister's Questions – his group of MSPs is simply too small. His best moments were when he challenged the SNP government on college funding, and he gained some

[219] Andy Maciver, 'Too little too late for Tories?', *The Scotsman*, 31 January 2012.

[220] Michael Settle and Brian Currie, 'Tories fear 2014 poll may lose them next election', *The Herald*, 27 February 2012.

[221] Jason Allardyce, 'Osborne leans to devo-plus policy', *The Sunday Times* (Scotland), 18 March 2012.

[222] Tim Montgomery. 'Cameron must make brave steps towards a federal UK', *The Guardian*, 20 February 2012.

concessions from John Swinney in the 2012 budget – but that may have had more to do with massaging the potential student referendum vote than with bowing to Lib Dem pressure.

In the local elections in May, the downward spiral continued. The Lib Dems lost 59% of the seats they had won in 2007, local councillors paying the price for the austerity coalition at Westminster. According to a poll in February, the Lib Dems would have held only 3 seats had there been a Holyrood election in 2012.[223]

In the constitutional debate, ex-Borders-MSP Jeremy Purvis played a prominent role as the leader of the cross-party Devo Plus Group. The party also tried to bolster its federalist profile with *Federalism: the best future for Scotland*, a report compiled under the convenership of Menzies Campbell MP.[224] It was jointly presented in October by Campbell and Willie Rennie and is to form the basis of the Lib Dem manifesto for the 2015 UK elections. 'Home Rule' for England and new regional assemblies are part of the plan. For Scotland,

> Campbell's blueprint – which assumes that Alex Salmond will lose the 2014 referendum on Scottish independence – would include giving Holyrood control over about two thirds of its tax-raising, including setting its own income tax rates, while sharing common UK-wide policies such as foreign affairs, defence, pensions and VAT overseen by a federal parliament.[225]

The Lib Dems were thus the first among the pro-union parties to publish their counter-proposals to the SNP's independence plans.

THE SCOTTISH GREEN PARTY

The Greens, with two MSPs, have been relegated to the sidelines. No longer in a parliament of minorities, their bargaining power has seriously diminished. In the local elections, the party made modest progress: they gained six seats, which brings them up to a total of 14 – of the 1223 councillors in Scotland. Not exactly a sensational break-through...

---

[223] Jason Allardyce, 'Union at risk as support for SNP hits 50%', *The Sunday Times* (Scotland), 5 February 2012.

[224] <scotLib Dems.org.uk/homerule>.

[225] Severin Carrell, 'Liberal Democrats in Scotland propose "home rule all round"', *The Guardian*, 17 October 2012.

The party's co-convener Patrick Harvie MSP shared a platform with Alex Salmond, when the Yes Scotland campaign was started in May. But the relationship between the Greens and the fledgling campaign was not exactly plain sailing. In June it was widely reported that the Greens had pulled out of the campaign, because, as Harvie put it, Yes Scotland was 'an entirely SNP vehicle.'[226] Margo MacDonald, the independent MSP, also voiced her reservations about a campaign to closely 'aligned to a political party.'[227]

At their party conference, in October, the Greens then formally voted to participate in Yes Scotland. However, 'the party reasserted its strong opposition to an independent Scotland remaining a party of NATO and to the SNP's proposal to spend at least £2.5 billion a year on defence.'[228]

Assessing the state of the parties in 2012, Campbell Gunn summed it up: 'While the Labour Party's fortunes have rallied to a degree since their disastrous Scottish parliamentary elections, the same cannot be said for the Conservatives or the Lib Dems.'[229]

CAMERON'S REFERENDUM

Prime Minister David Cameron's speech on Britain and Europe in January 2013, Michael Keating has argued,

> changes the game in the Scottish independence debate. The SNP has been cautious on Europe, recognising the EU is not greatly loved in Scotland. But the Europhobia of the home counties has no counterpoint here. There has been a campaign to scare Scots with the threat of exclusion from the EU should they vote for independence. Now it seems independence is the only way to stay in the EU. It is the British Conservatives who now look like separatists and isolationists.[230]

---

[226] Severin Carrell, 'Scottish Greens pull back from SNP pro-independence campaign', *The Guardian*, 11 June 2012.

[227] Andrew Whitaker, 'Now Margo snubs "Yes Scotland" over SNP dominance', *The Scotsman*, 11 June 2012.

[228] 'Scottish independence: Greens join Yes Scotland campaign', *BBC News Scotland*, 6 October 2012, <www.bbc.co.uk/news/uk-scotland-19858857>.

[229] Campbell Gunn, 'Opposition draw up battle lines in fight for union', *The Sunday Post*, 17 June 2012.

[230] Michael Keating, 'The West Lothian question taken to new level', *Scotland on Sunday*, 27 January 2013.

David Cameron's announcement that, in the event of a Conservative victory in the UK elections of 2015, he would renegotiate the UK's role in the European Union and offer an In/Out referendum on the result of any new deal in 2017, has thrown up all kinds of hypothetical complications for both Westminster and Holyrood. Mostly due to the time table.

If the Yes campaign were to win the 2014 Scottish referendum, the SNP believes that negotiations with the UK could be finalised by 2016, so that the 2016 Scottish elections could be the first elections to an independent Scottish Parliament. If Cameron were to win the 2015 UK elections, the UK would begin negotiations about repatriating powers from the EU to the UK, while the Scottish government would, 'from the inside', negotiate the terms of its continuing membership of the EU. Is it really feasible to believe that parallel negotiations with Westminster and Brussels could be completed within two years? Could Scotland, despite a Yes-vote in 2014, still be part of the UK come the 2016 elections? Salmond's former adviser John Kay, who is a Visiting Professor of Economics at the London School of Economics, spoke of 'five years of uncertainty,' following a Yes vote, and that negotiations on the terms of independence alone would take three years to complete.[231] Could the outcome of the 2016 Scottish elections potentially change the negotiations?

Moreover, Scotland would still elect MPs in 2015 – what would be their role in all of this? Would they be involved in negotiating Scotland's terms of independence? Could the UK exit the EU while Scotland was not yet independent? And would Scotland then have to apply for EU membership as an 'outsider'? What if Ed Miliband were to win a majority in 2015, but only thanks to Scottish Labour MPs? Would that Scottish contingent be involved in the independence negotiations? Would there have to be a new rUK election as soon as Scotland had established its independence?

FROM PROCESS TO SUBSTANCE

During the past year, 'the independence debate moved firmly to the top of the Scottish political agenda,' said John Curtice, when presenting the findings of the latest Scottish Social Attitudes Survey.[232] Much has been about process. And the important of his must not be underestimated. Brian Taylor emphasised that:

---

[231] Eddie Barnes, 'Scotand's "uncertain" five years following Yes vote', The Scotsman, 20 June 2012.

[232] Ian Dunt, 'Poll: Having SNP in power dampens support for independence', politics.co.uk, 24 January 2013, <www.politics.co.uk/news/2013/01/24/poll-having-snp-in-power-dampens-support-for-independence>.

I have heard this described as 'process' – as if it were, somehow, secondary and trivial. As if it were thwarting authentic debate. The reverse is true: untrammelled debate on the issues surrounding independence will not be possible while any doubts remain about the rules.[233]

In the Edinburgh Agreement, the Scottish Government conceded that the Electoral Commission would have a consultative say on the wording of the question, but the final decision would lie with the Scottish Parliament. Since then, the opposition parties have urged the SNP to accept the verdict of the Electoral Commission. Even the Yes Scotland's chief Blair Jenkins indicated that whatever wording the Electoral Commission approves should be the one on the ballot.[234]

'Do you agree that Scotland should become an independent country?'– the preferred option of the SNP Government – may seem simple and straightforward. But it has been criticised as a 'leading' question. A YouGov poll in February 2012 found that 8% more said Yes if the question was prefixed with 'Do you agree'.[235] There could also be a problem with 'independent country'. Does it refer to a sovereign state, or to greater autonomy?[236]

On 30 January, the Electoral Commission published its assessment. It suggested scrapping the 'Do you agree?' bit of the question and, lo and behold, harmony broke out at Holyrood. The UK government, the Yes Scotland campaign and Deputy First Minister Nicola Sturgeon all agreed to accept the findings of the Electoral Commission. Nicola Sturgeon declared that the Scottish government would accept 'in full' the commission's recommendations, which include higher spending limits for the campaign than mooted by the Scottish Government in order to create a level playing field for the two campaigns – a cap of £1.5 million instead of £750,000 for each side.[237]

The two items that are not settled are the exact date of the referendum (to be revealed in the Referendum Bill) and the Commission's concern

[233] Brian Taylor, 'Scottish independence: Propose, test, dispose', BBC News Scotland, 29 January 2013, <www.bbc.co.uk/news/uk-scotland-21248965>.

[234] Tom Gordon, 'Indy allies to Salmond: don't fight with the Electoral Commission', Sunday Herald, 27 January 2012.

[235] Eddie Barnes, 'Independence support falls 8% with different question', The Scotsman, 3 February 2012.

[236] See Robert Hazell and Alan Trench, 'Scottish independence: the battle lines are drawn', Monitor: Constitution Unit Newsletter, 51 (June 2012) <www.ucl.ac.uk/constitution-unit/publications/tabs/monitor/edit/monitor-newsletter/monitor-51.pdf>.

[237] Andrew Black, 'Scottish independence: SNP accepts call to change referendum question', BBC News Scotland, 30 January 2013, <www.bbc.co.uk/news/uk-scotland-scotland-politics-21245701>.

about clarity and the need for the Scottish and the UK government to work together to achieve this. Sturgeon and Salmond have challenged Westminster to have pre-referendum talks about post-referendum Scotland, but hitherto to no avail.[238]

Alex Salmond used a speech in London to outline a written constitution for an independent Scotland, which would guarantee housing for everybody and free education, and enshrine a ban on nuclear weapons.[239] While his opponents accused him of 'posturing', and constitutional experts weighed in on the pros and cons of a written constitution, the intent is clear:

> Discussing the nuts and bolts of implementing a Yes vote or the first tasks of the 'first independent Parliament' in 2016 creates a sense of momentum, an impression the SNP is on course for victory. That is badly needed with the Yes camp 20 points behind in the polls.[240]

Here is, of course, a paradox. In reality, a Yes vote followed by independence would mean that an elected government of an independent Scotland would decide about the Scottish constitution. And would not be bound by any pre-referendum projections. On the other hand, most Scots do not want to vote for a 'pig in a poke' – they want to know, as exactly as possible, to what kind of Scotland a Yes vote would lead them.

That explains that Nicola Sturgeon recently made a clear switch from the procedural and constitutional questions, and from identity politics, to the core issues of democracy and social justice:

> For me the fact of nationhood or Scottish identity is not the motive force for independence. Nor do I believe that independence, however desirable, is essential for the preservation of our distinctive Scottish identity. (…) I ask you, as you make up your minds over these next two years, to base your decision, not on how Scottish or British you feel, but on what kind of country you want Scotland to be and how best you think that can be achieved.[241]

---

[238] Tom Peterkin, 'UK says no to talks on independence', *Scotland on Sunday*, 13 January 2013.

[239] Scott Macnab, 'Salmond pushes for new rights for Scots', *The Scotsman*, 17 January 2013.

[240] Magnus Gardham, 'Have the Nationalists stolen a march on 2014 debate?', *The Herald*, 19 January 2013.

[241] Quoted in Ian Bell, 'Why Cameron won't force me into an identity crisis', *The Herald*, 9 January 2013.

That obviously takes into account the Scottish Social Attitude Survey's findings, that feeling Scottish, as opposed to British, bears little correlation with enthusiasm for independence. Alastair Darling spoke of 'a proud nation within a wider state.'[242] Of those who think independence will improve the economy (34%), the vast majority favour independence, which 'supports the view … that perceptions of Scotland's future economic prospects inside or outside the union will decide the referendum.'[243]

In January, Yes Scotland started a leafletting campaign, putting fairness and inequality at the centre of the independence message, flanked by a speech in which Alex Salmond attacked the 'brutal' welfare cuts inflicted by the Westminster government, hoping that the Scottish Social Attitudes Survey's finding that inequality was way down the Scots' list of priorities was, in Blair Jenkins' words, 'already out of date, because the impact of the UK government's welfare reforms and the reduction in people's benefits have not yet fed though to their pockets.'[244] Iain Macwhirter observed last September that he found 'an increasing number of natural Labour voters intrigued with the idea that a[n independent] Scottish Parliament might be the only way to ensure a social democratic Scotland. The phrase I kept hearing over the summer was: 'I'm not a Nationalist, but… '[245]

OUTLOOK

So, what will 2013 bring? It is a somewhat 'strange' year – apart from the quincentenary of the Battle of Flodden, there are no major events – no Royal Jubilees (well, there is a Royal baby due, of course), no big sporting events (there's always Andy Murray at Wimbledon) and, crucially, no scheduled elections in Scotland. A bit of a holding operation – preparing for the big events in 2014, the Commonwealth Games, the Football World Cup in Brazil (surely with Scotland, now that Gordon Strachan is in charge?), the centenary of the outbreak of the First World War, 700 years Bannockburn, the European Elections and, of course, the Referendum. The three years from 2014 promise to be frantic – the European elections in May '14, the referendum in the autumn of 2014, the

---

[242] 'Alistair Darling warns of "no way back"', *BBC News Scotland*, 25 June 2012, <www.bbc.co.uk/news/uk-scotland-scotland-politics-18572750>.

[243] 'Independence and the economy' (Leader), *The Herald*, 12 January 2013.

[244] Eddie Barnes, 'Fighting for Scotland's independence using fairness and inequality is a huge gamble for Yes campaign', *The Scotsman*, 30 January 2013.

[245] Iain Macwhirter, 'So, enter stage left: Nicola Sturgeon with the key role', *The Herald*, 6 September 2012.

Westminster elections in May '15, the Scottish elections in May '16, and a potential UK referendum on the EU in 2017…

But in 2013 the referendum campaign has only itself to maintain momentum. In the autumn, the SNP government will publish its White Paper on the referendum. Until then, the remaining procedural question – how to enable 16- and 17-year-olds to vote, and the exact date, will occupy some more column space. And all those issues discussed in 2012 will, in some form or other, come back this year – Europe, the currency, defence, pensions, etc. Christine Jardine is not alone when she muses:

> … it sometimes seems as if we have talked about little else and I find myself wondering whether both politicians and the media are actually giving the issue 'too much time' … And is our government at Holyrood in danger of losing the interest of those in the public who do not share their constitutional goal?[246]

Is too much time spent on Bill Jamieson's 'Planet Indyref'? As the *Herald* suggested,

> Discussions on issues such as a hypothetical independent Scotland in Europe and its membership of Nato have taken centre stage, relegating the ongoing business of government in Scotland to second rank. Questions of 'what if' are eclipsing the reality of what is.[247]

Even SNP MSPs and researchers are frustrated that the party's absolute majority at Holyrood is not used to greater effect in bolder law making. And the *Herald* fired another warning shot, only three days after the intervention quoted above:

> Mr Salmond's argument in favour of independence rests on demonstrating his party's competence in government. In general, it has passed that test. However, it is nearly two years before the Scottish electorate will vote on the issue. Is the campaign already distracting Scottish Government ministers from the day-to-day business of governing the country? If Mr Salmond has a fault, it is hubris. Recent faux pas and an apparent resistance to constructive criticism

---

[246] Christine Jardine, 'SNP is leading us along the road to nowhere', *The Scotsman*, 5 January 2013.

[247] 'Taxing question for Scots and HMRC' (Leader), *The Herald*, 20 November 2011.

risk undermining the trust on which he hopes to build his campaign for an independent Scotland.[248]

Regardless, the 'what if' questions will continue to dominate the discourse. The speculation about Scotland's EU status will rumble on, against the backdrop of Cameron's own referendum strategy. Thanks to the two looming referendums, Peter Jones quipped, politics 'increasingly looks like an advanced and extremely tortuous form of the prisoners' dilemma game'[249] – who competes with whom, who cooperates with whom – with very surprising constellations.

'Every poll agrees that support for independence has fallen over the past year,' Brian Wilson wrote in the *Scotsman*, 'while skepticism about Nationalist claims and assertions has intensified.'[250] Why are the poll ratings for independence so low?

> Twenty-three per cent for independence, at a time when the central mantra of unionism – that Scotland needs the embrace of the big, economically successful United Kingdom – is laid bare by facts of decline, poverty, collapsing pillars of the British state, and economic weakness and failure. How come?

Jim Sillars blames an 'ineffective campaign' with a 'vacuum where pro-independence information should be', and urges Yes Scotland to go beyond 'assertions' and 'opinions' – 'Scots need information, not just assertions.'[251] But convincing the Scots to take the plunge in an economic situation full of uncertainties is what Martin Kettle has called 'the daunting task of selling the feelgood philosophy of independence amid the feel-bad reality of continuing economic stagnation.'[252]

A *caveat* may be apposite at this juncture. Did the SNP not turn around a 16-point deficit in the polls before the 2011 landslide? Could the Yes campaign not do something similar when the campaign proper gets under way in 2014? Possible – but the fact that the polls on the constitutional preferences have been remarkably stable over the past two decades, and none of the big events – the arrival of Holyrood, SNP minority, then majority government, the financial crash and the deepest recession and

---

[248] 'Is Salmond's eye off the ball?' (Leader), *The Herald*, 23 November 2012

[249] Peter Jones, 'Game of two polls poses new questions', *The Scotsman*, 29 January 2013.

[250] Brian Wilson, 'Majority must reclaim their rights', *The Scotsman*, 30 January 2013.

[251] Jim Sillars, 'Educate, agitate, organise', *The Scotsman*, 29 January 2013.

[252] Michael Kettle, 'Salmond's wish is for a home rule option – and he'll get it', *The Guardian*, 26 January 2012.

slowest economic recovery in decades – have changed that make it hard to envisage a total turn-around in the next 18 months or so.

'Will the Scots push this elephant out of bed?', asked Tom Devine.[253] Well, there are two problems with Devine's analogy – first, he dates it from 1707, and second, he seems to neglect that Pierre Trudeau coined the phrase for (independent) Canada's relationship with its powerful neighbour to the south. Independence would neither change demography nor geography. I am afraid the elephant – which was there long before 1707 and, arguably, one of the reasons for negotiating the Union – will stay in the bed – but, as Macwhirter suggests, Scotland might have even less steer over the beast come independence.

What if the poll ratings for a Yes-vote stay where they are, or even fall further? May the third option on the ballot be resurrected? Blair Jenkins has predicted that the polls will narrow over the coming year, but he refused to 'estimate by how much or how quickly.'[254] Or will the Devo Plus, More or Max by then offer, in the words of Lesley Riddoch,

> A guaranteed third option (albeit with an uncertain implementation date) that transfers taxation, economic and welfare powers to the Sottish Government in the event of either party [Labour or Lib Dems] forming a government at the next UK election. Nothing less is acceptable now. And nothing less should prompt a 'No' vote by any of those now disenfranchised by Scotland's single question referendum.[255]

While Alex Salmond predicted a record turnout for the 2014 referendum, backed by John Curtice who said that turnout could reach 70 or 80 per cent,[256] Joyce McMillan begged to differ and nearly despaired:

> Increasingly, it seems as though the most likely outcome, 20 months from now, will be a referendum with an embarrassingly low turnout, as Scots turn away in droves from a vote which deliberately asks them the wrong question, and denies them their preferred political option. As the wiser old heads of Scottish politics said when the devolved parliament was first elected in 1999, devolution

---

[253] Tom Devine, 'Will the Scots push this elephant out of bed', *The Times*, 1 March 2012.

[254] Tom Gordon, 'Indy allies to Salmond: don't fight with the Electoral Commission', *Sunday Herald*, 27 January 2012.

[255] Lesley Riddoch, 'Opportunity knocks, but no answer', *The Scotsman*, 15 October 2012.

[256] 'Salmond predicts record turnout for referendum', *Edinburgh Evening News*, 22 September 2012.

is not an event, but a process. The next step in the process should have been more powers in areas such as pensions and welfare, and real fiscal responsibility for taxes raised in Scotland; but our politicians have conspired to keep that option off the 2014 ballot paper, condemning us, in all likelihood, to a massive No vote, followed by at least a decade of stagnation.[257]

'Experience says that the SNP and its allies have a lot more cause for optimism,' Ian Bell opined, 'than Labour and its new friends. Apathy in those erstwhile Labour heartlands is at historic levels.' He concludes: 'The referendum will omit an important question, so we must pose it ourselves. The United Kingdom is dysfunctional and in headlong decline. Yes or No? How many will rally, come 2014, to proof a cheerless alternative?'[258]

Even political anoraks have mixed feelings about the permanent merry-go-round of the referendum campaign, visiting and re-visiting topics *ad nauseam*. Still, it is the bread and butter of the chattering classes. Too bad that the recalcitrant *hoi polloi* seem less enamoured. Trailing through 1978 editions of the *Scotsman* – pre-referendum just as now – Paul Cockburn found a timely warning: 'Since the arguments for and against devolution have already been extremely well-rehearsed, the main danger is that this extension of debate will generate only boredom.' He added: 'Regardless of whether our sympathies lie with Yes Scotland, Better Together or Still Undecided, can any of us really say we're actually looking forward to the arguments that must be stretched out across the next 18 months?'[259]

Well, there are alternative pastimes. We must surely owe the fact that 2013 is the dedicated 'Year of Natural Scotland' to the 175th birthday of the great John Muir of Dunbar, the pioneering naturalist and author who is best known for his role in founding American national parks like Yosemite. A coast-to-coast John Muir Trail is being developed, and a John Muir Day is to be celebrated across Scotland on 10 April. Who says there is nothing happening in 2013? And what could be a better cure for bouts of referendum campaign fatigue than taking to the great outdoors? Just follow the great man's advice:

> Climb the mountains and get their good tidings. Nature's peace will flow into you as sunshine flows into trees. The

---

[257] Joyce McMillan, 'Scotland wants nae sinking ware', *The Scotsman*, 25 January 2013.

[258] Ian Bell, 'So many imponderables from just one question', *The Herald*, 17 October 2012.

[259] Paul F Cockburn, 'How the Scotsman used to be a very different newspaper', *Scottish Review*, 29 January 2013, <www.scottishreview.net/PaulCockburn53.shtml?utm_source=Sign-Up.to&utm_medium=email&utm_campaign>.

winds will blow their own freshness into you, and the storms their energy, while cares will drop away from you like the leaves of Autumn.[260]

[January 2013]

---

[260] John Muir, *Our National Parks*, Boston and New York: Houghton, Mifflin and Company (The Riverside Press), p.56.

Chapter X

THE YEAR AT HOLYROOD
2013-2014

The year 2013 began as it ended – with storms and floods. Oddly becalmed, by contrast, were the polls for the independence referendum. While the poll of polls of 2012 showed a division of 59 (No) to 41 (Yes), the same exercise in 2013 produced a 60 to 40 split (excluding the undecided). Unperturbed, the campaigns, Yes Scotland and Better Together, ground on. Then, in the first quarter of 2014, the polls began to move, the gap between Yes and No narrowed and, at long last, the rest of the UK seemed to wake up to the possibility that, come 18 September, the Ayes could have it.

Throughout 2013 the Scottish media, clearly in overdrive in the year before, seemed to be slightly less excited about the referendum debate, but still the papers and online journals were full of stories and comments anent the big date in Scottish history. And both BBC Scotland and STV pummelled us with TV panels and debates. By contrast, stories about the referendum were still scarce in the English media (apart from their 'kilted' editions). Either the political establishment and the media down south were, in view of the poll lead of the No camp, complacent to the point that they thought they need not engage, or they simply did not (yet?) care.

The year's focus was on the Scottish Government's White Paper which was promised for the autumn, and eventually published on 26 November. It would, the Government promised, answer all the questions. Otherwise 2013 was, after the peaks of the previous years – the UK General Election in 2010, the Scottish Parliament election in 2011 and the Local Elections in 2012 – a year where the campaigns had to make do without big political events. Three Holyrood by-elections, including the latest in January 2014, generated only little momentum. Two of them were necessitated by the tragic deaths of sitting MSPs.

THE GRIM REAPER

In April, the Aberdeen Donside MSP, Brian Adam, died at the age of 64 after a battle with cancer. First elected in 1999, he had served as SNP

chief whip from 2007 to 2011, one of the 'crucial people,' as First Minister Alex Salmond commented, 'who ... sustained the minority government',[1] and as the Minister for Parliamentary Business from May 2011 until September 2012.

On the last days of the Dunfermline by-election campaign (triggered by the resignation of the disgraced MSP Bill Walker), Helen Eadie MSP fell ill, was diagnosed with cancer, and succumbed to the disease only two weeks later, on 9 November, aged 66. The Cowdenbeath by-election was called for 24 January 2014. I may be allowed a personal word of gratitude to Helen Eadie: a widely respected MSP known for her feisty representation of her Fife constituents, she was also, since she was first elected in 1999, of immense help to me, as a staunch supporter of Edinburgh University's Parliamentary Programme.

In August, the former Scottish Tory leader David McLetchie lost his battle with cancer, aged only 61. An MSP since 1999, he served as party leader for the first seven years of the Scottish Parliament. Later, he returned to the front bench and also represented the Conservatives in the anti-independence Better Together campaign. As a List MSP, he was replaced by Cameron Buchanan, who combines his role as an MSP with being Honorary Consul of Iceland. On 26 January 2014, the former Lib Dem MSP John Farquhar Munro died at the age of 79. Always a champion of his native Highlands, he was 'a Gaelic speaker who fought for his fellow crofters, for land reform and for the survival and furtherance of his mother tongue.'[2]

On 4 April 2014, Margo Macdonald died, aged 70. She was one of the 'two charismatic female Nationalists (the other being Winnie Ewing) who helped establish the SNP as a serious political force' in the 1970s.[3] Demoted by her party to list position five for the 2003 Holyrood elections, she decided to stand as an Independent, and received the overwhelming support of her Lothian regional constituents in 2003, 2007 and 2011. A campaigning MSP (safety for sex workers, assisted suicide), she was one of the few politicians who would be pointed out by the tourist guides in the open double-deckers: 'There goes Margo'. At her memorial service, Alex Neil reminded us that the Conservative Scotland Office Minister David Mundell had described her as a 'one-woman second chamber'.[4] The watering hole in the Parly is already known as 'Margo's Bar' – a plaque there dedicated to the fearless, independent and irrepressible free spirit of the Scottish Parliament would be a fine way of commemorating her.

---

[1] Lana Montgomery, 'Aberdeen MSP Brian Adam dies of cancer, aged 64', *Daily Record*, 25 April 2013.

[2] Phil Davison, 'John Farquhar Munro – (Obituary)', *The Herald*, 28 January 2014.

[3] David Torrance, 'Margo MacDonald – (Obituary)', *The Herald*, 5 April 2014.

[4] Tom Peterkin, 'Margo MacDonald loved to challenge government and MSPs should follow suit', *The Scotsman*, 15 May 2014.

As she was an independent List MSP, Margo's seat will remain vacant until the next election in 2016.

When Margaret Thatcher passed away on 8 April 2013, her demise divided people just as her premiership had done. And nowhere more so than in Scotland. Here, the Tories have yet to recover from her reign. 'It is clear from the newspapers this week that she has not been forgiven for presiding over the de-industrialisation of Scotland,' John Knox summed up the reaction:

> Steel, coal, engineering and textile jobs turned into part-time service employment and short-lived computer factories. No doubt this would have happened anyway but she drove through the changes too quickly – 250,000 people were made redundant, unemployment rose to 12%. Whole communities were destroyed. The turmoil and bitterness of the miners' strike cannot be forgotten or forgiven by those of us who reported it at the time.[5]

Thatcher's policies, monetarism, privatisation and deregulation, cutting taxes for the rich and, above all, introducing the Poll Tax in Scotland,

> drove the Scots to insist on devolution as a protection against such 'high Tory' policies and today it still fires the campaign for independence. Certainly the Tories in Scotland have never recovered from Mrs Thatcher's toxic legacy. They have fallen steadily from 31% support when she came to office to 24% when she left and now to 16% and only one MP north of the border.[6]

'Thatcher's Sermon on the Mound in 1988, with its crass celebration of wealth, offended something deep in Scotland's Presbyterian soul,' Ian Macwhirter pondered: 'It convinced the Scots that they really were a different country and began the process that could still lead to Scotland leaving the United Kingdom for good.'[7] Canon Kenyon Wright once called her 'the unwilling and unwitting midwife' of he Scottish Parliament. 'But for her we might well not have had a Scottish Parliament today,' he wrote in a letter to the *Herald* after her passing.[8]

---

[5] John Knox, 'Letter from Scotland', *Caledonian Mercury*, 12 April 2013, <caledonianmercury. com/2013/04/12/letter-from-scotland-12th-march-2013/0038653>.

[6] *Ibid.*

[7] Iain Macwhirter, '"She convinced us Scotland was a different country"', *Sunday Herald*, 14 April 2013.

[8] Canon Kenyon Wright, 'Why we should give thanks to mother of Scottish Parliament', Letter to the Editor, *The Herald*, 9 April 2013.

No friend of Thatcher's was the writer Iain Banks, who died on 9 June 2013, aged 59, only two months after announcing he had terminal cancer. He was one of Scotland's most popular novelists, in both mainstream literature and – as Iain M Banks – science fiction. The latter made him a favourite of the former Scottish Labour leader Iain Gray who wrote a very perceptive and affectionate piece about the left-leaning, independence-supporting author in the *Scotsman*, particularly praising his 'Culture' novels.[9]

The shock-resignation of Cardinal Keith O'Brien from the post as Archbishop of St Andrews and Edinburgh, after allegations of sexual misconduct by three priests and one retired priest, threw the Catholic Church in Scotland into turmoil or even, according to the historian Tom Devine, 'its gravest crisis since the reformation.'[10] On a much more positive note, the Noble Prize in physics, bestowed on Professor Peter Higgs, was cause for celebrations way beyond Edinburgh University.

In December, the world mourned the passing of Nelson Mandela, perhaps the greatest statesman of his generation. And there is a great Scottish story to tell about him, from Hamish Henderson's 'The Men of Rivonia', written under the impression Mandela's speech from the dock at the Rivonia trial made on the Scottish writer, to Glasgow bestowing the Freedom of the City on the Robben Island prisoner in 1981 and Nelson Mandela's day in Glasgow in 1993, when he picked up his award.[11]

In May 2014, the Scottish Parliament marked its 15th anniversary. John Knox tried to sum up its record:

> The parliament we have built over the last 15 years is not without its flaws. Its successes I think have included free personal care, free university education, the national parks, the smoking ban and being a national forum. But its failures are legion: the cost, the expenses scandals, its timidity over taxation, its failure to spread power down to local communities and its turgid and ineffective committee system.[12]

[9] Iain Gray, 'Iain Banks: A writer of the first rank', *The Scotsman*, 18 June 2013.

[10] Gerry Braiden, 'Catholic Church facing "gravest crisis since Reformation"', *The Herald*, 26 February 2013.

[11] See Eberhard Bort, '"Free Mandela! Free Mandela!": Hamish Henderson, Nelson Mandela, and the Fight Against Apartheid in South Africa', Edinburgh People's Festival Hamish Henderson Lecture (7 August 2013), revised and updated, 24 January 2014, <www.edinburghpeoplesfestival.org/wp-content/uploads/2014/01/Hamish-Henderson-Memorial-Lecture-2013.pdf>.

[12] John Knox, 'Letter from Scotland', *Caledonian Mercury*, 16 May 2014, <caledonianmercury.com/2014/05/16/letter-scotland-16th-may-2014/0045599>.

BUDGET 2013

Given the SNP's absolute majority at Holyrood, there was never any doubt that the Government's £30bn budget for 2013 would be passed by Parliament, and so it did, by 68 to 56 votes. And yet, there was quite a bit of drama. In a series of last-minute changes, Finance Secretary John Swinney said there would be:

- A £61m increase in college funding over the three-year spending review period, putting the college budget at £522m in 2013/14 and £522m in 2014/15.
- An additional £38m for housing, bringing total budget for housing supply to £859m.
- £2m to bring empty town centre properties into residential use.
- An extra £10m for vital trunk road and bridge repairs.
- And £1m to double support for entrepreneurship.

Against the backdrop of a cut to the Scottish Government's budget – funded by the Treasury block grant – of about 8% in real terms, between 2010-11 and 2014-15, Swinney set his record:

> We are building on our original spending plans having listened to the views of parliament and the country and are delivering extra funding for housing, creating jobs and cutting emissions, funding to regenerate our town centres, more support for entrepreneurship, investment in our trunk road network and a decisive further investment into our colleges. [13]

Despite those concessions to demands from Labour, Tories and the Lib Dems, Swinney's 'best possible deal' faced a barrage of criticism from the opposition parties. Whereas he insisted that he had delivered a 'budget for growth', Labour finance spokesman Ken Macintosh's verdict was:

> There is nothing new here, nothing fresh, we are stuck with the same prescription the SNP have offered us for two years running, and for two years running they have promised jobs and growth and yet there have been no jobs and no growth. [14]

---

[13] 'Scottish budget: MSPs pass government spending plans', *BBC News Scotland*, 6 February 2013, <www.bbc.co.uk/news/uk-scotland-scotland-politics-21343192>.

[14] *Ibid.*

While John Henderson, the chief executive of Scotland's Colleges, expressed his delight that £61m more would be available for colleges over two years, both the Conservatives and the Lib Dems criticised what amounts to a cut of £24.6m to colleges. 'The SNP continue to make the wrong choices with precious resources,' Green MSP Patrick Harvie joined in the chorus of disapproval.[15]

WATER, HEDGES, LANDFILL: A SPOT OF LEGISLATION

In January 2013, MSPs unanimously voted through the Freedom of Information (Amendment) (Scotland) Bill, designed to bring the original decade-old Act up to date with recent developments. Infrastructure, Capital Investment and Cities Strategy Secretary Nicola Sturgeon said the bill was an 'important landmark in the life of freedom of information' but 'not the end of the journey' – but some MSPs and campaigners said it did not go far enough.[16] Likewise, in February Parliament unanimously approved the Water Resources (Scotland) Bill. It covers a broad range of areas relating to water and sewerage services. The Scottish government also renewed its commitment to keeping Scottish Water in public ownership.[17]

In March, Holyrood passed the SNP backbencher Mark McDonald's High Hedges (Scotland) Bill, which makes provision about hedges which interfere with the reasonable enjoyment of domestic properties. 'It might not be the most exciting piece of legislation to come out of Holyrood,' Kate Shannon commented, 'but there is no doubt the … High Hedges Bill could make a big difference to local authorities across Scotland' by helping them 'resolve disputes regarding garden hedges of a certain height which encroach on neighbouring properties.'[18]

In May, the Aquaculture and Fisheries (Scotland) Bill, designed to improve the management of Scotland's farmed and wild fisheries, passed its final parliamentary stage. Members of Holyrood's Rural Affairs Committee said the 'adversarial' dealings between the two parts of the industry had hindered their scrutiny of new legislation. Improving the

---

[15] Tom Peterkin, 'Colleges get extra £61m but still lose out, say critics', *The Scotsman*, 7 February 2013.

[16] 'FOI (Amendment) Bill passed unanimously', *BBC Democracy Live*, 16 January 2013, <news.bbc.co.uk/democracylive/hi/scotland/newsid_9785000/9785795.stm>.

[17] 'Water resource laws passed by MSPs', *BBC News Scotland*, 27 February 2013, <www.bbc.co.uk/news/uk-scotland-scotland-politics-21602451>.

[18] Kate Shannon, 'Hedging your bets: the High Hedges (Scotland) Bill', *Holyrood*, 28 January 2013, <www.holyrood.com/2013/01/hedging-your-bets-the-high-hedges-scotland-bill/>.

relationship between the two sectors was, they contended, 'perhaps of equal significance for Scotland in the long-term' as changing the law.[19] Also in May, the National Trust for Scotland (Governance etc.) Bill found unanimous approval. The bill, which concerns changes to the governance structure of the National Trust for Scotland, was 'small but perfect', said the National Trust for Scotland (Governance etc.) Bill Committee convener Fiona McLeod MSP.[20]

The Forth Road Bridge Bill was passed by the Parliament on 23 May 2013. It set up a new company to manage the Forth Road Bridge, the new Forth Crossing and the surrounding roads. Two weeks later, the name of the new bridge was disclosed: the popular vote fell on the prosaic Queensferry Crossing, beating Caledonia Bridge.[21] In June, the Crofting (Amendment) (Scotland) Bill was passed, correcting a defect in the 2010 crofting legislation, namely that owner-occupier crofters were unable to apply to the Crofting Commission to decroft land. 'Decrofting land can enable a house to be built on the land and facilitate croft land being passed from one generation to the next.'[22]

With the Land and Buildings Transaction Tax (Scotland) Bill, approved by Parliament on 25 June 2013, Holyrood 'passed its first bill to create a distinctive Scottish tax,'[23] in expectation of the powers to be transferred from Westminster under the Scotland Act 2012. A second bill to establish Scotland's own tax regime was passed on 17 December 2013: the Landfill Tax (Scotland) Bill makes provision to tax disposals to landfill sites.

The Post-16 Education (Scotland) Bill, passed on 26 June, includes provision for the regionalisation of colleges. The legislation is mainly aimed at widening access to higher education, and as such was welcomed by the University and College Union as well as by the National Union of Students. But Labour's Neil Findlay was scathing in his criticism: 'This is a bad bill. Much of it could have been achieved without legislation. It centralises power in the hands of the cabinet secretary, compromises autonomy and accountability, confuses college governance, and has limited ambition on widening access.' He had earlier called on the Scottish government to withdraw the legislation: 'At the time, I called the Bill a dogs breakfast,' he said. 'I want to withdraw that charge as I now realise it was an unfair slight on the pet food industry. But the bill should have been withdrawn

---

[19] 'MSPs criticise volatile relationship between sectors of fish farming industry', *Daily Record*, 4 February 2013.

[20] 'National Trust for Scotland (Governance etc.) Bill passed unanimously', *BBC Democracy Live*, 23 May 2013, <www.bbc.co.uk/democracylive/scotland-22641155>.

[21] Tom Peterkin, 'New Forth bridge named Queensferry Crossing', *The Scotsman*, 27 June 2013.

[22] 'Amendment to Crofting Act', *Stornoway Gazette*, 26 June 2013.

[23] 'Land and buildings transaction tax set to become law', *The Journal of the Law Society of Scotland*, 26 June 2013, <www.journalonline.co.uk/News/1012781.aspx#.Uu3PJCgx9Hg>.

and brought back in a more coherent and comprehensible state.'[24] The opposition parties voted against the bill, accusing the government of trying to interfere in the running of universities.

The Scottish Independence Referendum (Franchise) Bill, also passed on 27 June 2013, cleared the way for 16- and 17-year-olds to vote in the Independence Referendum. The Scottish Independence Referendum Bill, passed on 14 November 2013, created the legal basis for the holding of that referendum.

The Victims and Witnesses (Scotland) Bill, which finished its Stage 3 passage through Parliament on 12 December 2013, was bringing Scottish legal practice in line with EU law. It provides vulnerable witnesses in cases involving sexual offences, domestic abuse, stalking and human trafficking with new rights to special measures when giving evidence, including video links and screens. 'For too long, victims have been treated and been made to feel like bystanders in the criminal justice system,' Justice Secretary Kenny MacAskill said: 'The passage of this bill will see more consideration given to the rights of victims and witnesses of crime, and will improve their experience of the system to which they turn to see justice served.'[25] The legislation was welcomed as 'historic' by Victim Support Scotland. Its acting deputy chief executive, Alan McCloskey, said: 'For the first time ever, crucial rights for victims will be enshrined in law.' For Labour's Graeme Pearson MSP, the legislation could have gone further. And a Tory bid to amend the legislation to give rape victims the right to legal advice before personal information is accessed by lawyers was rejected in Parliament.[26]

On 21 January 2014 the Parliament gave green light for the Burrell Collection to travel while its home in Glasgow's Pollok Country Park is being refurbished, against the wishes laid down in the Burrell bequest. The Marriage and Civil Partnership (Scotland) Bill was approved by an overwhelming majority on 4 February 2014, in 'one of the Scottish parliament's genuinely historic moments.'[27] It removes the last remaining major issue of sexual discrimination from Scots law by legalising same-sex marriages. But while in England the wedding bells for same sex couples were ringing in March, campaigners in Scotland are disappointed that the date for the first gay marriage in Scotland, which was expected to be in September or October, may now have slipped from autumn to Christmas time.[28]

---

[24] 'MSPs back post-16 education reforms', BBC News Scotland, 26 June 2013, <www.bbc.co.uk/news/uk-scotland-scotland-politics-23054513>.

[25] 'Police attackers will be charged £10,000', The Scotsman, 13 December 2013.

[26] Ibid.

[27] 'A proud day for Scotland' (Leader), Sunday Herald, 2 February 2014.

[28] Judith Duffy, 'No gay wedding bells until Christmas', The Herald, 13 April 2014.

The Children and Young People (Scotland) Bill was passed on 19 February 2014, providing an increase in free childcare for three, four and vulnerable two-year-olds, from 475 to 600 hours – around 16 hours per week – from August 2014. A Labour proposal to give vulnerable two-year-olds a legal right to care was defeated at the committee stage, as was a Tory bid to guarantee that all children get two years of nursery care before school, regardless of when their birthday falls. The bill will also extend free school meals to all children in the first three years of primary school, from January 2015. Most controversial was the plan to appoint so-called guardians – specific named persons from the NHS and councils – to monitor every young person's well-being from birth to age 18. Among others, the Church of Scotland and the Conservatives opposed the scheme, saying that it raised concerns about diminishing the position of parents and increasing the role of the state in modern society. Children's Minister Aileen Campbell insisted that the appointment of a named person – such as a health visitor, midwife or teacher – for every child will 'provide a safety net for those who need one'.[29]

The Bankruptcy and Debt Advise (Scotland) Bill was passed on 20 March 2014. The most controversial point was that people who become bankrupt in Scotland will now be made to pay debts for four years instead of three. That, according to Labour's Jenny Marra MSP, gives Scotland 'the longest period of bankruptcy in the whole of the United Kingdom.'[30] Her claim was rejected by Enterprise Minister Fergus Ewing.

The third reading of the Procurement Reform (Scotland) Bill took place on 13 May. Labour and the trade unions had pressed, in vain, for the introduction of a living wage, and the Federation of Small Businesses challenged the Scottish Government over its claims that SMEs win a higher share of public contracts in Scotland than in most EU countries.[31] Labour made 'a last-ditch attempt' to force all companies bidding for public contracts to pay their staff the Living Wage – currently £7.65 an hour in Scotland. The party's infrastructure spokesman James Kelly argued such a move would 'give a pay boost to thousands of workers on low pay.' He said such a change would mean thousands of low-paid workers would be as much as £2600 a year better off, and almost two-thirds of those who would benefit were female workers: 'This is an opportunity not only to help women but an opportunity to tackle low pay in public contracts.' But Deputy First Minister Nicola Sturgeon insisted that 'making its payment a mandatory part of public contracts did not

---

[29] 'Scottish parliament passes children's bill', *The Scotsman*, 19 February 2014.

[30] 'Scotland bankruptcy reform law passed at Holyrood', *The Scotsman*, 20 March 2014.

[31] Simon Bain, 'Row over counteracts awarded to small firms', *The Herald*, 19 May 2014.

meet European laws.' After a heated debate, MSPs voted by 44 to 74 against introducing a 'Living Wage duty'.[32]

Further Government bills passed between January and March of this year were the Public Bodies (Joint Working) (Scotland) Bill, the Regulatory Reform (Scotland) Bill and the Tribunals (Scotland) Bill.

There is also a ream of legislation still going through the stages in Parliament, among them the second attempt by the late Margo MacDonald to get assisted suicide onto the statute books. The Criminal Justice (Scotland) Bill, with its highly contested plans, following the Lord Carloway Report, of abolishing corroboration, has been delayed, as Justice Cabinet Secretary Kenny MacAskill announced in April 2014 that stage two of the bill would not be considered until after Lord Bonomy's review group (which is looking into safeguards) has reported. That report is expected for April 2015.[33]

Also in the mix is the Criminal Verdicts (Scotland) Bill, with the equally controversial provision of removing the not proven verdict as one of the available verdicts in criminal proceedings; and for a guilty verdict to require an increased majority of jurors. In February and March, the Courts Reform (Scotland) Bill, the Food (Scotland) Bill and the Historic Environment (Scotland) Bill were introduced in Parliament. There are also members' bills like the Defective and Dangerous Buildings (Recovery of Expenses) (Scotland) Bill and the Disabled Persons' Parking Badges (Scotland) Bill.

THE LAST LEGISLATIVE PROGRAMME BEFORE THE REFERENDUM

On 3 September 2013, First Minister Alex Salmond introduced the Scottish government's legislative programme for the coming year, consisting of a total of 13 new bills.[34] Apart from the annual Budget Bill, there was a Revenue Scotland and Tax Powers Bill, setting up – in anticipation of the tax powers coming to the Scottish Parliament through the Scotland Act 2012 – Revenue Scotland as the tax authority which will

---

[32] 'MSPs have rejected a bid to force firms bidding for public contracts to pay staff the Living Wage', *Daily Record*, 14 May 2014.

[33] Brian Taylor, 'Quiet surrender over corroboration', *BBC News Scotland*, 24 April 2014, <www.bbc.co.uk/news/uk-scotland-scotland-politics-27131817>. The Justice Secretary was heavily criticised by the opposition parties for his handling of the bill. See Magnus Gardham and Jody Harrison, 'Salmond facing questions over MacAskill legal U-turn', *The Herald*, 24 April 2014, and Magnus Gardham, 'Salmond urged: Sack MacAskill over U-turn on corroboration', *The Herald*, 25 April 2014.

[34] 'At-a-glance: Scottish legislative programme 2013/14', *BBC News Scotland*, 3 September 2013, <www.bbc.co.uk/news/uk-scotland-23951293>.

be responsible for collecting taxes on land transactions and on waste disposal to landfill and any other taxes which may be devolved in future. A Bankruptcy Consolidation Bill seeks to put Scotland's bankruptcy legislation in one place in order to ensure that it is readable, accessible and easier for both practitioners and those affected by the law to use. The Conclusion of Contracts etc. Bill is to modernise Scots law in order to promote business and economic growth, allowing companies to conclude contracts by using email.

The Community Empowerment and Renewal Bill aims at making it easier for communities to take over public sector assets that are not used or underused and to help communities deal more effectively with vacant and derelict property in their areas. The Scottish Welfare Fund Bill give the fund, established in April 2013 to mitigate the effects of Westminster welfare cuts, a 'more secure statutory footing'. The Housing Bill will end the right-to-buy for social housing tenants. The Mental Health Bill is to help people with mental health issues access effective treatment quickly and easily.

Following the horsemeat scandal, a Food Standards Scotland Bill is to establish a new body to take over all of the old functions of the Food Standards Agency, with consumer protection as its primary concern. A Courts Reform Bill, based on the recommendations of Lord Gill and described by the Government as 'the most radical shake-up of the courts system for a generation,'[35] will remove low value claims from the Court of Session and give it the status it deserves as a senior civil court. Many civil cases, including personal injury cases, will be redistributed to the sheriff courts and the new personal injury court. New summary sheriffs will relieve sheriffs of some of the work, freeing them up to concentrate on complex civil cases and solemn crime.

The Damages Bill seeks to reform the law on key aspects of damages for personal injury, particularly under what circumstances a claim for damages can be brought and also the limitation period within which a claim should usually be made. The Licensing Bill will extend regulation for scrap metal dealers in an attempt to reduce metal thefts and introduce an offence of supplying alcohol to under-18s. New licensing regimes will be introduced for air weapons and sexual entertainment venues. Finally, the RCAHMS and Historic Scotland Merger Bill will combine the functions of Historic Scotland and the Royal Commission on the Ancient and Historical Monuments of Scotland (RCAHMS).

As he set out his plans, the First Minister also made a commitment that automatic early release from prison for the most serious violent and sexual offenders will be scrapped. The plan will be taken forward in an amendment to the Criminal Justice Bill, announced on top of the 13 new

---

[35] Gareth Rose, 'Courts reform to give quicker, cheaper justice', *The Scotsman*, 28 February 2013.

pieces of legislation in the SNP government's programme. It was an SNP manifesto pledge in 2007 and again in 2011 and, as 'a piece of populist policymaking,'[36] is supposed to attract Yes votes in the referendum campaign.

The opposition was not impressed by the programme. 'It was an opportunity to show us that we could take him seriously as Scotland's first minister,' Labour leader Johann Lamont responded: 'He could do that by bringing forward a legislative programme that met this one crucial test: that it would put the interests of the people of Scotland before the interests of the SNP. With this unambitious, lacklustre and moribund programme he has completely failed.' Ruth Davidson, the Conservative leader, concurred: 'This programme is notable not for what it achieves but for what it does not. It does little to extend the advantages he has because it's not in his interest to make devolution work we believe it can.'[37]

Not contained in the programme was a scheme rolled out in England and Wales in early 2014 which allows people to find out whether their partner has a history of domestic violence, known as Clare's Law.[38] The issue of a Scottish version of Clare's Law had been raised with the First Minister by the Scottish Conservative leader Ruth Davidson in March, and in May he responded saying at First Minister's Questions that such a law will be piloted in Scotland. Further, he announced, his government was also considering a new domestic abuse offence. Police recorded 60,080 incidents of domestic abuse in Scotland in 2012-13, up slightly from 59,847 in the previous year.[39]

Justice Secretary Kenny MacAskill announced new legislation that will affect the owners of the 500,000 air weapons he estimates are used in Scotland. The Air Weapons and Licensing (Scotland) Bill introduced in May at Holyrood[40] seeks to introduce strict licensing measures which, as the gun lobby predictably complains, 'will penalise law-abiding citizens and do nothing to cut misuse of the weapons by criminals.'[41]

---

[36] 'Salmond woos voters with populist policies' (Leader), *The Scotsman*, 4 September 2013.

[37] 'Alex Salmond outlines SNP government plans for year ahead', *BBC News Scotland*, 3 September 2013, <www.bbc.co.uk/news/uk-scotland-scotland-politics-23931772>.

[38] named after Clare Wood, who was murdered by her ex-boyfriend in Salford, Greater Manchester, in 2009.

[39] 'Scotland to pilot 'Clare's law' to tackle domestic violence', *BBC News Scotland*, 8 May 2014, <www.bbc.co.uk/news/uk-scotland-27315418>.

[40] 'Scottish airgun licensing bill introduced;, *BBC News Scotland*, 15 May 2014, <www.bbc.co.uk/news/uk-scotland-scotland-politics-27420858>.

[41] Jody Harrison, 'Opponents claim new airgun laws will not cut crime', *The Herald*, 16 May 2014.

BUDGET 2014

John Swinney's Budget Bill confirmed plans for £59m over two years to provide more free childcare places, taking the total additional money for childcare to approximately £250 million over this period. Funding of £55 million over two years for free school meals for youngsters in primaries one to three is also set out in the bill, as part of a £114 million package of help for young people. It further proposes spending £68 million in each of the next two years to mitigate welfare reforms introduced by Westminster, as well as £20 million this year and next year to limit the impact of the so-called 'bedroom tax', which affects about 80,000 Scots.

Swinney went on to confirm that the SNP's 'free' offers – no tuition fees, no prescription charges, and free bus travel for pensioners – would continue to be paid for by the state. His budget also provided funds to expand a rates relief scheme for small businesses, as well as to maintain the council tax freeze. But funding for Scotland's 32 councils will be slashed for the next two years, with a real terms reduction of £624 million by 2015-16. John Swinney said his spending plans would help Scotland's children, tackle poverty and assist those affected by welfare reforms:

> Within our limited powers we are doing everything possible to tackle the effects of Westminster's cuts to the Scottish budget on our economy and their relentless austerity agenda. This budget contains proposals that will help Scotland's children, tackle poverty, increase the opportunities for parents to work and protect some of our most vulnerable people from the impact of welfare reform. They are proposals that the whole of Parliament should be able to endorse.[42]

Labour were calling on John Swinney to provide more funding to help those who have had their housing benefit cut because they are deemed to have a spare room in their council or housing association property. The party's Finance spokesman Iain Gray said:

> Labour have consistently made clear that the single most important improvement to the budget we wish to see is funding to fully mitigate the impact of the bedroom tax, thus effectively abolishing this iniquitous policy in Scotland. Based on recent research this would require £50 million

---

[42] 'Finance Secretary urges MSPs to support budget for 2014/2015 which will include spending on childcare places', *Daily Record*, 22 January 2014.

each year. So far the government have found only £20 million.[43]

But then came the surprise announcement by Iain Gray that talks with Finance Secretary John Swinney were taking place that could result in the axing of the bedroom tax. Labour agreed to support the Budget, despite having previously voted against central measures for extra childcare and free school meals for younger primary pupils, in the hope that the final Budget will 'consign the bedroom tax to history in Scotland, right here and right now.'[44] At the beginning of May, the Westminster government transferred powers to Holyrood that mean that control over the money needed to bail out struggling tenants lies now with the Scottish Parliament.[45]

THREE BY-ELECTIONS: DONSIDE, DUNFERMLINE, COWDENBEATH

In June, November and January, three Holyrood by-elections were necessitated by the death of Brian Adam MSP, the resignation of Bill Walker MSP, and the death of Helen Eadie MSP. None of them turned out to be very dramatic. None of them brought any big surprises.

The SNP's Mark McDonald won the Aberdeen Donside by-election on 21 June 2013. He secured 9,814 votes, while Labour's Willie Young in second got 7,789, meaning the SNP majority was slashed by over 5,000, compared with the 2011 result.[46] Perhaps the biggest talking point of the campaign was First Minister Alex Salmond's 'unplanned' visit to Bramble Brae Primary School, which led to accusations by the Labour-led Aberdeen Council, demanding an investigation into the First Minister's conduct. In August, Sir Peter Housden, the head of Scotland's civil service, cleared the First Minister of breaking parliamentary rules with his school visit.[47]

The Dunfermline by-election became necessary when the former SNP MSP Bill Walker resigned his seat, some two weeks after he was convicted of 23 charges of domestic abuse against his three former wives and a

---

[43] *Ibid.*

[44] Scott Macnab, 'SNP and Labour will agree to end bedroom tax', *The Scotsman*, 23 January 2014.

[45] David Clegg, 'Taxi for bed tax', *Daily Record*, 3 May 2014.

[46] 'SNP's Mark McDonald wins Aberdeen Donside by-election', *BBC News Scotland*, 21 June 2013, <www.bbc.co.uk/news/uk-scotland-north-east-orkney-shetland-22986202>.

[47] Frank Urquhart, 'Alex Salmond Aberdeen by-election conduct cleared', *The Scotsman*, 8 August 2013.

stepdaughter.[48] He had been suspended and later expelled from his party after the allegations had surfaced in March 2012. He had remained for some time as an independent MSP, but resigned after facing pressure from campaigners and MSPs following his conviction. He was sentenced to twelve months in jail, of which he served six. Just before Easter 2014, he lost a bid to overturn one of his convictions for domestic abuse against a former wife.[49]

The by-election on 24 October was comfortably won by Labour's Cara Hilton, on 10,275 votes, with the SNP candidate, former MSP Shirley-Anne Somerville, coming second with 7,402 votes.[50] Johann Lamont hailed the victory as 'emphatic', claiming that political fortunes in Scotland were turning in Labour's favour.[51] And yet, the seven per cent swing would, according to John Curtice, not be enough for Labour to get ahead of the SNP if it were repeated across Scotland.[52]

Helen Eadie's death on 9 November triggered the Cowdenbeath by-election which was held on 23 January 2014. Labour's Alex Rowley, council leader in Fife, romped home with a two-to-one victory over his opponents. He received 11,192 votes; Natalie McGarry of the SNP came second with 5,704. Rowley's 55.8% meant an 11.25% swing from the SNP.[53] Noteworthy also that the Lib Dems finished fifth – behind Ukip. For Torcuil Crichton, this called into question whether the Lib Dems have an electoral future in Scotland.[54]

PARTY CONFERENCES 2013

When Scottish Labour MPs, MSPs and activists gathered for the party's annual conference at the Eden Court in Inverness in April, Johann Lamont faced a rebellion of senior Labour frontbenchers who reacted angrily to an interim report of the party's Devolution Commission

[48] Severin Carrell, 'Salmond: Bill Walker MSP should stand down after assault conviction', *The Guardian*, 22 August 2013.

[49] Dave Finlay, 'Ex-MSP Bill Walker loses abuse conviction appeal', *The Scotsman*, 17 April 2014.

[50] David Clegg, 'Dunfermline by-election: Labour's Cara Hilton wins race to replace shamed Bill Walker', *Daily Record*, 25 October 2013.

[51] Robin Dinwoodie, 'Lamont: Dunfermline shows we're competing again as SNP vote slumps', *The Herald*, 25 October 2013.

[52] Auslan Cramb, 'Comfortable win for Labour in Dunfermline by-election', *The Daily Telegraph*, 25 October 2013.

[53] Robin Dinwoodie, 'Labour increase majority in Cowdenbeath by-election', *The Herald*, 25 January 2014.

[54] Torcuil Crichton, 'Lib Dems' existence as electoral force called into question by Cowdenbeath by-election humiliation', *Daily Record*, 24 January 2014.

which recommended the devolution of all income tax to the Scottish Parliament. Lamont had to concede that the proposal had provoked internal divisions but called devolving income tax 'the most compelling' proposal in the report, simply building on measures which were already coming into force through the Scotland Act 2012, which gives Holyrood the limited right to set Scottish rates of income tax. Anas Sarwar, Scottish Labour's deputy leader and effective head of the party's 40 MPs, insisted he was not yet persuaded that entirely devolving income tax was necessary.[55]

The Scottish Conservatives met in June in Stirling, gave Alistair Darling, the leader of the Better Together campaign, a standing ovation (seen with a degree of unease among Labour followers who are uncomfortable with Labour's partnership with the Tories in Better Together)[56] and heard David Cameron's pledge to fight 'head, heart, body and soul' for the Union, renewing his promise of more devolution after a No vote. The party under Ruth Davidson, he said, was 'focused on securing Scotland's place within a strong UK but not afraid to look at how devolution can be improved.'[57]

The Lib Dems were the only UK-wide party to hold their UK conference in Scotland. They gathered in Glasgow in mid-September, where Nick Clegg came under fire when delegates overwhelmingly condemned the bedroom tax for 'discriminating against the most vulnerable in society.'[58] The Autumn Conference of the Scottish Green Party took place in early October 2013 in Inverness, under the overarching theme 'A Green Scotland in a Green Europe'. The Greens voted that Scotland should have its own currency after independence. They also formally adopted a proposal to ditch the monarchy – two issues where they clearly differ from the SNP's indy-lite agenda.[59]

The SNP shindig in Perth was overshadowed by the Grangemouth crisis. Ineos, the owner of the oil refinery and petrochemical plant, had announced on the previous Wednesday that the site was to close, with the loss of 800 jobs, after Unite members had refused to sign up to the company's survival plan. Roger Seifert of the University of Wolverhampton explained the potential impact: 'The Grangemouth plant accounts for 10% of Scottish manufacturing but less than 1% of the UK's. Where you have a small economy and small country they are much more

[55] Severin Carrell, 'Scottish Labour leaders face revolt over income-tax proposals', *The Guardian*, 19 April 2013.

[56] Angus Howarth, 'Scots Tories give Alistair Darling standing ovation', *The Scotsman*, 8 June 2013.

[57] Severin Carrell, 'PM: I'll fight Scottish independence head, heart, body and soul', *The Guardian*, 7 June 2013.

[58] Rowena Mason, 'Liberal Democrat activists condemn bedroom tax', *The Guardian*, 16 September 2013.

[59] Tom Peterkin, 'Greens back Scots currency', *The Scotsman*, 6 October 2013.

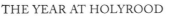

vulnerable to blackmail.'[60] On 24 October, after intense negotiations led by the Scottish Finance Secretary John Swinney and the newly appointed Scottish Secretary Alistair Carmichael (he had replaced Michael Moore on 7 October), the unions accepted a survival plan put forward from the management of the plant, agreeing to taking no strike action for three years, the introduction of a new pension scheme and the acceptance of a three-year pay freeze.[61] As Unite were forced into these humiliating concessions to reopen the facility, there were claims that public confidence in unions had been badly shaken. 'There is no question Unite has suffered a bloody nose,' Gregor Gall commented, 'but I don't think it's broken.'[62] No doubt, 'the reopening of Grangemouth has saved Yes Scotland and the First Minister from an embarrassment that could have derailed efforts to win the referendum in September 2014.'[63] The crisis cost the Scottish economy up to £65m and slowed economic growth in Scotland down to 0.7% in the final quarter of 2013.[64]

But the situation was also tied up with the Labour party's botched selection process for a candidate to succeed the disgraced Falkirk MP Eric Joyce in 2015, in which the local Unite leader played a decisive role, as Alan Cochrane pointed out:

> Complicating the issue in a massive sense for Mr Salmond is that he is stepping straight into a row that involves his oldest enemies – the Scottish Labour Party, whose local chairman in Falkirk, Stephen Deans, is at the centre of the dispute. A long-time worker at the plant, Mr Deans is being investigated by Ineos for allegedly 'fixing' votes in an MP selection contest on company time and using company emails.[65]

And the trouble is not over: in April 2014 Unite threatened to withdraw financial support for Labour at Westminster and Holyrood if it does not support the nationalisation of Ineos without compensation.[66]

---

[60] Janet Boyle, 'Salmond has a lot riding on Grangemouth', *Sunday Post*, 20 October 2013.

[61] Alistair Osborne, 'Grangemouth to stay open after union caves in', *The Daily Telegraph*, 25 October 2013.

[62] Gordon Blackstock, 'Grangemouth: death knell for unions?', *Sunday Post*, 27 October 2013.

[63] Matt Qvortrup, 'Embarrassment saved by reopening', *The Scotsman*, 26 October 2013.

[64] Scott Macnab, '£65m cost of refinery dispute to Scotland's economy', *The Scotsman*, 17 April 2014.

[65] Alan Cochrane, 'SNP conference overshadowed by fear of crisis', *The Daily Telgraph*, 18 October 2013.

[66] Paul Hutcheon, 'Union considers plans to withhold its support for Labour candidates', *The Herald*, 21 April 2014.

PUSH FOR LOCAL DEMOCRACY

An interesting development since the summer of 2013 has been the intervention, in three stages, of local government on behalf of their interests in what they perceive as a discourse falsely limited to the power relations between Westminster and Holyrood. First, the three island councils of Shetland, Orkney and the Western Isles added their demands for greater autonomy to the debate; then the cities chimed in; and, finally, CoSLA installed a Commission on Strengthening Local Democracy with the remit of looking into the purpose of local government.

The main demands of the three island councils of Shetland, Orkney and the Western Isles, as outlined in their document *Our Islands – Our Future*, are:

- Control of the sea bed around the islands, allowing revenues currently paid to the Crown estate to be channeled in to local needs.
- New grid connections to the Scottish mainland to allow world class wave, tidal, and wind energy resources to generate maximum benefits for the islands.
- New fiscal arrangements to allow the islands to benefit more directly from the harvesting of local resources, including renewable energy and fisheries.[67]

The Scottish Government responded to the demands with the 'Lerwick Declaration', installing a ministerial group under Local Government Minister Derek Mackay which is supposed to look into the possibility of devolving powers to the three councils – if the Scots vote Yes in the independence referendum. Labour used its Spring Conference to pledge more powers to the islands, and Alex Salmond took his cabinet to Stornoway in April.[68]

Next, Glasgow City Council published a Report by its chief executive George Black, which contrasted the UK government's handing of greater powers to English city authorities 'in recognition of their pivotal role in supporting economic growth' with Scotland 'where there has been increasing centralisation of powers to the Scottish Government'.[69] The report recommended that the council should seek assurances from the Scottish Government that if the referendum brings a Yes vote, Glasgow should have 'at least the same or greater powers as English cities and

---

[67] <www.orkney.gov.uk/Council/C/our-islands-our-future---faq.htm>.

[68] Scott Macnab, 'Salmond bid to win over islanders as they demand more powers', *The Scotsman*, 14 April 2014.

[69] See Craig Brown, 'Report on Glasgow autonomy', *The Scotsman*, 7 September 2013.

greater subsidiarity, given its significance as Scotland's largest city'.[70] The Scottish Cities Alliance, made up of all seven Scottish cities, followed Glasgow's lead, pressing for 'Scottish City Deals' modelled on a system south of the Border which transfers funding and powers from central to local government in return for meeting agreed economic targets.[71]

On 9 October 2013, CoSLA launched its Commission on Strengthening Local Democracy in Scotland which, ahead of the independence referendum, is to look at reforming local government in Scotland.[72] CoSLA president David O'Neill warned the 'centralising' Scottish Government against future power grabs and called for the role of councils to be enshrined in law. Among the issues set out for the commission is the funding of local government. 'The council tax freeze has been in place since 2007 and that is going to go on until the end of this parliament which will be 2017,' said O'Neill. 'During that time, local government's ability to raise its own finances has been reduced from only 20% down to 14-ish per cent.' That, he argued, is 'not a sustainable future.'[73] Whatever happened to the SNP's local income tax bill?

CoSLA's 'vision for stronger local democracy in Scotland' speaks of 'local services that are built around local democratic choice.' It rejects the increasing 'centralisation' of services epitomised by the council tax freeze, the merger of the eight regional police forces into a single force, and the loss of powers on public health and economic development. 'Over the decades,' according to David O'Neill, 'we have moved away from the local aspect of almost everything. More and more services are being run by distant bureaucracies and often those services are being done to people rather then delivered with them.'[74] The Commission's interim report, published in April, called for a 'radical overhaul' of Scottish democracy so that more decisions over tax and spending are made locally.[75] The final report is due before the referendum in September, setting out CoSLA's position on the constitutional debate. Alison Johnstone, Green MSP for Lothian, said:

> This report strengthens the case for a new deal for local democracy in Scotland. The Commission has clearly identified that people just don't feel very engaged with local decision-making and now the challenge is for them

[70] Ibid.

[71] Magnus Gardham, 'Increased power call for cities', The Herald, 11 September 2013.

[72] <www.cosla.gov.uk/sites/default/files/documents/local_matters.pdf>.

[73] Scott Macnab, 'Warning council tax rates freeze not sustainable', The Scotsman, 7 October 2013.

[74] Ibid.

[75] Andrew Whitaker, 'Scotland most "centralised" in Europe – Cosla', The Scotsman, 24 April 2014.

to identify bold solutions. As Scotland debates whether powers should shift from London to Edinburgh we must come up with new ideas for passing more control to local communities.[76]

The Scottish Parliament's Local Government and Regeneration Committee launched its own Inquiry into the Flexibility and Autonomy of Local Government. Issues such as the legal, constitutional and funding mechanisms in place will be explored during the course of the inquiry. The committee will consider public engagement and turnout at local elections, while also comparing the structures in place in Scotland with other jurisdictions. It will also look at how remote communities, such as rural or island communities, are accommodated within local government structures. It is unfortunate that at this crucial time for local democracy CoSLA itself is under threat from within, with rebel councils leaving the organisation, and Labour split as to how CoSLA is to deal with the SNP's funding cuts.[77]

At their conference in Nairn this February, the Scottish Greens presented a Local Democracy Report, authored by Andy Wightman, calling for a move towards much smaller units of government that would be able to raise the majority of their funding locally. The aim is to emulate the kind of stronger democracy other European countries such as Denmark, Germany and the Netherlands take for granted.[78]

Scottish Labour's Devolution Commission makes much of Labour's rediscovered love of local democracy, mentioning enhanced autonomy for the island councils specifically. A pamphlet published by the Scottish Fabians also explores ways Labour ought to push for more decentralisation, while critically noting that the party had a lot to answer for its centralising tendencies in the past.[79]

Local Government's push for more powers is a welcome reminder, in the run up to the referendum, that devolution of more (or all) power to Holyrood is not the only item on the agenda, that devolution was never meant to stop at the Edinburgh Parliament,[80] and that the Parliament's founding principle of sharing power with the people has, so far, not extended to sharing power with local democracy. On the contrary, as

---

[76] <www.scottishgreens.org.uk/uncategorized/greens-praise-cosla-report-on-local-democracy/#sthash.oE9Yos61.dpuf>.

[77] Gerry Braiden, 'Cosla walkouts divide Labour', *The Herald*, 30 May 2014.

[78] <www.scottishgreens.org.uk/news/scottish-greens-launch-local-democracy-report/#sthash.oLoH9ORb.dpuf>.

[79] Trevor Davies (ed.), *Towards the Local: Devolution and democratic renewal in Scotland*, Edinburgh: Scottish Fabians, 2014.

[80] Eberhard Bort, 'Arrested Devolution', *Product*, 9 August 2013, <www.productmagazine.co.uk/index.php/ideas/P1/>.

Andy Wightman has commented: 'At the same time as Scotland is on a journey to greater autonomy as a nation, the opposite is happening at the local level.'[81] Whichever way the vote goes this year, there seems to be a growing consensus that addressing the Scottish local democracy deficit ought to be a top priority of any Scottish government.

LAND REFORM

Another issue which transcends the referendum is land reform. The Scottish Government's Land Reform Review Group published its final report on 23 May 2014, recommending 'an integrated programme of land reform measures to take forward the changes required to modernise and reform Scotland's system of land ownership.' It criticises the Scottish Government: 'At present, the Scottish Government has no integrated approach to land reform and Scotland has not had a land reform programme for ten years.'[82] As Brian Wilson commented in the *West Highland Free Press*:

> Recommendations in the report which commend themselves to common sense and early action include the reform of Scotland's compulsory purchase legislation with a public right of pre-emption; 'a more integrated and ambitious' programme of land acquisitions for forestry; a 'strategic framework to promote the continued growth of local community land ownership'; a more 'solution-focused and less risk-averse' approach to EU state aid rules; the establishment of a National Housing Corporation charged with acquiring sufficient land to meet house-building needs.[83]

In a Report published on 20 March 2014, the Scottish Affairs Committee at Westminster stressed the need for a proper Land Register as the essential building block of land reform: 'Any government which is serious about land reform needs full and clear information on existing land ownership and values made widely available.' The Committee further found that 'Scotland lags behind most comparable European countries in providing such data' and called on the Scottish and UK Governments 'to address this

---

[81] <www.andywightman.com/?p=336>.

[82] <www.scotland.gov.uk/About/Review/land-reform/events/FinalReport23May2014>.

[83] Brian Wilson, <www.andywightman.com/docs/WHFP_BW_20140530.pdf>.

as a priority.'[84] The authors who briefed the Scottish Affairs Committee spell out the problem:

> Scotland has the most concentrated pattern of private land ownership in the developed world. The degree of concentration is evident from the fact that a mere 432 landowners account for half of all Scotland's privately owned land – such land (since not much more than 10% of Scotland is in public ownership) accounting, in turn, for the bulk of the country.[85]

'Land reform is not a referendum argument,' wrote Claire Baker MSP, 'Progress can be achieved under devolution and within this parliament.'[86]

WHITE PAPER

L ast year saw the completion of the procedural issues of the referendum – we now knew which question will when be asked (Should Scotland be an independent country?, and 18 September 2014 – 'Scotland's date with destiny'[87]), who will be entitled to vote (British and EU citizens over 16 resident in Scotland – but not the 800,000 Scots living south of the Border), how much money the campaigns may spend (up to £1.5m in the 16 week 'regulated' period prior to the referendum each for Yes Scotland and Better Together) and how much the parties (£3.15m on the 'Yes' side, and £4.2m on the 'No' side),[88] and that it is all legally above board – thanks to the Referendum Bills passed by the Scottish Parliament, in accordance with paragraph 5A of Part 1 of Schedule 5 to the Scotland Act 1998 – and that it will be supervised by the Electoral Commission.

Process being dealt with, the issues at stake could take centre stage. And here we go again – our old acquaintances: EU membership, the

---

[84] 'MPs call for open books on land ownership', Commons Select Committee, 20 March 2014,<www.parliament.uk/business/committees/committees-a-z/commons-select/scottish-affairs-committee/news/land-reform-substantive/>.

[85] James Hunter, Peter Peacock, Andy Wightman and Michael Foxley, *432:50 – Towards a comprehensive land reform agenda for Scotland* (A briefing paper for the House of Commons Scottish Affairs Committee), London: House of Commons, 2013, p.5, <www.parliament.uk/documents/commons-committees/scottish-affairs/432-Land%20Reform%20Paper.pdf>.

[86] Claire Baker, 'Devolution can deliver land reform that offers fairer ownership model', *The Herald*, 23 May 2014.

[87] According to the *Scotsman* front page, 22 March 2013.

[88] Eddie Barnes, 'Scottish independence referendum: spending limits at a glance', *The Scotsman*, 30 January 2013.

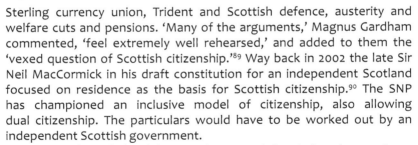

Sterling currency union, Trident and Scottish defence, austerity and welfare cuts and pensions. 'Many of the arguments,' Magnus Gardham commented, 'feel extremely well rehearsed,' and added to them the 'vexed question of Scottish citizenship.'[89] Way back in 2002 the late Sir Neil MacCormick in his draft constitution for an independent Scotland focused on residence as the basis for Scottish citizenship.[90] The SNP has championed an inclusive model of citizenship, also allowing dual citizenship. The particulars would have to be worked out by an independent Scottish government.

Despite the whole debate going round in circles, 'many Scots say they haven't enough information to make up their minds about independence.'[91] The moment everyone was waiting for (I may exaggerate) was *Scotland's Future*, the Scottish Government's 'Guide to an Independent Scotland'.[92] A curious mix between White Paper and Election Manifesto, it was published on 26 November 2013, and by March of this year more than 100,000 copies had been ordered by the public, and the cost had run to a grand total of £1.25 m.[93]

It was touted throughout the year by the SNP, and first and foremost by Nicola Sturgeon, as the 'comprehensive' document that would 'answer all the questions that people can reasonably expect.'[94] Did it live up to these expectations? James Maxwell in the *New Statesman* was impressed: 'The whole document was designed to highlight the governance-focused nature of modern Scottish nationalism – and largely succeeded in doing so.'[95] Over 10 chapters, 648 pages and 170,000 words, it includes a Q & A section where 650 questions are addressed, including the current and future shape of Scotland's finances, the SNP's defence plans, its economic and welfare policies, and Holyrood's policy options

[89] Magnus Gardham, 'The vexed question of Scottish citizenship', *The Herald*, 5 October 2013.

[90] See Jo Shaw, *Citizenship in an independent Scotland: legal status and political implications*, Edinburgh: The University of Edinburgh, School of Law (CITSEE Working Paper 2013/34), <www.citsee.ed.ac.uk/working_papers/files/CITSEE_WORKING_PAPER_2013-34.pdf>, p.6.

[91] Lesley Riddoch, 'Will the white paper on Scottish independence make any difference?', *The Guardian* (Comment is free), 25 November 2013, <www.theguardian.com/commentisfree/2013/nov/25/white-paper-scottish-independence>.

[92] Scottish Government, *Scotland's Future: Your Guide to an Independent Scotland*, Edinburgh: Scottish Government, 2013. <www.scotland.gov.uk/Publications/2013/11/9348/0>.

[93] 'White Paper cost hits £1.25m', *BBC News Scotland*, 11 March 2014, <www.bbc.co.uk/news/uk-scotland-scotland-politics-26528814>.

[94] Mandy Rhodes, 'Destiny's child: Interview with Deputy First Minister Nicola Sturgeon', *Holyrood*, 26 August 2013; see also Tom Gordon, 'Sturgeon: white paper on yes vote to be published', *The Herald*, 15 September 2013.

[95] James Maxwell, 'The Scottish independence White Paper passed the political test', *New Statesman*, 28 November 2013.

after Scotland leaves the British state. It does give a clear direction of travel.

But there are problems. A lot of the answers given are mere assertions and statements of outcomes, envisaged but not yet negotiated. That pertains to Scotland's passage from an integral part of the UK towards EU and NATO membership after independence as well as to the assurance that Scotland would be in a currency union with the rest of the UK. And, regarding policies, there are contradictions. 'An independent Scotland will not replicate the economic structure of the UK,' states the White Paper. How can that be squared with the proposed currency union based on the very similarity of productivity and employment rates north and south of the Border? Or the avowed commitment to a shared system of financial regulation, to 'fiscal discipline' and to securing 'credibility with the financial markets,' all of which are, as Maxwell argues, 'entirely in keeping with the Westminster consensus.' He sums up the White Paper's economic strategy: 'It assumes revenues generated by a dynamic free market should fund a generous welfare state. Hence the simultaneous pledges to cut corporation tax and deliver Swedish-style childcare provision.'[96]

The biggest problem of the White Paper is its assertive character. As Nicola Sturgeon explained, 'on issues where negotiation will be required, we set out the rational, reasonable and responsible case that serves the interests of both Scotland and the rest of the UK.'[97] But negotiations do not always go according to plan. And they involve two (or more) partners – who will themselves determine what is in their best interests. No caveat is allowed into the SNP government's document. Imagine David Cameron publishing a White Paper on EU reform, stating bluntly that repatriation of wholesale powers from the EU to member states was, as his experts corroborate, in every state's best interest, and that therefore the UK will succeed, within two years, in a far-reaching reform that will see intergovernmentality restored across the EU, agreed by all other 28 states because he had 'set out the rational, reasonable and responsible case that serves the interests of both' the UK and all member states and the EU itself? And that it was therefore a given that he would win an In/Out referendum in 2017. My guess is that the SNP would be among the first ridicule him for such a conceit.

Two major interventions undermined two of the main assertions of the White Paper. On the currency union, while the Bank of England Governor Mark Carney on his visit to Edinburgh at the end of January only said that Scotland would need to give up significant areas of its sovereignty and reach a watertight deal with the UK on banking, taxation and spending if a new sterling zone were to avoid the risks and instability which had

---

[96] *Ibid.*

[97] Nicola Sturgeon, 'Unveiling the White Paper', *The Scotsman*, 23 November 2013.

plagued the Euro, thus casting a degree of doubt on its workability[98] – which, as it did not rule out a currency union, was hailed by the SNP as a constructive contribution –, Chancellor George Osborne, in Edinburgh a fortnight later, said: 'The pound isn't an asset to be divided up between two countries after a break-up like a CD collection. If Scotland walks away from the UK, it walks away from the UK pound.'[99] He made this statement on the basis of advise to him made by the permanent secretary to the Treasury Sir Nick Macpherson. Robert Peston remarked on this 'significant constitutional event, as

> It is unusual for to write a public letter on any issue at all, let alone one as momentous as whether institutional arrangements should be put in place so that an autonomous Scotland could have an influence on monetary and financial-regulation policy while continuing to use the pound.'[100]

In May, he went even further, declaring that would not even be negotiations about a currency union and threatening that Scottish banknotes would cease to exist. In a series of grave warnings about the consequence of a Yes vote, the Chancellor also claimed that Scotland could run out of hard cash in the event of independence, the financial-services sector would not survive, and average mortgage payments north of the Border would increase by £5,400 per year. And he repeated: 'No ifs, no buts, there will not be a sterling zone.'[101]

He was backed up by Labour Shadow Chancellor Ed Balls and Lib Dem Chief Secretary to the Treasury Danny Alexander. [102] The SNP called it 'bluff and bluster', particularly when the edict of Osborne, Balls and Alexander was undermined by a ministerial leak that a currency union might well be possible, as a *quid pro quo* for greater flexibility by the Scottish Government on Trident.[103] Alex Salmond's response was:

---

[98] Severin Carrell, 'Mark Carney raises doubts over Scotland's plan to share the pound', *The Guardian*, 29 January 2014.

[99] Andrew Black and Aidan James, '"Yes" vote means leaving pound, says Osborne', *BBC News Scotland*, 13 February 2014, <www.bbc.co.uk/news/uk-scotland-scotland-politics-26166794>.

[100] Robert Peston, 'Analysis', *BBC News Scotland*, 13 February 2014, <www.bbc.co.uk/news/uk-scotland-scotland-politics-26166794>.

[101] David Maddox, 'Osborne: Independence will kill Scottish banknotes', *The Scotsman*, 15 May 2014.

[102] David Maddox, 'UK says no to formal currency union', *The Scotsman*, 12 February 2014.

[103] Magnus Gardham and Robbie Dinwoodie, 'No camp minister: we would do deal on currency', *The Herald*, 29 March 2014.

> This is a concerted bid by a Tory-led Westminster establishment to bully and intimidate – but their efforts to claim ownership of sterling will backfire spectacularly in terms of reaction from the people of Scotland, who know that the pound is as much theirs as it is George Osborne's. (…) The reality is that a formal currency union with a shared sterling area is overwhelmingly in the rest of the UK's economic interests following a 'Yes' vote, and the stance of any UK government will be very different the day after a 'Yes' vote to the campaign rhetoric we are hearing now.[104]

And if not? The SNP has steadfastly refused to publish a Plan B. The most likely outcome then would be 'Dollarisation', i.e. Scotland using the pound, but without a formal arrangement, the way Panama uses the Dollar.

On EU membership, the White Paper had stated that Scotland would gain membership through Article 48 of the Treaty of the European Union; it would not have to apply as a new state, and that the process could be concluded within 18 months of a 'Yes' vote. In reality, it is more likely that Article 49 will be used. 48 is for Treaty amendments, 49 for the accession of new states. The outgoing President of the European Commission, José Manuel Barroso said, when interviewed by Andrew Marr on 16 February, that it would be 'extremely difficult' for Scotland to join the EU. He reiterated that Scotland, after independence, would, 'as a new state' have to apply for membership, and that all EU member states would have to agree: 'Of course it will be extremely difficult to get the approval of all the other member states to have a new member coming from one member state:

> We have seen Spain has been opposing even the recognition of Kosovo, for instance. So it is to some extent a similar case because it's a new country and so I believe it's going to be extremely difficult, if not impossible, a new member state coming out of our countries getting the agreement of the others.[105]

The comparison with Kosovo infuriated the Scottish Government. John Swinney called the remarks 'pretty preposterous' – 'Scotland has been a member of the EU for 40 years – we're already part of the European Union.'[106]

---

[104] Andrew Black and Aidan James, see fn 98.

[105] Andrew Whitaker, '"Impossible" for Scotland to join EU, says Barroso', *The Scotsman*, 17 February 2014.

[106] *Ibid.*

As David Martin MEP remarked during the European election campaign, there is little doubt that an independent Scotland would become an EU member state – what is not so clear is what the price would be.[107] Would Scotland have to sign up to Schengen, the Euro, and would it keep the UK rebate, even while the SNP is claiming that Scotland is the 14th-richest country in the world?

Who's right? Who can be trusted? In truth, as Lesley Riddoch commented, 'all the white papers in the world won't produce more than an educated guess on key questions. So Scots in search of unimpeachable certainty may be in for a disappointment.'[108] There is no crystal ball. Who can tell how the economies of the Eurozone, of the US, Russia, China, India or Brazil will develop in the next few years? Or the price of oil? We just saw an unexpected dip in oil revenues of nearly £5bn in one year – that is a good sixth of the Scottish budget.[109] What will the situation in the Middle East look like in half a decade? Or in Ukraine, for that matter? Who knows how the UK election will go in 2015? Clear answers are impossible to give. Predictions can be made, assurances be given. As Brian Taylor pointed out, the whole referendum campaign is a game of 'doubt and assurance'[110] – the Yes campaign assuring that Scots will be better off under independence; the No campaign sowing doubt about these assurances, claiming that we are 'better together' in the UK union – a claim in turn disputed by Yes Scotland.

BENDING BOOKSHELVES

But there are other sources. Apart from countless websites which offer information and debate[111] – from the campaigns themselves to academic bodies, the media (e.g. the BBC's 'Scotland Decides'), think tanks and the third sector, but also individual and partisan domains – and some outright whacky, a plethora of books have been published on the

---

[107] Angus Roxburgh, 'Labour MEP: "independence no barrier to EU membership"', *Sunday Herald*, 18 May 2014.

[108] Lesley Riddoch, 'Will the white paper on Scottish independence make any difference?', *The Guardian* (Comment is free), 25 November 2013, <www.theguardian.com/commentisfree/2013/nov/25/white-paper-scottish-independence>.

[109] Scot McNab, 'Scotland's cash from North Sea drops by £4.4bn', *The Scotsman*, 13 March 2014.

[110] Brian Taylor, 'Contest of doubt and assurance', *BBC News Scotland*, 29 March 2014, <www.bbc.co.uk/news/uk-scotland-26800420>.

[111] To mention only the more important ones: <www.yesscotland.net>, <bettertogether. net>, <www.scottishconstitutionalfutures.org>, <www.futureukandscotland.ac.uk>, <www.futureofscotland.org>, <whatscotlandthinks.org>, bellacaledonia.org.uk>, <wingsoverscotland.com/>, <www.votenoborders.co.uk/>.

referendum, and a few more are expected before the crucial polling date – some by activists, some by journalists, and some by academics. They range from overviews, with lots of history and scene-setting, to partisan and polemical interventions.

In terms of overviews and historical perspectives, there is Andrew Marr's reissue of *The Battle for Scotland*,[112] with a new introductory chapter which is, unfortunately, marred (excuse the pun) by an unacceptable number of clangers – 'riddled with errors ... and only superficially insightful'.[113] Far grittier and Whiggishly to the point is Iain Macwhirter's *Road to Referendum*, partly based on his STV three-part series broadcast in 2013.[114] It is an eminently readable mix of history, memoir and political analysis, which reflects Macwhirter's deep-set belief in some form of Devo Max and a federal or confederal future for a looser UK union. There seems to be some controversy about a STV repeat and update in 2014 which, apparently, was planned but subsequently shelved,[115] perhaps because some perceived it, as Alex Massie had it in the *Spectator*, 'as an endorsement of the nationalist view of Scottish post-war history.'[116] David Torrance's *The Battle for Britain*, well researched and, given the author's Unionist credentials, unexpectedly unbiased, concludes that 'independence – however defined – was now a serious proposition.'[117] He followed that with a short treatise on the possibilities of a federal UK: *Britain Rebooted: Scotland in a Federal Union* tries to make the case that the UK is already quasi-federal and that the best way forward would be for Scotland to become part of a rebooted federal Union.[118]

There were two more reissues in revised and expanded form, representing very different perspectives by two Scottish historians: Christopher Whatley's *The Scots and the Union: Then and Now* and Murray Pittock's *The Road to Independence* – the former closer to a Unionist analysis, the latter on the Nationalist side.[119]

[112] Andrew Marr, *The Battle for Scotland*, London: Penguin, new ed., 2013.

[113] David Torrance, 'Weighing up the Evidence', *Scottish Review of Books*, vol.9, no.4, 2013.

[114] Iain Macwhirter, *Road to Referendum*, Glasgow: Cargo Publishing, 2013.

[115] Phil Miller, 'Has acclaimed referendum show been shelved?', *The Herald*, 19 April 2014.

[116] Alex Massie, 'Prime Time for Nationalists: STV screens a 60 minute advert for the SNP', *The Spectator* (Blog), 5 June 2013, <blogs.spectator.co.uk/alex-massie/2013/06/prime-time-for-nationalists-stv-screens-a-60-minute-advert-for-the-snp/>.

[117] David Torrance, *The Battle for Britain: Scotland and the Independence Referendum*, London: Biteback Publishing, 2013, p.341.

[118] David Torrance, *Britain Rebooted: Scotland in a Federal Union*, Edinburgh: Luath Press, 2014.

[119] Christopher Whatley, *The Scots and the Union: Then and Now*, Edinburgh: Edinburgh University Press, 2nd new edition, 2014; Murray Pittock, *The Road to Independence?: Scotland in the Balance*, London: Reaktion, 2nd new and expanded edition, 2014.

Linda Colley manages to cover a lot of ground in her slim *Acts of Union and Disunion*,[120] based on a series of fifteen short talks on BBC Radio 4. She examines the historic unions between the nations of this archipelago and concludes that, if the present Union is to have a future, it would need radical reform: the establishment of an English parliament, preferably located in the North, some sort of federation, and a written constitution. *Scotland's Choices: The Referendum and What Happens Afterwards*, by Iain McLean, Jim Gallagher and Guy Lodge, is, given the authors' well-known commitment to Devo More, an admirably even-handed exploration of the history that has led us to where we are, the intricacies of the question poised, and potential outcomes.[121]

A lively collection, documenting not only the lectures but also public debates around them, is the Royal Society of Edinburgh and the British Academy's *Enlightening the Constitutional Debate*,[122] based on a series of events in Edinburgh, London, Glasgow and Aberdeen, covering the whole spectrum from Scotland and the EU; taxation and spending; defence and international relations; the real economy; currency, banking and financial services; culture and broadcasting; borders, immigration and citizenship; science and higher education; welfare and public services; to historical, legal and constitutional issues.

Andrew Goudie's lucid and competent compendium *Scotland's Future*, written by a team of economic experts, explores, as the shorter *Scottish Independence: Weighing Up the Economics* by Gavin McCrone, the economic perspectives of constitutional change. David Torrance called the latter 'the best (and admirably brief) account of the economics of independence.'[123] Michael Keating and Malcolm Harvey look at the limited sovereignty available to a small nation in the twenty-first century in *Small Nations in a Big World*.[124]

James Mitchell's *The Scottish Question* argues that the referendum in September will actually solve very little – it may prove an important event, but it will not answer 'the Scottish Question'.[125] Gerry Hassan, too, wants to look beyond the current independence debate, and a simple Yes/No dichotomy, with his major contribution, *Caledonian Dreaming*.[126] The title of his book harks back to David Greig's *Caledonia Dreaming*, a play written

[120] Linda Colley, *Acts of Union and Disunion*, London: Profile Books, 2013.

[121] Iain McLean, Jim Gallagher and Guy Lodge, *Scotland's Choices: The Referendum and What Happens Afterwards*, Edinburgh: Edinburgh University Press, 2013.

[122] <www.royalsoced.org.uk/cms/files/events/reports/2013-2014/The%20Book.pdf>.

[123] David Torrance, see fn 112.

[124] Michael Keating and Malcolm Harvey, *Small Nations in a Big World: What Scotland Can Learn*, Edinburgh: Luath Press, 2014.

[125] James Mitchell, *The Scottish Question*, Oxford: Oxford University Press, 2014.

[126] Gerry Hassan, *Caledonian Dreaming: The Quest for a Different Scotland*, Edinburgh: Luath Press, 2014.

around the 1997 UK election and the prospect of Devolution, but makes do without the Sean Connery running gag. His main thesis, expounded in countless articles as well as in this tome, is that the referendum changes what is possible, regardless of its outcome. Yet, he fears that not enough of the tougher questions are addressed, and that an emphasis on continuity could hamper Scottish democracy with the British-style dysfunctional qualities that a Yes vote was supposed to liberate us from. Mitchell and Hassan have also edited a collection of essays curiously titled *After Independence*, another attempt by a 'diverse assembly' of contributors at giving pointers beyond 18 September, arguing that constitutional change, as the editors see it, is 'less an end in itself but ... something that has the potential, but we stress only the potential, to offer new opportunities but will also present new challenges.'[127]

The late Stephen Maxwell's *The Case for Left Wing Nationalism*, a collection of essays ranging over four decades, edited by his son Jamie, is a challenge to the often repeated lazy assumptions about Scotland's 'social-democratic consensus' and its alleged egalitarianism, as amply demonstrated by an often cited quote ffrom the essay which gives the collection its title, written in 1981:

> The Edinburgh advocate in his New Town Flat and the Glasgow bus driver in a Red Road high rise may share a sentimental attachment to Scotland on the football field or athletics track and feel a similar irritation when 'England' is used for 'Britain' by TV newsreaders. But in their everyday concerns – their jobs, their incomes, their hopes for their children, their anxieties about retirement, the quality of their housing, their health – they might as well live in different countries. When Nationalists talk of Scotland the nation they must expect the questions: whose nation, what kind of Scotland?[128]

For Maxwell, as we also know from his *Arguing for Independence: Evidence, Risks and the Wicked Issues*,[129] Scottish independence had to be about more than flag-waving, it had to embrace social justice and be a force for peace in the world.

Class, Nation and Socialism: The Red Paper on Scotland 2014, a collection echoing the famous Gordon Brown-edited *Red Paper on Scotland* of 1975,

---

[127] Gerry Hassan and James Mitchell (eds), *After Independence*, Edinburgh: Luath Press, 2013, p.2.

[128] Stephen Maxwell, *The Case for Left Wing Nationalism: Essays and Articles*, ed. by Jamie Maxwell, Edinburgh: Luath Press, 2013.

[129] Stephen Maxwell, *Arguing for Independence: Evidence, Risks and the Wicked Issues*, Edinburgh: Luath Press, 2012.

is edited by Pauline Bryan and Tommy Kane, who give the direction of the book in their introduction: 'What is on offer in this referendum would break the class unity of working people across the nations of Britain without breaking the chains of economic control that bind them.'[130] Most authors argue for working-class solidarity and left-wing politics for the whole of the UK. Likewise, *Scotland's Road to Socialism: Time to Choose*, edited by Gregor Gall, sounds a similar trumpet call, criticising the short-comings of the SNP's 'social democracy', even questioning whether the SNP's economic prospectus adds up to, in Margaret and Jim Cuthbert's words, 'any meaningful concept of independence'. Also as an intervention in the referendum debate, the Child Poverty Action Group published *Poverty in Scotland*, an indictment of the impact of austerity policies and how they relate to the constitutional debate.[131]

Democracy Max: A Vision for a Good Scottish Democracy sums up the intermediate results of an ongoing independent inquiry under the aegis of the Electoral Reform Society Scotland, involving deliberative discussions, a 'People's Gathering' and a series of round tables.[132] Lesley Riddoch's *Blossom*, with its emphasis on participatory democracy at local and regional level, social justice, sustainable economic growth and co-operative partnership, argues that the constitutional debate is in danger of putting the cart before the horse. Do we not first need to know what kind of Scotland we want, before we address the question of what constitutional framework will allow us to get there? 'A change of constitutional control will not be enough to transform Scotland.'[133] In the tradition of a Scottish flyting is the two-hander by and Alan Cochrane, *Scottish Independence: Yes/No*,[134] in which the *Scotsman* journalist and former SNP-candidate George Kerevan and the *Daily Telegraph*'s Scottish editor and former SNP-voter (!) cross pens.

I share Paul Salveson's disappointment in Jim Sillars' *In Place of Fear II: A Socialist Programme*.[135] He called it 'the political equivalent of the grim grey Scottish council houses which still disfigure much of central belt Scotland' and contrasted it with *Yes: The Radical Case for Scottish*

[130] Pauline Bryan and Tommy Kane (eds), *Class, Nation and Socialism: The Red Paper on Scotland 2014*, Glasgow: Glasgow Caledonian University Archives, 2013.

[131] John H McKendrick, Gerry Mooney, John Dickie, Gill Scott and Peter Kelly (eds), *Poverty in Scotland: The independence referendum and beyond*, London: Child Poverty Action Group, 2014.

[132] Electoral Reform Society Scotland, *Democracy Max: A Vision for a Good Scottish Democracy*, Edinburgh: Electoral Reform Society Scotland, 2013.

[133] Lesley Riddoch, *Blossom: What Scotland Needs to Flourish*, Edinburgh: Luath Press, 2013, p.9.

[134] George Kerevan and Alan Cochrane, *Scottish Independence: Yes/No*, London: The History Press, 2014.

[135] Jim Sillars, *In Place of Fear II: A Socialist Programme*, Glasgow: Vagabond Voices, 2014.

Independence, by James Foley and Pete Ramand,[136] which 'presents a case for independence from the left but its socialism is a more co-operative and decentralised one than that of Jim Sillars.'[137] And I have to declare an interest in the forthcoming Jimmy Reid Foundation collection of essays on the *Common Weal*, as I have been involved in the process. Robin McAlpine has also explained the outlines of the 'Common Weal' approach in a contribution to Chris Harvie's Festschrift *View from Zollernblick*.[138]

Robert Crawford follows the theme of the Battle of Bannockburn, the 700th anniversary of which is commemorated this year, through Scottish literature and culture in *Bannockburns*[139] – an ever so slightly lopsided view which gives relative short shrift to 'unionist' writers, while writers with nationalist sympathies are thoroughly embraced. It is, expectedly, very good on Burns, but not so good at explaining the flourishing Scottish Enlightenment (under the dreaded Union) and the fact that never before or after were more monuments erected in the memory of Robert the Bruce than in nineteenth-century 'unionist nationalist' Scotland. Alexander Moffat and Alan Riach claim in *Arts of Independence* that 'all arts work for independence.'[140] The arts in Scotland, they argue, 'are more than essential in the argument for an independent Scotland':

> They are preeminent. Economic, political and social questions need to be asked and answered but without the cultural argument, they are merely the mechanics. (...) Cool, reasoned arguments are required but we want more than that. We want the passion and emotional investment that gives us the courage of our dispositions.[141]

So much for the civic, 'governance-focused nature of modern Scottish nationalism'. Another polemic we can look forward to is Alasdair Gray's wee book on the case for Scottish independence, *Independence: An*

---

[136] James Foley and Pete Ramand, *Yes: The Radical Case for Scottish Independence*, London: Pluto Press, 2014.

[137] Paul Salveson, *The Northern Weekly Salvo*, no.141, 20 April 2014, <www.paulsalveson.org.uk/2014/04/20/illustrated-weekly-salvo-141/>.

[138] Robin McAlpine, 'Common Weal and a State of Disorientation', in Eberhard Bort (ed.), *View from Zollernblick: Regional Perspectives in Europe* (A Festschrift for Christopher Harvie), Ochtertyre: Grace Note Publications, 2013, pp. 75-88.

[139] Robert Crawford, *Bannockburns: Scottish Independence and Literary Imagination, 1314-2014*, Edinburgh: Edinburgh University Press, 2014.

[140] Alexander Moffat and Alan Riach, *Arts of Independence for an Independent Scotland: The cultural argument and why it matters most*, Edinburgh: Luath Press, 2014, p.7.

[141] *Ibid.*, p.11.

Argument for Home Rule, which is promised for July.[142] And Gordon Brown will add his pennyworth in book form with *My Scotland: Our Britain*, advising his countryfolk to stick with the Union. 'The best future for Scots is not to leave Britain,' he argues in a very personal account, 'but to continue to shape it.'[143]

THE GAP NARROWS

Was it that Scots have read all these books – and ploughed through the White Paper – that the opinion polls started to move around the turn of the year? Over the past years, the constitutional preferences of the Scots had been very stable, despite all kinds of events and shocks to the political system, from the advent of the Parliament through various forms of government (coalition, minority, majority), the breakthrough of the SNP in 2007, trumped by the absolute majority of 2011, the financial crash, the change of government at Westminster, the 'Edinburgh Agreement' on the referendum... you name it, it did not significantly impact on the polling figures. The trend was, if anything, regressive. And, surprisingly, young people seemed to be even less in favour of independence. An online poll in May 2014 showed that almost two-thirds of Scots aged 16 and 17 were worried about the economic future of Scotland.[144]

But the polls did begin to change since late last year. The gap between Yes and No narrowed. While the poll of polls of 2012 and 2013 were nigh identical – 59: 41 and 60 : 40 respectively, the poll of polls for the first quarter of 2014 narrowed to 56 : 44.[145] An ICM poll conducted on 16 April for *Scotland on Sunday* and published by the paper on Easter Sunday had the gap down to three percentage points[146] – the best result recorded for the Yes side up to that point, leaving aside one Panelbase poll of last autumn which had Yes narrowly in front but was widely criticised for using lead-in questions.[147] Was this the turning point? But in May the No

[142] Alasdair Gray, *Independence: An Argument for Home Rule*, Edinburgh: Canongate, 2014.

[143] Gordon Brown, *My Scotland, Our Britain: A Future Worth Sharing*, London: Simon and Schuster UK, 2014.

[144] Michael Settle, 'Referendum poll reveals teenagers fear for the economy', *The Herald*, 19 May 2014.

[145] John Curtice, 'Depending on the pollster, it looks like a photo finish', *The Independent*, 25 April 2014.

[146] Tom Peterkin, 'Referendum race on knife edge as No support slides', *Scotland on Sunday*, 20 April 2014.

[147] See John Curtice, 'SNP/Panelbase Poll Shows One Point Yes Lead', 2 September 2013, <blog.whatscotlandthinks.org/2013/09/snppanelbase-poll-shows-one-point-yes-lead/>.

side established an 8 to 14% lead again, and after the Euro elections the picture resembled that of last year again.[148]

Graph 2: Scottish Independence Referendum Polls

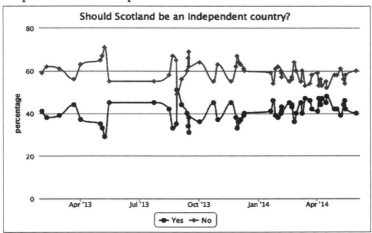

[including ICM for *Scotland on Sunday* conducted on 16 April – published on 20 April, and up to 1 June] [149]

Memories of 2011 were conjured up. Had not the SNP also been way behind until a few weeks before the Scottish Parliament election, and eventually swept the board on polling day? Are we in for a repeat of that astonishing feat? This year, of course, the Scots will not be voting for a government they can vote out of office four or five years later. Simple analogies might therefore be misplaced. The polling news jolted politicians and media commentators south of the border into the shock realisation that they may have been too complacent in their assumption that the Scots would vote No. There was, suddenly, an awareness that 'once things change they can change very fast, and in ways for which few of us are in any way prepared.'[150] A further boost for the Yes camp came when the *Sunday Herald* declared its support for independence on its front page – the first Scottish newspaper to do so. It may only have

---

[148] Stephen Daisley, 'STV referendum poll shows swing to Yes but No still in the lead', *STV News*, 2 June 2014, <news.stv.tv/scotland-decides/news/277620-ipsos-mori-poll-for-stv-shows-gap-between-yes-and-no-closing/>.

[149] <whatscotlandthinks.org/questions/should-scotland-be-an-independent-country-1#line>.

[150] Martin Kettle, 'The UK is on shifting sands. We cannot assume survival', *The Guardian*, 17 April 2014.

a circulation of 25,000, but its online presence has continuously grown over the past years.[151]

The Better Together campaign seemed to be in crisis. Was it too negative?[152] Were the interventions of coalition politicians on day trips to Scotland counter productive? Toffs telling Scots they cannot have the pound, that their pensions are in danger, that energy prices will rise and defence jobs go if they dared to vote Yes – was the gut reaction to those pronouncements a swing towards Yes? 'Salmond is a brilliant late-stage campaigner,' the *Spectator* editor Fraser Nelson said in an interview, 'and I absolutely think that it [independence] could happen.' He added, from his London perspective:

> A lot of people down here underestimate how the SNP activists have waited their whole lives for this – this is not just another election for them. The battle is fought in ways they just don't understand down here. The unionists have deployed their nuclear weapons – EU membership and the pound – and all this has served just to increase nationalist support. These were the biggest cards the unionists have to play, they played them early, and they seem to have backfired. Nobody in the Better Together campaign has worked out how to win the argument yet.[153]

'If, by some chance, the polls continue to narrow, and the Yes vote prevails come September,' Joyce McMillan concluded acerbically,

> It will be that indictment that will be carved on the gravestones of the current generation of Labour, Conservative and Liberal Democrat politicians: that in their intellectual laziness, their institutional complacency and their craven compliance with an increasingly unjust and reactionary political climate, they betrayed the finest aspects of the union they claim to defend and helped to consign it to the dustbin of history, perhaps well before its time.[154]

---

[151] Mure Dickie, 'Sunday Herald backs campaign for Scottish independence', *Financial Times*, 5 May 2014.

[152] Michael Settle, 'Darling under pressure over poll predictions', *The Herald*, 22 April 2014.

[153] Decca Aitkenhead, '"I'd put £1,000 on Ed to win"', Interview with Fraser Nelson', *The Guardian*, 19 April 2014.

[154] Joyce McMillan, 'Is the No camp killing the Union?', *The Scotsman*, 18 April 2014.

Against that backdrop, the Scottish parties embarked on their Spring conferences in March and April.

SPRING CONFERENCES

The Scottish Conservatives kicked off Scotland's spring party conference season with a passionate appeal by Ruth Davidson to stay 'better together' in the Union. The party also united on the need to devolve more powers to the Scottish Parliament.[155] Its devolution proposal would only be published in May, but Tory MEP Struan Stevenson went on record saying that Scotland should be raising all the money it spends to stop the 'drift to independence'.[156]

The Scottish Labour conference in Perth a week later was initially threatened by a boycott from Labour MPs over the Devolution Commission's proposals to devolve income tax to Holyrood.[157] But a watered-down plan, allowing Holyrood to raise about 40% of its own revenues, avoided that scenario. A year earlier, 'the party had been palpably divided – with sundry MPs criticising a proposal to devolve the whole of income tax as tantamount to independence by the back door. This year in Perth the revised plan was endorsed by the conference unanimously.'[158] But will it be enough to persuade voters who want a stronger parliament? Could the Labour Party be overtaken by the Tory proposals for further devolution, and especially further tax powers to be announced in May by the Conservatives' Strathclyde Commission?

The acceptance of the compromise was prepared in a speech Gordon Brown made in Glasgow in advance of the conference. In it, he backed substantial, but not full fiscal powers for Holyrood, but also called for a new constitutional framework to set out the purpose of the UK as pooling and sharing resources, a constitutional guarantee of the permanence of the Scottish Parliament, the replacement of the Barnett formula with a new tax-sharing agreement and extra powers for Holyrood.[159] That

---

[155] Mure Dickie, 'Scottish Conservatives unite on need for more devolution', *Financial Times*, 17 March 2014.

[156] Andrew Black, 'Scottish Tory conference: MEP Struan Stevenson makes more fiscal powers call', *BBC News Scotland*, 16 March 2014, <www.bbc.co.uk/news/uk-scotland-scotland-politics-26601300>.

[157] Kate Devlin, 'Labour MPs plan conference boycott amid income tax row', *The Herald*, 6 February 2014.

[158] Brian Taylor, 'Labour tries to blend principle and pragmatism', *BBC News Scotland*, 21 March 2014, <www.bbc.co.uk/news/uk-scotland-26690123>.

[159] Severin Carrell, 'Gordon Brown calls for Scotland to have right to set tax and welfare policies', *The Guardian*, 10 March 2014.

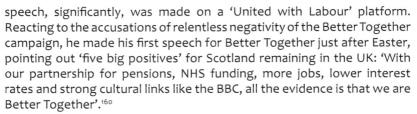

speech, significantly, was made on a 'United with Labour' platform. Reacting to the accusations of relentless negativity of the Better Together campaign, he made his first speech for Better Together just after Easter, pointing out 'five big positives' for Scotland remaining in the UK: 'With our partnership for pensions, NHS funding, more jobs, lower interest rates and strong cultural links like the BBC, all the evidence is that we are Better Together'.[160]

Johann Lamont's conference speech tried hard to wrest the social-democratic high ground from the SNP. 'Seven years of nationalism in Scotland – and not one policy which distributes wealth from rich to poor – in fact the opposite.' She claimed: 'Those in the richest houses saving most. Those with the most getting more. Those with the least getting less. That isn't just a betrayal of social justice – it is a betrayal of everything we believe Scotland stands for.'[161] When Ed Miliband hit the Euro election campaign trail in Dundee in May, he promised 'first year, first term, more powers' – if he became Prime Minister in 2015. A new Scotland act would transfer 40% of tax-raising powers to Scotland.[162]

At the end of March, the Scottish Liberal Democrats tried to spread 'a little constitutional sunshine' in Aberdeen. Willie Rennie, clearly concerned about the tone of the debate over independence, told his party to 'ack-cen-tu-ate' the positive.[163] He also changed his position on the so-called Bedroom Tax, now calling for it to be scrapped, with Nick Clegg indicating that that could be facilitated for Scotland.[164] Nick Clegg also spoke of an 'ever hardening consensus' between the Lib Dems, Labour and the Conservatives on greater devolution to Scotland:

> A Scottish parliament that doesn't just spend the cheque handed over from Westminster, but which has the power to raise the majority of its budget too – creating greater accountability and the power to affect radical change here in Scotland. Where the UK parties have promised powers to Scotland, we have worked together and delivered. And if

---

[160] Magnus Gardham, 'Brown's top five positive reasons to stay in the UK', *The Herald*, 23 April 2014.

[161] Andrew Black, 'Scottish Labour Party conference: Lamont lambasts SNP's pro-Yes campaign', *BBC News Scotland*, 22 March 2014, <www.bbc.co.uk/news/uk-scotland-scotland-politics-26692674>.

[162] Torcuil Crichton, 'Vote no and I'll deliver Home Rule', *Daily Record*, 9 May 2014.
163 Peter McMahon, '"Sunshine Strategy" at Scottish Lib Dem conference' (Blog), *ITV Border*, 28 March 2014, <www.itv.com/news/border/2014-03-28/sunshine-strategy-at-scottish-lib-dem-conference/>.

[164] Robbie Dinwoodie, 'Clegg in promise to tackle bedroom tax cap', *The Herald*, 29 March 2014.

Scotland makes the positive choice this September to stick with the UK family, we will come together again.[165]

With taxation powers amounting to 40 to 50% of Scotland's revenue – will the SNP still argue that Holyrood is a 'pocket-money parliament', as they did when the Calman proposals were introduced?[166]

The SNP conference in April, celebrating the party's 80th birthday and buoyed by the improving polls for the referendum and being very comfortably ahead in Holyrood polls,[167] was more akin to a rally than a traditional party conference. Besides attacking the Better Together campaign for its negativity (hot on the heels of Lord Robertson's remarks that a Yes vote would have 'cataclysmic' consequences and be welcomed by the global 'forces of darkness'[168]) – Alex Salmond branded it 'the most miserable, negative, depressing and thoroughly boring' campaign in modern times[169] – the central theme of the SNP's gathering in Perth was the wooing of Labour voters, urging them to 'reclaim their party' by voting Yes in the referendum.[170] Salmond referred to a 'Labour Party leadership that has totally lost its way, that has lost touch with the values of Labour voters.'[171] 'Independence will be good for Scottish Labour,' he said: 'The Labour Party, freed from Westminster control, will have the chance to return to its core values: many of which we in this party agree with and share.'[172]

But both Nicola Sturgeon and Alex Salmond also targeted women, as the polls show that among them the Yes campaign is lagging behind. Among Scottish business women, 70% intend to vote No in the

[165] Andrew Black, 'Scottish Lib Dem conference: Clegg to outline Union case', BBC News Scotland, 28 March 2014, <www.bbc.co.uk/news/uk-scotland-scotland-politics-26751361>.

[166] Andrew Grice, 'Scottish Parliament may win greater tax powers', The Independent, 25 November 2009.

[167] Robbie Dinwoodie, 'No mid-term blues as SNP stay ahead in Holyrood poll', The Herald, 1 January 2014.

[168] Scott Macnab, 'Scottish independence "cataclysmic" – Robertson', The Scotsman, 9 April 2014.

[169] Andrew Black, 'SNP conference: Salmond attacks "negative and depressing" No campaign', BBC News Scotland, 12 April 2014, <www.bbc.co.uk/news/uk-scotland-scotland-politics-26997887>.

[170] David Clegg, 'Independence referendum: Nicola Sturgeon urges Labour supporters to 'reclaim' their party by backing Yes campaign', Daily Record, 11 April 2014.

[171] Kieran Andrews, 'SNP spring conference: Nicola Sturgeon woos Labour voters for the "last mile of our journey"', The Courier, 12 April 2014.

[172] Peter Lynch, 'Salmond courts women and Labour voters – and keeps a close eye on Ukip', The Conversation, 14 April 2014, <theconversation.com/salmond-courts-women-and-labour-voters-and-keeps-a-close-eye-on-ukip-25569>.

forthcoming referendum.[173] Sturgeon pledged not only increased child benefits, but also to undo 'the worst impacts' of UK Government welfare reforms, particularly those affecting women, should Scotland vote for independence. And Alex Salmond promoted Angela Constance and Shona Robison, two of his female ministers, to cabinet rank so that 40% of his Cabinet are now female.[174]

PARLIAMENTARY INTERLUDE

Ever since the din over the referendum began to dominate the political and media discourse in 2012, commentators have repeatedly warned that Scotland's day-to-day politics did not get the attention, coverage and scrutiny they deserve. Has Johann Lamont perhaps been ill-advised to go for independence-related questions Thursday after Thursday, instead of holding Alex Salmond to account over the running of Scottish governance?

This lack of accountability, it was feared, could be exacerbated by the absolute majority of the SNP at Holyrood. In May, there were claims that the inbuilt SNP majority in Holyrood committees was 'blocking scrutiny'.[175] Accusations have ranged from SNP committee members attempting to suppress a public petition calling for independence referendums for Orkney, Shetland and the Western Isles to withdrawing an expert's invitation to give evidence in the Finance Committee after he submitted a report that contradicted government claims about an independent Scotland's membership of the EU. Then a row broke out at the Public Audit Committee, with opposition MSPs taking the unprecedented move of publishing a 'minority' version of an official report, after SNP members had blocked criticism of how the merger of eight regional forces into Police Scotland in 2013 had been handled.[176]

The biggest stushie concerned the European Committee's report on Scotland's EU membership. SNP committee members used their majority to add extra evidence into the final report supporting Alex Salmond's claim that Scotland could retain EU membership under 'Article 48' – a position contested by Westminster. SNP members also wanted to add extra quotations from committee witnesses about how being a small state in the EU is advantageous. Many of these amendments were

---

[173] Scott Wright, 'Businesswomen go for no vote', *The Herald*, 14 May 2014.

[174] Tom Gordon, 'Rallying cry: Salmond inspires troops at last SNP conference before referendum', *Sunday Herald*, 13 April 2014.

[175] Magnus Gardham, 'Claims SNP are blocking scrutiny', *The Herald*, 15 May 2014.

[176] Chris Marshall, 'SNP "tried to suppress damning dossier on Single Police Force"', *The Scotsman*, 14 May 2014.

opposed by the three opposition MSPs on the committee, but overruled by the four SNP members and added nonetheless. Labour and Tory MSPs also wanted to publish the original draft of the report as a minority report but were blocked from doing so by the SNP members, who used their majority to stonewall the move. The opposition MSPs said they were concerned about a 'cult' of 'obedience and slavishness' forming around the SNP which was undermining the Scottish Parliament.[177]

Following renewed concerns about an A&E waiting time crisis, with the number of patients waiting for four hours or more for emergency care almost trebling from 36,000 in 2009 to 104,000 last year, the *Daily Record* titled 'Referendum is bad for nation's health'.[178] A week later, Health Secretary Alex Neil became only the third cabinet member in Holyrood history to face a no-confidence vote in the Scottish Parliament, over a controversial reorganisation of acute mental health services in his constituency. Johann Lamont claimed he had 'deceived' Parliament in 2012 by telling MSPs he would not take part in the decision-making, when he had in fact already communicated his decision to the health board. Four times she called on the First Minister to 'sack' the Health Secretary – four times the answer was 'No'.[179] After a bad-tempered debate, in which Alex Neil was accused of an 'abuse of power compounded by misinforming parliament', the SNP used its majority in the first vote of no confidence in a minister at the Scottish Parliament for 13 years. It was defeated by a margin of 67 to 57, with all opposition parties backing the motion lodged by Labour.[180]

That out of the way, we could return to the referendum.

TOO CLOSE TO CALL

At the time of writing, in May, some four months before the referendum, the outcome seems, as the poll at Easter showed, too close to call. Doubtless, there will me many more twists and turns until polling day. More organisations and celebrities will declare their support for one or the other side. The CBI got into considerable trouble when it registered with the No campaign, lost 18 of its member organisations, and

[177] Ben Riley-Smith, 'SNP uses majority to stifle criticism of Alex Salmond's EU membership stance', *The Daily Telegraph*, 13 May 2014.

[178] David Clegg, 'Referendum is bad for nation's health', *Daily Record*, 9 May 2014.

[179] Magnus Gardham, 'Salmond rejects calls to fire Neil over emails row', *The Herald*, 16 May 2014.

[180] Andrew Whitaker, 'SNP majority saves Neil in vote of no confidence', *The Scotsman*, 21 May 2014.

then performed an embarrassing U-turn.[181] Standard Life, the Weir Group and others who have questioned independence, received short shrift from the SNP – bluster and bluff, had they not been against devolution as well? Academics have come out for Yes – and for No.[182]

Less of a backlash was experienced by David Bowie who urged the Scots to stay with the UK.[183] Nor does coming out for No seem to have harmed Kermit the Frog's popularity.[184] J K Rowling, Alex Ferguson, James McMillan and Robin Harper are other supporters of Better Together. Billy Connolly and Andy Murray have vowed to keep shtum on the issue. A small army of writers and artists – many of them as part of the National Collective – are campaigning on the Yes-side, from Elaine C Smith, Eddie Reader and Irvine Welsh to Alasdair Gray, Sean Connery and James Robertson, Allan Cumming, Brian Cox and Liz Lochhead. It is, of course, questionable how big an effect all these celebrity endorsements do actually have?

What we, apparently, will not see is a TV debate between Alex Salmond and David Cameron. The SNP has repeatedly called for such an occasion, but it has always been rejected by No. 10. Last autumn, Cameron wrote to Salmond declining the invite. The referendum was for the Scots to decide – he should debate with the leader of the Better Together campaign, Alistair Darling. But the SNP renewed its pressure at the beginning of May when it transpired that Cameron was willing to publicly debate with Nigel Farage on TV. Nicola Sturgeon called it 'astonishing that David Cameron is happy to have a head-to-head debate with Nigel Farage, whose party doesn't have a single seat in the House of Commons, but continues to run scared of a debate on the future of Scotland with First Minister Alex Salmond.'[185]

But we have a new BBC programme: *Scotland 2014* replaced *Newsnight Scotland* in the last week of May. Gone the abrupt cuts from Paxman to Brewer. But the new flagship news programme, going head to head with STV's *Scotland Tonight*, sank to just 22,000 viewers in the first week, having started with an audience of 89,000. Presented by former Channel 4 News presenter and correspondent Sarah Smith, the daughter of John

[181] Terry Murden, 'CBI does U-turn over No vote sign-up', *The Scotsman*, 26 April 2014.

[182] Kate Devlin, 'Academics divided on impact of Yes vote', *The Herald*, 6 May 2014.

[183] Conal Urquhart, '"Scotland, stay with us" – David Bowie weighs into independence debate at Brits', *The Guardian*, 20 February 2014.

[184] Kate Devlin, 'Kermit the Frog joins Bowie in opposing independence', *The Herald*, 25 March 2014.

[185] David Maddox, 'Cameron "will face Farage but not Salmond"', *The Scotsman*, 5 May 2014.

Smith, it was billed as 'cheeky and fun', but was described as 'bland' and met with a lukewarm reception.[186]

This comes hot on the heels of a report by Professor John Robertson, of the School of Creative and Cultural Industries at the University of West Scotland, which claimed there was a pro-union bias on BBC Radio Scotland's *Good Morning Scotland*.

> Robertson, who favours independence, said a study of the programme throughout April 2014 suggested it was 'balanced in crude numerical terms but, in every other respect, unfair to the "yes" campaign and favouring the "Better Together" campaign'.[187]

Criticism of the BBC's news coverage in Scotland was fuelled further after it was revealed longstanding *Good Morning Scotland* radio host Gary Robertson was being dropped. Robertson's exit, believed to be part of cost-cutting measures at the corporation, comes after *Today* presenter Jim Naughtie joined the Good Morning Scotland team in the runup to the independence vote on 18 September.

Labour's poll lead in the UK is slim – a recent poll had them even behind.[188] Just before the Euro elections, Labour plummeted to a four-year low in a Guardian/ISM poll. For the first time in two years, the Conservative were in the lead (33 to 31).[189] And yet, extrapolated from the English council elections, the BBC projection was that Labour would be just 4 seats short of a majority in the House of Commons in 2015. If Scotland voted Yes – and the Scottish MPs were eliminated – Labour would still be the strongest party, now 17 seats short of an overall majority. According to a survey conducted by Lord Ashcroft of 26,000 voters in marginal seats, Labour was 'on course to win next year's general election because the UK Independence Party is hitting the Tory vote in key marginal constituencies,' which 'would leave Labour with a healthy majority in Parliament, potentially as large as 70 or 80 MPs.'[190]

The Tories hope that the economic recovery will trump the 'cost of living crisis', and nearly two-thirds of UK voters do not see Ed Miliband as

[186] Daniel Sanderson, 'Viewers vote with remotes against BBC's referendum show', *The Herald*, 31 May 2014.

[187] John Plunkett, 'BBC's Scottish independence coverage accused of pro-union bias', The Guardian, 2 June 2014.

[188] Tom Clark, 'Tories on top as Labour poll rating sinks to four-year low', *The Guardian*, 13 May 2014.

[189] *Ibid.*

[190] Peter Dominiczak, 'Lord Ashcroft poll: Labour on course to win general election', *The Sunday Telegraph*, 25 May 2014.

a PM in waiting.[191] The prospect of a Tory government in 2015 is, according to an ICM survey for *The Scotsman*, boosting the Yes vote to the tune of five per cent, tempting more Labour voters to back independence.[192]

If the vote on 18 September is narrow, the focus could be on particular groups of voters. How about the young? By May, already 98,000 (or 80%) had registered to vote, and a majority of them looked likely to vote No.[193] Jan Eichhorn summarised survey results from 2013:

> Young people in Scotland do not appear to be any less interested in politics than the overall population, though they are much less likely to identify with a political party. Turnout in the referendum amongst this group looks set to be high, albeit perhaps somewhat lower than amongst eligible voters in general. In contrast, support for independence itself seems set to be relatively low, because young people are more likely to have a reasonably strong sense of British identity and more likely to be worried about the practical consequences of independence.[194]

Or the 450,000 English-born living in Scotland?[195] Some 66% of them said, according to a Panelbase poll, that they would vote against independence.[196] Or the deprived? More than 700,000.[197] They are more favourably disposed towards independence. But they are also the least likely to use their vote. Or the over 160,000 European citizens living in Scotland?[198] Or immigrant communities? Above all, turnout is expected to reach 70, perhaps 80% – 20 or even 30% more than in Holyrood elections.[199] Who are these extra voters? What will they vote for?

---

[191] Sam Coates, 'Miliband is not fit for No 10, say most voters', *The Times*, 26 March 2014.

[192] Andrew Whitaker, 'Scots "are driven to vote Yes by Tory success"', *The Scotsman*, 21 April 2014.

[193] Michael Settle, 'Referendum poll reveals teenagers fear for the economy', *The Herald*, 19 May 2014.

[194] Jan Eichhorn, 'Will 16 and 17 year olds make a difference in the referendum?' Edinburgh: ScotCen Social Research, November 2013, <www.scotcen.org.uk/media/205540/131129_will-16-and-17-years-olds-make-a-difference.pdf>.

[195] Iain Macwhirter, 'To make No a positive, first resolve the English Question', *The Herald*, 11 July 2013.

[196] Michael Settle, 'Referendum poll reveals teenagers fear for the economy', *The Herald*, 19 May 2014.

[197] Scottish Index of Multiple Deprivation 2012, <simd.opendatascotland.org/using>.

[198] Scottish Government, *Scotland in the European Union*, Edinburgh: Scottish Government, 2013, <www.scotland.gov.uk/Resource/0043/00439166.pdf>, p.2.

[199] Alan Wilson, 'Nicola Sturgeon optimistic of high turnout for independence vote', *The Courier*, 3 December 2013.

EURO ELECTION EARTHQUAKE

On 22 May, the European Parliament elections did again not generate a huge turnout (33% in Scotland), but a trifle more excitement than usually. As polling day approached, it seemed increasingly likely that Ukip might snatch one of the six Scottish seats. With the help of 'Madame Ecosse' Winnie Ewing, Alex Salmond pitched it as a contest between the SNP gaining a third seat and Ukip getting a foothold in Scotland.[200] That strategy may have backfired, as his opponents suggested afterwards.[201] While Salmond laid the blame on the doorstep of the media, particularly the BBC for 'beaming' Farage into every household.[202] He has a point – one got the impression that the Ukip leader had a season ticket for *The Daily Politics*, *Question Time* and *This Week*. John Curtice summed it up:

> The SNP had hoped that UKIP success in England and Wales would be accompanied by the party's failure to win a seat in Scotland. Symbolically there seemed no better way of demonstrating that the attitudes and values of people in Scotland are very different from those of their neighbours south of the border. Alas the plan went awry when UKIP managed to win a seat north of the border – ironically, because the SNP themselves were two or three points short of what was needed to keep UKIP out.[203]

The 29% for the SNP meant that, even after seven years of government, the party again topped the poll (with a miniscule minus of 0.1%); Labour came second with 25.9% (a plus of 5.1%). Both retained their two seats: Ian Hudghton and Alyn Smith for the SNP, David Martin and Cathrine Stihler for Scottish Labour. The Conservatives gained slightly (17.2%, up by 0.4%) and held their seat, Ian Duncan replacing Struan Stevenson who had not stood in this election. Ukip came fourth, with 10.5%, up by 5.2%, which secured the sixth Scottish seat for David Coburn. The Scottish Greens reached 8.1% (up slightly by 0.8%). The Scottish Liberal Democrats met another Waterloo. Their 7.1% (a minus of 4.4%) meant that George Lyon lost his seat. South of the border, they retained only 1 (of formerly

---

200 Tom Peterkin, 'Voting SNP keeps Ukip out of Scotland, urges Ewing', *The Scotsman*, 21 May 2014.

201 Simon Johnson, 'Scottish Ukip MEP thanks Alex Salmond for breakthrough', *The Daily Telegraph*, 26 May 2014.

202 David Torrance, 'Ukip catch SNP by surprise', *The Scotsman*, 26 May 2014.

203 John Curtice, 'Implications of the Euro Result in Scotland', What Scotland Thinks, 27 May 2014, <blog.whatscotlandthinks.org/2014/05/implications-of-the-euro-result-in-scotland/>.

10) MEPs – and there were calls for Nick Clegg's resignation. Although Labour gained 9% (and 7 seats) compared to 2009, the leadership's tactic of not attacking Ukip and the poor poll ratings of Ed Miliband caused a fair deal of soul searching after the vote.

Many were surprised, or even shocked, that Ukip, a party that, in Scotland, had hitherto always lost their deposit (but beat the Lib Dems in the Cowdenbeath by-election), got over ten per cent of the vote north of the Border. When Nigel Farage came to Edinburgh in May for another encounter with protesters, he was adamant that Ukip could win that seat and also change the referendum debate, claiming that the SNP's support for the EU made true independence impossible.[204]

Coming fourth in Scotland was bad enough, but only a political tremor compared to the earthquake down south. There, Ukip came first in England (and a close second to Labour in Wales), despite the party's chaotic campaign.[205] Immediately, discussions ensued about informal or even formal electoral arrangements – a 'coupon' election, local pacts – between Farage's motley crew of anti-European right-wingers and the Conservatives.[206] Any such talk is bound to raise alarm bells in Scotland. It could not only make a Tory-led UK government after 2015 more likely, but also the In/Out EU referendum – and in turn make Scots much more prone to vote Yes on 18 September. If, as Brian Taylor had observed before the election, 'the European Elections … result in a disparate approach north and south of the Border,' meaning 'that Ukip may triumph in England while the SNP head the polls in Scotland,' it would make it 'feasible to argue once again that politics in Scotland and England are diverging and require distinct treatment. In short, independence.'[207]

Now the Scottish referendum debate turned on the question whether the Euro result had somewhat eroded that divergence, and thus posed more of a problem to the Yes campaign, or whether Ukip's shock success would reinforce the Yes side. But a few days later, the economy was back on the front pages. Two diametrically opposite projections were published on the same day by the UK Treasury and the Scottish Government. The Treasury Report, accentuating the positive that the 'Union dividend' would make every Scot £1400 richer (in other words, independence would cost every Scot £1400) – and the SNP's claim that

[204] Magnus Gardham and Brian Donnelly, 'Police keep the peace as Ukip leader returns to Edinburgh', *The Herald*, 10 May 2014.

[205] Jane Merrick, Ian Johnston and Kitty Knowles, 'Ukip under repeated fire – but it's not putting off the voters, say the polls', *The Independent on Sunday*, 27 April 2014.

[206] As mooted during election night by the likes of Jacob Rees-Mogg MP, Peter Bone MP and Daniel Hannan MEP in order to avoid a 'rift in the Conservative family' in the 20125 General Election.

[207] Brian Taylor, 'Don't work with children or tapeworms', *BBC News Scotland*, 30 April 2014, <www.bbc.co.uk/news/uk-scotland-27224157>.

Scots would be £1000 better off becoming independent. The Treasury report was seriously flawed as it misquoted figures about the set-up costs of an independent Scottish state of £1.5bn from research by Professor Patrick Dunleavy of the London School of Economics (which were condemned by him as misrepresented and greatly overblown – he came up with a 'guestimate' of £150m to £300m). Accordingly, Alex Salmond declared the Treasury's report 'blown to smithereens'. Although neither he nor John Swinney had any detailed figures for those set-up costs. Salmond picked Dunleavey's £250m, which would be trifling, set against the £100bn estimated share of UK assets.[208] His government's paper promising the 'independence bonus' in fifteen years' time, based on a growing economy and greater productivity as well as a growing population (24,000 immigrants per year)[209] in an independent Scotland, was promptly denounced by Danny Alexander as a 'bogus bonus'.[210] Tom Farmer was close to despair:

> The 28th of May was supposedly the day we the voters were to gain clarity on the impact of independence in or out of the Union. … What has been presented today is farcical, and how any undecided voter could pick through the claims and counter-claims and make any sense of them is well beyond me. We as voters have been disrespected.[211]

'I think that UK ministers and the Treasury potentially have a point arguing that the Scottish Government has not been very forthcoming, they might even say evasive, about clarifying some of the costs of independence,' Patrick Dunleavy himself commented. 'But there is no point in putting into public circulation misinformation to try to counteract that.'[212]

THE FINAL MILE

There is little doubt that 'the final mile' will be eventful. At long last, the Edinburgh Trams are carrying their first passengers – on the first

[208] Magnus Gardham, 'Salmond backs economist's £250m start-up price tag for independence', *The Herald*. 29 May 2014.

[209] Magnus Gardham, 'Salmond sets immigration target of 24,000 per year', *The Herald*, 29 May 2014.

[210] Tom Gordon, 'Fog descends on both Scotlands', *The Herald*, 29 May 2014.

[211] Magnus Gardham, 'Salmond sets immigration target of 24,000 per year', *The Herald*, 29 May 2014.

[212] Magnus Gardham, 'Treasury shot Danny Alexander in the foot', *The Herald*, 31 May 2014.

weekend 40,000 bought tickets to be part of the tram renaissance after nearly 60 years. In fine sunny weather they enjoyed what Chris Harvie – adding his voice to calls for the system to be extended – has described as 'potentially the most glamorous stretch of European public transport – barring the vaporetto on Venice's Grand Canal.'[213] We can also look forward to the long-delayed public inquiry into the 'trams fiasco', which was widely expected after the Scottish local elections of 2012, but is sure to happen now that the trams are up and running.

After the Euro elections, politics now have to share the stage with commemorative and sports events over the summer. Bannockburn 700 is the main reason for another Year of Homecoming and, like its predecessor in 2009, it has run into difficulties. The event in Stirling at the end of June had to be scaled down, due to extremely poor ticket sales, and the competition from National Armed Forces Day, commemorating the centenary of the outbreak of World War I, to be held also in Stirling on the same weekend in June.[214]

From 12 June the Football World Cup in Brazil beckons – with England, but without the Scots. It gave Johann Lamont one of her best lines in her party conference speech:

> We are not there – again. But there is one thing you can be certain of. Within the first five minutes of England's opening game John Motson will have mentioned 1966. That's a good reason to change the channel. It's just not a good reason to change the constitution.[215]

The action then moves back to Scotland. From 23 July to 3 August, the Commonwealth Games will hit Glasgow, and here Scotland has its own team in the competition! The extraordinary idea of blowing up the Red Road high rises as part of the Opening Ceremony was, luckily, dropped, following a public backlash.[216] In excess of a thousand culture events are planned to be part of this mega-event, which could, like Bannockburn 700, provide the patriotic feel-good factor the Nationalists would hope will take them over the winning line come September, when punters will

---

[213] Alastair Dalton, '"Glamorous" Edinburgh trams the envy of Europe', *The Scotsman*, 27 September 2013.

[214] Brian Donnelly, 'Holyrood to quiz organisers of Bannockburn showcase', *The Herald*, 21 April 2014.

[215] Johann Lamont, 'Leader's Speech at Party Conference', 22 March 2014, <www.scottishlabour.org.uk/blog/entry/speech-to-scottish-labour-conference-by-johann-lamont-msp#sthash.NGW1HHqy.dpuf>.

[216] Alison Rowat, 'Much to be gained by calling off the Red Road big bang', *The Herald*, 11 April 2014.

also look forward to the Ryder Cup coming to Gleneagles.

The long shadow of Günter Grass inspired the bipartisan Bus Party 2014, a tour of artists, writers and musicians round Scotland for a 'two-way listening exercise', which started in early May. Neal Ascherson, who as a young reporter had witnessed the Grass charabanc enlivening the otherwise dull 1964 German election campaign, introduced the concept to Scotland for the 1997 referendum. 'This isn't about yes or no,' he said at the launch, 'but the campaign itself. It's humbling after covering the past two referendums to see what is happening now. Scotland at the end of this campaign will be a different country.'[217]

The National Theatre of Scotland will treat us to a 24-hour show, co-curated by playwright David Greig (a Yes campaigner) and David MacLennan (a No man): 'The Great Yes, No, Don't Know, Five Minute Theatre Show', live broadcast online on 23 June, will feature 840 performances, with contributions from 'poets, school pupils, film-makers, families, community groups, teenagers, visual artists and expectant mothers, with ages ranging from three months to 80 years old.'[218] And, no doubt, the Edinburgh Fringe and the International Edinburgh Book Festival in August will offer further explorations, only weeks before the referendum.

OUTCOME SCENARIOS

If we wake up on 19 September and realise that Scotland has voted No, we will all have a pretty good idea why that outcome was predictable – or so the expert pundits will tell us. If we wake up to a Yes vote, again, we will have all the explanations why that happened. Allow us to speculate.

If Better Together prevailed, as nearly all the polls still suggest, then we can assume that fear of uncertainty and economic disadvantage played a major part in making up voters' minds, but also a sense of Britishness and loyalty anent the Union. Did they want what the Better Together campaign called 'the best of both worlds' – a strong Scottish Parliament combined with the security of the UK?

The Government's White Paper, with all its assertions, would have failed to persuade enough voters. What if all those statements about Europe, the currency, etc, all depending on negotiated outcomes, did not materialise in the end? Fears about the money in one's pocket, the security of pensions, the status of Scotland in Europe, and under what terms EU membership could be secured? Did voters calculate that an

---

[217] Libby Brooks, 'Artists go on "listening" bus tour ahead of Scottish vote', *The Guardian*, 2 May 2014.

[218] Phil Miller, 'Theatre shows to place referendum under the spotlight', *The Herald*, 13 May 2014.

independent Scotland might make an EU exit of rUK more likely – which in turn raised fears that they might end up with an external EU frontier marking the Anglo-Scottish border? Could the fact that both sides did not allow for a measure of doubt in their pronouncements have rebounded more on the Yes side?[219] And, if the negotiated independence package differed substantially from the assertions made in the White Paper – there would be no chance of voting on it again, on account that the first vote was on a 'false prospectus'.

If UK polls by September showed a likelihood of a Labour government at Westminster in 2015, that could have further diluted the urge to translate anti-austerity, anti-Tory votes into Yes votes. The pledges for further devolution by the 'Westminster parties' must have been credible enough to bolster the 'No' vote. All three party leaders had made a firm promise of new powers for Holyrood – Ed Miliband: 'First year, first term, more powers';[220] David Cameron: more powers after No vote, but no guarantee that such powers would be included in the first Queen's Speech;[221] and Nick Clegg: further powers 'inevitable' after No vote.[222] Maybe they will even have managed to agree a common platform before the Referendum? Had the SNP's stereotypical retort that you cannot trust the Tories – remember 1979? – perhaps lost some salience after the Scotland Act 2012?[223] Did voters feel that there is some mileage in the process of devolution yet, and was there a feeling that the Scottish polity was perhaps not (yet) ready for independence? Sure, some just did not want to give the SNP its prize. Others might have been happy with a strong SNP, but in a devolved Scotland. And maybe some thought that an independent Scotland would need more politicians, new ministerial departments, perhaps a second chamber, and that all of that would cost too much? Did the SNP's softly-softly approach not work – keep the pound, keep the Queen, stay in EU and NATO – independence – you won't notice the Difference? Or did it even turn off folk with a more radical vision for Scotland? If we won't notice the difference – what's the point? Maybe Alex Salmond's (qualified) respect for Putin reminded folk of his close relations with the likes of Rupert Murdoch and Donald Trump and that put them off from voting Yes?[224]

---

[219] David Torrance, 'The avoidance of doubt and a lack of candour in Yes camp', *The Herald*, 5 May 2014.

[220] Torcuil Crichton, 'Vote No and I'll Deliver Home Rule', *Daily Record*, 9 May 2014.

[221] Tom Peterkin, 'Cameron promises new powers for Holyrood', *The Scotsman*, 16 May 2014.

[222] Michael Settle, 'Clegg promises more powers for Holyrood in event of No vote', *The Herald*, 19 May 2014.

[223] See David Torrance, 'Nationalists determined to rewrite inconvenient history', *The Herald*, 19 May 2014.

[224] Kate Devlin, 'Salmond: My respect for Putin', *The Herald*, 28 April 2014.

Was the yes camp over-optimistic about the progressive, social-democratic consensus in Scotland, when a survey suggested that nearly seven out of ten Scots back stricter immigration control, more than half want international aid budgets cut, and six out of ten want benefits restricted to people who have lived in the UK for at least five years?[225] And was Dennis Canavan, the Yes chairman, on shaky ground when he claimed, appearing before MSPs at Holyrood, that 'Scots are ready to accept tax hikes after a Yes vote to help bring about a "radical redistribution" of wealth and create a fairer Scandinavian-style state'?[226] A statement the SNP government did clearly not endorse.

If, on the other hand, the outcome is Yes, what would have changed the mind of those undecided and quite a few of those who, over the years, had been in the 'No' camp? A triumph of hope over fear, belief in the possibility of a better, fairer, more equal Scotland? 'Vibrant optimism' trumping 'old pessimism'?[227] Trust in the White Paper's direction of travel and envisaged outcomes, trust built up over seven years of SNP government at Holyrood? Was it the Yes campaign's superior organisation on the ground?

Or was the No campaign simply too negative? Too much 'Project Fear'? The tendency of the No side to threaten Scotland with dire economic and budgetary consequences if it dares break with London, increasingly resented by many Scots as bullying? Was it a sense that the UK had become unreformable, regardless whether Ed Miliband or David Cameron would win in 2015? A UK of austerity, foodbanks, the marketisation of everything, rampant populism, unequal and unfair and, as David Marquand pithily laments, bereft of moral purpose?[228] Somewhat along the lines of Alex Salmond (who can do 'negative' as well as any No campaigner) when he branded David Cameron a 'fearmonger who personifies everything that is wrong in British politics today.'[229]

Or was independence seen as the only way of getting rid of nuclear weapons on Scottish soil? Fear of a Tory-Ukip unholy alliance not only winning in 2015, but taking the UK out of the EU – independence, as Alex Salmond never tired to argue, as the only way of securing continuing EU

[225] Magnus Gardham, 'Seven out of ten Scots "back Ukip policy on immigration"', *The Herald*, 21 May 2014.

[226] Scott Macnab, 'Scots are "happy to pay extra tax after Yes vote"', *The Scotsman*, 22 May 2014.

[227] Colin Bell, 'Vote pitches old pessimism against a vibrant optimism', *The Herald*, 3 May 2014.

[228] David Marquand, *Mammon's Kingdom: An Essay on Britain, Now*, London: Allen Lane, 2014.

[229] Michael Settle, 'Salmond: PM sums up all that is wrong in UK politics', *The Herald*, 14 May 2014.

membership for Scotland?[230] Could the 'purple peril' have been a decisive force in making the Scots vote Yes?

Or did the feel-good factor, maybe even patriotic fervor, of Bannockburn and the Commonwealth Games help – a mood of optimism which chimed with the Yes Scotland and Common Weal vision? Did, in the end, the softly, softly approach of the SNP work – offering continuity and change as a reassuring message? While everyone waited for the big game changer, was it the slow burn that did it?

AFTER THE VOTE

There have ben concerned voices warning that the campaign was turning into a real dog fight, potentially leaving Scotland deeply scarred, despite assurances from leading politicians that, as laid down in the Edinburgh Agreement, the voters' verdict would be accepted in good faith by both sides, and that, immediately after 18 September, all Scots would work together, regardless which side they had backed. Margo MacDonald's memorial service turned into 'a plea for understanding and respect from both sides of the independence campaign – for the sake of all our futures.'[231] The Church of Scotland has even called for a service of national reconciliation in St Giles Cathedral in the immediate aftermath of the referendum.

A lot will depend on the margins of victory. A clear No would, it can be assumed, be accepted by the Yes side – in accordance with Alex Salmond's dictum that an independence referendum is a 'once in a generation opportunity', which was repeated in the White Paper. Would a No mean no change, as the White Paper claims? All Better Together parties will have published their devolution proposals, which all go beyond the Scotland Act 2012. Carwyn Jones in Wales and Douglas Alexander have talked up the need for a Constitutional Convention across the UK, following a No vote.[232] Would the SNP accept a role in it, and perhaps, for the time being, a greater role in UK politics?

Maybe such a Convention could address the fundamental fault of devolution: that it does not reconnect the devolved territories to the decision-making at the centre. Sir Neil MacCormick always used to say that the missing link in the British system was the lack of a Bundesrat –

---

[230] Eddie Barnes, 'EU stay "needs" Yes vote', *The Scotsman*, 15 May 2013.

[231] 'Margo's legacy: "Intolerance on both sides has to stop"' (Leader), *Edinburgh Evening News*, 26 April 2014.

[232] Alan Robertson, 'National convention needed post-2014, urges Alexander', *Holyrood*, 1 March 2013, <www.holyrood.com/2013/03/national-convention-needed-post-2014-urges-alexander/>.

regional/national representation at the centre. Colin Kidd revived he idea in a recent piece for the *London Review of Books*:

> For all the constitutional tinkering of the Blair years the House of Lords remains a problem shelved. The English regions are lukewarm at best about regional assemblies, not least as few taxpayers want to support an additional layer of costly legislators. However, were the House of Lords to be transformed ... into a German-style Bundesrat, with a membership drawn from the governments of the nations and regions of the United Kingdom, ... then the powers of what is effectively England's House of Commons might at last be clipped by a reinvigorated second chamber.[233]

If Labour, the Lib Dems and the Tories did not honour their pledges, it would give the SNP the perfect platform to put independence back on the agenda for the 2016 Scottish parliament elections – perhaps asking the Scottish electorate for a mandate to negotiate independence, with a view of putting the negotiated package to a new referendum. That would avoid the present situation, where people are asked to make up their minds on pre-negotiated prospectuses rather than agreed deals. All would then depend on the SNP again getting a majority at Holyrood.

A narrow No vote would resolve very little. There are plenty SNP politicians and activists who would push for a rerun of the referendum as soon as possible.[234] Alistair Carmichael may believe that a No vote followed by the transfer of substantial powers to Holyrood 'will kill the public appetite for independence forever,'[235] but he should bear in mind George Robertson's prediction that devolution would 'kill nationalism stone dead'. A narrow No vote would widely be interpreted as a 'Not Yet'. Even in the wake of a No vote, the SNP might be in with a very good chance to win the 2016 elections.

A Yes vote, decisive or narrow, would trigger independence negotiations between the Scottish and UK governments. The SNP's position is that the Better Together parties would be invited to participate in these negotiations, which will, in the White Paper's rather optimistic scenario, be concluded within 18 months, so that 26 March 2016 could become Scotland's 'Independence Day' – five weeks before the Scots would elect the first Parliament of an independent Scotland. But will

---

[233] Colin Kidd, 'A British Bundesrat?', *London Review of Books*, vol.36, no.8, 17 April 2014, pp.13-14.

[234] Simon Johnson, 'SNP MSPs back second independence referendum', *The Daily Telegraph*, 23 December 2012.

[235] Tom Gordon, 'No vote will kill appetite for separate Scotland for good, says Carmichael', *Sunday Herald*, 18 May 2014.

negotiations be as easy, amiable and consensual as the White Paper tries to make out?

What would happen to the UK elections in 2015? Would the Scots elect 59 MPs for just one year? Could the elections be delayed, as the SNP's Westminster leader Angus Robertson suggested?[236] Or would David Cameron have to resign after losing the Union under his watch, and maybe trigger an earlier UK election?[237] Echoing his refusal to debate Alex Salmond head-on, Cameron would have none of that. The referendum, he said, is 'not about my future, it is about Scotland's future.'[238] Would that position be tenable after a Yes vote?

A House of Lords constitution committee report published in May concluded that the proposed date of Scottish independence could be delayed in the event of a Yes vote if it is not in the best interests of the rest of the UK. The peers also suggested Scottish MPs should be allowed to keep their seats beyond a Yes vote in the independence referendum, but recommended that they should not be allowed to negotiate for the rest of the UK on the terms of independence. Would there be a scramble of Scottish MPs who saw their future at Westminster for English constituencies? The committee also recommended that Scotland should be seen as a successor state, meaning the UK would keep its existing international agreements while Scotland has to renegotiate. Angus MacNeil, the SNP MP, said the House of Lords was an 'undemocratic anachronism stuffed to the gunnels with over 800 peers of the realm who answer to no electors and are often there because of privilege or patronage'. He added: 'It will be elected representatives who will lead Scotland's transition to independence.'[239]

As the EU can only negotiate with sovereign states, would Scotland's accession to the EU be postponed till after independence is achieved? Or would the UK, while negotiating with Scotland, also negotiate on behalf of Scotland in Brussels? There is little doubt that Scotland would, eventually, become a member state of the EU, but the terms are a different question. Does the Scottish Government really think that they can claim, on the one hand, that an independent Scotland would be one of the richest nations of the world and, at the same time, expect the EU to extend the UK rebate to a country which receives more than its fair

---

[236] Kieran Andrews, 'Angus Robertson calls for delay of UK elections', *The Courier*, 30 November 2013.

[237] Kate Devlin, 'Politicians always say No to thoughts of losing', *The Herald*, 22 April 2014; Jane Merrick and John Rentoul, 'No 10 silent on Cameron future if Scots vote Yes', *The Independent on Sunday*, 27 April 2014.

[238] Andrew Woodcock, 'Cameron says he won't quit after yes vote', *The Scotsman*, 10 May 2014.

[239] Auslan Cramb, 'Peers suggest UK could delay proposed date of Scottish independence', *The Daily Telegraph*, 16 May 2014.

share of agricultural and regional subsidies (in contrast to England – the reason in the first place that the rebate was grudgingly granted)?

How would UK and NATO negotiations affect the determination of the Scottish Government, as expressed in the White Paper, to get rid of Trident by the end of the first independent Parliament, i.e. by 2020 or 2021? Defence Minister Philip Hammond has already indicated that that timetable was unrealistic, saying that it 'would take at least ten years and cost tens of billions of pounds to move the UK's nuclear deterrent from the Clyde.'[240] And he reiterated an independent Scotland would lose thousands of Defence jobs, and that Alex Salmond's promises that Navy ships would still be built in Scotland after a Yes vote were unsubstantiated.[241]

Finally, how would the parties campaigning for a No vote, and so long in a commanding lead, adapt to a Yes vote? Would they fare much better than the Scottish Tories post 1997? Relegated to the margins? Or, would it, as the SNP mischievously insinuates, be a liberation from the Westminster corset for them?

Regardless of the referendum outcome, the campaign has already changed Scotland. We have seen thousands of Scots attending town hall meetings, getting involved, particularly in the grassroots Yes campaigns.

> The Yes campaign on the ground is really hundreds of autonomous local campaigns, each raising their own money and running their own events. They put on meetings for non-political audiences and they are constantly trying to make sure that platform speakers are mainly non-politicians. They want people who are not giving prepared answers or reading from a script.[242]

That gives hope that the push for more local democracy as well as the new efforts at land reform will transcend the referendum and perhaps gain momentum, either as part of the participative debates around a Scottish constitution after a Yes vote, or as part of improving devolution, in case of a No vote.

For many in the SNP, the referendum is the culmination of a livelong dream. They will pull out all the stops until the finishing line. The law of referendums may favour the status quo, the devil you know – but not

---

[240] Scott Macnab, 'UK draws battle lines on nuclear weapons', *The Scotsman*, 15 April 2014; Kate Devlin, 'Trident to stay on Clyde until at least 2026 says Hammond', *The Herald*, 9 May 2014.

[241] Michael Settle, 'Salmond: Scotland would still build Navy ships after yes vote', *The Herald*, 16 April 2014.

[242] Robin McAlpine, 'Taking politicians out of politics reaps rewards', *The Scotsman*, 26 April 2014.

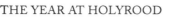

necessarily, as history shows.[243] Will the Scots, as the Social Attitudes Surveys tell us, vote primarily with their head, with their personal economic prospects firmly guiding their decision, or will they be guided by their heart, gut instinct and emotion, fired up by the dream of a fairer, more prosperous Scotland, as promoted by the Yes campaign?[244] Grassroots campaigners and the big beasts in Scottish and UK politics will battle it out over the summer. 'We all have to live with each other after September 18,' wrote Iain Macwhirter: 'And what is increasingly clear to me is that Scotland will be a different country whatever the outcome.'[245]

Ten years after the MSP's moved into their shiny new building at Holyrood, and more than 15 years since the first elections for the new Scottish Parliament, we are approaching a crossroads – either a new chapter on the devolution journey, or a break with devolution, striking out as an independent country. The Scots will decide on 18 September.

Beyond September – whatever the result of the referendum – working out the relationships between the nations of this archipelago will continue. The referendum may solve less than some people expect, but the campaign will have a long aftermath, and the decision will be watched way beyond Scotland and the UK as an example of democratic self-determination.

Meanwhile – I'm off to catch an Edinburgh tram.

[May 2014]

---

[243] See Matt Qvortrup, 'History tells sceptics Yes can win', *Scotland on Sunday*, 13 April 2013.

[244] 'Better Together faces difficult job on taxes' (Leader), *The Scotsman*, 2 April 2014.

[245] Iain Macwhirter, 'Yes or No, road to referendum will lead us to a new Scotland', *The Herald*, 1 May 2014.

Made in the USA
Charleston, SC
21 June 2014